Microsoft

MICROSOFT®
ASP.NET
PROGRAMMING WITH MICROSOFT
VISUAL C#™ .NET
STEP BY STEP

Microsoft
.net

G. Andrew Duthie
Douglas J. Reilly

PUBLISHED BY
Microsoft Press
A Division of Microsoft Corporation
One Microsoft Way
Redmond, Washington 98052-6399

Copyright © 2003 by G. Andrew Duthie

Library of Congress Cataloging-in-Publication Data
Duthie, G. Andrew, 1967-
     Microsoft ASP.NET Programming with Microsoft Visual C# .NET Step by Step / G. Andrew Duthie, Douglas Reilly, Microsoft Corporation.
          p. cm.
     Includes index.
     ISBN 0-7356-1815-1
     1. Internet programming.   2. Active server pages.   3. C# (Computer program language)
     4. Microsoft .NET.   I. Reilly, Douglas J.   II. Microsoft Corporation.   III. Title.

     QA76.625 .D89   2002
     005.2'76--dc21   2002071819

Printed and bound in the United States of America.

1 2 3 4 5 6 7 8 9   QWT   7 6 5 4 3 2

Distributed in Canada by H.B. Fenn and Company Ltd.

A CIP catalogue record for this book is available from the British Library.

Microsoft Press books are available through booksellers and distributors worldwide. For further information about international editions, contact your local Microsoft Corporation office or contact Microsoft Press International directly at fax (425) 936-7329. Visit our Web site at www.microsoft.com/mspress. Send comments to *mspinput@microsoft.com*.

Acquisitions Editor: Anne Hamilton
Project Editor: Denise Bankaitis

SubAssy Part No. X08-90254
Body Part No. X08-90263

For Ali...

I keep the picture of you and me in NYC on my desk;
I think of you often, and miss you all the time...

See my eyes, don't see what I see,
Touch my tongue, don't know what tastes good to me,
The human condition is what keeps us apart,
Everybody's got a story that could break your heart.

— *Amanda Marshall*

Like the song says, everybody's got a story that could break your heart. I actually have several. Here is one.

My work on the book is dedicated to Alison Reilly. Ali was the daughter of my brother Bobby. Back in 1997, as Bobby was dying of a hereditary condition called Familial Adenmoatous Polyposis (FAP), I promised him I would look after Ali, if anything happened to him. From that point on, I kept a special eye out for Ali, and tried to help her as best I could with school, programming (she became a Computer Science major) and anything else. We lived some distance away, however, we kept in touch through e-mail and instant messaging. We talked about her health, music we both enjoyed, computers, and life in general.

Ali previously had surgery to try and eliminate any chance of the cancer that had killed her dad and my dad before that. Unfortunately, in an irony that is really too great for words, that very surgery was the cause of the desmoid tumor that finally took her from us October 10, 2001. She was 20 years old. For more on Ali, see *http://ali.accessmicrosystems.com*. For more about FAP and related diseases, see *http://www.hereditarycc.org*.

I have been kept healthy, even though I have the same condition, due to good medicine, good doctors, and good luck. First among those good doctors is Dr. Hans Gerdes, of Memorial Sloan-Kettering Cancer Center in NYC.

Contents

Douglas J. Reilly
Acknowledgements

Andrew Duthie is one of perhaps two people with whom I could actually collaborate on a book. Thank you for inviting me to work on the C# version of the book! In many respects, the experience of working on this book was like Gilligan's "Three hour tour." It took *lots* longer than either of us expected, but in the end it is a lot better than either of us expected as well. Thanks to Denise Bankaitis of Microsoft Press, the long (and I emphasize *long*) suffering editor of the book. Thanks to Aaron L'Heureux of Online Training Solutions, Inc., the tech editor of the book.

Last, and certainly not least, I need to thank my family. Many a night, I have been toiling away in the basement while they were out and about doing the normal things families do. Tim, you are the best son a Dad could ask for. In two years, it will be my pleasure to refer to you as *Dr.* Tim! Erin, neither of us could have predicted the paths your life would take, but I am very proud of how far you have come, even as you have a way to go. I am rooting for you! Jean, I am sure that sometimes being my wife is not easy, but I do hope that there are other times that make up for it. I love you, and can't wait for vacation!

Douglas J. Reilly
September 3, 2002

G. Andrew Duthie
Acknowledgements

First and foremost, I'd like to thank my co-author, Doug Reilly, for his contributions to this book. Without his hard work and assistance, this book would have taken far longer to complete (and might not have been finished at all!).

I'd also like to thank my project editor at Microsoft Press, Denise Bankaitis, for the support and assistance she cheerfully provided. Thanks to Tess McMillan for her work setting up the practice files, and in particular to Anne Hamilton for providing this opportunity to Doug and me.

Last but not least, I thank my wife Jennifer. Her love, patience, and support make my work possible and worthwhile.

G. Andrew Duthie
September, 2002

Finding Your Best Starting Point

Microsoft ASP.NET Programming with Microsoft Visual C# .NET is designed to provide a comprehensive introduction and overview of developing Web applications with ASP.NET. The goal of this book is to help you become competent at the basic skills necessary for creating and using ASP.NET applications. To help you get there as quickly and easily as possible, this book has been divided into four parts, each composed of chapters related to a specific topic. Over the course of these parts and chapters, you'll learn about the new .NET development platform and the part ASP.NET plays in it. You'll also learn the skills necessary to take advantage of ASP.NET Web Forms, Server Controls, and XML-based Web services.

Depending on the skills and experience you bring to this book, you might want to start with a particular part that is of interest to you or skip over certain parts entirely. The following table can help you decide where to start in this book.

If you are	Follow these steps
New to programming	**1** Install the sample files as described in "Installing the Sample Files" on page xvii.
	2 Learn about the background of the .NET Framework and ASP.NET by reading Chapters 1–6. Then either work through Part 3 if you want to know more about the technologies underlying ASP.NET, or work through Part 4 if you want to get straight into the coding.
	3 Work through the rest of the parts and chapters based on your interest in their topics.

If you are	Follow these steps
Switching from classic ASP or similar technologies	**1** Install the sample files as described in "Installing the Sample Files" on page xvii. **2** Read or scan Parts 1 and 2 if you're interested in the background of .NET and ASP.NET. If you do not have any experience with a language derived from C++, pay special attention to Chapter 3, "Understanding Programming Basics." **3** Work through Part 3 for basic Web Forms skills as well as an introduction to using ASP.NET Server Controls and accessing data with ADO.NET. **4** Work through Part 4 for additional ASP.NET application skills.

If you are	Follow these steps
Referencing this book after working through the chapters	**1** Use the index to locate information about specific topics, and use the table of contents to locate information about general topics. **2** Read the Quick Reference at the end of each chapter for a brief review of the major tasks in each chapter.

Corrections, Comments, and Help

Every effort has been made to ensure the accuracy of this book and the contents of the sample files. Microsoft Press provides corrections and additional content for its books through the World Wide Web at the following Web site:

http://microsoft.com/mspress/support

Microsoft Press maintains a database with up-to-date information about its books. To query this Knowledge Base directly, connect to

http://www.microsoft.com/mspress/support/search.asp

If you have problems, comments, or ideas regarding this book or the sample files, please send them to Microsoft Press.

Send e-mail to:

mspinput@microsoft.com

Or send postal mail to:

Microsoft Press
Attn: Developer, Step by Step Series Editor
One Microsoft Way
Redmond, WA 98052-6399

Please note that product support is not offered through this addresses. For help with Visual C# .NET, you can connect to Microsoft Technical Support on the Web at *support.microsoft.com/directory*, or for additional developer information about ASP.NET, go to *www.microsoft.com/net* and search on ASPNET.

Visit the Microsoft Press World Wide Web Site

You are also invited to visit the Microsoft Press World Wide Web site at the following location:

http://www.microsoft.com/mspress

You'll find descriptions for the complete line of Microsoft Press books (including others by G. Andrew Duthie and Douglas J. Reilly), information about ordering titles, notice of special features and events, additional content for Microsoft Press books, and much more.

Installing the Sample Files

The sample code used in this book is available on the book's Web site at *www.microsoft.com/mspress/books/6326.asp*. To download the sample files, simply click the Companion Content link on the More Information menu on the right side of the Web page.

System Requirements

To use the sample code provided at the Web site, you'll need a computer with the following configuration:

- Microsoft Windows 2000 (SP2 recommended), XP Professional, or .NET Server
- Microsoft SQL Server 2000 (Personal, Standard or Enterprise Edition, SP2 recommended) or the Microsoft SQL Server Desktop Engine (MSDE), included with Visual C# .NET.
- Microsoft Internet Explorer 5.5 or later
- Internet Information Services (IIS). To access the ASP.NET features, IIS must be installed prior to installing the .NET Framework.
- The .NET Framework SDK, which can be downloaded from the MSDN Web site at *http://msdn.microsoft.com/netframework /prodinfo/getdotnet.asp*. (Because Microsoft Visual Studio .NET includes the SDK, you don't need to install the .NET Framework SDK separately if you install Visual Studio .NET.)

note

Note that to run some of the command-line tools in the .NET Framework (such as wsdl.exe and the command-line compilers) more easily, you might also need to add the paths to these utilities to the PATH environment variable, as described in Appendix C. If you have problems running any of the command-line tools, you can use the Windows Search facility (located on the Start menu) to search for their location. Then add the path to their location to the PATH environment variable.

Conventions Used in This Book

You can save time when using this book if you understand how instructions, keys, notes, and so on are used *before* you start the first chapter. Please take a moment to read the following list, which explains the conventions for these and other elements.

- Hands-on exercises for you to follow are given in numbered steps (**1**, **2**, and so on). A round bullet (●) inidicates an exercise that has only one step.
- A plus sign (+) between two key names means that you must press those keys at the same time. For example, Press Alt+Tab means that you hold down the Alt key while pressing the Tab key.
- Text that you are to type appears in **bold**.
- Notes provide additional information about a topic.
- Notes labeled IMPORTANT alert you to essential information that you should check before continuing the chapter.
- Tips can help save you time and trouble as you use the technologies being described.

PART 1

Getting Started with ASP.NET

CHAPTER

1

Opening and Running an ASP.NET Web Application

In this chapter, you will learn how to

✔ *Start Microsoft Visual Studio .NET.*

✔ *Open and run an ASP.NET application.*

✔ *Work with tool windows.*

✔ *Exit Visual Studio .NET.*

ASP.NET is not just an upgrade—not by a long shot. ASP.NET provides the most advanced Web development platform created to date. What's more, ASP.NET has been rebuilt from the ground up to create an entirely new and more flexible infrastructure for Web development.

What makes ASP.NET so revolutionary is that it's based on Microsoft's new .NET platform, or more accurately the Microsoft .NET Framework. To understand clearly where and when to use ASP.NET, let's take some time to go over the .NET platform, the products that comprise it, and where ASP.NET fits within Microsoft .NET.

Understanding Microsoft .NET

Microsoft .NET is an umbrella term that describes a number of recently released technologies from Microsoft. Taken together, these technologies are the most substantial changes to the Microsoft development platform since the transition from 16-bit to 32-bit development.

Microsoft .NET includes the following technology areas:

- The .NET Framework
- .NET languages and language tools

In the next section, you'll learn about these technologies and how you can use them to speed up your development of robust, high-performance Web-based or Windows Forms-based applications on the Microsoft Windows platform.

The .NET Framework

The .NET Framework is an essential technology for ASP.NET development. It provides the basic system services that support ASP.NET, as well as Windows Forms development, the new rich client development technology provided by .NET. Much like the Microsoft Windows NT 4.0 Option Pack, an add-on to Windows NT 4.0 that added Microsoft Internet Information Server 4.0 and Active Server Pages (ASP) technologies to NT 4.0, the .NET Framework is an add-on to Windows 2000, Windows NT 4.0, and Windows 98/Me that adds the basic supporting system services for .NET technologies. The framework will also be built into newer releases of the Windows server operating system line, including the Windows .NET Server line.

important

Although Microsoft Visual Studio .NET will be supported on the Windows 9x, Windows NT, Windows 2000, and Windows XP platforms, the full framework won't be available on all platforms. Most importantly, although other platforms can be used as ASP.NET clients, ASP.NET applications will run only on Windows 2000 and later versions.

The .NET Framework consists of two main parts:

- The common language runtime
- The .NET Framework class library

The Common Language Runtime

The common language runtime (CLR) provides a runtime environment for the execution of code written in .NET languages. The CLR manages the execution of .NET code, including memory and object lifetime management. In addition to these management services, the CLR enables developers to perform debugging, exception handling, and inheritance across multiple languages. Performing these tasks requires that the language compilers follow the Common Language Specification (CLS), which describes a subset of the data types supported by the CLR that are common to all of the languages used in .NET.

The individual language compilers compile the code written by developers into an intermediate language called Microsoft Intermediate Language (IL or MSIL). This IL is then either compiled to native code by the CLR at install time or compiled Just-In-Time (JIT) at first execution.

Code that is compiled to IL and managed by the CLR is referred to as *managed code*. It's called this because the CLR takes responsibility for managing the execution of the code, including the instantiation of objects, allocation of memory, and garbage collection of objects and memory.

Components written in managed code and executed by the CLR are referred to as *.NET managed assemblies*, or *assemblies* for short. Assemblies are the basic unit of deployment in the .NET world and are quite similar to COM components. The difference is that whereas a COM component is associated with or contains a type library to describe how clients should interact with it, an assembly contains a *manifest*, which is the set of metadata that describes the contents of the assembly. Among other advantages, the self-describing nature of .NET components means that they don't need to be registered on a computer in order to work!

This metadata also describes the dependencies and version information associated with an assembly. Not only does this make it much easier to ensure that all necessary dependencies of an assembly are fulfilled, but it also means that multiple versions of the same assembly can be run side by side on the same computer without conflict. This is a major step in resolving "DLL Hell," the bane of many developers' existence. Just ask any Web developer who's worked with more than one version of Microsoft ActiveX Data Objects (ADO), and you're sure to get an earful about applications being broken by a new version of ADO. With .NET, this issue should be a thing of the past. As long as the consuming application knows which version of an assembly it's designed to use, it can locate the correct version among multiple versions of the same assembly by querying the assembly's metadata.

There's a great deal more to the CLR, which you'll learn about in future chapters. If you need information on the CLR, search on "common language runtime" in either the .NET Framework SDK documentation or the MSDN Library documentation for Visual Studio .NET.

The .NET Framework Class Library

The .NET Framework class library is designed to support the efforts of developers by providing base classes from which developers can inherit. This class library is a hierarchical set of .NET classes that developers can use in their own applications. The classes, which are organized by containers referred to as *namespaces*, provide both basic and advanced functionality that developers can easily reuse. They include classes that support basic common datatypes; classes that provide access to data; and classes that support such system services as drawing (good news for anyone who's had to use a third-party component for dynamically creating graphics in an ASP application), network functionality (including DNS (Domain Name System) and reverse DNS lookups), and many others.

The library also contains the classes that form the basis of ASP.NET, including the *Page* class (a part of the *System.Web.UI* namespace) from which all ASP.NET pages are derived, as well as many other classes in the *System.Web* namespace and its children. Future chapters will discuss several of these classes.

note

The ASP.NET QuickStart Tutorial (installed with the .NET Framework SDK samples) contains a useful Class Browser sample application that you can use to view the various classes of the .NET Framework class library.

Inheritance

Inheritance is a central concept in the .NET Framework. It provides a way for developers to use existing code in classes. A class can expose both properties and methods that clients can use. Classes that are inherited from a particular base class are said to be *derived* from that class. By inheriting from this class, a developer can reuse the functionality that it exposes without having to rewrite the code.

In addition (and more important), a developer using the inherited class can override one or more of the methods exposed by the class in order to provide a specialized implementation of that functionality. This capability will come in handy when you learn about custom server controls in Chapter 10.

.NET Languages and Language Tools

One of the best things about the .NET platform is that, whereas classic ASP restricted developers to using scripting languages (with their inherent limitations), ASP.NET lets you work with *any* .NET-compliant language. This means that the code you write in ASP.NET is compiled for better performance, and you can take full advantage of advanced language features.

For the .NET platform, languages (and the tools with which you'll use them) are probably one of the most important topics to discuss. Let's take a high-level look at some of the languages and tools that will be available for developing .NET applications.

Notepad and Other Text Editors

Believe it or not, many developers, particularly ASP developers, still do much of their development in Microsoft Notepad (which I used to lovingly refer to as "Visual" Notepad) or other free or inexpensive text editors. While Notepad has the substantial advantage of being ubiquitous, it's not exactly what you'd call a robust development environment. That said, if you're working with the .NET Framework SDK (rather than Visual Studio .NET), there's no reason you can't use Notepad (or another favorite text editor) to do all of your .NET development. The .NET Framework SDK includes command-line compilers for C# (pronounced "C sharp"), Microsoft Visual Basic .NET, and JScript .NET. So you can create your classes, ASP.NET pages, and so on in Notepad and then either compile them explicitly using the command-line compilers or, in the case of ASP.NET, allow the ASP.NET runtime to dynamically compile each page when it's requested for the first time.

Visual Studio .NET

For simpler and faster development, most developers will probably want to work in Visual Studio .NET, which provides a single integrated development environment (IDE) for all of Microsoft's .NET languages (with the exception of Microsoft Visual FoxPro 7.0, which does not use the CLR or .NET Framework). This means that developers of C#, Visual Basic .NET and Microsoft Visual C++ will all share the same IDE, including the capability to perform debugging and error-handling across languages in the same environment.

Visual Studio .NET provides a substantial number of new features, including:

- A single, unified programming model for all .NET languages and for both Windows and Web applications
- Drag-and-drop development for the server using Server Explorer

■ Dynamic Help

■ A robust customization and extensibility model for the IDE

■ Strong support for XML

■ Web services with dramatically easier cross-platform application integration

You'll learn more about the Visual Studio .NET environment later in this chapter.

C#

A new member of the Visual Studio family, C# is a descendent of the C language. It's much like C++, but designed with greater simplicity and ease of use in mind. Although C# isn't necessarily as easy to learn as Visual Basic, it's far easier than C++ and provides nearly all of the power available to C++ developers. It also doesn't require you to manage the allocation and deallocation of memory, as C++ does, nor does it expose pointers in ways that have caused generations of C programmers great difficulty. Because C# is a managed language, all of the memory management is taken care of by the CLR. This advantage is important because memory management is one of the most troublesome areas of C++ development and is responsible for many application crashes.

Developers familiar with C, C++, and Java will quickly become productive using C#. This book includes plenty of C# code examples that will give you a taste of this exciting new language and help you get started.

Visual Basic .NET

As mentioned earlier, ASP.NET developers are no longer restricted to a watered-down version of Visual Basic like VBScript. They can now take advantage of the full power of the Visual Basic .NET language, which has been increased substantially by the addition of structured exception handling and support for inheritance and multithreaded programming, to name just a few improvements.

Like C#, Visual Basic .NET is a managed language, which means that the CLR manages the execution of Visual Basic .NET code. You no longer need to explicitly destroy your object references using *Set object = Nothing*, as you did when using COM components in Visual Basic 6 and earlier versions. The .NET garbage collector automatically recovers the memory used by the component as soon as no clients are referencing it.

Visual Basic .NET has many new features, but users of VBScript and Visual Basic 6.0 should have little trouble using it once they're familiar with the .NET programming model. This book includes some Visual Basic .NET code examples that will give you a taste of this exciting new language.

Additional .NET Languages

In addition to C# and Visual Basic .NET, Visual Studio .NET ships with JScript .NET, Visual C++, and the managed extensions for Visual C++, which enable C++ developers to target their applications to the CLR.

Visual Studio .NET also provides an extremely flexible plug-in architecture that allows other languages that are written for or ported to the .NET platform to easily use the power of the Visual Studio IDE. The current list of third-party languages planned for Visual Studio .NET includes:

- APL
- COBOL
- Eiffel
- FORTRAN
- Haskell
- Mercury
- Mondrian
- Oberon
- Pascal
- Perl
- Python
- RPG
- Scheme

Some of these languages are commercial implementations, but some are university research projects that might never reach commercial status. Still, between the languages that will ship with Visual Studio .NET and the third-party languages that will be available, there should be a language to please just about any developer.

Getting Oriented

Although this book will focus on building ASP.NET applications with Visual C# .NET, the development environment you'll be working in is Visual Studio .NET. Because Visual Studio .NET now supports all of the .NET languages in a single IDE, many of the tasks you'll learn in this book are applicable to Visual Basic .NET, Visual C++, and JScript .NET, as well as to Visual C# .NET. You'll begin by starting the Visual Studio .NET IDE.

Starting Visual Studio .NET

The exercises in this chapter require that you have installed at minimum the Visual C# .NET Standard Edition (included with the Deluxe Learning Edition of this book), as well as the practice files for the book, which you can download from the book's Web site at *http://www.microsoft.com/mspress/books/6326.asp*. If you have not installed both, please do so now and then return to this chapter.

Start Visual Studio .NET

Start button

1   Click the Start button, point to All Programs (or Programs in Windows 2000), and then point to Microsoft Visual Studio .NET.

The icons for Visual Studio .NET are displayed.

2   Click the icon for Microsoft Visual Studio .NET.

The Visual Studio .NET IDE starts and displays its Start Page, which provides links and tools to help you configure the IDE, open recent projects, create new projects, and many other tasks. If this is the first time you've run Visual Studio .NET, the IDE displays the MyProfile portion of the Start Page, enabling you to configure the layout of the tool windows in Visual Studio .NET, as well as the keyboard shortcuts used to accomplish common tasks.

3   Change the setting in the Profile drop-down list from Visual Studio Developer to Visual C# Developer.

This setting configures the IDE windows and keyboard configuration to use the default Visual Studio .NET keyboard configuration, the default Visual Studio .NET window layout, and the Visual C# .NET Help filter. You can change the Profile setting back to Visual Studio Developer if you want to restore the original settings later.

4   Click the Get Started link to switch to the Get Started portion of the Start Page.

This section provides links for opening projects or creating new projects, as well as for searching for sample code in the Visual Studio documentation and online.

Search for sample code

1 Click the Find Samples link to switch to the Find Samples tab.

Here you can search for samples based on the developer profile (Visual Studio, Visual C#, Visual C++, or Visual Basic) and filtered by keyword or type.

2 Type **ASP.NET** in the textbox, and then click Go.

A list of matching samples from the documentation is displayed.

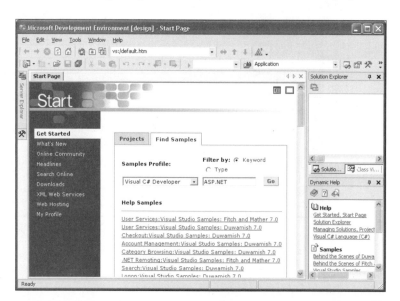

important

Sample applications and code can be useful tools for learning how to develop applications, including ASP.NET applications. But keep in mind that samples are often designed to illustrate a limited set of specific concepts, and might not always use best practices for security and design. Before using sample code in your applications, be sure you understand the security and architectural implications of doing so.

Open a Web application project

1   Switch back to the Projects tab of the Get Started section by clicking the Projects link, and then click Open Project.

The Open Project dialog box is displayed.

2   Browse to the location where you installed the practice files (the default is C:\aspnetsbs), open the Chapter_01 folder, select the Chapter_01.csproj file, and then click Open. (Alternatively, you can open all the projects installed with the practice files by selecting the aspnetsbs.sln file located in the aspnetsbs folder.)

The Chapter_01 project is loaded.

note

By default, Windows 2000 and Windows XP hide file extensions for known file types. If this setting is turned on, you will not see the .csproj and/or .sln extensions to the mentioned in step 2. You can modify this setting in the Folder Options dialog box. In Windows Explorer, click Folder Options on the Tools menu, and click the View tab. Clear the Hide Extensions For Known File Types check box, and then click OK or Apply. The file extensions now appear in the Open Project dialog box.

Solutions and Projects

Applications in Visual Studio .NET are organized in containers called *projects* and *solutions*. Projects are containers for the files associated with a single application type, such as a control library, whereas solutions are containers for one or more projects. The projects that make up the sample files for this book are contained in a single solution named aspnetsbs.sln. Solutions are useful tools for organizing all of the projects associated with a larger application, such as Web applications, and the control projects or component projects associated with them.

Start button

Running Web applications is a little different than running Windows applications or console applications. With Windows and console applications, running the application in the IDE is as simple as clicking the Start button on the Visual Studio .NET toolbar. Although you can also run a Web application using this technique, it is more common to simply browse to the page in the application that you want to test. If you want to run a Web application using the Start button (or by clicking Start on the Debug menu), you need to select a page in your application that will be the start page, or the first page loaded when the application is run. You'll learn about these techniques in Chapter 14, which covers debugging ASP.NET applications. For now, let's just test a page by browsing it.

Browse a Web page

1   If you've already loaded the Chapter_01 project, skip to the next step. If not, return to the previous section, follow the steps to load the project, and then return to this section.

2   To build the application, on the Build menu, click Build Chapter_01.

3   In Solution Explorer, right-click the Welcome.aspx file, and then click View In Browser.

The Welcome.aspx page is loaded into a browser window that is integrated into the IDE. You can browse pages in an external browser window, or with browsers other than Internet Explorer, by right-clicking a page, clicking Browse With, and then choosing your desired browser and other options. Close this page when you are done by right-clicking the tab.

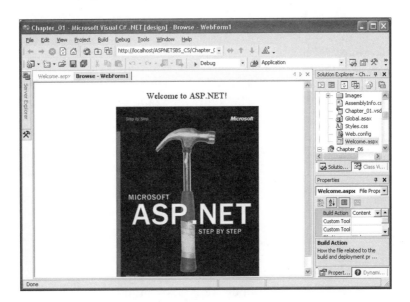

The Visual Studio .NET IDE

The Visual Studio .NET IDE includes a wide array of tool windows, toolbars, and menus that provide developers with a great deal of flexibility in performing their development tasks. You can perform any given task, such as adding an item to a project, using a tool window, a toolbar button, or a menu selection. Although this flexibility is a good thing, it can be overwhelming at first. To make it easier for you to find your way around, let's take a tour through the new enhancements, tool windows, toolbars, and menus of the Visual Studio .NET IDE.

IDE Enhancements

The new enhancements you'll find in the Visual Studio .NET IDE include the following:

■ **Start Page**   The Start Page, which you saw earlier in the chapter, is displayed by default each time you start Visual Studio .NET. It enables you to set your preferences for the IDE, access recent and existing projects, and create new projects.

■ **Multilanguage IDE**   Unlike Visual Studio 6.0, where each language used a different IDE (except for Microsoft Visual InterDev and Visual J++, which shared an IDE), in Visual Studio .NET, all languages share the same IDE. This means that standard features such as Find and Replace, debugging, and so on work consistently across different languages. This alone is a big productivity enhancement over Visual Studio 6.

■ **Command window**   A cross between Visual Basic's Immediate window and a command line, the Command window lets you execute Visual Studio commands or code statements, depending on the mode of the window. The following graphic shows a Command window that's been switched to immediate mode using the *immed* command.

The Command window has two modes:

■ **Command mode**   Enables you to execute Visual Studio commands without using the menu system, or to execute commands that don't appear in any menu.

■ **Immediate mode**   Enables you to evaluate expressions, check the value of variables, execute program statements and functions, and so on. This is used in debugging.

■ **Tabbed documents**   Designed to simplify the management of multiple files being edited simultaneously, the Tabbed Documents interface enables you to see all of the files you're editing at once. This makes it much simpler to switch back and forth between open editing windows. You can still set up Visual Studio .NET to use the old method used by Visual Studio 6, however. Click Options on the Tools menu, select the General option in the Environment folder, switch from Tabbed Documents to MDI environment, and then click OK. You'll need to restart Visual Studio .NET for this change to take effect.

Pushpin button

■ **Auto-hide**   My personal favorite, auto-hide works much as it does with the Windows taskbar. To enable auto-hide for a window, click the pushpin icon in the window's title bar. Then when you move the mouse away from the window, the window hides itself at the side of the IDE where it's docked leaving only a tab with the window title visible. Hovering over the tab causes the window to reappear. This is a great feature for preserving the maximum amount of screen real estate for the code window, and it can make life much easier in terms of managing multiple windows in the IDE.

- **Improved HTML editor**   Like Visual InterDev before it, the Visual Studio .NET HTML editor provides both a design view and an HTML (source) view. Visual Studio .NET has eliminated the Quick View window provided by Visual InterDev. Instead, you preview pages in an embedded browser window, which provides a truer view of how a page will look. The improved editor also supports specifying the HTML schema you're writing for via the *targetSchema* property. Setting *targetSchema* determines which elements will be made available via the editor's statement completion features and allows the IDE to provide you with feedback on syntax that's incorrect in the context of your chosen target schema.

Explore Tabbed Documents

1   With the Chapter_01 project open in the IDE, double-click the Welcome.aspx file in Solution Explorer.

A new tab is added to the editor.

Scroll buttons

Close button

2   Switch between open documents (including the Start Page) by clicking the tab for the document you want to switch to.

If there are more tabs than will fit onscreen, you can scroll to view the hidden tabs using the scroll buttons at the top of the editor window. You can close the currently selected document by clicking the Close button at the top of the editor window.

New Features

In addition to the IDE enhancements, a number of entirely new features have been added to the Visual Studio .NET IDE:

- **XML editor**   This editor enables you to edit XML data (.xml) and schema (.xsd) files in source, data, or schema views, depending on the type of XML file you're editing.

- **Dynamic Help**   This feature provides context-sensitive help. While you work in the IDE, it suggests topics of interest as you add files, controls, and code to your project.

note

Although the Dynamic Help window can be very useful, it also levies a performance penalty because each time you perform some action in the IDE, the Dynamic Help window searches for topics of interest related to that action. If you're familiar with most of the tasks you need to perform, or if you're running Visual Studio .NET on an older machine, closing the Dynamic Help window (by clicking the Close button in the top right corner of the window) might make the IDE more responsive.

■ **Support for Windows Installer**   Visual Studio now supports this much-improved setup technology for Windows applications, including support for installation rollback in case of setup issues. You can even create deployment packages for Web applications that enable you to install and run ASP.NET applications on a machine that does not currently have the .NET Framework installed. The deployment package installs all necessary runtime files for you.

Windows

While working with the Visual Studio .NET IDE, you'll encounter a wide variety of windows used for a wide variety of purposes. Some are new, like the Dynamic Help window described in the previous section, and others will be familiar to users of previous versions of Visual Studio. This section takes a look at the most common windows.

■ **Designer/Source Editor**   This is the pane where you'll spend most of your time in the Visual Studio environment. It integrates almost all of the designers and source-code editors that you'll use in Visual Studio, including the Web Forms, XML schema, and HTML designers, as well as a unified source-code editor that provides support for XML, HTML, SQL, Cascading Style Sheets (CSS), and all of the .NET languages. The editor provides enhanced features specific to each language. Two particularly exciting new features of the HTML and CSS editors are IntelliSense statement completion for both HTML and CSS, and better control over how (or if) the editor modifies the format of your HTML and CSS documents. To change the formatting settings, click Options on the Tools menu, select the Text Editor folder, select the HTML/XML (or CSS) folder, and then select the Format option. Buttons at the bottom of the designer/editor window enable you to switch between Design and HTML views of ASP.NET pages, as well as between different modes for other document types. You can step through this process using the steps described in the section Switching from HTML to Design Mode.

■ **Solution Explorer**   Solution Explorer should be familiar to anyone who's used Visual InterDev 6. It's one of the primary tools you'll use to manage project files and resources, including adding, removing, opening, renaming, and moving files, as well as setting a start-up page or project, switching between code and design view for a file, and viewing status information (for example, Source Code Control status) about your files. The graphic on the next page shows Solution Explorer.

Running a Web Application

1

- **Class View**   The Class View pane, which by default shares a window with Solution Explorer, contains a listing of all classes (contained in .vb or .cs modules) in your projects and the methods, properties, and interfaces implemented in those classes. If Class View is not visible, click the Class View tab in the window it shares with Solution Explorer.

- **Server Explorer**   Server Explorer is a new feature of Visual Studio .NET that enables you to view resources on both your local machine and remote servers, including configured data connections, event logs, message queues, and performance counters. Server Explorer also lets you drag and drop resources onto Web Forms pages or .NET components, enabling some of the most productive server-side development available to date. In the Standard Edition of Visual C# .NET, Server Explorer is limited to connecting to and viewing database objects.

*Alphabetic
(AZ) button*

■ **Properties**   The Properties pane should be immediately familiar to anyone who's used any of the Visual Studio development tools. It provides access to the properties of the object currently selected in the IDE. The Properties pane enables you to collapse or expand categories of properties to better view the categories you're interested in. You can also view the properties in alphabetical order by clicking the alphabetic button (with AZ on it), just below the object selection drop-down menu. When an ASP.NET document is open in Visual Studio .NET and an object such as a Label is selected, you can also see what events are available by clicking on the lightning bolt button to see a list of events or add event handlers.

For those who haven't used the Properties pane in previous versions of Visual Studio, you can take a look at how you can modify the properties of a control in the section "Exploring Properties" later in this chapter.

■ **The Visual Studio .NET Toolbox**   The Visual Studio .NET Toolbox is another element modeled closely on the Visual InterDev environment. It provides access to a wide variety of controls, components, and HTML elements. You can add Toolbox items (essentially, the HTML tags or text elements used to implement controls or components) to Web Forms or components either by double-clicking the item name in the Toolbox (in which case the item is inserted at the current cursor location) or by using drag-and-drop (enabling you to place the item where desired). Note that some items do not have a visual representation when used in a Web Form. These items are usually displayed in a separate area at the bottom of the Designer window. The graphic on the following page shows the Toolbox displaying the Web Forms controls.

Running a Web Application

tip

You can add your own items or categories (called tabs) to the Toolbox. To add a tab, right-click the Toolbox, click Add Tab on the shortcut menu, and give the tab a name. To add your own items, make sure the desired tab is selected, select the desired item in the Designer (or select the desired text in the code editor), and drag it to the Toolbox. If you want, you can give the new item a descriptive name by right- clicking it and clicking Rename Tab.

Task List An underrated and often underutilized tool from Visual InterDev, the Task List window enables you to create, sort, and track tasks to be completed for the current solution. The Task List also can contain tasks automatically generated by Visual Studio to help you locate and correct build errors. Tasks can be categorized and prioritized according to your needs. Categories include Comment tasks (indicated by comment tokens such as *TODO*, *UPGRADE_TODO*, and so on), User tasks, Build Errors, Shortcuts (created by right-clicking a line of code in the editor and clicking Add Task List Shortcut), and IntelliSense tasks, which are displayed when IntelliSense detects an error in your code. The following graphic shows a Task List with a Shortcut task, a User task, and a Comment task. To display the Task List, on the View menu, point to Other Windows, and click Task List menu option.

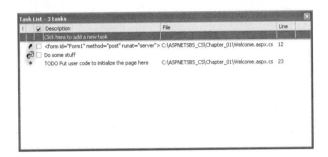

Switch from HTML to Design mode

1   If the Welcome.aspx page is not open in the editor, open it by double-clicking the file in Solution Explorer.

2   Click the HTML button to switch to HTML view. (You can switch back by clicking the Design button.)

When you click the HTML button, the HTML code for the page is displayed.

HTML button

Design button

Explore the Properties pane

1   If it isn't already open in the editor, open the Welcome.aspx file by double-clicking it in Solution Explorer. Make sure you're in Design view; if you're not, click the Design button to switch to Design view.

2   Click the text "Welcome to ASP.NET!" to select the control it represents.

This is an ASP.NET Label server control. When you select the control, its properties are displayed in the Properties pane. (You'll learn more about ASP.NET server controls in later chapters.)

3   Click the + sign next to the *Font* property to expose its subproperties.

4   Select the *Bold* property, and then click its drop-down list box to change the property value to True.

5   Select the *Size* property, and then click its drop-down list box to change the property value to Large.

Notice how the text displayed is modified.

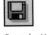

Save button

6 Center the Label control over the image by dragging the control in the designer window, and then save the file by clicking the Save button on the toolbar.

7 Browse the page by right-clicking Welcome.aspx in Solution Explorer and clicking View In Browser.

The result should look similar to this graphic:

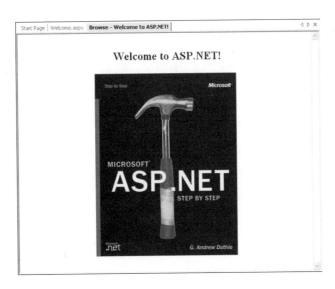

The Output window will be familiar to developers who've used Microsoft's Visual C++ or Visual J++ tools. One of the primary purposes of the Output window is to display messages related to project builds. (A build is the process of compiling all of the code files that make up a project.) Because you need to build your ASP.NET Web applications before code modifications will appear, you'll be seeing a lot of this window. The following graphic shows the output of a build of a sample project. In this case the build was successful, with no errors or warnings. Had there been build errors or warnings, they would have been displayed in this window.

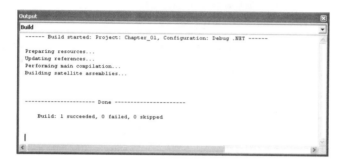

Toolbars

To accomplish tasks in Visual Studio .NET, you'll most likely use a combination of the IDE's toolbars and menus. This section takes a look at the most commonly used toolbars, and the next section looks at the most commonly used menus. You can view the full list of available toolbars by right-clicking any toolbar (or empty toolbar area). In keeping with the customizable nature of the Visual Studio .NET IDE, all toolbars can be customized by adding, removing, or rearranging buttons, moving toolbars, and showing or hiding toolbars.

note

Given the flexibility of the Visual Studio .NET toolbars, it's easy to end up with your toolbars looking nothing like they did when you installed Visual Studio. If you want to restore your toolbars to their original configuration, click the Options button found at the right end of each toolbar, click Add Or Remove Buttons, click the menu item for the toolbar name, and then click Reset Toolbar.

Some of the more common toolbars include:

- **Standard**   The Standard toolbar, shown in the following graphic, contains buttons for common file and project commands, including opening files and projects, creating new files and projects, and accessing various windows in the IDE.

- **Formatting**   The Formatting toolbar, shown in the following graphic, contains buttons related to the formatting of text, including font and font size, text alignment options, and background and foreground colors. This toolbar is enabled only when you're entering or editing text in Design view.

- **Text Editor**   The Text Editor toolbar, shown in the following graphic, contains buttons related to the operation of the Text Editor, including access to IntelliSense features, indenting and commenting of code, and bookmarks. (You use bookmarks to navigate quickly to specific sections of your code.)

- **Debug**   The Debug toolbar, shown in the following graphic, contains buttons related to Debugging commands—from Start, Stop, and Break commands to buttons for accessing the various Debug windows. (Debugging is covered in Chapter 14.)

Menus

Many menus are available in Visual Studio .NET. Which specific menus are available depends on the task you're working on at any given time. Although we won't go over all of them here, the menus you'll encounter most frequently in your Visual Studio travels are listed here.

- **File menu**   The File menu is used to create, open, and save files and projects, as well as to print files and to exit the program.

- **Edit menu**   The Edit menu contains commands for working with text and objects, such as Cut, Copy, and Paste, as well as text-specific commands, such as Find and Replace, and formatting commands, such as Make Uppercase or Make Lowercase.

- **View menu**   The View menu is used to access windows or views that are currently hidden. You use this menu to switch from source code to design view or to open up windows such as the Task List, as well as to choose which toolbars are displayed.

- **Project menu**   The Project menu is used to add items to a project, add references to assemblies or XML Web services, and set the start page and start-up project used for debugging.

- **Build menu**   The Build menu is used for building and rebuilding a project or projects, as well as commands for deploying projects.

- **Debug menu**   The Debug menu is used to start, stop, and pause (break) debugging, and to set breakpoints and access debugging windows.

- **Data menu**   The Data menu is used to generate datasets and preview data.

- **Format menu**   The Format menu is used to control styles, alignment of controls and Z-Order (controlling how overlapping controls appear on the display).

- **Table menu**   The Table menu is used for working with HTML tables. You use this menu to insert or delete tables, rows, columns, and cells, as well as to merge or split cells.

- **Tools menu** The Tools menu contains commands related to customizing the IDE and to external tools such as the OLE/COM Object Viewer and Spy++. You use this menu to access the Customize dialog box discussed earlier, as well as the Options dialog box, discussed in the next section.

- **Query menu** The Query menu is used for creating and running database queries using Visual Studio's database tools.

- **Window menu** The Window menu is used to navigate and manage the open document windows being used by the application.

- **Help menu** The Help menu is used to access the Visual Studio .NET documentation, as well as to access product support. This menu also contains a link to the Visual Studio .NET start page that appears by default when you open Visual Studio. If you accidentally close the start page, you can use this menu item to get it back.

tip

You can create your own custom menus by right-clicking anywhere in the menu bar and clicking Customize. In the Customize dialog box, click the Commands tab. Under Categories, select New Menu. Under Commands, click and drag the New Menu item to the desired location in the menu bar. Next, right-click the new menu heading, and use the Name entry to give your new menu a name. You can then drag items from the other menu categories to your new menu. To create a submenu, drag another copy of the New Menu item to the desired location on your menu.

Options

One of the most dramatic areas of improvement in Visual Studio .NET is in customization. Much of the customization available in Visual Studio .NET is controlled from the Options dialog box, shown in the graphic on the next page. As mentioned earlier, you can access this dialog box by selecting Tools and then Options. Not only has the number of options increased significantly, but the degree of control over particular options has increased as well.

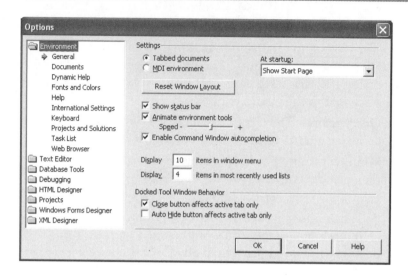

One good example of this increased control is in the area of code formatting. Visual InterDev developers will no doubt remember the frustration of having the Visual InterDev editor reformat their ASP code when switching from Design to Source view. Visual Studio .NET still performs code formatting, but you have language-by-language control over how this formatting is done. (Not all languages use auto-formatting, so they won't all have these options.) Go to the Text Editor option folder, choose the language (for example, HTML or CSS), and set the options as you prefer. In this way, you can determine how formatting is applied to your code or, for some languages, you can turn off reformatting entirely.

note

One new option that will appeal to longtime BASIC users is having the IDE display line numbers in the text editor. Unlike in BASIC, however, in Visual Studio .NET the line numbers are only for reference; they're not actually a part of the code file. You can turn this option on or off for individual languages, or you can turn it on globally for all languages.

Exiting Visual Studio .NET

When you're finished working with a given project, naturally you'll want to exit from Visual Studio .NET.

Shut down the program

Save All button

1 Save any open files, either by using the Save All button on the toolbar or by clicking Save All on the File menu.

2 Click Exit on the File menu.

Visual Studio .NET shuts down.

What's New in ASP.NET

Although there are plenty of familiar features in ASP.NET, some significant changes have been made to the ASP.NET architecture, including many improvements and new features. The following section takes a high-level look at what's new in ASP.NET.

Familiar Features

Many ASP.NET features will be familiar to Web developers who've used classic ASP. The much-used *Request* and *Response* objects are still there, as are the *Application*, *Session*, and *Server* objects, albeit with some new properties and methods. You can still use either *<script runat="server">* blocks or the *<% %>* ASP script delimiters to denote server-side script. In fact, for the most part you can write an ASP.NET page exactly the same way you would write a classic ASP page. Once you get used to the new programming model of ASP.NET, though, you'll never go back to coding your ASP applications the old way.

Bear in mind that you don't need to migrate all of your existing ASP applications at once. ASP.NET is designed to run side by side with classic ASP. So while you're working on your first new ASP.NET application, your current ASP applications can still be running right alongside the new one.

What's New

There's a lot of new stuff in ASP.NET, and it will take time to learn all of it. But once you've learned it, your productivity will be far greater than it was with classic ASP. Let's look at a list of some of the new features of ASP.NET.

■ **Web Forms** This is the new programming model of ASP.NET. Web Forms combines the best of ASP with the ease of development and productivity of Visual Basic. You can drag controls onto a page and then write code to provide interactivity, call business objects, and so on. You'll learn about Web Forms in Chapter 7.

■ **Server controls**   A major component of the Web Forms programming model, the ASP.NET server controls map approximately to HTML elements (plus some additional controls you'll learn about later) and provide powerful server-side programmability. Server controls are run on the server and can output HTML that's tailored for uplevel browsers, such as Internet Explorer 5.x or later, or for any HTML 3.2–compliant browser. Chapter 8 and Chapter 10 will cover server controls in depth.

■ **Web Services**   This key part of ASP.NET enables you to make programmatic services available to other developers over the Internet (or a local intranet). Web Services are based on the emerging Simple Object Access Protocol (SOAP) standard, so they will allow relatively painless interoperation across diverse platforms. You'll learn more about Web Services in Chapter 11.

■ **Caching**   ASP.NET includes a powerful new caching engine that enables you to improve the performance of your applications by reducing the Web server and database server processing loads. You'll learn more about caching in Chapter 12.

■ **Configuration Improvements**   ASP.NET uses a new method of storing configuration information for Web applications. Instead of IIS storing this information in a hard-to-access database, it's stored in XML-based human- and machine-readable configuration files. You'll look at how these configuration files work in Chapter 5.

■ **State Management Improvements**   If you've had to build an ASP application to run on a Web farm, you know all too well that classic ASP has major limitations when it comes to state management. ASP.NET overcomes these limitations, providing support for distributing session state across Web servers, persisting state information in a SQL Server database, and providing state management without the use of cookies. You'll learn how to take advantage of these features in Chapter 4.

■ **Security**   This function is extremely important in today's Web applications. The security model in ASP.NET has been substantially improved, including new and improved authentication methods, code access security, and role-based authorization. You'll look at the ASP.NET security model and how to implement security in your ASP.NET applications in Chapter 6.

■ **Improved Reliability**   ASP.NET contains new features aimed at improving the reliability of Web applications, including proactive restarting of applications and automatic process recycling to resolve deadlock conditions and memory leaks.

We've only scratched the surface in describing some of the new offerings of the .NET platform and the substantial advantages offered by ASP.NET. In subsequent chapters you'll get detailed information on using ASP.NET to create faster, more robust, and more functional Web applications. In the next chapter, you'll learn about the various development tools that you can use to create your Web applications, from simple text editors to powerful IDEs like Visual Studio .NET.

Chapter 1 Quick Reference

To	Do this	Button
Start Visual Studio .NET	Click the Windows Start button, point to All Programs, point to Microsoft Visual Studio .NET, and then click the Microsoft Visual Studio .NET icon.	*start*
Change how the IDE tool windows are configured	Click the My Profile link on the Visual Studio .NET Start Page, and modify the settings as desired.	HTML *HTML*
Switch between Design and HTML views of an ASP.NET page	Click the Design or HTML buttons below the designer/editor window.	Design *Design*
Save a file	Click the Save button, or click Save *<filename>* on the File menu.	*Save*

Creating an ASP.NET Web Application

In this chapter, you will learn how to

✔ *Create a new Web application with Microsoft Visual Studio .NET.*

✔ *Add a Web Forms page to a Web application project.*

✔ *Add Server Controls to a Web Forms page and modify their properties.*

✔ *Write code in event handlers.*

✔ *Build and test a Web application.*

Now that you've learned about some of the features of Visual Studio .NET, the next step is to take advantage of them in your own applications. Conveniently enough, that's precisely what you're going to learn about in this chapter.

We'll begin with an overview of the two major project types used for ASP.NET applications, followed by a look at the file types used in ASP.NET, and the purpose of each. Then you'll learn how to create a new Web application, add a new Web Forms page, add controls to the page, and manipulate their properties. Finally you'll learn how to add event handler code to the page, build the project, and test the page.

ASP.NET Project Types

There are two basic types of ASP.NET applications, each with a distinct purpose. For a Web application that will provide its own HTML-based UI, there are ASP.NET Web applications. For Web-based functionality that will be accessed programmatically, there are ASP.NET Web Services. Both of these application types can be developed with or without Visual Studio .NET, although the Visual Studio environment makes developing either type of application significantly easier and faster. The following graphic shows the ASP.NET Web application and ASP.NET Web Services project templates for Visual Basic .NET:

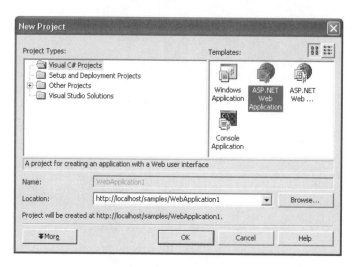

ASP.NET Web Applications

ASP.NET applications, at their simplest, are much like classic ASP applications. A simple ASP.NET application consists of the following four parts:

- A virtual directory in IIS, configured as an application root, to hold the files that comprise the application and to control access to the files

- One or more .aspx files

- A Global.asax file (analogous to the Global.asa file in classic ASP) to deal with Session and Application start-up and clean-up logic (optional)

- A Web.config file used to store configuration settings (new in ASP.NET and optional)

For Visual Studio .NET users, the good news is that all the preceding files are created for you when you create a new Web application project.

ASP.NET Web Forms

Web Forms are an important part of any ASP.NET Web application. Put simply, they are ASP.NET pages that use ASP.NET Server Controls. The Web Forms programming model makes it possible (and relatively easy) to develop Web-based applications in much the same way that today's Visual Basic programmers develop Windows-based applications that have a graphical user interface (GUI).

Web Forms in Visual Studio .NET enable you to create rich, interactive applications simply by dragging controls onto a page and then writing minimal code to handle user interaction, events, and so on. In addition, the Visual Studio .NET environment enables you to work on your pages visually, using the Web Forms Designer, or textually, using Visual Studio .NET's powerful source-code editor.

The code you write in your Web Forms can be written in one of two ways: inline in the .aspx file (as is typical of a classic ASP page), or using a code-behind module. Although it's possible to write your application with code in the actual .aspx file and still take advantage of compiled code and the other improvements of .NET, it's recommended that you get in the habit of using code-behind modules. Visual Studio .NET defaults to using code-behind for UI-specific programming logic.

Code-Behind

Code-behind is a new feature in ASP.NET that enables developers to truly separate the HTML UI code from the code in Visual Basic .NET, C#, or other languages that are used to provide user interaction, validation, and so on. There are a number of advantages to using code-behind modules, including the following:

- **Clean separation of HTML and code** Code-behind enables HTML designers and developers to do what they do best independently, while minimizing the possibility of messing up one another's work (something that happens all too frequently when developing classic ASP applications).

- **Easier reuse** Code that isn't interspersed with HTML in a .aspx page can be more easily reused in other projects.

- **Simpler maintenance** Because the code is separated from the HTML, your pages will be easier to read and maintain.

- **Deployment without source code** Visual Studio .NET projects using code-behind modules can be deployed as compiled code (along with the .aspx pages), enabling you to protect your source code if you want. This can be very useful if you're creating applications for clients but want to retain control of your intellectual property.

If you are using Visual Studio .NET, there is an additional advantage to using code-behind. Many features of the Visual Studio .NET editor, such as code completion and IntelliSense, work only for code that is in a code-behind file.

All in all, it's worthwhile to get into the habit of using code-behind. You'll see examples of how code-behind is used throughout this book. Part III of the book will discuss Web Forms in detail.

ASP.NET XML Web Services

Although no one would deny that Web applications created with ASP.NET (or even with classic ASP) can be very useful, one of the things that has long been missing from it is an easy way to provide programmatic functionality over the Internet or an intranet without tying the client to a specific UI. This is where ASP.NET XML Web Services come in.

An XML Web Service, at its simplest, is a chunk of programming code that is accessible over the Web. XML Web Services are based on the World Wide Web Consortium's (W3C) SOAP specification. This allows computers on varying platforms, from Windows servers to UNIX workstations, to offer and consume programmatic services over the HTTP protocol.

> **note**
>
> SOAP can use other protocols, such as FTP or SMTP, but HTTP is the most common protocol used with SOAP and XML Web Services because most firewalls allow communication through the HTTP protocol.

ASP.NET makes it remarkably easy to implement XML Web Services. In fact, all you need to do is add a declaration to any methods that you want to make available as XML Web Services. Visual Studio .NET makes it even easier by taking care of all the work necessary to make your XML Web service available to potential clients. Part IV covers XML Web Services in detail.

ASP.NET File Types

There are a number of new file types you'll see in your ASP.NET applications. To avoid any confusion, let's take a minute to go over the ones you'll see most often and discuss how they're used.

- **.aspx** The extension you'll see most often is .aspx. It's used for Web Forms pages, and it's analogous to the .asp extension in classic ASP.
- **.ascx** The extension used for Web Forms user controls is .ascx. User controls provide one of the many ways available in ASP.NET

to reuse code. They're somewhat similar to the include files in classic ASP in that they can be as simple as a few HTML tags or can include complex logic that the author might want to reuse in many pages. User controls are added to a Web Forms page using the @ Register directive, which is discussed in Part III.

- **.asmx**   The extension used for files that implement XML Web Services is .asmx. XML Web Services can be accessed directly through .asmx files, or the .asmx file can direct the request to a compiled assembly that implements the Web service.

- **.cs**   The extension for Visual C# .NET code modules is .cs. All Web Forms pages (.aspx) added to a Visual Studio .NET Web application that are written in Visual C# .NET will have a corresponding .cs code-behind module with the same name as the Web Form page to which it's related (*pagename.aspx.cs*).

- **.resx**   The .resx extension denotes a resource file. These files are used primarily in Windows Forms applications, but are also available to Web application developers for storing resources such as alternative text strings for internationalization of applications.

- **Global.asax**   Like Global.asa in classic ASP, Global.asax is a file used to define Application-level and Session-level variables and start-up procedures. Note that although Global.asax can be structured like Global.asa with start-up procedures such as *Session_OnStart* (*Session_Start* in ASP.NET) coded directly in the Global.asax file in a *<script runat="server">* block, Visual Studio implements these procedures in a .cs (or .vb) code-behind module rather than in the Global.asax file itself (*global.asax.cs*).

  In addition to the functionality available in a classic ASP Global.asa file, ASP.NET also enables you to import namespaces, link to assemblies, and perform other useful tasks. You'll learn more about Global.asax in Chapter 7.

- **Web.config**   Web.config is a new file type in ASP.NET. It's used to solve one of the major hassles with classic ASP applications: configuration. The Web.config file is a human-readable and machine-readable XML-based file that stores all the configuration settings for a given application (or segment of an application). Web.config files are interpreted hierarchically; that is, a Web.config file in a subdirectory of your application will override the settings of the Web.config file(s) in its parent directories. The advantage is that configuration settings can be inherited where that is desirable, but you also have very granular control over configuration.

Visual Studio .NET

It's certainly possible to create ASP.NET Web applications in Notepad or another text editor, but if you're doing serious ASP.NET or component development, you'll probably want to work within the Visual Studio .NET environment. The advantages of Visual Studio .NET over simple text editors include

- Robust management of project files and multiple projects.
- Integration with Microsoft's Visual SourceSafe source-code control environment.
- Visual Tools for working with Web Services, Web Forms Server Controls, and database tools.
- Packaging and deployment services for Web applications.
- Support for multiple languages within a single IDE, including cross-language inheritance and debugging.

That's just a partial list. There's much more to the tool than can be covered in a single chapter. So without further ado, let's look at how to create projects and pages in the Visual Studio .NET environment.

Creating Applications

One of the first things you'll want to do to work with ASP.NET in Visual Studio .NET is create a new project, or in Visual Studio .NET parlance, a Web application.

Create an ASP.NET Web application

1   Launch Visual Studio .NET, using the techniques you learned in Chapter 1.

2   To open the New Project dialog box, use one of the following three methods:

- Click the Create A New Project link on the Visual Studio .NET Start Page (displayed by default when you first open Visual Studio .NET).
- Click the New Project button, located on the standard toolbar.
- On the File menu, point to New, and click Project.

New Project button

3   In the New Project dialog box (see the following graphic) click the Visual C# Projects folder, click the appropriate template (ASP.NET Web Application), set the location to **http://localhost/Chapter_02**, and then click OK.

Note that this application is separate from the Chapter_02 project included with the practice file installation, which is contained in the aspnetsbs_cs solution.

Visual Studio .NET creates a new Web application as well as physical and virtual directories for the project.

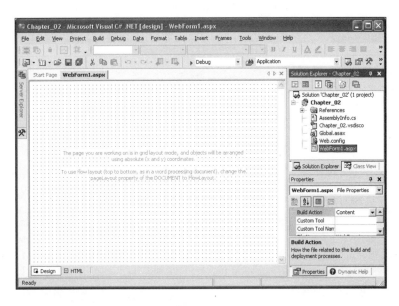

That's it! You've now created your first ASP.NET Web application. Next we'll look at how to add new pages.

In your new Web application, you'll notice that Visual Studio .NET has already added a page to the project for you, named WebForm1.aspx, and opened it in the editor. However, because one page is rarely enough for most sites, let's look at how to add a new page to your Web application.

Create a new ASP.NET page (Web Form)

1   Add a new Web Form to your application.

As with creating a new project, there are several ways to add a new ASP.NET page (also referred to as a Web Form) to your application. Which one you should use is largely a matter of how you like to work. Here are several ways to accomplish this task, although there are others:

■   In Solution Explorer, right-click the application name, point to Add, and then click Add Web Form, as shown in the graphic on the next page. You can also click Add New Item, and then click Web Form in the Templates area of the Add New Item dialog box.

Creating Web Applications

Add New Item

- On the Visual Studio .NET toolbar, click the Add New Item button. You can also click the down arrow next to this button, and then click Add Web Form in the drop-down menu.

- On the Project menu, click Add Web Form (or Add New Item).

The last two of these methods will open the Add New Item dialog box, shown in the following illustration:

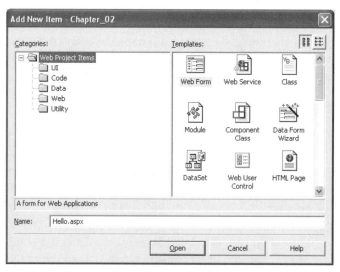

2   In the Add New Item dialog box, click the Web Form template, and specify **Hello.aspx** for the new page. Before finishing up, you might want to take a look at some of the other template types that are available, making sure that Web Form is selected when you're done. After you're done looking, click the Open button.

Visual Studio .NET creates the page, adds it to the project, and opens it in the Web Forms Designer.

Adding Server Controls

Now that you've created a start page for your new application, what can you do with it? Well, let's start by creating a simple page to display a "Hello World!" greeting to the client. By default, Web Forms are opened in Grid Layout mode. Because Grid Layout relies on Cascading Style Sheets, which are not supported in all browsers, you might want to change the page layout to Flow Mode. To do so, follow these steps.

Modify Web Form properties

1   With the Web Form open in the Visual Studio .NET designer, click the Web Form page to ensure it is selected.

If this is the first time you have used the IDE, the word *DOCUMENT* should appear in the drop-down list at the top of the Properties pane when the page is selected.

2   Click the *pageLayout* property in the Properties pane, and click FlowLayout in the drop-down list, as shown in the following graphic.

note

When you place components on a page while the page is in grid layout, a style attribute is added to the control to enable precise placement on the page. If after you place a component on the page and change from grid layout to flow layout, the style attribute with positioning information is not removed. If you want to remove the style attribute, you can go to HTML mode and manually delete the style attribute.

3   Save the page by clicking Save Hello.aspx on the File menu (or by clicking the Save button on the toolbar).

Until you add controls (or HTML elements), the page will display the message shown in the following graphic in Design view.

Add controls to a Web Form

1   With the Web Form open in design mode, position your mouse pointer over the Toolbox tab. (By default, it's found to the left of the code editor/designer.)

2   When the Toolbox appears, ensure that the Web Forms palette is active. (The title bar of the active palette is shown immediately above the controls displayed in the Toolbox.) If it isn't active, you can click its title bar to activate it. Note that the Web Forms palette is only available when a page is in design mode.

3   With the Web Forms palette active, double-click Label control (see the following figure) to add an ASP.NET Label control to the page. After you've added the label, it should be selected by default.

4   To make the Label control display the text you want, you need to change its *Text* property. Click the Text property in the Properties pane, and then change the text (by default, Label) to **Enter a name:**, as shown in the graphic on the next page.

5   Click the background of the page to place the mouse pointer after the *Label* control you added to the page.

6   Using the Toolbox as in Step 3, add a *TextBox* control to the page, and then add a Button control to the page.

7   Using the same technique as in Step 4, change the *Text* property of the *Button* control to **Submit**.

Save button

8   Save the page by clicking the Save button on the toolbar. You can also save by clicking Save <filename> on the File menu.

Add event handler code

1   To make the page do anything useful, we need to add some code, so double-click the *Button* control.

This will open up the code-behind module for the Web Form and create an event handler procedure called *Button1_Click*, placing your cursor in the handler.

2   Add the following code to the Button1_Click procedure.

```
Label1.Text = "Hello, " + TextBox1.Text + "!";
TextBox1.Visible = false;
Button1.Visible = false;
```

3   Save the code-behind module, which should now look like the following graphic.

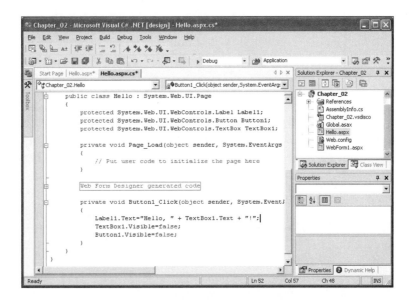

Building and Testing Your Page

Because you modified the code-behind module for the Web Form, you need to build your project before you can browse the page. (You'll learn more about code-behind in later chapters.) *Building* is the process of compiling all the code modules in the project so they'll be available to the pages and modules that call them. To build the project, click Build Chapter_02 (or Build Solution, which will build all projects in the solution) on the Build menu.

After you've saved the Web Form page and its code-behind module and built the application, you can test the page using the following steps.

Test your page

1   Right-click the page in Solution Explorer, and click View In Browser.

The result should look like the graphic on the following page. (You can close the Output pane if you want to see more of a page.)

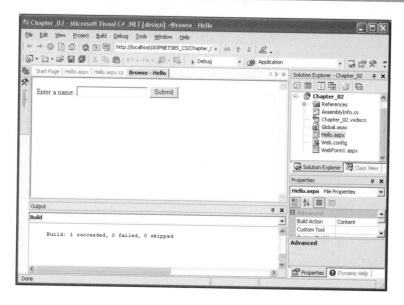

2   Enter your name in the text box, and click Submit.

The result should be similar to the following graphic. (Note that the Web toolbar shows the address of the page being browsed. You can enter this address in a browser window on your computer to view the page in a nonembedded browser window.)

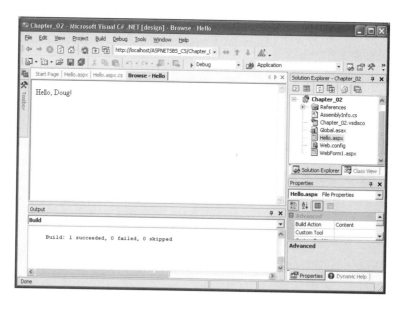

Chapter 2 Quick Reference

To	Do this	Button
Create a new project in Visual Studio .NET	Click the New Project Button, select the project language and template, and then provide the name and location for the new project.	
Create a new Web Forms page	Click the Add New Item button (or click the arrow to the right and click Add Web Form). Provide a name for the new Web Form, and click OK.	
Save a file	Click the Save button, or click Save *<filename>* on the File menu.	

3

Understanding Programming Basics

In this chapter, you will learn how to

✔ *Use expressions, variables, and constants.*

✔ *Use methods.*

✔ *Use flow control statements.*

✔ *Handle errors.*

✔ *Use object-oriented programming techniques.*

This chapter is intended for readers who have little or no direct programming experience. It's designed to give a brief overview of some basic programming concepts that will help you better understand the examples presented throughout the book. Readers with programming experience might wish to skip this chapter and move on to Chapter 4.

Although this chapter provides an overview of basic programming concepts, I encourage readers with little hands-on programming experience to use other resources to supplement this information. These resources include books on programming basics, Web sites such as the Microsoft Developer Network site (*http://msdn.microsoft.com*), and newsgroups and mailing lists that can be helpful to the inexperienced. (Microsoft maintains a large number of newsgroups on development topics related to Microsoft tools at *http://msdn.microsoft.com /newsgroups/*. You can read from and post to these newsgroups using a news-reader such as Outlook Express.) And the ASP.NET development team at Microsoft has just launched a set of discussion forums on ASP.NET that promise to be a great resource as well. These forums can be found at *http://www.asp.net /forums/*. Of course, one of the best (and most overlooked) resources for programming concepts in C# is the MSDN documentation that ships with Microsoft Visual C# .NET (a subset of which is also available as part of the quarterly MSDN library, which can be ordered from *http: //msdn.microsoft.com/subscription*). The MSDN documentation contains samples, tutorials, language references, and specifications for C#, Microsoft Visual Basic .NET, managed extensions for C++, and JScript .NET.

This chapter will discuss how these basic programming concepts apply to ASP.NET, and how you can use them to create effective ASP.NET applications. Although most of these concepts aren't language-specific, there are some subtle differences in how they're implemented in C# vs. Visual Basic .NET or other .NET languages.

note

In ASP.NET, all code is contained in either Web Forms pages, code-behind modules, or modules that make up class libraries that are external to your ASP.NET applications. The term *module* in this sense refers to the .cs file that contains the code.

A *class*, as you'll see in "Using Classes as Containers for Code" later in this chapter, is a special type of code container that provides a number of useful features. Classes are contained within modules (that is, files with the extension .cs).

A *namespace* contains one or more classes and can be defined in one or more modules. Namespaces can be used to prevent name collisions when two classes have the same name.

Expressions, Variables, and Constants

Expressions, variables, and constants are some of the most basic building blocks of computer programs, and you'll use them all extensively in your ASP.NET applications.

Expressions

Expressions are central to virtually all computer programs. Expressions enable you to:

- Compare values to one another.
- Perform calculations.
- Manipulate text values.

An expression can be as simple as the following:

```
1 + 1
```

An expression like this isn't very useful by itself, however. Unlike people, who can easily recognize "one plus one" and fill in the blank ("equals two"), computers aren't capable of that kind of leap of logic. For the expression to be useful, it needs to tell a computer not just to add one and one, but to store the result somewhere so that we can make use of it later (either by displaying it to the user or using it in another expression later). This is where variables come in.

Variables

As with the preceding example, at some point during the execution of most programs, you'll need to store values of some sort. Examples include the results of mathematical operations (as in the preceding example), text input from users, and the results of comparisons. Simply put, *variables* are storage areas for data. This data can be numeric, text, or any one of a number of special data types.

Data Types

The *data type* variable defines the type of data that can be stored in it, as well as the format in which that data is stored (and the amount of memory that the system needs to allocate for the variable). The following table lists the data types supported by C# and Visual Basic .NET, as well as the Microsoft .NET Framework SDK types to which they map. The data types marked with an asterisk don't have a native representation, but you can still access these data types by using the appropriate *System* type when declaring the variable. Why cover Visual Basic .NET types? If you are creating a class to be used by other developers, knowing how the types match between C# and Visual Basic .NET is critical, both to ensure that the correct type is used, and to document the class in a Visual Basic .NET programmer-friendly way. The good news is that, unlike in the 32 bit Win32 world of Visual Basic 6 and Visual C++ 6, an integer in both environments is the same size and has the same numeric range.

The data type of a variable is determined at the time the variable is declared. This will be discussed further in the section titled "Declaring Variables" later in this chapter. Some data types (such as the Date type) do not have language specific implementations. In Table 3-1, there is an asterisk (*) in the cells of types without the corresponding language-specific data types. Some data types are not Common Language Specification (CLS) compliant, and are noted with a cross (†) in the .NET data type column.

Table 3-1.   Data Types

C# data type	VB.NET data type	.NET data type	Size
bool	Boolean	System.Boolean	1 byte
byte	Byte	System.Byte	1 byte
sbyte	*	System.SByte †	1 byte
char	Char	System.Char	2 bytes
*	Date	System.DateTime	8 bytes
decimal	Decimal	System.Decimal	12 bytes
double	Double	System.Double	8 bytes
int	Integer	System.Int32	4 bytes
uint	*	System.UInt32 †	4 bytes
long	Long	System.Int64	8 bytes
ulong	*	System.UInt64 †	8 bytes
object	Object	System.Object	4 bytes
short	Short	System.Int16	2 bytes
ushort	*	System.UInt16 †	2 bytes
float	Single	System.Single	4 bytes
string	String	System.String	10 bytes, plus (2 x string length)
struct	User-Defined Type	System.ValueType (inherited)	Sum of member sizes

important

ASP.NET contains both framework-specific data types and language-specific data types for specific .NET languages, such as C# and Visual Basic .NET. To take advantage of some of the multilanguage features of the .NET environment, you need to limit your use of data types to those supported by the CLS, a subset of the data types supported by the common language runtime. In the preceding table, data types marked with a † are not CLS-compliant. Avoid using them in classes that you want to make available for use with other .NET languages.

Note that C# does not have a native type that maps to the DateTime data type, but using the .NET data type is just as easy.

Value Types vs. Reference Types

In .NET development, there are two categories of data types: value types and reference types. Although understanding the distinction between these types isn't absolutely necessary if you want to develop ASP.NET applications, it can help you better understand how these data types operate and how to deal with error messages resulting from coding errors. (Not that those ever happen, right?)

Value types are data types that store their data directly as values in memory. They include all the numeric types (*int32*, *short*, *single*, and so on), structures (custom data types based on *System.ValueType*), and enumerations (custom types that represent a defined set of values), as well as *boolean*, *char*, and *date* types. Value types are accessed directly, as in the following example:

```
int myInt;  // C# declaration for an int32
// Expression to assign the value 123 directly to the variable
myInt = 123;
```

note

C++ programmers will recognize all the syntax used to declare and assign variables, as well as comment delimiters. If instead you are using C# and have a Visual Basic background, several elements of C# syntax might require explanation.

Virtually all C# statements end with semicolons (;). Multiple C# statements can appear on a single line as long as all statements are terminated with semicolons. Unlike Visual Basic .NET, you can spread a single statement over as many lines as needed without using any sort of line extender (such as the underscore character (_) used by Visual Basic .NET). C# ignores whitespace characters, such as spaces, tabs, and new lines.

Comments in C# can be single line comments that begin with two slash characters (//) or multiline comments that begin with slash-star (/*) and end with star-slash (*/).

Reference types are data types that store a reference to another memory location that contains the data, which is usually based on a class, such as the *String* class in the .NET Framework. Reference types include *Object* (which acts as a replacement for Visual Basic's *Variant* type, no longer supported in .NET), *String*, and all *Arrays*, as well as instances of custom classes. Reference types are accessed through members of the class to which the type holds a reference, as in the following example:

```
// Define a class
class myClass {
    public int myInt;
}
// declare an instance of the class
myClass myClassInstance;
// Allocate space for the class
myClass = new myClass();
// Expression to assign the value 123 to myClass member myInt
myClass.myInt = 123;
```

Unlike value types, in which all you need to do is declare the variable and set a value, reference types must be declared and then have space allocated for them, using the new keyword in the example.

> **note**
>
> Conversion between value types and reference types is accomplished through a process called *boxing* and *unboxing*. *Boxing* is the process of creating an instance of the reference type object and assigning the value of a value type to the object (as well as storing information on the value's data type). *Unboxing* is the process of assigning the value of the boxed object type to a variable of the appropriate type (or a compatible type, such as assigning a boxed *int16* to a variable of type *int32*). Boxing and unboxing variables enables you to use the most lightweight variable possible, while still being able to box that variable into an object.

Declaring Variables

Before you can use variables in your programs, you need to declare them. *Variable declaration* is the process of specifying the characteristics of the variable (data type, lifetime, scope, and visibility) so that the runtime system knows how much storage space to allocate for the variable, which actions to allow on the variable, and who can take those actions. A variable declaration takes the following form in C#:

```
int x; // Declares a variable of type int
```

> **note**
>
> The previous example uses *x* as the name of the variable. Although this is perfectly acceptable as far as the language compilers are concerned, you should consider giving your variables more meaningful names, such as *FirstName* (for a string variable holding a first name), *LoopCount* (for a numeric variable used in a looping structure), or *Person* (for a reference to a class representing data on a person). This naming convention makes it much easier to remember the purpose of a variable, and it will make your code much easier to maintain.

The preceding declaration specifies a variable of type *int* (which maps to the *System.Int32* type). In addition to simple declarations like these, you can use the placement of the declarations, as well as C# keywords, to modify the lifetime, scope, and accessibility of your variables.

Lifetime

Lifetime refers to the span of time from when the variable is declared to when it is destroyed. The lifetime of a variable depends on where it is declared.

> **note**
>
> The following examples in this chapter write text into the *Text* property of a label control named *Message*. Labels and other server controls will be explained more completely in Chapter 9.

For example, the lifetime of a variable declared inside a procedure is limited to the execution of the procedure. After the procedure has finished executing, the variable is destroyed and the memory it occupied is reclaimed. An example is shown here:

```
// C# method
private void HelloWorld()
{
    String HelloString;
    string hellostring;
    HelloString="Hello World!";
    hellostring=HelloString;
    Message.Text+=HelloString;
    Message.Text+="<br>";
    Message.Text+=hellostring;
    // Both HelloString and hellostring will disappear
    //    after the next line...
}
```

> **important**
>
> There are two strings in this example, one declared as a *String* and the other declared as a *string* to remind you that C#, like C++, is case sensitive. In this example, the first string, *HelloString*, is declared as a System.String because in searching for the type *String* (note the upper case 'S'), C# will find System.String. The second variable, *hellostring*, is declared as a string (note the lower case 's'). This means that *hellostring* is declared using the C# alias for System.String. C# considers *HelloString* and *hellostring* to be entirely different objects. This is an important point to remember if you are a beginning C# programmer.

When this procedure completes, the variables *HelloString* and *hellostring* no longer exist. Their lifetime has ended. If *HelloString* had been declared outside the procedure, as in this next fragment of code, its lifetime would be until the instance of the class containing it was destroyed.

```
// Declare string outside of method
String HelloString;
// C# method
void HelloWorld()
{
    HelloString="Hello World!";
    Message.Text+=HelloString;
    // HelloString will still exist
    //    after the next line...
}
```

C# variables can also be declared as *static*. Static variables exist for the life of the class, and even if there are many instances of the class, there is only a single instance of the static variable. Static variables must be declared as members of the class rather than inside a single method.

note

The C# documentation recommends using whole words when naming your variables. You should use mixed case, with the first letter of each word capitalized, as in *HelloString*. This is called *Pascal-case*. This is one of many possible naming conventions you can use for variables and other elements in your programs. *Naming conventions* are simply agreed-upon standards for how elements will be named in a program. For instance, making the first character of the first word in a phrase lower case and capitalizing the first character of each subsequent word is called *Camel-case*. The particular naming convention you choose isn't important, but you must choose one and use it consistently. Doing so will make it easier for you to maintain your code and will help others understand what it's doing.

Scope

Scope, also known as *visibility*, refers to the region of code in which a variable can be accessed. The scope of a variable depends on where the variable is declared, and in Visual Basic .NET it can include the following levels.

- **Block-level**   Variables declared within curly braces, for instance in an *if* or *while* statement are referred to as block-level variables. Although the scope of block-level variables is limited to the block in which they're declared, their lifetime is that of the procedure in which the block appears.

- **Procedure-level**   Also known as local variables, these are visible only within the procedure in which they're declared.

- **Module-level**   In modules, classes, or structures, any variable declared outside of a procedure is referred to as a module-level variable. The accessibility of module-level variables is determined by any accessibility keywords used in their declaration (see the section titled "Accessibility" later in this chapter).

- **Namespace-level**   Variables declared at module level but given public accessibility (*public* or *internal*), are referred to as namespace-level variables. They're available to any procedure in the same namespace that contains the module in which the variable is declared.

Namespaces

A namespace is a container used for scoping. Namespaces can contain classes, structures, enumerations, interfaces, and delegates. By using namespaces, you can have more than one class in a given program with the same name, so long as the classes reside in different namespaces. Using namespaces can help ensure that code created by multiple teams of developers can be combined to create larger systems without name collisions.

Namespaces declared in C# uses the *namespace { }* syntax, where the classes and other types to be contained within the namespace are bracketed by the curly braces.

Namespaces can also be nested within other namespaces, forming a hierarchical tree structure. This structure enables you to combine classes in logical groupings, making it easier for those using your namespaces to find the classes they're looking for.

Following these guidelines will make your application more memory efficient and will make maintaining your code easier.

There is one significant difference in how scope works in C# vs. C++. The following code would work in C++, but fail in C#:

```
private void ScopeTest()
{
 int foo;
 foo=2;
 if ( foo!=2 )
 {
        // This would work in C++, fail in C#
        int foo;
        foo=7;
 }
 // In C++, foo would now be equal to the number 2, and the
 //    foo declared inside the if statement is not visible
 //    or available.
 /* In C#, if the only instance of foo was declared inside
 the if statement, foo would not be visible or
 available, but you would still be unable to
 declare a variable named foo.
 */
}
```

In this contrived example, even though the second copy of foo is declared within the braces of the *if* statement, the compiler will generate an error and fail to compile the code because that second instance of foo would hide the first instance. In C++, the second declaration of foo would declare a variable visible only inside the *if* statement, hiding the previous value of foo. You can, however, declare a variable at the class level and then declare a variable of the same name, even with a different type, within a method of that class.

There are a couple of guidelines to follow regarding lifetime and scope:

- Limit your variables to the narrowest possible scope that will allow you to accomplish your objectives.
- Avoid using the same name for variables of different scope within the same module even where it is allowed. Using the same name in such situations can lead to confusion and errors.
- Because module-level and *static* variables all continue to consume memory as long as the class or module is running, you should use them only when necessary.

Programming Basics 3

Accessibility

The last important concept in variable declaration is accessibility. The accessibility of a variable determines whether it can be accessed from outside the module (or application) in which it's declared. In C#, accessibility is determined through the use of one the following modifiers.

- *public*   Variables declared with the *public* keyword are accessible from anywhere in the same module (or class) in which they're declared, the namespace containing that module, and any other applications that refer to the application in which they're declared. They can only be used at the module or class level.

- *internal*   Variables declared with the *internal* keyword are accessible from anywhere in the same module (or class) in which they're declared, as well as the namespace containing that module.

- *protected*   Variables declared with the *protected* keyword are accessible only within the class in which they're declared or a class that inherits from that class. (See the section titled "Using Inheritance" later in this chapter.) The *protected* keyword can be combined with the *internal* keyword and can be used only to declare class members.

- *private*   Variables declared with the *private* keyword are accessible only from the module, class, or structure in which they're declared. In classes or modules, declaring a variable with no modifier or as *private* has the same effect on the variable's accessibility, but *private* makes your intentions more explicit. The *private* keyword cannot be used within a procedure.

> **note**
>
> In C#, all variables must be declared before they can be used. Failure to declare a variable will result in a compiler error. In Visual Basic .NET and some other languages, it's possible (but not advisable) to use variables without first declaring them.

Operators

In addition to the normal operators you are familiar with ('+' for addition, '-' for subtraction, '/' for division, '*' for multiplication and '=' for assignment), there are several operators borrowed from C and C++ that require some explanation.

- ++ Increment operator, incrementing the value by 1 (i++ is the same as i=i+1)
- — Decrement operator, decrementing the value by 1 (i— is the same as i=i-1)
- += Increment assignment operator (i+=5 is the same as i=i+5)
- -= Decrement assignment operator(i-=5 is the same as i=i-5)
- == and != `Equality` and Inequality operator
- % Modulus (remainder) operator. (17%5 equals 2)

There are other, less essential operators that are fully described in the MSDN documentation, and even the common operators can have other meanings. For instance, the plus sign (+) is also used as a string concatenation operator. In addition, operators can be overloaded, enabling you to define new meanings for them when used in combination with your class.

Constants

Constants are similar to variables, except for one important detail: After a constant has been declared and initialized, its value cannot be modified. Constants are very useful when you have a literal value that you want to refer to by name. For example, if you're a fan of Douglas Adams, you might want to create a constant to refer to the literal value *42*.

```
const int TheAnswer = 42;
```

Anywhere within your program (subject to the same scope, lifetime, and accessibility rules as variables) you can use the constant name *TheAnswer* instead of the literal value *42*.

Constants are particularly handy in place of literal values used as the arguments to methods of components you might use. For example, in classic ADO (ActiveX Data Objects), the data types of stored procedure parameters were represented by numeric values. Trying to remember all those values would be unrealistic, so the developers of ADO also made it possible to use constants (*adInteger*, *adVarChar*, and so on) in place of the literal values.

In other words, constants let you substitute easy-to-remember names for difficult-to-remember literal values. This can make your code easier to write and maintain.

Enumerations

Many constants used with ASP.NET are actually created using enumerations. Using enumerations, you can locate all related constants together, and the enumerations can be used in a type-safe way. For example, enumerations would be handy if you have a method that accepts numeric values representing a color numbered between 1 and 3. For instance, you might want to set a color:

```
private void SetColor(int color);
```

This method will, in fact, happily accept any integer value. You could declare an enumeration as follows:

```
enum ColorType {
  Red=1,
  Green,
  Blue
}
```

By default the first element of an enumeration is equal to 0. In this example, because I need an enumeration that contains 1 through 3 I set the first value in the enumeration to 1, and then the subsequent values are each incremented by one. So Green is 2 and Blue is 3. Now, rather than the previous method declaration, you could use the following:

```
private void SetColor(ColorType color);
```

This method will require an instance of the ColorType enumeration passed as the parameter, ensuring that the value is a valid member of the enumeration, and thus the value represents a valid color. The following is an example of calling SetColor with a ColorType enumeration member:

```
SetColor(ColorType.Blue);
```

Methods

Methods (functions inside of a class—all functions must be inside a class in C#) are an important tool in ASP.NET development because they enable you to determine at the time you write the code the order in which sections of code will run at runtime. Methods also enable you to better organize your code into discrete units based on the functionality provided by each one. For example, if you write code that multiplies two numbers and returns the result, that code is much more useful if it's wrapped in a procedure. Using a method allows the code to be called from more than one place in your application as necessary, which enables you to reuse the code rather than rewrite it each time you need to multiply two numbers.

Unlike Visual Basic, which has a *Sub* and a *Function* as distinct concepts, C# has only a single type of method, a function. Of course, you can create a method in C# without returning a value by declaring the function return type *void*. *void* is a special "type" in C#, used to specify that a method does not return a value as in this example:

```
// C# procedure that writes output to the browser
private void WriteHello1(string FirstName)
{
    Message.Text+="Hello, " + FirstName + "!<br>";
}
```

Receiving Input Parameters

Note that in a C# function, the name of the procedure is followed by a set of empty parentheses. These parentheses have a purpose other than simply taking up space. You can place code between these parentheses to define one or more parameters that users must pass when they call the procedure. Parameters can be passed either by value (a copy of the value is passed to the procedure) or by reference (a reference to the location of the value is passed to the procedure, which allows the procedure to modify the original value). You use the keyword *ref* to specify that the parameter is to be passed by reference. If no keyword is used, the parameters will be passed by value. The following code shows some examples:

```
private void ModifyInt(int MyInt)
{
 MyInt+=42;
 // Modified value will not be available
 // once this method returns.
}
private void ModifyInt(ref int MyInt)
{
 MyInt+=42;
 // Modified value will be available to
 // calling method.
}
```

You can pass more than one parameter to a procedure simply by separating each parameter with a comma, as in the following example:

```
private void WriteHello(string Name1, string Name2)
{
    Response.Write(?Hello to both ? + Name1 + ? and ? + Name2)
}
```

Programming Basics

Note that you explicitly type the parameters by declaring the data type of each parameter as *string*. If any data type other than *string* is passed to the procedure, the method will not compile. Because the C# *string* type is just an alias for the *System.String* type, you could pass in a *System.String* instance as a parameter and there would be no type violation.

Early vs. Late Binding

One difference between C# and Visual Basic .NET is that C# forces early binding whereas Visual Basic .NET allows late binding by default. Late vs. early binding is a concept that is difficult to grasp without an example. Imagine the following method in Visual Basic .NET (don't worry—this is a very simple function that requires no Visual Basic .NET experience):

```
Private Sub foo(ByRef bar As Integer)
    bar = 2
End Sub
```

This method is very straightforward; accept a single parameter as an integer and set it equal to the number 2. Because the variable is passed by reference (note the ByRef keyword), the changed value will be available to the calling method.

Imagine now that you call the method as follows:

```
foo("1");
```

Will this work? That depends. With the default settings, Visual Basic .NET will compile this and work at runtime. This is late binding. One consequence of this (beside the overhead of converting the string "1" to a number at runtime) is that it is possible that a failure can occur that will not be detected at compile time. For instance, if you call foo as follows:

```
foo("One");
```

What we intend here is clearly less obvious. The string literal "One" cannot be converted to a number, and so if Visual Basic .NET is set up to use late binding, an exception will be thrown at runtime.

The moral of the story is that using C# (with its forced early binding) is a good thing!

Function Overloading

C# does not allow optional parameters, however, much of the same effect can be realized by using function overloading. Function overloading means that there is more than one method with the same name, but different parameters.

For instance, imagine that you have a method that accepts a person's first name, like so:

```
private void WriteHello1(string FirstName)
{
    Message.Text+="Hello, " + FirstName + "!<br>";
}
```

Now lets say that you embed this all over an application and then discover that you really need to make the last name available in some cases. One solution would be to create an additional method, as follows:

```
private void WriteHello(string FirstName,string LastName)
{
    Message.Text+="Hello, " + FirstName + " " + LastName + "!<br>";
}
```

Now you can call WriteHello and pass in either a single string or two strings. In a more complex example, rather than having each overloaded method actually do some work, you would likely make all methods except one (the one that passes the largest number of parameters) into shell methods that simply call the version with the most parameters, adding default values when called. So you might re-create the WriteHello method that accepts a single string as follows:

```
private void WriteHello(string FirstName)
{
    // Default to an empty string for last name
    WriteHello(FirstName,"");
}
```

This is not quite as convenient as optional parameters as implemented in Visual Basic .NET, but does allow the same functionality.

3

Programming Basics

All the previous examples used the void return type, meaning that no value was returned from the method. There are two ways of getting values back from a method call. The first is by declaring a non-void return type. For instance, to safely divide two numbers we could do the following:

```
private int Divide(int Numerator,int Divisor)
{
 if ( Divisor!=0 )
 {
        return(Numerator/Divisor);
 }
 else
 {
        return(0);
 }
}
```

This method prevents me from dividing by 0, and returns 0 if division by 0 is requested. One thing to remember about returning values from a C# method is that there is no default return value. Every logical path in the method must return a value of the correct type. Thus, if I rewrite the method as follows, it will fail to compile:

```
private int Divide(int Numerator,int Divisor)
{
 if ( Divisor!=0 )
 {
        return(Numerator/Divisor);
 }
 else
 {
        Response.Write(?Error! Division by 0 requested!?);
 }
}
```

The compile time error that C# will return for this method is "Not all code paths return a value." If you say a method will return an int, it really must return one! This example returns an integer, but you can return any type, including complex types like classes and structures.

The second way to return a value from a method is to use a *ref* parameter. When you say a parameter is passed by ref, rather than the actual value being passed to the method, a reference (very much like a pointer) is passed, so that changes to the parameter's value will be visible back in the calling method. For instance:

```
private void RefTest(ref int Number)
{
      Number+=5;
}
private void CallRefTest()
{
      int foo=5;
      RefTest(ref foo);
      // Now foo is 10!
}
```

Note that when you pass a ref parameter you must precede the variable name with the keyword *ref*. When calling by reference, you must pass a variable, not a constant. Thus, the following will be invalid:

```
RefTest(ref 5);
```

The compiler message related to this error is "An out or ref argument must be an lvalue." An *lvalue* is an expression that can be places on the left side of an equal sign used for assignment. Saying 5=x (where we are using the single equal sign for assignment rather than the double equal sign used for testing equality) makes no sense, so 5 is not an lvalue.

In addition to ref, you can pass a parameter as an *out* parameter. This is similar to a ref, but unlike a ref, the parameter need not be initialized before being passed to the method. For example:

```
private void OutTest(out int Number)
{
  Number=5;
}
private void CallOutTest()
{
  int foo;
  // Now foo is not initialized!
  // If I tried to use foo here, a compile time error
  //     will occur.
  OutTest(out foo);
  // Now foo is 5!
}
```

In this example, foo is declared but not initialized in CallOutTest. In OutTest, foo is assigned a value, and OutTest makes no assumptions about the value of Number being passed as a parameter. If rather than assigning a value to Number, I tried to use the value first, or even tried to increment the value using += rather than just assigning a value, a compile time error occurs.

Finally, you can change the accessibility of a method using the public, private, internal, and protected keywords. Methods are private by default, which means they can be called only from the module, class or struct they reside in. This is the exact opposite of the default in Visual Basic .NET, where methods are public by default.

Flow Control

Another important part of any program is flow control, which enables you to determine at runtime which sections of your code will run, and in what order. Flow control statements are the foundation of business logic and consist of conditional logic (including *if* and *case* statements), looping structures (*for...* and *do...* loops), and error-handling statements.

if Statements

if statements are the form of conditional logic, also known as decision structures, that you will probably use most in your programs. They enable you to look for a defined logical condition in your program and execute a specific block of code if that condition is *true*. The following code checks a *Session* variable for the logged-in user name (set in the login page) to prevent a user who has not logged into your ASP.NET application from viewing pages that require a login:

```
if ( Session[?LoggedInUserName?] == ?? )

{

    Response.Redirect(?Login.aspx?);

}
```

In C#, *if* statements consist of the keyword *if* (case sensitive!), a *predicate* or condition expression, followed by the expression or block to be executed if the predicate evaluates to true. The *if* keyword is self explanatory.

> ## note
>
> To index into the ASP.NET objects such as Session and Application, C# uses square brackets ([and]) rather than parentheses. If you use parentheses instead, you will get the not crystal clear compile time error message " 'Session' denotes a property where a 'method' was expected." What this is telling you is that *Session* is a property that needs to be indexed using square brackets rather than a method, called with parentheses.

A predicate is an expression that can be simple (as in the previous example) or quite complex, spanning multiple lines as needed. (Recall that C# ignores white space such as spaces, tabs, and newlines.) A predicate can contain multiple expressions that evaluate to *true* or *false* chained by && (logical AND) or || (logical OR) operators. For instance, the following predicate checks for the same *Session* variable as the previous example AND that a variable called *Tries* is not equal to 7:

```
if ( Session[?LoggedInUserName?] == ?? && Tries!=7 )
{
    Response.Redirect(?Login.aspx?);
}
```

In this example, if Session["LoggedInUserName"] is not equal to an empty string, the test for Tries!=7 will not be evaluated. This is called *Short-Circuit Evaluation*. After C# determines that no matter whether an expression evaluates to *true* or *false*, the predicate will still evaluate to *true* or *false*, the additional expressions are not evaluated. In this example it would not matter, but in other examples one of the expressions might have a side effect of being evaluated (changing some variable or calling a method that does). Short-Circuit evaluation also enables you to test expressions that might run quickly first, and then test those expressions that might take some time to run only if testing the expression could make a difference.

If the predicate evaluates to *true*, the single line or the block immediately below the *if* statement is executed. The following example would work exactly the same as the previous example:

```
if ( Session[?LoggedInUserName?] == ?? && Tries!=7 )
    Response.Redirect(?Login.aspx?);
```

This *if* statement is different from virtually all other examples in this book in that it does not use curly braces. Why do I always use curly braces and have a single line *if* statement enclosed within a block? Imagine that I added one more line of code and ended up with the following:

```
// Bad example of what can happen when your indentation says one
//        thing, but the code something else.
if ( Session["LoggedInUserName"] == "" && Tries!=7 )
 Tries++;
    Response.Redirect("Login.aspx");
```

Although my indentation means "If there is no logged in user and *Tries* is not equal to 7, increment *Tries* and redirect to Login.aspx," what will really happen is that *Tries* will be incremented only if the predicate evaluates to *true*, and the user will **always** be redirected to Login.aspx. Trust me here. Always use curly braces, no matter how simple the expression.

You can also provide code that will execute if the defined condition is *false* by adding the *else* statement. You can nest *if* and *else* statements as needed. These techniques are shown in the following example:

```
if ( Session[?LoggedInUserName?] == ?? )
{
    Response.Redirect(?Login.aspx?);
}
else
{
if ( Session[?LoggedInUserName?] == ?SuperUser? )
{
Response.Write(?You are a superuser!?);
}
else
{
Response.Write(?Hello, ? + Session[?LoggedInUserName?] + ?!?);
 }
}
```

> **note**
>
> C# enables you to place en entire *if* statement on a single line, such as the following:
>
> ```
> if ( 1 < 2 )  Response.Write(?1 is less than 2?);
> ```
>
> This syntax should only be used for very simple *if* statements because it is inherently harder to read and debug single-line *if* statements. On occasion I might use such a construct when I need to have lots of *if* statements in a row and want to conserve space. Generally, rethinking the logic is a better solution.

switch case Statements

Another form of conditional logic you'll use frequently is the *switch case* statement. This statement is useful in situations where you can reasonably expect the defined condition you're testing to evaluate to one of a limited number of values (or ranges of values). Unlike *switch case* statements in C++, C# *switch case* statements can switch not only on integer values, but on strings as well. For example, the following code checks to see which item of a listbox was chosen by a user and then it takes appropriate action:

```
switch(ColorString)
{
case "Red":
   Message.Text+="<font color='" + ColorString + "'>";
   Message.Text+="You chose Red";
   Message.Text+="<font>";
   break;
case "Green":
   Message.Text+="<font color='" + ColorString + "'>";
   Message.Text+="You chose Green";
   Message.Text+="<font>";
   break;
case "Blue":
     Message.Text+="<font color='" + ColorString + "'>";
   Message.Text+="You chose Blue";
   Message.Text+="<font>";
   break;
}
```

You can also add a *default* statement to execute specific code when the tested expression doesn't match any of your listed values, as the following code demonstrates:

```
switch(ColorString)
{
   case "Red":
   ?
   case "Green":
   ?
   case "Blue":
    ?
  default:
      Message.Text+="<font color=\?black\?>";
      Message.Text+="You did not chose a color";
      Message.Text+="<font>";
    break;
}
```

It's good programming practice to always have a *default* statement just in case there are unexpected values for the expression you're testing (such as *ColorString* in this example). Note also that *default* is a C# keyword, so naming a class *default* (with a lower case 'd') can be a problem. You might inadvertently end up trying to use *default* as a class name if you create a page default.aspx. Use Default.aspx (note the upper case 'D') to avoid this, or better yet, use a different page name!

> **note**
>
> C++ Programmers are used to sometimes not using a *break* statement at the end of every *case* to allow processing to "drop through" to the next *case*. Although there are some cases in which C# does allow this (documented in the C# Language Reference in the MSDN documentation), it is always safer to just include the *break*.

Let's actually use the *switch case* statement in a real Web Form. I will use several components that will be explained later in Chapter 9.

Use the *switch case* statement

1 Open Visual Studio .NET.

2 On the File menu, point to New, and then click Project.

3 In the New Project dialog box, click the ASP.NET Web Application icon from the C# Project Type.

4 Name the project Chapter_03 as shown in the following graphic, and click OK.

5 You should see the Visual Studio .NET screen, as shown in the following graphic:

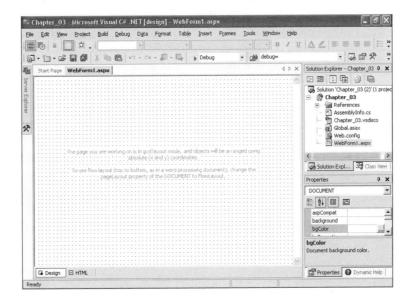

6   Move the mouse pointer over the Toolbox along the left side of the screen. It will expand. Drag a label onto the form, and then click DropDownList and place it on the form next to it. Click another label and place it on the form below the drop-down list and the other label. The form should look like the following graphic:

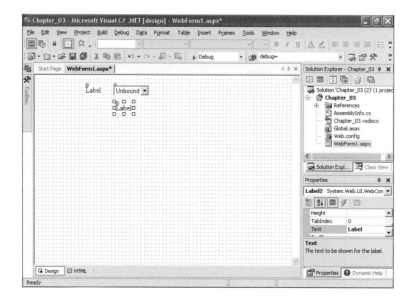

7   Click the drop-down list, and then in the Properties pane, change the ID from *DropDownList1* to **Color**. Change *AutoPostBack* from False to **True**. In the drop-down list, scroll down to the *Items* property, click the ellipses (…), and enter items for the drop-down list by clicking the Add button four times. Then click the Text box in the Properties pane for the first item and change it to **Select**. Change the text box of the second item to **Red**, the third item to **Green**, and the fourth item to **Blue**. When the screen looks like the following graphic, click OK.

8   Change the text of the label next to the drop-down list to **Color**. Change
     the ID of the label below the drop-down list to **Message**.

9   Double-click the drop-down list and a screen will appear, as shown in the
     following graphic:

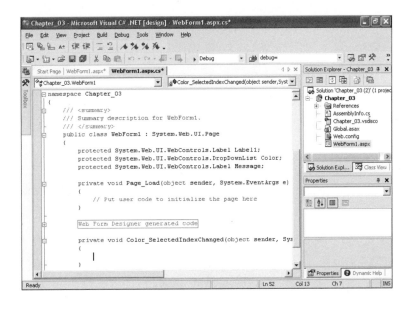

This is the event handler that is called when the item in the drop-down list is changed. This is covered more fully in Chapter 9.

10 Add the following code to the *Color_SelectedIndexChanged* event handler:

```
Message.Text="";
// Initialize label.
switch(Color.SelectedItem.Text)
{
    case "Red":
        Message.Text+="<font color='" +
Color.SelectedItem.Text + "'>";
        Message.Text+="You chose Red";
        Message.Text+="<font>";
        break;
    case "Green":
        Message.Text+="<font color='" +
Color.SelectedItem.Text + "'>";
        Message.Text+="You chose Green";
        Message.Text+="<font>";
        break;
    case "Blue":
        Message.Text+="<font color='" +
Color.SelectedItem.Text + "'>";
        Message.Text+="You chose Blue";
        Message.Text+="<font>";
        break;
    default:
        Message.Text+="<font color=\"black\">";
        Message.Text+="You did not chose a color";
        Message.Text+="<font>";
        break;
}
```

11 On the File menu, click Save All to save the page, and then on the Build menu, click Build Chapter_03 to compile the application.

12 To run the application, on the Debug menu, click Start.

13 To select a color other than the default, click the down arrow to the right of the drop-down list, and click a color. A screen similar to the one shown in the following graphic will appear:

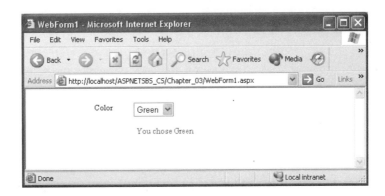

This simple example shows several features of ASP.NET and C# within Visual Studio .NET, including:

- **RAD development** Drop controls on the form, and then handle events.
- **Codeless Development** The ability to set many properties on controls without any coding.
- **Automatic postbacks by controls other than buttons** Every time you select an item from the list, the form actually posts back to the server. This allows for a much richer user interface than classic ASP.

Looping Statements

Looping statements are useful features that enable you to perform actions repeatedly, by either specifying explicitly at design time the number of times the code should loop, deciding at runtime how many times to loop, or looping through a collection of objects and taking a specific action on each item. There are several different types of looping statements, each of which has its own particular syntax and is useful for a different situation. Loop types include

- *for...* loops
- *foreach...* loops, a special case of *for...* loops
- *do...while* loops
- *while...* loops

Programming Basics

3

Using *for...* Loops

for... loops are useful for repeating a given set of statements a number of times. The number of times the statements are executed can be determined either explicitly or by evaluating an expression that returns a numeric value. The following example (from the *ASP.NET QuickStart Tutorial*) uses a *for...* loop that counts from 1 to 7, and for each pass of the loop, outputs a message with a font size equal to the counter variable:

```
int i;
for ( i = 0 ; i<7 ; i++ )
{
 Message.Text+="<font size=\"" + i + "\">Welcome to ASP.NET</
font><br>";
}
```

> **note**
>
> In this example, I use a backslash (\) inside the string to escape the quotation mark ("). Quotation marks around the font size are required for properly formed HTML because they are used as the string delimiter.

In this example, in addition to using the variable *i*, *i* could also be declared within the *for...* loop, as in this example:

```
for ( int i = 0 ; i<7 ; i++ )
{
 Message.Text+="<font size=\"" + i + "\">Welcome to ASP.NET</
font><br>";
}
```

Every *for...* loop in C# consists of three parts, any of which can be empty:

- **Initialization** in the previous example, *int i = 0*
- **Expression** the test expression, evaluated like the predicate in the *if* statement
- **Iterators** a statement to be run during each iteration of the loop.

You can also use a *for...* loop to loop through the elements of an array by specifying the length of the array as the loop count expression, as follows:

```
string[] s = new string[5];
s[0] = "A";
```

```
s[1] = "B";
s[2] = "C";
s[3] = "D";
s[4] = "E";
for ( i = 0 ; i<s.Length - 1 ; i++ )
{
    Message.Text+="<font size=\"" + i + "\">";
    Message.Text+=s[i];
    Message.Text+="</font><br>";
}
```

note

In C#, all arrays are zero based. Therefore, to use the *Length* property of the array for a looping statement, you should use *Length – 1*. Checking for *Length* instead will result in a runtime exception. Unlike Visual Basic .NET, declaring an array as I do in the example just shown creates an array of 5 elements, *not* an array with 0 as the lower bound and 5 as the upper bound (in fact 6 elements).

Using *foreach...* Loops

foreach... loops are a specialization of *for...* loops that enable you to loop through a collection or group of elements and take action on each item. The following example demonstrates looping through the items in an array of dates:

```
DateTime[] Dates;
Dates = new DateTime[3];
Dates[0]=DateTime.Now;
Dates[1]=Dates[0].AddDays(7);
Dates[2]=Dates[0].AddYears(1);
foreach (DateTime dt in Dates)
{
    Message.Text+=dt.ToShortDateString() + "<br>\n";
}
```

This code outputs each date to the browser using *Response.Write*. Because the DateTime type contains a date and a time, I use ToShortDateString to format the date in a way that shows only the date. Using *foreach...* loops completely eliminates any problem with indexing outside the bounds of the array.

Using *do...while* Loops

do...while loops enable you to execute a set of statements repeatedly for as long as a test condition remains true. The condition contained in the *while* part of the statement is evaluated at the end of each cycle, and so code inside the loop is executed at least once. For example:

```
// Do?While syntax:
int i = 1;
do
{
    Message.Text+="<font size=\"" + i + "\">Welcome to ASP.NET</
font><br>";
    i++;
} while ( i<=5 );
```

Using *while...* Loops

while... loops do essentially the same thing as *do while...* loops; they enable you to execute a given set of statements while a given condition is true. A *while...* loop that does the same thing as the preceding *do...while* loop would look like the following:

```
// while syntax:
i = 1;
// Declared previously?
while ( i <= 5 )
{
    Message.Text+="<font size=\"" + i + "\">Welcome to ASP.NET</
font><br>";
    i++;
}
```

Most programs will use a variety of loop types. No matter which loop type you choose, the important thing is that you use it correctly and consistently for a given task. This will make your code easier to read and maintain.

Error Handling

In any application, one challenge faced by developers is dealing with the inevitable errors. Application errors come in three varieties:

■ **Syntax errors** These include misspelled or missing keywords or symbols (such as a missing *closing bracket*), or other mistakes relating to the syntax of the language you're using. Syntax errors are typically flagged by the IDE and can be easily fixed at design time.

■ **Runtime errors**   These are errors that appear after your code is compiled and running. Runtime errors are caused by code that appears correct to the compiler, but that cannot run with certain values. For example, code that divides one integer variable by another will appear to be correct to a compiler, but it will cause a runtime error if the second variable is zero.

■ **Logic Errors**   These are errors in which a program that works correctly under some (or most) circumstances gives unexpected or unwanted results based on certain input values. This type of error can be extremely difficult to track down and fix because it doesn't stop the execution of the program.

One thing all three types of errors have in common is that they must all be handled in some fashion, lest they provoke grave dissatisfaction on the part of your users. An important first step is prevention.

Selecting C# as your language to develop ASP.NET pages is the first step in eliminating some classes of errors that have plagued classic ASP applications. A properly compiled ASP.NET application will not contain undeclared variables or method calls that will compile correctly but could fail with type violations at runtime.

Ways to Handle Exceptional Situations

No matter how careful you are when developing an application, eventually there will be a situation that your application is not prepared to handle. For instance, your application might request access to a database when the database is unavailable. There are two general ways to react to this situation in C#:

■ Check return codes from methods that could fail

■ Use Structured Exception Handling

Checking return codes to all methods is the way that COM implemented error handling. Checking for HRESULT was a significant part of any COM program written in C or C++. C++ allows Structured Exception Handling, where the flow of control is more straightforward. Exception handling brackets the section of code, allowing explicit handling of specific types of exceptions, as well as code that will always run, regardless of whether an exception occurs.

Checking Return Values

Checking return values seems initially to be the easiest way to handle errors. You can, in a very straightforward way, know exactly what failed and react to it in code very close to where the error occurs. The problems that occur are:

- The error handling code interrupts the clean flow of what is happening in the normal case where the process proceeds without error.
- It is too easy to forget about checking for error return codes.
- Given a large number of operations that require checking, the level of nesting can become ungainly.

For example, the code to check three levels of return values shows how confusing this kind of error handling can get:

```
if ( OpenDB()==NO_ERROR )
{
  if ( OpenTable()==NO_ERROR )
  {
        if ( FetchRow()==NO_ERROR )
        {
              // Actually do something?
        }
  }
}
```

This type of error handling is best suited for the sort of errors that would occur often. For instance, if you are prompting a user for the name of a file, the method that does that might best be handled by checking a return code.

Using Structured Exception Handling: *try...catch...finally*

The *try...catch...finally* form of exception handling, also known as structured exception handling, should be familiar to C++ and Java developers.

In C#, the *try...catch...finally* syntax enables you to enclose code that can cause an exception in such a way as to catch and deal with specific exceptions and/or provide generic exception handling. The following code shows a simple *try...catch* block:

```
int a, b;
double c;
try // Start monitoring for exceptions
{
    //Code that may cause an exception
    a = 1;
    b = 0;
    c = a / b;
}
catch ( DivideByZeroException )
{
    // Code to handle divide by 0 exception
}
finally
{
    // Code that executes after any code in the Catch block(s)
}
```

You can define *catch* blocks for as many specific errors as you want to handle. The *finally* block can be used for any code you want to run after the exception-handling code, including cleanup code, such as code to close a file. The *finally* block of code is always run, whether or not an exception has occurred.

In addition to catching exceptions, your code can actually throw an exception. To do so, you use the *throw* keyword. For example, if you wanted to catch only the divide by 0 exception and then rethrow any other exception, you could use the following code:

```
int a, b;
double c;
try // Start monitoring for exceptions
{
    //Code that may cause an exception
    a = 1;
    b = 0;
    c = a / b;
}
catch ( DivideByZeroException )
{
```

```
    // Code to handle divide by 0 exception
}
catch ( Exception e )
{
  throw(e);    // Rethrow exception e
}
finally
{
    // Code that executes after any code in the Catch block(s)
}
```

One thing worth noting is that in the second *catch* block, rather than just declaring the exception type, I specify an instance of the exception that I can then manipulate. In this example, I get a named instance of the exception so that I can rethrow it. This can also be useful when you have exceptions that contain details that you need to look at to properly handle the exception. It is also worth noting that the most specific *catch* blocks should be first, followed by any more general *catch* blocks. If the *catch* for the most general exception type (*Exception* in this example) was first, all exceptions would be caught in that block, including the more specific exception, the *DivideByZeroException*.

What happens if an exception is thrown and your code does not catch it? Probably not what you would like. This next example will step you though the process of creating a page that generates an unhandled exception, and then adding exception handling to properly handle the exception.

Add exception handling

1   Open Visual Studio .NET if it's not already open.

2   If Chapter_03 is not already open, on the File menu, point to Open, and then click Project. Click the project Chapter_03 created earlier in this chapter. This project can also be selected by pointing to Recent Projects on the File menu and clicking the project.

3   Right click the Chapter_03 project in the Solution Explorer on the right side of the screen. On the shortcut menu, point to Add, and click Add Web Form. When prompted, name the form **Exceptions.aspx**, and click the open button. In the Solution Explorer, right click Exceptions.aspx, and click Set As Start Page on the shortcut menu. This makes Exceptions.aspx the page that will load when the application is run.

4   Position the mouse pointer over the Toolbox until it expands. Drag a button from the Toolbox onto the form. Drag a label onto the form just below the button.

5   In the Properties pane on the right side of the screen, change the text of the button from Button to **Divide By Zero**, and click Enter. The button conveniently expands to show all the entered text.

6   Change the ID of the label from Label1 to **Message**. The screen should look like the following graphic:

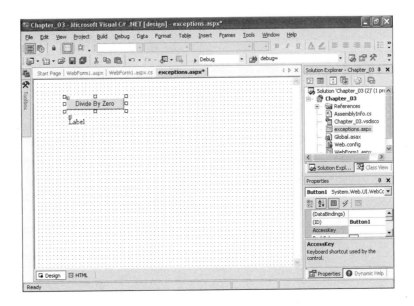

7   Double-click the button in the designer, and you will see the code view showing the *Button1_Click* event handler.

8   Add the following code to the handler:

```
int divisor = 0;
Message.Text=(4/divisor).ToString();
```

9   On the File menu, click Save All to save the page, and then on the Build menu, click Build Chapter_03 to compile the application.

10 To run the application, on the Debug menu, click Start. When you see the screen with the Divide By Zero button, click the button. You will see a screen similar to the following graphic:

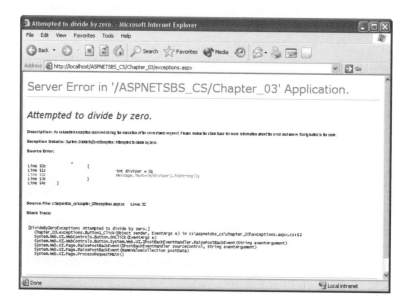

11 Close the application. Find the *Button1_Click* event handler and change the code to the following:

```
int divisor = 0;
try
{
    Message.Text=(4/divisor).ToString();
}
catch( DivideByZeroException )
{
    Message.Text=?Cannot divide by 0!?;
}
```

12 On the File menu, click Save All to save the page, and then on the Build menu, click Build Chapter_03 to compile the application.

13 To run the application, on the Debug menu, click Start, click the Divide By Zero button and the Message label will display a message telling you that you cannot divide by 0.

You'll see more examples of exception handling throughout the book.

Understanding Object-Oriented Programming Basics

Object-oriented programming will probably be new to some C# programmers, as well as to those new to programming entirely. C++ allows object oriented programming, but C#, with the .NET Framework as a model really encourages object orientation. C++ allows code to exist outside of any class, whereas C# mandates that all code must exist inside classes. The .NET Framework is not a perfect model for studying how to structure classes to achieve best object orientation, but it is a place to start.

This section provides an overview of object-oriented programming, particularly as it relates to the .NET development platform. Object-oriented programming is a substantial topic, so it's highly recommended that you do some additional reading to supplement the material provided here. There are also many books on both object-oriented programming and *design patterns*, related subjects.

In the simplest terms, an *object* is an instance of a class in an object-oriented language such as C++, C#, and Visual Basic .NET. Objects typically mirror their real world counterparts: employees, invoices, and purchase orders are all examples of real world entities that can be modeled as objects in your programs. Objects typically provide both *properties*, which describe some attribute of the object (for example, an employee might have an *EmployeeID* property), and *methods*, which allow actions to be taken by the object (for example, an *Invoice* object might expose a *Process* method). Properties and methods make it easier for programmers to know how to use a given object.

In addition to properties and methods, object-oriented programming offers three helpful features: inheritance, polymorphism, and encapsulation.

Inheritance is the ability to create new classes that are derived from existing classes. A derived class "inherits" all the properties and methods of the class from which it is derived (referred to as the *parent class*). Programmers can then add additional properties and methods to the derived class, or in some cases override the implementation of an existing method inherited from the parent class.

Polymorphism lets programmers have identically named methods in different classes, and it allows the correct method to be executed based on the context of the call. For example, a programmer could define an *Invoice* class with a *Process* method. The programmer could then define separate *TimeInvoice* and *MaterialsInvoice* classes that derived from the *Invoice* class, but which might or might not use the same implementation of the *Process* method exposed by the parent class. A method calling the *Process* method on a class that is descended from Invoice does not need to know exactly which implementation of *Process* will be called.

Encapsulation allows objects to be treated as "black boxes" in that only the properties and methods defined by the programmer as publicly available are visible outside of the object. Internal object state and the implementation of the publicly available methods are hidden by encapsulation. This limited visibility lets developers freely modify the internal state and implementation of their objects, as long as they don't change the publicly defined interface used to access the object. For instance, an *EmployeeList* class might expose methods *FirstEmployee*, *NextEmployee* and so on. Internally, such a list could be managed using a simple array, a linked list (in which each item points to the next item in a list), or a database table. To the consumer of the class, it should not matter exactly how the list is maintained internally, so long as the public methods such as *FirstEmployee* returns the correct information.

Using Classes as Containers for Code

Classes are the basic unit of an object-oriented application. A class in C# typically contains property and method definitions, as well as event handlers (a special class of methods). Classes are often grouped into useful collections through the use of namespaces. *Namespaces* can contain classes and other namespaces. For example, the *System.Web* namespace defined by the .NET Framework SDK contains not only classes such as the *HttpRequest*, *HttpResponse*, and *HttpServerUtility* classes (which provide the equivalent functionality of the ASP Request, Response, and Server intrinsic objects), but also a number of namespaces, including the *System.Web.UI*, *System.Web.Caching*, and *System.Web.SessionState* namespaces, each of which also contains classes and/or namespaces.

By using classes as containers for code and namespaces, the .NET architecture makes it very easy to create a rich, yet intuitive application hierarchy that can make your code easier to use, debug, and maintain.

> ### note
> When you develop applications in the Visual Studio .NET environment, a root namespace will be created with the same name as your project. If you specify additional namespaces within your code modules, these will become child namespaces of the root namespace. You can change the root namespace by right-clicking your project in Solution Explorer and clicking Properties. The *Root Namespace* property appears under Common Properties, General.

Using Inheritance

Now that you know a bit about object-oriented programming, let's take a look at a simple example of how to put it to use. First let's define a class based on a real world entity, an animal.

```
public class Animal
{
 public virtual void Eat()
 {
       Console.WriteLine(?Yum!?);
 }
 public virtual void Sleep()
 {
       Console.WriteLine(?Zzzzz??);
 }
}
```

You use the *virtual* modifier to let C# know that the behavior can be overridden by a derived class.

> **note**
>
> Unlike C++, C# allows only single inheritance. Although some C++ program-mers will find this to be a problem, the reality is that in virtually all cases, there are better alternatives to using multiple inheritances. C# does enable you to implement multiple interfaces, something that is often useful.

Next create a more specific animal class, *Cat*, that derives from the Animal class. Note the use of the listing of the Animal class after the name of the new class and a colon on the first line of the declaration. This is how you let C# know that the class inherits from another class. Inheriting from another class is really that simple. This class will override the behavior of the Eat method, but not the Sleep method, as follows:

```
public class Cat : Animal
{
 public override void Eat()
 {
       Console.WriteLine("Yum, Yum?Meow, Meow!");
 }
}
```

Programming Basics

3

The *override* modifier is used to let C# know you intend to override the method in the base class.

You'll also create a *Dog* class that derives from *Animal* and that overrides the *Sleep* method, but not the *Eat* method, as follows:

```
public class Dog : Animal
{
 public override void Sleep()
 {
        Console.WriteLine("Zzzzzz?woofwoofwoofwoof?zzzzzz!");
 }
}
```

Finally, use the *Cat* and *Dog* classes in the following code. Note that you use the imports statement to access the members of the *Animals* namespace without fully qualified names (such as *Cat* instead of *Animal.Cat*).

```
class Class1
{
 static void Main(string[] args)
 {
 Cat cat;
        Dog dog;

        cat=new Cat();
        cat.Eat();
        cat.Sleep();

        dog=new Dog();
        dog.Eat();
        dog.Sleep();
 }

}
```

This code, when run from a command line, provides the following output:

```
Yum, Yum?Meow, Meow!
Zzzzz?
Yum!
Zzzzzz?woofwoofwoofwoof?zzzzzz!
```

Even though you called the same two methods on both the *Cat* and *Dog* classes, when you overrode a method of the parent *Animal* class, you got the behavior that you specified for the particular animal. When you didn't override, the output shows that you got the behavior inherited from the parent *Animal* class. You can find the full source code for this example, including a project file to use in Visual Studio .NET, in the source folder for this chapter (Chapter_03) in the source archive for this book.

Inheriting from the .NET Base Classes

The preceding example might not seem terribly useful, and admittedly, creating your own *Cats* and *Dogs* by inheriting from *Animal* won't help you much in your development efforts. Fortunately, the same principles demonstrated in that example apply to the classes that make up the .NET Framework. Many of these classes can be used to derive your own specialized classes. You'll see specific examples of this in Chapter 10.

Inheriting Across Languages

Another nifty feature of the .NET Framework and the common language runtime is that they enable you to inherit from classes written in other languages. Why is this important? Because it means that development teams can make better use of the existing skill sets of their developers, as well as the company's existing code base. For example, a company with experienced Visual Basic developers (and existing code in Visual Basic) can have those developers continue to write in Visual Basic .NET. If the company also has a group of skilled Java developers, they can easily make the transition to C# and use the existing class resources created by the VB developers through inheritance.

Programming Basics

Chapter 3 Quick Reference

To	Do this	Code
Declare a variable	Use the data type, followed by the variable name.	`int MyInt;`

Modify the accessibility of a variable or procedure	Use the public, private, internal, or protected keywords	`public void myProc()`
		`{`
		`}`

To use structured exception handling	Create a *try...catch...finally* block.	`Try`
		`{`
		`// Code to try?`
		`}`
		`catch ( System.Exception )`
		`{`
		`// Handle error`
		`}`
		`finally`
		`{`
		`// Code that will ALWAYS run`
		`}`

Inherit from a base class	Append the base class name to the name of the derived class, separated by a colon	`class Dog : Animal`
		`{`
		`}`

Declare a method that will be over-ridden in classes that descend from the current class	Use the *virtual* modifier	`public virtual void myProc()`
		`{`
		`}`

Override a method declared in a base class	Use the *override* modifier	`public override void myProc()`
		`{`
		`}`

PART 2

ASP.NET Infrastructure

4

Managing State

In this chapter, you will learn how to

✔ *Use application state.*

✔ *Use session state.*

✔ *Configure state storage.*

✔ *Use client-side cookies for state storage.*

✔ *Manage state and scalability.*

✔ *Use ASP.NET server control state.*

Most applications of any significance use pieces of data, or *variables*, that must be maintained across a series of requests or shared between multiple users of an application. This data is referred to as *state*. In a rich client application, it's relatively simple to maintain individual user state simply by allocating space in memory on the client machine. In Web applications, managing user and application state is more challenging. The primary reason for this is that the Hypertext Transfer Protocol (HTTP), the protocol used to send and receive requests through a Web browser, is inherently stateless. That is, HTTP doesn't provide a way for the Web server to identify a series of requests as coming from the same user, making it difficult for the Web server to maintain state and associate it with an individual user.

In classic ASP, this limitation was overcome through an in-memory collection of key-value pairs associated with the *Session* intrinsic object. The *Session* collection, however, had a number of important limitations of its own, which are discussed later in this chapter.

In addition to individual user state, many applications need to store and retrieve *application-level* state information that is global to all users of the Web application. Classic ASP exposed a collection similar to that of the *Session* collection on the *Application* intrinsic object.

Using Application State

Application state refers to any data that you want to share among multiple users of your application. This can include connection string information for databases (although this information is often better limited to the business tier of an application), shared variables, and cached datasets (although these might be better stored using the ASP.NET cache engine, which is discussed in more detail in Chapter 12). In fact, one of the difficulties in managing application state is choosing from the many available options for storing such state.

Like classic ASP, ASP.NET provides a collection of key-value pairs that developers can use to store values and object instances. This collection can be accessed in much the same way as in classic ASP.

```
// Setting and getting Application Variables
Application["MyApplicationVar"] = "MyValue";
MyLocalVar = Application["MyApplicationVar"];
```

Application state storage in ASP.NET is supplied by the .NET *HttpApplicationState* class, an instance of which is exposed as the *Application* property of the *Page* class. Because every ASP.NET page has as its ancestor the *Page* class, you can access the *Application* property as if it were an inherent property of the page, as shown in the preceding code.

For backward-compatibility with classic ASP, the ASP.NET *Application* object exposes a *Contents* property that can be used to access individual values, using the appropriate key.

```
Application.Contents["MyApplicationVar"] = "MyValue";
MyLocalVar = Application.Contents["MyApplicationVar"];
```

New in ASP.NET is the ability to add items to the *Application* collection using the *Add* method exposed by the *Application* object. You can use the *Remove* method (exposed by the *Application.Contents* collection in classic ASP) to remove items from the *Application* collection.

```
// Using Add and Remove on Application Object
Application.Add("MyApplicationVar", "MyValue");
Application.Remove("MyOtherApplicationVar");
```

You can also clear the contents of the *Application* collection by using the *Clear* method exposed by the *Application* object (or the *RemoveAll* method, which provides backward-compatibility in classic ASP).

```
// Either line below will clear the application state
Application.Clear();
Application.RemoveAll();
```

The *Application* object exposes several other ways to access and modify the values stored in the *Application* collection, as shown in Table 4-1.

Table 4-1. Application Object Methods and Properties	
Method or Property	**Use**
AllKeys property	Returns a collection of all the keys by which the Application collection values can be accessed.
Count property	Returns the number of objects stored in the Application collection.
Get method	Returns an item from the Application collection by key or by index.
Set method	Updates an item in the Application collection by key or by index.
GetKey method	Returns the key for an item based on a supplied index.
ToString method	Returns a string that represents an item in the Application collection. Useful when a string value is required, rather than an object reference.

In addition to storing values in the *Application* collection, you can instantiate and store references to .NET components in application state using the *<object runat="server">* tag syntax in the Global.asax file (or its associated code-behind file), as described in the previous chapter. These objects then become part of the application's *StaticObjects* collection and can be referenced in your ASP.NET Web Form pages by referring to the *id* attribute associated with the object.

```
'Global.asax
<object runat="server" id="MyClassInstance" class="MyClassName"
   scope="Application">
</object>
//Web Forms page
Response.Write("Value = " + MyClassInstance.MyValue);
```

> **note**
>
> Global.asax (or its associated code-behind file) is the only mechanism for creating object instances with *Application* scope. When you're using either the *Application* or *Session* collections, it's a good idea to initialize the variables you're using to a default value (such as " " for a string or *0* for a numeric) in the *Application_Start* and *Session_Start* event handlers in Global.asax. You can then test for the default value as a way of determining whether it has been altered.

Synchronizing Access to Application State

One challenge in managing state information that's shared between multiple users is ensuring that no two users can attempt to update the state information simultaneously, which could lead to corruption of the data being stored. Like classic ASP, the ASP.NET Application object provides *Lock* and *Unlock* methods that developers can use to ensure that only a single user can update application state information at any given time. Developers should call *Application.Lock()* prior to modifying any data stored in the *Application* collection, and call *Application.Unlock()* after the modification is complete. To prevent scalability problems, while the application is locked, no other users can modify data stored in the *Application* collection. For this reason, you should make sure to keep the application locked for the shortest time possible and perform as little work as possible while the application is locked.

Read and write application state

1   Open Microsoft Visual C# .NET. Create a new project called *Chapter_04*. On the File menu, point to New, and click Project. Select ASP.NET Web Application from the application templates window.

2   Place your mouse pointer over the Toolbox on the left side of the screen and when the Toolbox expands, click a label and drag it onto the screen.

3   With the label control selected, change the ID of the label from Label1 to **Message**. The screen should look something like the following illustration:

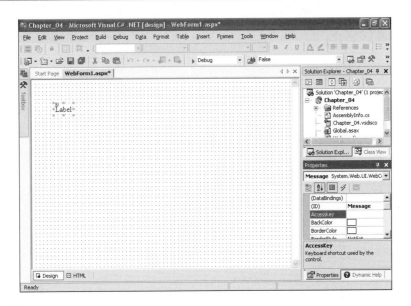

4   On the View menu, click Code or press F7 to open the Code Editor. Alternately, you can double click anywhere on the form to open the Code Editor in the *Page_Load* event handler.

5   Find the *Page_Load* method, and add the following code:

```
// Test the Application object
int loop;
// Lock the application object before we manipulate it
Application.Lock();
Application["TestString"]="Hello";
    Application.Add("TestNumber",43);
// Now unlock the Application, since we will now
//just read from the Application object.
Application.UnLock();
Message.Text="There are " +
    Application.Count.ToString() +
    " items in the Application collection.<br>\n";
for ( loop=0 ; loop<Application.Count ; loop++ )
{
    Message.Text+="Application(" +
        loop.ToString() +
        ")=" + Application[loop] + "<br>";
}
```

6   To save the application, on the File menu, click Save All (or press Ctrl+Shift+S).

7   To build the application, on the Build menu, click Build Chapter _04.

8   To run the application, on the Debug menu, click Start (or press F5). The resulting screen should look like the following illustration:

Recommendations for Application State

Information stored in application state can be easily shared between all users of an application. This can make it very tempting to use application state to store all manner of data, from application settings such as database connection strings to cached datasets containing frequently used data. In many cases, however, there are more efficient means of storing this data than application state. Table 4-2 shows some examples of situations when you might not want to store information in application state, as well as alternatives for storing such information.

Table 4-2.   Application State Recommendations

State information	Issues	Alternative
Database connection strings or other application configuration settings	Typically, these settings are accessed infrequently. Storing this information in application state is not very efficient.	Use the Web.config configuration file to store this information, and retrieve it with the GetConfig method of the Context object.

State information	Issues	Alternative
Datasets containing frequently read data	Caching frequently used data at the application level can be efficient but there's little automatic control over when the data is refreshed.	Use the ASP.NET cache engine to cache expensive or frequently read data. The ASP.NET cache engine provides fine-grained control over how and when data is refreshed or purged from the cache. (See Chapter 12 for more information.)
Shared application flags or counter variables	Shared values that can be updated by multiple users of an application can present major scalability issues, as discussed in "State and Scalability" on page 110.	Consider storing shared application flags in a database, which will provide finer-grained control over the reading and updating of individual values.
References to object instances	Storing references to objects with the wrong threading model (such as legacy COM components created with Visual Basic) can have a severe impact on the scalability of an application.	If it's absolutely necessary to store a reference to an object instance, ensure that the class from which the object is created is thread safe.

Limitations of Application State

Application state has several limitations that you should consider when deciding how to manage your state information:

- **Durability** Application state lasts only as long as the Web application is running. If the Web application or Web server is shut down or crashes, any state information stored at the application level will be destroyed. Any information that needs to persist between application restarts should be stored in a database or other persistent storage.

- **Web farms** Application state is not shared across multiple servers in a Web farm (nor across multiple processors in a Web garden). If you need to store values that must be available to all users in these scenarios, application state is not an appropriate choice.

■ **Memory** Any given server has a limited amount of physical memory available. Overuse of application state can result in information being swapped to virtual memory (a location on a hard drive used to provide supplemental "memory" storage). This can reduce performance significantly.

> ## note
>
> Web farms are groups of identically configured servers that share the load of serving user requests for a given Web application. Each server contains the same content and can fulfill any request. Requests are routed to individual servers by a hardware-based or software-based load-balancing algorithm that either determines which server is least loaded or assigns requests to a given server randomly.
>
> Web gardens are new to ASP.NET. Using a Web garden, an application can be set to run on specific processors on a multiprocessor server.

Using Session State

As challenging as it can be to manage application state information, the statelessness of HTTP makes maintaining state for individual users even more challenging. First the Web server needs to be able to identify a series of requests as coming from a single user. Then the Web server must associate these requests with the state information for that specific user.

In classic ASP, these challenges were met with the Session intrinsic object. Each user had his or her own session instance, identified by a session ID, which could be used to store per-user state information. The session ID, a unique, generated value for that run of the application was then stored in a cookie on the client machine. It would then be passed back to the server with each subsequent request, allowing the server to identify the session associated with that user.

Unfortunately, session state in classic ASP had several inherent limitations that made it less than ideal, particularly for applications requiring high scalability. These included the following:

■ **Web farms** In classic ASP, session state could not be scaled across multiple servers in a Web farm, limiting its usefulness in high-scalability situations.

■ **Durability** In classic ASP, session state would be destroyed by a server restart or crash. This made it a poor choice for such uses as shopping carts, whose contents should survive such events.

■ **Cookie reliance** Classic ASP offered no inherent solution for supporting session state with browsers that could not or would not accept cookies. Although aftermarket solutions were available, they often involved unacceptable performance trade-offs.

ASP.NET solves each of these limitations, providing per-user state storage that's scalable, reliable, and available on browsers that don't support cookies (or for users who choose not to accept cookies). For more information about the available options for ASP.NET session state and how they solve these limitations, see "Configuring Session State Storage" on page 111.

As with the ASP.NET Application object, the ASP.NET *Session* object is exposed as a property of the *Page* class, from which all ASP.NET pages inherit. This allows access to the *Session* object using the *Session* keyword.

```
// Setting and Getting Session Variables
Session["MySessionVar"] = "MyValue";
MyLocalVar = Session["MySessionVar"];
```

note

When accessing the *Session* or *Application* collections directly using a key, you must use square brackets with C#, as shown in the preceding code. When calling methods, such as the *Add* or *Remove* methods, parentheses are used in C#.

The *HttpSessionState* class, an instance of which is created for each user session for which session state has been enabled, provides the *Session* object functionality.

Like the *Application* object, the *Session* object exposes a *Contents* collection for backward-compatibility with classic ASP. Any values stored in the *Session* collection can also be accessed through the *Contents* collection alias.

```
// Using the Contents collection to access State
Session.Contents["MySessionVar"] = "MyValue";
MyLocalVar = Session.Contents["MySessionVar"];
```

The *Session* collection can also be used to store references to object instances, using syntax similar to that used to store object references at the application level. These objects then become part of the session's *StaticObjects* collection and can be referenced in your ASP.NET Web Form pages by referring to the *id* attribute associated with the object.

```
//Global.asax
<object runat="server" id="MyClassInstance" class="MyClassName"
   scope="Session">
</object>
//Web Forms page
Response.Write("Value = " + MyClassInstance.MyValue);
```

Table 4-3 lists some of the additional properties and methods provided by the Session object to retrieve and manipulate Session collection values.

Table 4-3. Session Object Properties and Methods	
Method or Property	Use
Keys property	Returns a collection of all the keys by which Session collection values can be accessed.
Count property	Returns the number of objects stored in the Session collection.
SessionID property	Returns a string containing the session ID for the current session.
Timeout property	Returns an Int32 value representing the current Session Timeout setting.
Abandon method	Destroys the current user session.
Clear method	Removes all items from the Session collection.
RemoveAt method	Removes a specific item from the Session collection, based on its index within the collection.
ToString method	Returns a string that represents an item in the Session collection. Useful when a string value is required rather than an object reference.

Enabling Session State

Unlike application state, which is always available to Web applications, session state must be enabled before you can use it. The good news is that the default configuration file at the server level (Machine.config) automatically enables session state, so you don't need to take any additional steps to enable it. Nonetheless, you should be aware that the settings in the Machine.config configuration file, as well as in the Web.config configuration file for your application, determine whether session state is enabled or disabled. The pertinent settings are detailed in Appendix B.

If you want to delay the creation of a session until it's necessary, you can add the *EnableSessionState* attribute to the @ *Page* directive of all pages not requiring session state.

```
<%@ Page EnableSessionState="False" %>
```

Any attempt to access the Session object from a page on which *EnableSessionState* has been set to *false* will result in an error. Note that after a session has been created for a given user, setting the *EnableSessionState* attribute to *false* doesn't result in the destruction of the existing session. It only prevents access to the *Session* object from that page.

You can set the session state to read-only for a given page by setting the *EnableSessionState* attribute to *ReadOnly*. Any attempts to update values stored in the *Session* collection from that page will be ignored.

Enabling Session State in Visual Studio.NET

Visual C# .NET makes it even easier to enable (or delay enabling) session state in your applications by exposing the *enableSessionState* attribute as a property of the *Document* object. This enables you to view and modify its value using the Visual C# .NET Properties pane, shown in the following illustration:

To change its setting, click *enableSessionState* in the Properties pane, click the down arrow, and then click the value you want in the drop-down list.

Read and write session state

1   Open Visual C# .NET. Open the project created previously, *Chapter_04*, if it is not already open. On the File menu, point to Open, and then click Project. Navigate to the project folder, and click the solution file.

2   To add a new page to the project, right-click the project root in Solution Explorer, point to Add, and then click Add WebForm. When prompted, change the name of the file from WebForm2.aspx to **SessionState.aspx**, and then click the Open button.

3 In Solution Explorer, right-click the newly created file, SessionState.aspx, and then click Set As Start Page on the shortcut menu.

4 Position your mouse pointer over the Toolbox on the left side of the screen and when the Toolbox expands, drag a label onto the screen.

5 With the Label control selected, change the ID of the label from Label1 to **Message**.

6 On the View menu, click Code or press F7 to open the Code Editor.

7 Find the *Page_Load* method, and add the following code:

```
// Test the Session object
int loop;
Session["TestString"]="Hello";
    Session.Add("TestNumber",43);
Message.Text="There are " +
    Session.Count.ToString() +
    " items in the Session collection.<br>\n";
for ( loop=0 ; loop<Session.Count ; loop++ )
{
    Message.Text+="Session(" +
        loop.ToString() +
        ")=" + Session[loop] + "<br>";
}
```

8 To save the application, on the File menu, click Save All (or press Ctrl+Shift+S).

9 To build the application, on the Build menu, click Build Solution (or press Ctrl+Shift+B).

10 To run the application, on the Debug menu, click Start (or press F5). The resulting screen should look like the following illustration:

Recommendations for Session State

Session state's ease of use makes it easy to overuse or abuse. Table 4-4 lists examples of when you might not want to store information in session state, as well as alternatives for storing such information.

Table 4-4. Session State Recommendations		
State information	**Issues**	**Alternative**
User-specific settings	Depending on how frequently these values are accessed, session state might not be the most efficient way to store these settings.	For infrequently accessed values, consider storing userspecific settings in a database.
Datasets containing frequently read data	Caching frequently used data at the session level can be efficient but there's little automatic control over when the data is refreshed. It's very important to consider the cost of storing a dataset for each user session over the cost of retrieving the dataset from the database.	Use the ASP.NET cache engine to cache expensive or frequently read data. The ASP.NET cache engine provides fine-grained control over how and when data is refreshed or purged from the cache. See Chapter 12 for more information about caching.
References to object instances	Storing references to objects with the wrong threading model (such as legacy COM components created with Visual Basic) can severely affect the scalability of an application. It's important to consider the cost of storing a reference to an object for each user session.	If it's absolutely necessary to store a reference to an object instance, ensure that the class from which the object is created is thread safe.

Limitations of Session State

Thanks to a number of new features in ASP.NET, the primary limitation of session state in ASP.NET is memory. As with application state, session state is limited by the memory available on the Web server. After the available physical memory on the Web server has been exhausted, information will be stored in much slower virtual memory.

State and Scalability

How and where you choose to store state information for your application can have a major impact on how scalable your application is. *Scalability* refers to the ability of an application to service requests from increasing numbers of users without any significant decrease in performance or response time.

Some of the factors affecting application scalability that result from poor decisions in state management include the following conditions.

- **Failing to disable session state when not used**   If you're not using session state within your application, disable it by changing the *mode* attribute of the *sessionState* configuration section of Web.config to *off*. For applications that make limited use of session state, ensure that any pages that don't use session state include the *EnableSessionState="false"* attribute as a part of the page's @ *Page* directive.

- **Misusing Application.Lock()**   The *Application.Lock()* method prevents access to all application values for any user other than the user whose request resulted in the call to *Application.Lock()*. This continues until the *Application.Unlock()* method is called. You should minimize the time that these values are locked by calling *Application.Lock()* immediately prior to updating a value and calling Application.Lock(). If you want to add a value that might require some time to calculate, generate the value, save it into a variable, lock the application, add the value from the variable, and then unlock the application.

- **Storing references to single (or apartment) threaded objects**   Storing references to objects that are not free-threaded at application or session level can interfere with IIS thread management capabilities and can result in severe scalability problems. Avoid storing objects that are not free-threaded at application or session level.

- **Using in-process session state**   To scale a Web application beyond a certain point, it's often necessary to use a Web farm to allow multiple servers to handle requests. In-process session state, the default is not available to all servers on a Web farm. To use session state with a Web farm, you should set your application's Session mode to either StateServer or SQLServer as described in the next section.

- **Overusing session or application storage**   Storing numerous object references or large datasets at the application level, and particularly at the session level, can rapidly exhaust the physical memory on a

Web server, causing it to store additional information in virtual memory. This can have a dramatic effect on the performance of an application. You should always ensure that any use of application state (and more importantly, session state) will not exceed the physical memory resources available on the Web server. Also remember that other applications will be using some of these resources.

Configuring Session State Storage

ASP.NET provides several new possibilities for storing session state. Each is designed to overcome one or more of the limitations of session state in classic ASP. The available settings include the following:

- **In-process (InProc)** This is the default setting. Its behavior is essentially the same as in classic ASP.
- **Out-of-process (StateServer)** This setting specifies that a server running the ASP.NET state NT service will store session state. The state server to connect to is specified by an attribute, as described in the following section, "Storing Session State Out-of-Process."
- **SQL Server (SQLServer)** This setting specifies that session state will be stored in a SQL Server database. The SQL Server to connect to is specified by an attribute, as described in the section "Storing Session State in SQL Server" on page 113.
- **Cookieless Sessions** This setting enables you to maintain session state even for users whose browsers cannot handle cookies.

The following sections describe how to configure each of these settings.

Storing Session State In-Process   *in memory of server*

By default, Web applications, whether created in Microsoft Visual Studio .NET or manually, will store session state in-process. As noted, this setting has several inherent limitations, including lack of scalability and durability. For applications requiring neither scalability beyond a single server nor durability of session state across server restarts or crashes, however, this setting might work just fine. It's also the simplest to deal with because it doesn't require any changes to the application configuration file.

Storing Session State Out-of-Process *in memory of the STATE SERVER*

The first solution to the problems of scalability and durability for session state is to store session state out-of-process in a dedicated ASP.NET state process provided by an NT service. One advantage of this method is that the ASP.NET state service can service requests from multiple servers, making it possible to scale session state across a Web farm. Another advantage is that the ASP.NET state service runs in a separate process (or even on a separate machine), so state information can survive restarts or crashes of a specific Web application process. Note that session state information stored by the ASP.NET state service does *not* survive a restart or crash of the machine on which it's running.

Store session state out-of-process

1   Open the Web.config configuration file for your application and locate the sessionState configuration section.

2   Change the *mode* attribute from InProc to **StateServer.**

3   Modify the *stateConnectionString* attribute so that it reflects the server name (or IP address) of the state server and the port that the ASP.NET state service is monitoring (by default, this is 42424).

4   The complete sessionState configuration section that uses the ASP.NET state service on the local machine would look like the following code. (Note that the *sqlConnectionString* attribute, which is not used in this example, and the *cookieless* and *timeout* attributes have been omitted. The full list of attributes is available in Appendix B.)

```
<sessionState
    mode="stateserver"
    stateConnectionString="tcpip=127.0.0.1:42424"/>
```

5   Start the Services Microsoft Management Console (MMC) snap-in by clicking Start, All Programs, Administrative Tools, Services.

Start Service button

6   Start the ASP.NET state service on the desired server by clicking on the Start Service button on the MMC Services snap in, shown in the following illustration:

ASP.NET will automatically connect to the specified state server to store session state for your application. If the state service on the specified server is not running, you will receive an error message.

Keep in mind that although storing session state in a dedicated server process can improve the overall scalability of your application, there are inherent performance implications of moving session state out of process. Retrieving state information from a different process (and especially from a different machine) is significantly more costly than retrieving it from within the same process. You should test the impact on the type and amount of session data you plan to store before implementing this type of session state storage in a production application.

Storing Session State in SQL Server

in hardrive of the SERVER

The second solution to the problems of scalability and durability for session state is to store it out-of-process in a SQL Server database. One advantage of this method is that the specified SQL Server can service requests from multiple servers, making it possible to scale session state across a Web farm. Also, the session state information is stored in a SQL Server database, so state information can survive restarts or crashes of any Web application process, any Web server, or even the SQL Server itself.

Store session state in SQL Server

1   Set up the SQL Server session state database by running the InstallSqlState.sql batch (located in the .NET Framework install directory, by default %windir% \Microsoft.NET\Framework\%version%) against the SQL Server you plan to use. (For more information about running batch statements, check with your database administrator or the SQL Server Books Online.)

2   Open the Web.config configuration file for your application and locate the sessionState configuration section.

3   Change the *mode* attribute from *InProc* or *stateserver* to **SQLServer**.

4   Modify the *sqlConnectionString* attribute so that it reflects the IP address of the desired SQL Server and the user ID and password used to access the SQL Server.

5   The complete sessionState configuration section that uses a SQL Server on the local machine would look like the following example. (Note that the *stateConnectionString* attribute and the *cookieless* and *timeout* attributes have been omitted.)

```
<sessionState
  mode="SQLServer"
  sqlConnectionString="data source=127.0.0.1;user id=sa;password="/
>
```

note

There are security implications to placing the SQL Server user ID and password in the connection string in Web.config. A better practice, where possible, is to use a trusted connection to SQL Server. Chapter 9 describes the steps necessary to use a trusted connection with SQL Server, as well as other connection techniques. Chapter 6 further explores the topic of security in ASP.NET, including good practices for storing connection string information.

Using Cookieless Sessions

One ongoing challenge for Web developers using classic ASP is handling session state for users whose browsers can't or won't accept cookies. Classic ASP provided no intrinsic solution for this situation. In ASP.NET, it's relatively simple.

Handle session state for browsers that don't accept cookies

1   Open the Web.config configuration file for your application and locate the sessionState configuration section.

2   Change the *cookieless* attribute from *false* to *true*.

3   The complete sessionState configuration section would look like the following. (Note that the *stateConnectionString*, *sqlConnectionString*, and *timeout* attributes have been omitted.)

```
<sessionState
  cookieless="true"/>
```

When the *cookieless* attribute is set to *true*, ASP.NET will automatically embed the SessionID value in the URL for all requests. For best results, always use relative URLs for internal links within your application. Relative URLs contain only the path and file information for the requested resource, and not the protocol and domain, which are assumed to be the same as the current page.

Formatting URLs for Cookieless Sessions

ASP.NET provides automatic embedding of session IDs in the relative URLs within your application, but not for absolute URLs, nor for URLs from applications outside yours. If a request for a page within an application set up for cookieless sessions is received that doesn't contain an embedded session ID, ASP.NET will create a new session ID and embed it in the URL for that request.

To prevent this problem, you can manually format URLs by calling the *ApplyAppPathModifier* method of the Response intrinsic object and passing it a virtual path. The method will return an absolute URL containing the embedded SessionID for use with cookieless sessions. An absolute URL includes the protocol, domain, path and file name necessary to request a given resource. The syntax for this method is as follows:

```
string myAbsoluteURL;
myAbsoluteURL = Response.ApplyAppPathModifier("foo.aspx");
```

Using Client-Side Cookies for State Storage

A discussion of state management would be incomplete without at least a brief mention of another option for storing application state: client-side cookies. This method doesn't work with users whose browsers cannot handle cookies (or who have turned off cookies), but it's the most lightweight method for storing certain types of state data because it requires no resources on the Web server.

Store user state in a nonpersistent cookie

1   Create a new instance of the *HttpCookie* class, using code like the following:

```
HttpCookie MyCookie = New HttpCookie("MyCookieName");
```

2   Set the *Value* property of the cookie to the desired value.

```
MyCookie.Value = "MyValue";
```

3   Add the cookie to the *Cookies* collection of the *Response* object (exposed by the *Page* class).

```
Response.Cookies.Add(MyCookie);
```

This sets a cookie called *My Cookie* that lasts until the user closes the browser.

Using Persistent Cookies

To store user state that will persist across multiple browser sessions, you need to use persistent cookies. In order for a cookie to be persistent, its expiration must occur in the future. To make the cookie created in the previous example persist for two days, add the following line of code, just prior to adding the cookie to the *Response.Cookies* collection:

```
MyCookie.Expires = Now.AddDays(2);
```

Here are some things to consider about using persistent cookies:

- Cookies have a bad reputation due to their misuse by some Web companies to track the surfing habits of Web users. It's a good idea to explain to your users exactly how and why you're using persistent cookies, and to describe the benefits of accepting those cookies.

- Keep the expiration of persistent cookies within a reasonable amount of time. For most sites, cookie expiration should be measured in hours or days, or at most months. Setting your cookie expiration to years in the future is likely to result in more users refusing your cookie.

- *Never* store user data, such as credit card numbers or other data that could be at risk if intercepted or otherwise compromised, in a cookie.

note

Although it might seem obvious to avoid storing information such as credit card numbers in cookies, it's equally important to consider the security implications of storing such information on the server side, whether in session state in memory, or in a database server. Although there's no single right answer to how to store sensitive data, here are some guidelines you should follow:

- Store sensitive data only if you must, and then only for the minimum length of time necessary.
  Encrypt sensitive data to better protect it from being compromised.

- When possible, archive sensitive data on systems that are not connected to the Internet (and are thus less vulnerable to being compromised).

- Make sure that you follow good security practices on all of your servers, particularly those exposed to the Internet. (We'll cover security in greater detail in Chapter 6.)

Although following these guidelines won't guarantee that your Web applications will never be compromised by crackers, they'll help you limit the damage.

ASP.NET Server Control State

Server control state is also managed by ASP.NET. Developers who used classic ASP to create data-driven applications had to figure out how to maintain the state of the various HTML form elements on their ASP pages from one page to the next, or even between submissions of a page that submits to itself. HTML provides no built-in mechanism for maintaining the state of individual form elements, so developers were left to come up with their own methods of maintaining and restoring this information.

ASP.NET provides a solution to this challenge with the server control architecture. All ASP.NET server controls are capable of maintaining their own state through a mechanism known as *ViewState*. ViewState is maintained on a page-by-page basis as a hidden form field that contains all the state information for all the form elements on that page.

ViewState and server controls are discussed in detail in Chapters 10 and 12.

Chapter 4 Quick Reference

To	Do this	Example
Store information in the Application collection	Use either the Application object, the Application.Add method, or the Application.Contents collection to add the item to the collection.	*Application[key] = value;* *Application.Contents[key] = value;* *Application.Add(key,value);*
Modify information in the Application collection	Use the Application object to access and modify the item by its key or index, or use the Application.Set method to access and modify the item by its key.	*Application[key] = newvalue;* *Application[index] = newvalue;* *Application.Set(key, newvalue);*
Create and store an object in the Application StaticObjects collection	Add an <Object> tag in Global.asax with the *runat=server* attribute and the *scope=application* attribute.	*<object runat="server"* *id="myObject"* *scope="Application"* *class="myClassName">* *</object>*

(continued)

To	Do this	Example
Store session state in a dedicated server process	Modify the sessionState configuration section of your application's Web.config file, changing the *mode* attribute to **StateServer** and the *stateConnectionString* attribute to the appropriate IP address and TCP port for the state server being used.	*<sessionState mode="StateServer" stateConnectionString= "tcpip=127.0.0.1:42424"/>*
Store session state in a SQL Server database	Modify the sessionState configuration section of your application's Web.config file, changing the mode attribute to **SQLServer** and the *sqlConnectionString* attribute to the appropriate data source name, user ID, and password for the SQL Server being used.	*<sessionState mode="SQLServer" sqlConnectionString= "data source=127.0.0.1; user id=sa; password="/>*
Provide support for session state without cookies	Modify the sessionState configuration section of your application's Web.config file, changing the *cookieless* attribute to *true*.	*<sessionState cookieless="true"/>*

Configuring an ASP.NET Application

In this chapter, you will learn how to

✔ *Edit ASP.NET configuration files.*
✔ *Override parent configuration settings.*
✔ *Lock down configuration settings.*

One of the most important new features of ASP.NET, given the advantages it provides developers, is the new configuration system it provides. This configuration system uses human-readable and machine-readable XML-based files to store configuration information. This chapter looks at how these configuration files work and how you can use them in your applications.

Understanding ASP.NET Configuration

Configuration in ASP.NET is based on a series of XML-based files that are hierarchical in nature. Each server contains a master (or root) configuration file called Machine.config that is stored in C:*windir*\Microsoft.NET\Framework *version*\CONFIG\Machine.Config (see the graphic on the following page). This master configuration file contains the default settings for all ASP.NET applications on that server. This file also contains settings for machine-wide configuration (such as assembly binding and remoting channels), as well as other settings. Use caution when you edit this file to avoid inadvertently making changes that affect other applications.

In addition to Machine.config, each ASP.NET Web application might have one or more files called Web.config in its folders. Each Web.config file must reside in its own folder, and each file overrides any settings of the configuration files in parent folders. Settings in Web.config apply only to content within the folder in which the file resides and any content in child folders. This enables you to set up a hierarchy of configuration files so you can set application-wide configuration options at the highest levels while still being able to override those settings at a lower level. For example, if you have a group of files whose access must be restricted, you can place those files in a separate folder within your application and then add a Web.config file that implements tighter security restrictions. You'll see how to do this later in this chapter.

note

If you decide to use multiple levels of configuration files within your application, you should consider using comments to make it clear that you're overriding settings from parent Web.config files or Machine.config. This way, those who need to maintain the application can understand your intent. Comments in ASP.NET configuration files use the same syntax as HTML comments: <!— —>.

Keep in mind also that many of the settings configured in Web.config and Machine.config can also be overridden at the page level using attributes of the @ Page directive. To avoid confusion, take care to ensure that all developers on a project (as well as those who will maintain the application) understand this.

Changes to configuration file settings are detected automatically by the ASP.NET runtime and integrated into the cached configuration settings for the application. When a change is made, all new requests for resources within the scope of a given configuration file use the new configuration settings automatically.

Introducing Web.config

Like the Machine.config file, Web.config is XML based. This means that each Web.config file is made up of tags and attributes, similar to HTML. (XML is a markup language based on Structured Generalized Markup Language or SGML, the same language on which HTML was based.) Unlike Machine.config, however, most Web.config files will not contain elements for every available configuration setting. In fact, an ASP.NET application doesn't actually require a Web.config file to function. If Web.config is omitted from an application, it simply inherits its configuration settings from the master configuration file, Machine.config.

A Web.config file has the following basic structure:

```
<?xml version="1.0" encoding="utf-8" ?>
<configuration>
   <system.web>
      <elementName1>
         <childElementName1
            attributeName1=value
            attributeName2=value
            attributeNameN=value />
      </elementName1>
      <elementName2
            attributeName1=value
            attributeName2=value
            attributeNameN=value />
      </elementName2>
      <elementNameN
            attributeName1=value
            attributeName2=value
            attributeNameN=value />
   </system.web>
</configuration>
```

Each Web.config file should begin with the standard XML declaration, though it will work without it. The file also contains opening and closing <configuration> tags. Nested within those tags are the opening and closing <system.web> tags, indicating that the content within is ASP.NET-specific configuration information. This configuration information is supplied in tags referred to as elements. Each element consists of either an opening and closing tag with one or more child elements to provide specific configuration values, or a tag pair with one or more attributes to provide specific configuration values. If an element doesn't have child elements, you can omit the closing tag by adding the forward slash (/) character at the end of the opening tag. (This is standard XML syntax.) You'll see this format in action later in this chapter, as well as in Appendix B.

> **note**
>
> Many developers found it frustrating when Microsoft Visual InterDev 6 reformatted code according to its preferred style. That feature was difficult, if not impossible, to turn off. In Microsoft Visual Studio .NET, not only can you control how code is validated and formatted, but in most cases, you can turn off autoformatting entirely.
>
> To view or change the formatting settings for a given language, on the Tools menu, click Options, and in the Options dialog box, click the Text Editor folder. Click the folder for the language of your choice. Note that for some languages, the formatting settings appear on more than one option page. For example, HTML/XML formatting options are set on the Format page, the HTML Specific page, and the XML Specific page, all under the HTML/XML folder.

Editing Configuration Files

At the time of this writing, the Visual Studio .NET environment's tools for editing configuration files are limited to syntax coloring, XML validation, and code formatting. Because the ASP.NET configuration files are XML-based, you can also use your favorite XML editor (or text editor) to edit ASP.NET configuration files.

Open Web.config

1   Either open the Chapter_05 project from the practice files or create a new project named Chapter_05 using the steps learned in Chapter 2.

2   Double-click the Web.config file in Project Explorer.

   The Web.config file will be opened for editing using the Visual Studio .NET XML editor. We'll look at examples of editing this file later in the chapter, so you might want to leave it open.

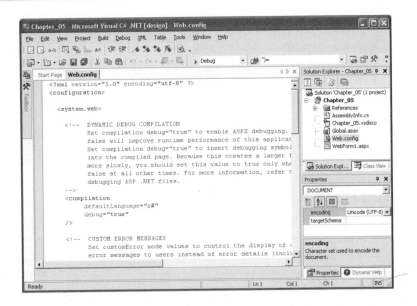

In addition to syntax coloring and validation, Visual Studio .NET also provides a default Web.config file for each new Web application project you create. This default file contains the most commonly used elements as well as comments that explain the available options for each element, as shown in the previous graphic. The default Web.config file is useful as a template for any additional Web.config files you want to place in subfolders of your Web application. Keep in mind that when you're using configuration files in subfolders of your application, it's a good idea to include only the elements for the configuration settings from the parent file that you want to override. This helps prevent overriding a configuration setting by accident, and it might help reduce parsing overhead for the configuration of your application.

Editing the Master Configuration File

Not only does the master configuration file, Machine.config, contain the default settings for all ASP.NET applications on the machine, it has machine-wide configuration settings as well. Be cautious when editing this file. It is prudent to create a backup copy of the file before you edit it. Also keep in mind that unless you're the only one who uses the machine on which you're developing, any changes you make to Machine.config will also affect other ASP.NET developers using the machine. Unless you enjoy dealing with unhappy colleagues, you should discuss any proposed changes with them first.

Configuring an ASP.NET Application

At the time of this writing there are no GUI tools available for editing the Web.config files and modifying configuration settings. Fortunately, the default

Web.config file created by Visual Studio .NET Web Applications, shown in the following graphic, contains comments specific to the most commonly used settings. These comments provide guidance for using the available parameters for a given configuration element (although not all configuration elements appear in the default Web.config file).

In addition to the comments found in the Web.config file generated by Visual Studio .NET, the Machine.config file also contains comments with specific settings for certain elements. These comments can guide you when you make configuration changes. The available ASP.NET configuration elements and their settings are described in Appendix B.

To illustrate how to configure ASP.NET applications, let's look at two examples. The first example shows how to use the <customErrors> element to define a custom page to handle 404-Not Found errors when a user requests a page that doesn't exist in your application. The second example shows how to use the <httpModules> element to remove the SessionStateModule for applications that do not use Session state.

Configure a custom 404 handler

1   If you did not do so in the previous exercise, create a new project named Chapter_05.

2   Add a new Web Form to the project. Name the file **fnf.aspx**.

The new Web Form will be displayed in Design view.

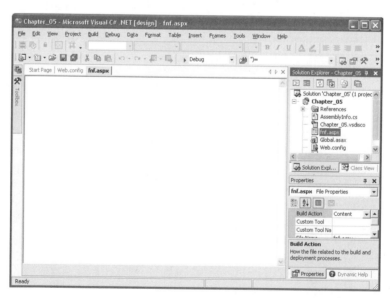

3   Add a Label control to the page.

4   Double-click the Web Form in the Design view window.

The code-behind module for fnf.aspx will be displayed in the Code Editor, with the cursor automatically moved to the *Page_Load* event handler. Note that a local declaration has been added to the code-behind for the Label control to allow access to the control by its name, *Label1*.

```
protected System.Web.UI.WebControls.Label Label1;
```

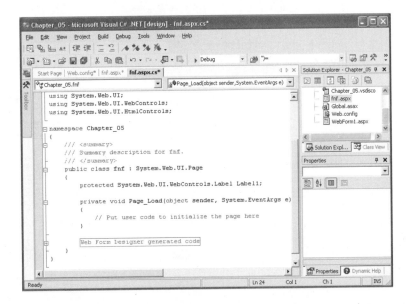

5 Replace the comment with the following code. (The ASP.NET runtime adds the *aspxerrorpath* query string variable automatically and populates it with the path requested by the user when redirecting from an HTTP error.)

```
Label1.Text = "We're sorry. The page you requested: " +
    Request.QueryString["aspxerrorpath"] + " does not exist.";
```

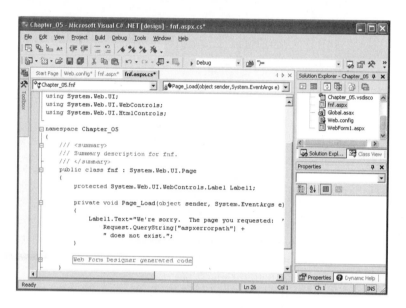

6 Save fnf.aspx and fnf.aspx.cs by either saving the individual files or clicking Save All on the File menu.

7 If it is not already open, open Web.config by double-clicking it in Solution Explorer.

8 Modify the <customErrors> element to look like the following code fragment. (The <error> child element maps the HTTP 404 (not found) error code to redirect to the Web Form created earlier.)

```
<customErrors mode="On">
    <error statusCode="404" redirect="fnf.aspx"/>
</customErrors>
```

The screen should then look like the following illustration. When you are through, save the file.

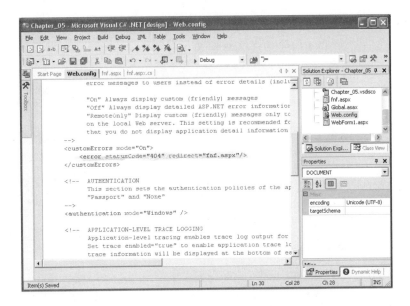

9 To build the project, click Build Chapter_05 on the Build menu.

10 Right-click WebForm1.aspx (the default Web Form added to the project when it was created), click Browse With, click Microsoft Internet Explorer in the Browser list, and then click the Browse button. (This will open the page in a separate browser window rather than one embedded in the IDE.)

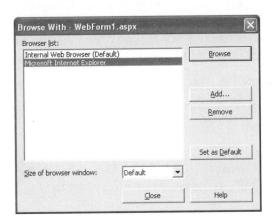

11 Using the Internet Explorer Address bar, change the file portion of the URL from WebForm1.aspx to WebForm.aspx (a file which does not exist), and then click the Go button.

The page will redirect to fnf.aspx and display a message similar to the following. (The path might vary depending on how you set up your project.)

You can use this technique to provide useful error messages to your users, as in this example, or expand on it by using the redirect page to send notification to an administrator of the error, using Microsoft .NET Framework's *SmtpMail* class. (You'll learn how to use the *SmtpMail* class in Chapter 8.)

HttpModules are classes that participate in the processing of every request made to an application. The built-in *HttpModules* in ASP.NET include the *SessionStateModule* and *OutputCacheModule* as well as modules for each of the built-in authentication methods in ASP.NET. These modules are added by default in machine.config using the *<httpModules>* element. You can use the *<httpModules>* element in your Web.config file to remove any of the modules you're not using or to add additional *HttpModules* (including your own custom *HttpModules*).

Remove an *HttpModule*

1 If it is not already open, open Web.config by double-clicking it in Solution Explorer.

2 Add an *<httpModules>* element to the file just below the opening *<System.Web>* tag, as follows:

```
<httpModules>
    <remove name="Session"/>
</httpModules>
```

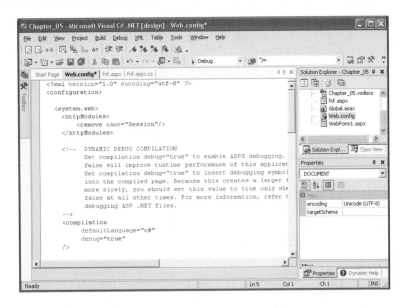

3   Change the *mode* attribute of the *<customErrors>* element to Off. (You'll see why in a few steps.)

4   Double-click the file WebForm1.aspx in Solution Explorer, and then double-click the page in the editor.

The code-behind module for WebForm1.aspx will be displayed for editing.

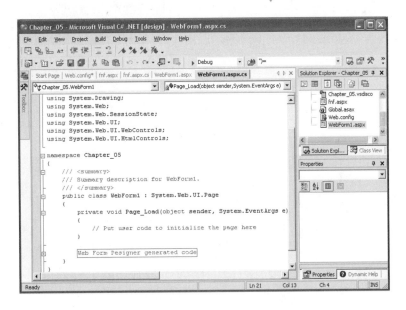

5   Replace the comment in *Page_Load* with the following code:

```
Session["foo"] = "Bar";
```

6   Save all open files and build the project.

7   Right-click WebForm1.aspx in Solution Explorer, click Browse With, click Microsoft Internet Explorer in the Browser list, and then click the Browse button.

The request will result in an exception because we've removed the *SessionStateModule* from the application. Had we not modified the *<customErrors>* element in step 3, you would see a generic error message instead of the detailed message shown in the following graphic:

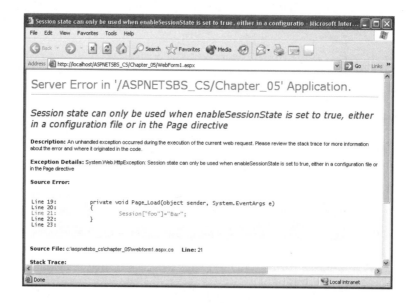

Overriding Configuration Settings for Subdirectories

After you've created the application-level Web.config file (or Visual Studio .NET has created it for you when you created a project) and modified its settings to suit your needs, you might want to modify the configuration settings for a subset of your application. For example, you might want to apply more stringent security requirements to a particular set of files. In ASP.NET, it's simple to override the application-level configuration settings. It takes only three steps.

Override parent configuration settings

1   Create a subfolder in your application and place the content to which the new configuration settings will apply in it.

2   Create a new Web.config file in the new folder.

3   Add the configuration settings you want to override to the new Web.config file.

Include only the configuration elements you want to override in the new Web.config file. All other settings are inherited from the Web.config file of the parent folder, or if that file doesn't exist (or doesn't contain settings for all available configuration elements), from the Machine.config file for your Web server.

Locking Down Configuration Settings

Clearly, there will be times when Web developers or administrators want to configure settings for an entire server or site, and prevent them from being overridden. This might be desirable for authentication and authorization settings or to prevent the overriding of security policy settings. Fortunately, ASP.NET provides the <location> tag for just this purpose.

The <location> tag has two attributes: *path* and *allowOverride*. The *path* attribute enables you to specify a path to which the settings within the <location> tag pair apply. This attribute enables you to use a single configuration file, such as Machine.config, to apply configuration settings for multiple applications, virtual directories, or files on the same machine. Some settings can only be set at the machine or application level. If you attempt to apply these settings at the directory or file level using the *path* attribute, an exception will be thrown.

> **note**
>
> When you're using the *path* attribute to apply configuration settings to multiple locations, use comments to clarify the intended purpose of each set of <location> tags. In shared server environments, use comments to note the person responsible for a given set of configuration settings.

The *allowOverride* attribute determines whether the settings within the <location> tag pair can be overridden by settings applied in a child configuration file. If this attribute is set to *false*, any attempt to change the specified setting in a child configuration file will result in an exception.

Use the <location> tag to lock down configuration settings

1 Open the configuration file (Web.config or Machine.config) from which you want to lock down a particular setting.

2 Add the following code within the <configuration> and </configuration> tags:

```
<location path="path to lock down" allowOverride="false">
    <system.web>
        <!-- Configuration elements to be locked down -->
    </system.web>
</location>
```

3 Add the desired configuration elements between the <system.web> and </system.web> tags.

Chapter 5 Quick Reference

To	Do this
Edit Web.config in Visual Studio .NET	Double-click the Web.config file in Solution Explorer, edit as desired, and save.
Override parent configuration settings	Add a new folder to which the new settings will apply, add a new Web.config file to that folder, add the desired configuration elements, and then save.
Lock down configuration settings	Wrap the settings to be locked down with a <location></location> tag pair with the *allowOverride* attribute set to *false*.

6

Security in ASP.NET

In this chapter, you will learn how to

✔ *Remove unused services to reduce security exposure.*

✔ *Create and apply security policies to simplify the configuration of OS security settings.*

✔ *Secure the system administrator account for an MSDE database instance.*

✔ *Validate and restrict user input.*

✔ *Enable logging of Web requests.*

✔ *Enable SSL encryption of Web requests.*

✔ *Enable Windows-based or Forms-based authentication for ASP.NET.*

✔ *Use ACL or URL-based authorization to control access to resources.*

✔ *Use trusted connections with SQL Server or MSDE databases.*

In days gone by, there were two primary types of applications: single-user applications in which presentation, business logic, and any necessary data handling all occurred on the user's client machine, and client/server applications, which removed much or all of the data handling to a separate database server. Back then, security was largely a matter of making sure that in a client/server situation, users only made modifications to data that they were authorized to change. Issues such as denial-of-service attacks, port sniffing, and so on were seldom faced by the typical application developer.

The Internet has changed all that forever. Applications that are exposed to the Internet are inherently vulnerable to a host of issues, from attempts at stealing data, to the defacing of Web sites, to denial of service attacks. No matter what operating system or other software you run, that vulnerability will never go away entirely. Software development is an imperfect science, and unfortunately, no one yet has created an operating system that is invulnerable to attack.

The good news is that most software, including Microsoft Windows 2000, Windows XP, and Internet Information Services (IIS), can be made quite secure if you follow best practices (a recognized set of recommended procedures and policies) for security, such as keeping track of and installing security patches as soon as they are released. One of the remarkable things about security practices in our industry is just how many servers (both Microsoft-based and otherwise) are sitting out there exposed to the Internet without patches installed that have been available for months or even years!

The Importance of Security

Security should be one of the first concerns a Web developer thinks about when designing and implementing an application. In many ways, designing an application without *considering* security is the same as designing an application *without* security. It is much harder to add security to an application after the fact than it is to do so up front.

Of course, there are different levels and types of security. The type and level you need for your application will vary depending on what your application does, the type and value of data (if any) that you store, the amount of risk you are comfortable with, and the amount of time, effort, and money you are willing to expend to have a secure application. The security needs of a personal home page, for example, are very different from those of a corporate intranet site or a retail e-commerce site. Table 6-1 describes the kinds of threats that are out there and the consequences of being underprepared for them.

Table 6-1. Security Threats		
Type of threat	**Primary target**	**Consequence**
Web server compromise		
▪ Defacement ▪ Substituting of incorrect or misleading information for valid information ▪ Unauthorized access to internal networks ▪ Installation of Trojan or Distributed Denial of Service (DDoS) code	All Web sites	This threat can be embarrassing for an individual, but it can be costly to a corporation, not only in terms of repairing damages, but also in the cost to the company's reputation of having its site defaced, or worse yet, having inaccurate or misleading information posted. Compromised systems can also be used to mount DDoS attacks on other systems—a potential source of liability.
Denial of service	Higher-profile sites	A denial of service attack can prevent users from accessing your site by flooding it with illegitimate requests, among other techniques. These attacks can be difficult to prevent.
Data loss or compromise		
▪ Data compromised through packet sniffing ▪ Server data compromised user impersonation or data forgery	All sites transmitting and receiving sensitive data	Consequences of not addressing this threat include compromise of credit card or other sensitive data, and illicit modification of server data.

Security Basics

With so many potential threats against Internet applications, it's often difficult to know where to start when designing a secure application. This section will discuss some of the strategies you can use to get started.

- **Server set-up and application design**   Preventing Web server and/or data compromise due to insecure server settings and poor application design

- **Patching**   Preventing Web server compromise due to vulnerabilities in server software

■ **Access control**   Preventing Web server and/or data compromise due to inappropriate access settings

■ **Auditing and logging**   Tracking who is hitting your site, what they're doing, and when

■ **SSL and other cryptographic security tools**   Preventing data compromise

Server Setup and Application Design

One of the first areas to concentrate on is how you set up your server. Designing an application that implements authentication and authorization properly is futile if someone can simply bypass all that security through some vulnerability for which you haven't applied the patch. This section will discuss a number of good practices for server set-up and application design, but it's no substitute for a solid understanding of IIS security. You should consult other sources for IIS security, such as the Microsoft Technet site (*http://www.microsoft.com/technet/*) and the security guides for Windows 2000 offered by the NSA (which include a guide to securing IIS 5, available at *http://nsa2.www.conxion.com/win2k /download.htm*). An especially good source of information about IIS (and Web application) security are the books of Michael Howard, who has been a security program manager for Microsoft IIS 4.0 and 5.0 and was on the Microsoft Windows XP team. His books include *Designing Secure Web-based Applications for Microsoft Windows 2000* (2000) and the recently released *Writing Secure Code* (2002), both from Microsoft Press.

Choosing an Operating System

When you're choosing an operating system (OS), the first thing to ask yourself is just how much security you need. As with many questions related to the design of a Web application, there are trade-offs to be made between security and cost. Although client operating systems such as the Windows 9x series might be able to act as Web servers on a limited basis through Personal Web Services (PWS), they are not acceptable when security is an important factor.

Workstation or server operating systems, such as Windows 2000 and Windows XP Professional, offer more robust scalability and better security features, including better access control (see "Access Control" on page 156), logging, and encryption.

note

One reason to choose Windows 2000, Windows XP, or Windows .NET Server to develop and/or host a Web application is that these operating systems can use the NTFS file system, whereas the Windows 9x series cannot. NTFS enables you to provide robust access control at both the file and folder level, and provides built-in support for file encryption (in Windows 2000 and later). FAT and FAT32 (available in the 9x series) are poor choices for Web applications requiring robust security.

Server operating systems offer the most robust security features, as well as better scalability, greater ease of configuration, and better features for developers.

Ultimately, your choice of operating system comes down to the following three factors:

- Features (in this case, security features)
- Cost
- Existing environment

Your evaluation should include an analysis of all these factors, with the goal of determining which OS meets your security needs (features), while allowing you to work within the constraints of cost and existing environment (if any).

important

Windows 2000 and Windows XP provide a number of major security improvements over previous Windows versions, including built-in support for file system encryption, security policies and templates (discussed later in this section), and a Security Configuration And Analysis tool. This tool can be very useful in determining whether your system will meet your security needs as configured, and can help you easily configure it if it doesn't. For these reasons, Windows 2000 (or later) should be the default choice for secure Web applications on the Microsoft platform.

Choosing a Purpose

Another important point to consider when choosing your operating system is the purpose of the server. For smaller applications with low scalability requirements, it might be acceptable to run your Web server, database server, and components all on the same machine. Because IIS and most databases make significant demands on both RAM and processor power, this model does not scale particularly well for larger applications. More importantly, however, placing a database on a Web server that is exposed to the Internet greatly increases the security risks to the data stored in that database. This can also be true for other server and application software, from mail server software to productivity applications such as Microsoft Office. The important point is that as you add more purposes to a server, you are also adding more security exposure. Keep all this in mind as you configure your servers and decide the purpose for each one.

Too Much Service

The next important set of decisions comes when you install your operating system (Windows 2000, for example), or when you add services to be used by your application. This choice concerns which services will be installed.

Unused running services can be a significant security risk. For example, if you install the FTP or SMTP services and have not protected the ports those services use, an attacker could detect the services and attempt to use them to compromise your server through various known vulnerabilities. (You can reduce the risk of compromise through diligent application of patches. See "Patching" on page 156 for more information.)

If you are not using a service, you should avoid installing it or use the Add Or Remove Programs applet to remove it. The following steps, which are specific to Windows XP (the procedure for Windows 2000 is very similar) show how.

Remove unused services

1   Log on using an administrative account.

2   Click Start, and then click Control Panel.

3   Double-click the Add Or Remove Programs icon.

4   In the left side of the window, click the Add/Remove Windows Components button.

5   Review the list of installed components (shown in the following illustration). Of particular interest is the IIS node. Select that item and click the Details button.

6   To remove a service or component, clear the check box next to it, as shown in the following illustration. Click OK to close the Internet Information Services (IIS) dialog box.

7   Click Next to apply your changes.

8   The final dialog box will look like the following illustration. Click Finish to complete the process.

Also, if you need to install services that are not used all the time, you should set them to be started manually rather than automatically. This way, you have control over when these services are running.

Be a Policy Maker

One unheralded feature of Windows 2000 and later is a robust set of tools for setting up a machine's security settings quickly and relatively painlessly. A full discussion of these tools is beyond the scope of this book (and could take up a book of its own), but let's look at a couple of them.

The Security Templates tool and the Security Configuration And Analysis tool when used together enable you to create, edit, and apply templates for defining security policies, from minimum password length to file system auditing policy. Both tools, shown in the following illustration, are implemented as Microsoft Management Console (MMC) snap-ins.

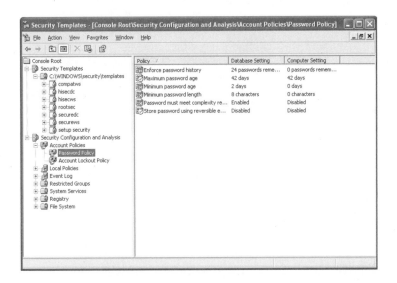

note

You can also define security policies manually by using the Local Security Policy editor, which you can find by opening the Control Panel folder, and then double-clicking the Local Security Policy icon. This tool enables you to adjust individual local security policy settings, as well as apply security templates to the local machine. In Windows XP, first change to Classic view in the Control Panel.

Access the Security Templates tool

1 Either open an existing MMC console or create a new one by clicking Start, and then clicking Run. Then type **mmc**, and click OK.

2 On the File menu (Console menu in Windows 2000), click Add/Remove Snap-in (Ctrl+M). Then click the Add button.

3 In the list of available snap-ins, click the Security Templates snap-in. Then click the Add button.

4 Click the Close button to close the Add Standalone Snap-in dialog box. Then click OK to close the Add/Remove Snap-in dialog box.

5 If desired, save your new or modified MMC console by clicking Save or Save As on the File menu (the Console menu in Windows 2000).

Security in ASP.NET

> **note**
>
> An infrequently used but useful feature of the MMC creates and saves custom consoles that contain the MMC snap-ins you use most frequently. You can use the same procedure outlined in the preceding steps to add the Security Configuration And Analysis snap-in (or any other snap-in) to a console.

The advantage of using the Security Templates tool to create and edit your security templates is that it enables you to create security policy templates without applying the template to the local machine.

Create a new security template

1   Expand the Security Templates node by clicking the Plus (+) sign to its left.

   This will display the template path folder(s) available on the machine, as shown in the following illustration.

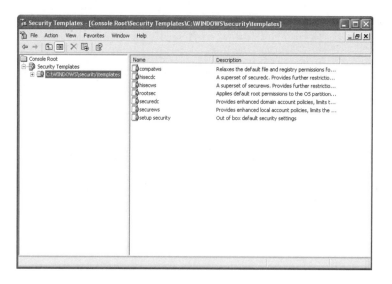

2   Right-click the template path folder for the path where you want to store your new template, and then click New Template.

   The following dialog box will be displayed:

3 Enter the name **TestTemplate** and the description **This is a test template** for the new template, and click OK. The new template will be displayed under the path folder you selected in step 1, as shown in the following illustration. (You might need to expand the node for the template folder to view the new template.)

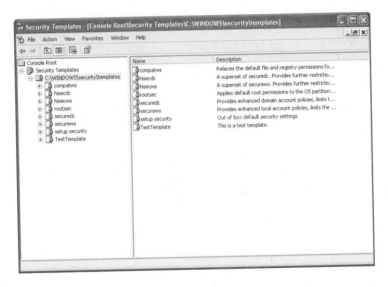

4 To display the options available for configuration with the template, double-click it or click the Plus (+) sign next to it.

5 Using the same technique as in step 4, expand the policy area you want to customize, such as the Password Policy (which can be found under the Account Policies node). Select the policy area to view its available Policy attributes in the right pane of the console window.

6   Double-click the Minimum password length policy.

7   Select the Define This Policy Setting In The Template check box, as shown in the following illustration. Then edit the value to your desired value.

8   Click OK to close the Template Security Policy Setting dialog box and apply your change to the template.

9   After making any additional desired changes to the template, save it by right-clicking the template node and clicking Save (or Save As, if this is the first time the template is being saved).

Of course, after you've created your custom template, you might want to use it to configure security for one or more machines. This can be accomplished using the Security Configuration And Analysis tool, which can also be used to determine which settings on the local machine are not in compliance with the template you've defined (or one of the predefined templates).

important

As with many security-related tasks, you must be logged in as an administrator to successfully analyze the current security settings and apply security templates. Non-administrators can start the Security Templates and Security Configuration And Analysis tools, but they will receive an error message if they attempt to perform actions for which they do not have the necessary permissions.

You can also use templates to define security settings for development, staging, and production security requirements. A development or staging server's security requirements are usually less restrictive than those for a production server environment where the completed application ultimately will be deployed.

Unfortunately, when an application is moved to the more restrictive environment of the production server, the application might not work due to security restrictions. By defining security templates for development, staging, and production environments, you can apply those templates to your development and/or staging servers to test whether the application will work with the greater restrictions of those environments. After testing is complete, you can restore the previous template to continue development work.

important

Because the Security Templates tool can affect a large number of security settings on a machine, it is very important that you configure and test your templates on development or staging systems before applying them to production systems. Certain security restrictions can prevent Web applications from functioning properly (for example, by restricting access to accounts used by the application), so you should always make sure your application works properly under the security policy defined by the template before applying the template to a production system.

note

If the Export Template command is unavailable on the shortcut menu of the Security and Configuration Analysis node in MMC, you need to create or open a Security Database, import a template, and then run Analysis. After you do this, you will be able to export the template. Follow these steps to enable the Export Template command:

1 Right-click Security and Configuration Analysis in MMC, and click Open Database on the shortcut menu.

2 Type the name of a new database, and click Open.

3 In the Import Template dialog box, click one of the templates, and click Open.

4 Right-click Security and Configuration Analysis in MMC, and click Analyze Computer Now on the shortcut menu.

5 When the Perform Analysis dialog box appears in the Error Log File Path text box, select a location for the log file, and then click OK.

After the analysis is complete, Export Template and most other options should be available on the shortcut menu of the Security and Configuration Analysis node in MMC.

Apply a security template

1   In a new or existing MMC console, on the File menu (Console menu in Windows 2000), click Add/Remove Snap-in (Ctrl+M). Then click the Add button.

2   In the list of available snap-ins, click the Security Configuration And Analysis snap-in. Then click the Add button.

3   Before selecting a new template, you might want to save your current settings as a template so you can restore them after applying a different template. To save a template containing the current settings, right-click the Security Configuration And Analysis node, click Export Template, provide a name for the exported template, and click Save.

4   Right-click the Security Configuration And Analysis node, and click Import Template.

5   Click the desired template in the dialog box, and click OK. For this exercise, click the built-in hisecws.inf template.

> **note**
>
> Microsoft has a template called hisecweb.inf available for configuring a high-security Web server. This template can be used as a starting point for creating your own security templates. You can download it from the following URL:
>
> *http://download.microsoft.com/download/win2000srv/SCM/1.0/NT5 /EN-US/hisecweb.exe*

6   To compare the settings in the template to those currently configured on the local machine, right-click the Security Configuration And Analysis node, click Analyze Computer Now, and then click OK in the Perform Analysis dialog box.

7   Expand the Account Policies node to display the Password Policy node. Then click the Password Policy node to view its settings, as shown in the following illustration. Where local settings match the template, there's a green check mark. Where settings do not match, there's a red X.

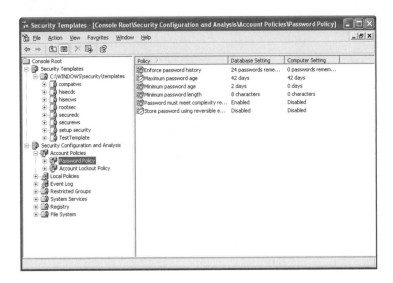

8 To configure the local machine with the settings specified in the template, right-click the Security Configuration And Analysis node, click Configure Computer Now, and then click OK in the Configure System dialog box.

9 If you want to view the settings modified by the template, you will need to reanalyze the computer as described in step 5.

Keep in mind that only settings for which a value has been defined in the template will be applied. All other settings will remain as they were previously configured. Also note that if a server you're configuring is part of a Windows 2000 domain, any settings configured in the domain-wide security policy will override settings in the local security policy.

Passwords, Please

One of the most common (and dangerous) areas overlooked in Web server security is password protection. Problems in this area include weak or nonexistent passwords for sensitive information or services, and placing passwords in plain-text files such as ASP and ASP.NET pages, Global.asa or Global.asax files, or configuration files in the Web space.

Weak or Blank Passwords

A simple rule of thumb for sensitive information on your Web server is that it should be protected by a password, and a strong one. Too often, developers wrongly assume that it's sufficient to put Web pages (or other sensitive content) that should be accessed only by certain authorized users in a separate directory that is only accessible by entering the URL directly. And worse, Web developers who are not sufficiently familiar with SQL Server (or its desktop equivalent,

MSDE, which is installed with the Microsoft .NET Framework QuickStart samples and can also be installed with Microsoft Visual Studio .NET) install these databases on a Web server or another server on their network without understanding the security ramifications.

SQL Server and MSDE both contain an extended stored procedure called *xp_cmdshell* that allows command-line commands to be run on the server. Why is this important? Because in many cases, people still install SQL Server or MSDE with a blank password for the system administrator (*sa*) account. For a server connected to the Internet, this is like begging to be hacked. In fact, one Web hosting company that hosts a site devoted to ASP and ASP.NET articles fell prey to precisely this problem (due to the default configuration of MSDE in the Beta 2 .NET Framework QuickStart samples, which included a blank *sa* password—a situation which has been corrected in the release version). This highlights the inherent risk of both beta software and of samples, which are rarely designed for high security. The result was that some malcontents used *xp_cmdshell* to delete much of the content on the affected server. The Web hosting company was fortunate enough to have backups of the content and was able to restore the server, but the damage could have been catastrophic.

important

It cannot be emphasized strongly enough: You must have a strong password on the *sa* account of any SQL Server or MSDE databases on your network. A malicious user with access through the *sa* account can do anything to your server that he could accomplish from a command line, including adding or deleting user accounts, installing and executing malicious code, and deleting content or system files.

Change the MSDE *sa* password

1   On the machine in which MSDE is installed, open a command prompt.

2   Type the following command, which uses the osql command line SQL tool to connect to the \VSdotNET named instance of MSDE that can be installed by the QuickStart samples using the osql command-line utility, and then click Enter:

```
osql -S(local)\VSdotNET -E
```

3 If the connection is successful, you'll see the following prompt (if the login fails, you'll get a failure message):

```
1>
```

4 If the login is successful, enter the following commands to modify the password for the *sa* account. Make sure you memorize the new password so you won't forget it. (Avoid writing it down if possible. But if you must, make sure you put it somewhere secure so prying eyes won't find it.) Replace *<new password>* with the new password you've chosen and press the Enter key after the final single quote of 'sa,' and follow the *go* command by pressing the Enter key:

```
1> sp_password NULL, '<new password>', 'sa'
2> go
```

5 If the result is successful, you should see the message shown in the following illustration. Also note that in this example, a password containing letters, numbers, and symbols has been chosen.

warning

Although it might seem obvious, you should NOT use the password shown in this example as the *sa* password for your SQL Server or MSDE instance. Instead, choose a unique value that will be difficult to guess.

6 Type **exit**, and then press the Enter key to exit the *oSql* utility.

> **tip**
>
> You can also use the Computer Management administrative tool to manage MSDE (and SQL Server) databases. To open this tool, open the Control Panel, double-click the Administrative Tools icon, and then double-click the Computer Management icon. (If you are not logged in as an administrator, you will need to right-click the icon, click Run As on the shortcut menu, and log in as an Administrator from the Run As Other User dialog box.) In the Computer Management tool, locate and expand the Services And Applications node, and then expand the Microsoft SQL Servers node. All instances of SQL Server and MSDE running locally will be listed. The Computer Management provides similar functionality to SQL Enterprise Manager.

You can also use the SQL Server Enterprise Manager utility, if it is available, to modify the login accounts and passwords for an MSDE database.

Almost as bad as blank passwords are passwords that are weak (easily guessable), such as

- Names or places
- Dates such as birthdays or anniversaries
- Words found in a dictionary
- Short passwords (eight characters or fewer)
- All letters, all lowercase, all uppercase, or all numeric

Weak passwords make it much easier for someone trying to hack a server to guess the password for an account. So-called *dictionary attacks* use a dictionary of common terms or words to rapidly attempt to log in to an account. *Brute force attacks* attempt every possible value until they find the correct one. Although a strong password won't necessarily eliminate brute force attacks, it can increase the time needed for such an attack to succeed. In combination with appropriate auditing and logging, this can give you time to deal with the attack.

Strong passwords meet minimum requirements for length and complexity. You can require secure passwords using a security template, such as the hisecweb.inf template, using the Security Configuration And Analysis tool as described in the section "Apply a security template." The hisecweb.inf template sets minimum and maximum password age, enforces password history (preventing users from reusing old passwords), sets minimum password length to eight characters, and requires passwords to meet minimum complexity requirements, including requiring passwords to include three of the following four categories of characters:

- Uppercase characters
- Lowercase characters
- Numeric characters
- Non-alphanumeric symbols (such as punctuation, special characters like *, #, and $, and so on)

Note that these settings control passwords only for NT security accounts. If you use your own authentication credentials in your application, you will need to implement your own solution for enforcing strong passwords, such as using the RegularExpressionValidator Server Control to perform pattern matching. (See Chapter 8 for more information on validation controls.)

Storing Passwords Safely

Another common problem in Web applications is storing passwords or other sensitive data in unsafe locations: plain-text files such as ASP and ASP.NET pages, Global.asa or Global.asax files, and configuration files in the Web space (those that are accessible by HTTP requests to the Web server). The problem usually occurs when developers place database login information including the password in a plain-text file on the Web server. These developers assume that because users are prevented from viewing the source of .asp, .aspx, .asa, and .asax files by default, this information will be safe.

Unfortunately, this is true only if the Web server is not compromised by a security vulnerability. If a server is compromised, a malicious user might be able to read any file in the Web space for an application and gain the password(s) stored there.

Sensitive information, such as database passwords, can be protected using one of the following options:

- If you're using SQL Server or MSDE, use a trusted connection to connect to your database. In doing so, you will use the *Trusted_Connection* attribute of a connection string to tell SQL Server to use the current user's NT login information to log in. This is most useful in intranet scenarios in which users log in to your application through NTLM with an NT user name and password. This method has the advantage of not needing to store a password at all.

■ Store the connection string information in the Machine.config file, which is not directly in the Web space of the application, using the appSettings configuration section (described in Appendix B). Although this method is still not ideal because password information is still being stored in plain text, the fact that the Machine.config file is stored outside of the Web space makes it that much harder for a malicious user to get to this file. For better security with this method, the directory containing Machine.config and the directory containing your Web application should reside on different drives.

■ For passwords used with Forms-based authentication, you can use the aptly (if awkwardly) named *HashPasswordForStoringInConfigFile* helper method of the *FormsAuthentication* class to hash a password for storing in a configuration file, a database, or an XML file. You can then use the same method to hash the password entered by the user at runtime and compare the two hashes to determine whether to allow the login to succeed. You'll learn how to store hashed passwords later in this chapter.

In addition, you can also use such methods as encryption to make a would-be hacker's job more difficult. The bottom line is that there is really no secure place that you can store passwords that is one-hundred-percent secure, but some methods are more secure than others. Balance your need for security against other factors when choosing how and where to store sensitive information.

note

Using a trusted connection with SQL Server requires either using Windows-based authentication and impersonation, as described in "Using Impersonation" on page 179, or setting up the default ASPNET account (the account used to run the ASP.NET worker processes) as a login account in the SQL Server database being accessed. This process is described in Chapter 9.

Limit Those Accounts

Account limitations are an important security strategy from the standpoint of Windows 2000 accounts, database accounts, and any custom accounts you create for your application. You should configure each account to have only the capabilities necessary for the type of user it represents. For example, it is usually a good idea to set up a database account with read-only access for pages (or components) in your application that need only to read and display data.

A good example of this practice is Microsoft's decision to change the default account for running ASP.NET worker processes. The default account used to be the SYSTEM account, which has numerous privileges and can perform almost any action on a machine. Now the default is the ASPNET account (specified by the *MACHINE* value for the *username* attribute of the *<processModel>* configuration element in Web.config), which has very few privileges on the system. This change makes certain techniques more difficult to use, but it also reduces the likelihood that a single compromised application would compromise an entire system or an entire network.

No Samples, Thank You

Another area of danger for the unwary IIS administrator or Web developer is sample applications. By default, some versions of IIS are installed with a set of sample applications designed to help developers learn to develop applications on an IIS server. The .NET Framework SDK also has samples that can be installed to help developers learn to develop .NET applications. These and other sample applications have their place, but *not* on a production Web server.

Sample applications are not designed to run on production servers, so typically they do not use best practices to prevent servers or applications from being compromised. For example, samples installed with one version of IIS included a utility that enabled users to view the source of ASP pages. Unfortunately, if this utility was installed on a server containing production applications, it could be used to view the source code and make them vulnerable to attack.

As mentioned earlier, the .NET QuickStart samples install an instance of the MSDE database software. In the Beta 2 release, this instance was installed with a blank password for the sa account. If these samples were installed on a server that is exposed to the Internet, this would result in a major vulnerability.

Additionally, some sample applications demonstrate extremely poor practices when it comes to security. Earlier versions of the QuickStart samples used the *sa* account with a blank password for database connections. This is an extremely bad practice. Not only does it re-inforce the bad habit of leaving the *sa* account with no password, but it also uses an account for data access that has much wider permissions than are necessary for data access alone. The good news is that the current versions of the QuickStart samples follow the best practice of using an MSDE account created especially for the sample applications. This account only has permission to access the databases used by the samples, and only the permissions on those databases necessary for the samples.

Although the changes in the .NET Framework QuickStart samples indicate that Microsoft is committed to demonstrating better security practices in sample applications, they still should not be installed on a production server (or any other server that is exposed to the Internet, for that matter) unless you have a very clear understanding of the risks involved and take the steps necessary to mitigate those risks.

You Need Validation

Validation is another area that is often overlooked in Web application security. For example, developers might include validation code to ensure that users enter an e-mail address or phone number in the correct format. But they might not consider that other text fields, particularly large text fields or those that are displayed elsewhere in the application, can expose the application to unacceptable risks.

The problem with not validating all text input by the user is that a malicious user can enter text, such as script commands, ASP.NET <% %> render blocks, or other text that in the wrong context, could be allowed to execute rather than being treated as plain text to be displayed. Additionally, input fields used to construct SQL statements for data access might be vulnerable to unexpected commands being entered. Validation can help you prevent this problem as well as prevent nuisance problems such as users attempting to post profanity in guest book or discussion list applications built with ASP.NET. In fact, ASP.NET makes it very easy to implement robust validation using a set of server controls designed specifically for this purpose.

The important thing to remember is that you should always treat any input from a user as suspect until it has been proven otherwise. Validate that the input from the user is what you're expecting *before* you use, store, or display it. You can do this by limiting the length of text input fields and/or using validation controls, a special group of ASP.NET server controls. You'll learn how to perform validation with these controls in Chapter 8.

Mind Those Ports!

Internet applications communicate through the TCP/IP protocol, which is the basis for all communication between computers on the Internet. TCP/IP uses two pieces of information to find the endpoints for a given communication: the IP address, which is a unique number assigned to a given machine, and a TCP port number, which for most applications is a well-known number used consistently by all applications of that type. For example, all Web servers use TCP port 80 as the default port for HTTP (Web) communications. The well-known nature of these port numbers and the services found on them makes it much easier for Web servers and clients to find one another.

Other well-known ports include File Transfer Protocol (FTP, port 21), Simple Mail Transport Protocol (SMTP, port 25), and POP3 (port 110). The full list of well-known ports and the services assigned to them can be found at *http://www.iana.org/assignments/port-numbers.*

Why is this important to the discussion of security and Web server set-up? Because the very ease of discovery that well-known port numbers makes possible also presents a security risk for the unwary. For example, in Windows 2000, the ports for services such as FTP, SMTP, and POP3 (among others) are left open by default. This gives hackers an engraved invitation to probe these ports and see if the software behind them is vulnerable to attack. Given the many vulnerabilities discovered in FTP, SMTP, and other Internet-based services, it is essential to close all ports that are not in use by your application.

Closing ports can be accomplished in a number of ways, the most common being packet filtering (either through firewall software or a hardware router) or using the IPSecurity Policy Management MMC snap-in in Windows 2000 or Windows XP. For many applications, the preferred solution is to set up a hardware firewall between the Web server and the Internet that only allows traffic on port 80 (HTTP), and optionally port 443 (HTTPS) if secure sockets Web traffic is required. (See " Using SSL to Protect Communications" on page 159 for more information about Secure Sockets Layer communication.) Then a second firewall is added between the Web server and the internal network that only allows traffic on ports necessary for the Web server to reach other servers (such as the database server) and that blocks ports 80 and 443 (and any other ports open in the other firewall). This method places the Web server in what is referred to as a DMZ (demilitarized zone), which is designed to prevent direct communication between the Internet and an internal network. This protects servers on the internal network from attack.

important

Whichever method you use to close unused ports on your Web server, it is imperative that you block traffic to any ports that your application or applications do not use. Remember, however, that the ports that remain open are still a security risk. Effective logging of server activity, frequent monitoring of logs, and prompt patching of vulnerabilities in software operating on the open ports are all important means of defending your server(s) from attacks.

A full discussion of packet filtering, routing, and IPSec management is beyond the scope of this book. Consult the manual for your firewall or router or the Windows 2000/XP Help files for more information about implementing these solutions.

Security in ASP.NET
6

Patching

After your server is set up correctly and securely and you've considered how the design of your application affects security, you might think you're home free. Not so! Even the most securely configured server and securely designed application can be compromised by a lax attitude toward ongoing maintenance. One of the most important aspects of ongoing maintenance of servers and applications is staying on top of patches released by vendors of any software you're using.

In an ideal world, the software we use would be perfect from the start. However, the reality is that there are few, if any, programs that do not contain vulnerabilities. When these vulnerabilities are discovered, typically the vendor of the program will issue a patch designed to correct the problem. Unfortunately, many server administrators do not apply these patches consistently, leaving their servers vulnerable to attack.

This is inexcusable. Most patches can be applied easily, and there are many ways that you can be notified automatically about new ones for Microsoft software. These include the following sources of information about patches.

- The Windows Update site (*http://windowsupdate.microsoft.com/*) lets you analyze the updates available for a given system and determine which of them are currently installed. Windows 98 and later install a link to Windows Update in the Start menu by default.

- The Microsoft Product Security Notification service lets you sign up for e-mail notification of vulnerabilities and available patches. This method is useful for administrators who need to keep track of patches without visiting multiple machines. You can sign up for this service at *http://www.microsoft.com/technet/treeview/default.asp?url=/technet/security/bulletin/notify.asp*.

- The Network Security Hotfix Checker is a command-line utility that will scan the local machine or machines on the local network for uninstalled patches for Windows NT 4.0, Windows 2000, IIS 4.0 and 5.0, SQL Server 7.0 and 2000 (and MSDE), and IE 5.01 and later. The Network Security Hotfix Checker is downloadable from *http://www.microsoft.com/downloads/release.asp?releaseid=31154&area=featured&ordinal=2* You can find more information about using the Network Security Hotfix Checker by going to *http://msdn.microsoft.com* and searching for Network Security Hotfix Checker. Windows XP also offers an automatic service to download fixes as they become available.

Access Control

Access control is the process of determining who can access resources on your server. This includes both **authentication** (determining the identity of a user making a request) and **authorization** (determining whether that user has permission to take the action requested). For an ASP.NET application, there are several different authentication and authorization methods. You'll learn how to implement authentication and authorization in ASP.NET later in this chapter.

It is important not to forget that access control also includes physical access to the machine being secured. The best authentication, authorization, and password practices won't help you a bit if someone can gain physical access to a machine and circumvent your security barriers or simply damage the machine beyond repair. Any machine that has value to you should be secured physically as well as through software from unauthorized use.

Auditing and Logging

As mentioned earlier in this chapter, even the best security practices and strongest passwords cannot provide 100 percent protection against attacks. For this reason, it is imperative to enable auditing and logging on exposed servers.

Auditing is the process of monitoring certain activities such as logon attempts for success or failure and then logging the results of this monitoring to the Windows event log. Auditing (and proper monitoring of the logs) enables you to determine when someone is attempting to attack your machine, such as by trying numerous incorrect passwords. In this case, by auditing login failures, you would be able to see the failed login attempts in the Security event log and take appropriate action to foil the would-be intruder (such as disabling the account being attacked). As with many of the other settings discussed in this chapter, the auditing policy for a Windows 2000 machine can be set using a security template through the Security Configuration And Analysis MMC snap-in.

Logging is the process of writing information about the activities being performed on a machine to a known location for later review. For our purposes, the most important logging (after the logging of audit information) is done by IIS for the Web, FTP, and SMTP services. Logging is performed at the site level. The following steps enable logging for a Web site, but the steps for FTP, SMTP, and other IIS services are similar.

Enable logging in IIS

1   Open the Internet Services Manager MMC snap-in by clicking Start, and clicking Control Panel. (In Windows 2000, the Control Panel is in the Settings submenu.) In the Control Panel folder, double-click the Administrative Tools icon. Finally, in the Administrative Tools folder, double-click the Internet Information Services (Internet Services Manager in Windows 2000) icon. (If you are not logged in as an administrator you will need to right-click the icon, click Run As, and then specify an administrative account, or log in as an administrator).

2   Select the server you want to manage, and expand the tree to find the site you want to manage. Right-click the desired site, and click Properties on the shortcut menu. The following dialog box will be displayed:

3   In the <*sitename*> Properties dialog box, ensure that the Enable Logging check box is selected.

4   You can modify the format of the logs using the Active Log Format drop-down list, and you can click the Properties button to modify where logs are kept, how frequently a new log file is created, and the specific information that is logged.

> **note**
>
> It is considered a good practice to modify the location of the Web server logs from their default of *%WinDir%\System32\LogFiles* because that makes it more difficult for a hacker who gains access to your system to cover his tracks. If the log files are in their default location, a hacker can easily alter them or delete them to hide their activity.

Using SSL to Protect Communications

By default, information sent through HTTP requests and responses is sent as clear text. This means that someone could capture the packets that make up these requests and responses and then re-create them, including any data passed from form fields on a submitted page. If such a form contained sensitive data, such as passwords or credit card numbers, this data could be stolen.

Encryption is an important tool for keeping this kind of information secure. The most commonly used form of encryption in Web applications is the Secure Sockets Layer (SSL) protocol. SSL is used by sites requiring secure communications between the Web server and the browser to create and exchange a key used to encrypt communications between the client and server, which helps protect this information from prying eyes. This is typically done by e-commerce sites to protect credit card information, for example. SSL can also be useful for protecting other information, including SessionID cookies and login information when using basic authentication, or ASP.NET Forms-based authentication. (See "Enabling Authentication" later in this chapter for more information about basic authentication.)

By default, SSL communications occur on port 443 (as opposed to non-SSL Web communications, which are on port 80 by default), and use the *https://* prefix for URLs that use SSL. Enabling SSL for your Web server requires obtaining a server certificate and binding that certificate to the Web sites on which you want to use SSL. To request a server certificate from a certification authority, follow these steps.

Request an SSL certificate

1   Open Internet Services Manager. (If you are not logged in as an administrator, you will need to use the Run As feature of Windows 2000 or Windows XP to run the Internet Services Manager using an admin account.)

2   Right-click the site you want to protect by using SSL and then click Properties.

3   On the Directory Security tab, shown in the following illustration, click the Server Certificate button. This will start the Web Server Certificate Wizard.

4   Use the Web Server Certificate Wizard to create a new certificate request. This method is useful if you want to create a certificate request to send to a third-party certificate authority, such as Verisign or Thawte. For a fee, these companies will verify the information in the request and send you a server certificate. Alternately, if you have Certificate Services installed on a machine on your network, you can use that service to create a certificate. (Note that your clients must have your Certificate Services CA listed in their browser as a trusted certificate authority to use this method.) See the Certificate Services documentation for more information about creating and installing your own certificates.

note

No matter which method you use to generate a certificate request, the common name of the certificate (identified by the Certificate Services Web request pages as Name) must match the fully qualified domain name of the site on which the certificate will be installed. Otherwise, users will get a warning that the server's certificate is valid but the name on the certificate doesn't match the requested URL.

After you've received the response from the certificate authority containing your certificate, follow these steps to install the certificate for use in IIS.

Install an SSL certificate

1   Locate the certificate file you received from the certificate authority. Right-click the file, and click Install Certificate.

2   Open Internet Services Manager. (If you are not logged in as an administrator, you will need to use the Run As feature of Windows 2000 or Windows XP to run the Internet Services Manager using an admin account.)

3   Right-click the site you want to protect by using SSL, and click Properties.

4   On the Directory Security tab, click the Server Certificate button. This will again start the Web Server Certificate Wizard.

5   Click Next to advance to the second page of the wizard.

6   On the Server Certificate page of the wizard, shown in the following illustration, click Assign An Existing Certificate, and then click Next.

7   The Available Certificates page should list all the certificates on the current machine, including the certificate you just installed. Click the desired certificate, and then click Next.

8   Review the Certificate Summary information to ensure that you are assigning the correct certificate. Then click Next.

9   Click Finish to complete the wizard.

After you've installed the certificate for a given site, you can use SSL to encrypt communications on any of the virtual directories under that site by having users request pages with *https://* rather than *http://*. To ensure that pages cannot be viewed without SSL, however, you must require SSL for the page or directory you want to protect.

Require SSL

1   Open Internet Services Manager. (If you are not logged in as an administrator, you will need to use the Run As feature of Windows 2000 or Windows XP to run the Internet Services Manager using an admin account.)

2   Right-click the site, virtual directory, or file you want to protect, and then click Properties.

3   On the Directory Security or File Security tab, click the Edit button, which should now be available. This will open the Secure Communications dialog box, shown in the following illustration:

4   In the Secure Communications dialog box, select the Require Secure Channel (SSL) check box. You can select the Require 128-bit Encryption check box for greater security but this requires that the client browser support 128-bit encryption.

5   Click OK to close the Secure Communications dialog box, and then click OK again to close the Properties dialog box for the site, directory, or file you are protecting. The resource should now be accessible only by using *https://*.

Enabling Authentication

As discussed earlier in this chapter, authentication is the process of validating the identity of the user making the current request. ASP.NET applications work with IIS to carry out authentication based on one of several authentication types, which are discussed in the following section.

Authentication and authorization in ASP.NET work hand-in-hand and operate on two distinct levels: the operating system/IIS level and the ASP.NET level. Here's an overview of how IIS and ASP.NET interact:

1   Request comes in to IIS for a resource associated with ASP.NET (such as a Web Form).

2   If one of the IIS authentication methods is enabled, IIS performs authentication and adds the authentication information to the request.

3   IIS passes the request to the ASP.NET runtime. From this point on, IIS plays no further role in the request.

4   If Windows-based authentication is enabled, authorization is performed on the request using the authenticated identity passed by IIS, and if the authorization (typically ACL authorization) succeeds, the request is processed.

5   If Forms-based authentication is enabled, ASP.NET checks for the Forms-based authentication cookie. If no cookie exists, the user is redirected to the configured login page. After the user successfully logs in, an authentication cookie is set, and if the authorization (typically URL authorization) succeeds, the user is redirected to the resource they requested.

6   If Passport authentication is enabled, ASP.NET checks for a Passport cookie, and if it does not exist, ASP.NET redirects the user to the Passport login page for the site. After the user successfully logs in, the Passport cookie is set and the user is redirected to the resource he or she requested.

Selecting an Authentication Type

There are three basic types of authentication available for ASP.NET applications: Windows-based, Passport, and Forms-based authentication. The authentication method you choose will depend on the types of clients you're dealing with, the level of control you have over the client browser choice, and a number of other factors. The next several sections will discuss the available methods, how they're implemented, and why you might choose one particular method over another.

> ### note
> The interaction between IIS and ASP.NET, in terms of authentication and authorization, can be somewhat confusing if you're inexperienced with these features. Until you understand how the various options work, you should practice the techniques and procedures discussed in this section on a machine that is not exposed to the Internet or other potential sources of compromise.

Requests for resources in an ASP.NET application go through two distinct levels of authentication: the IIS level and the ASP.NET application level. The type of authentication you choose determines which of these levels is used to determine whether the request is properly authenticated. As mentioned earlier, authorization also occurs on two levels, so it is important to choose the appropriate authorization method for the authentication type you're using.

The authentication type is determined by the <authentication> element in the Web.config file for an application. You'll see examples of this element later in this section. The full syntax of the <authentication> element is explained in Appendix B.

Using Windows-Based Authentication

In Windows-based authentication, ASP.NET relies on IIS to authenticate the incoming request using one of its available authentication methods.

■ **Basic authentication**   This method is compatible with most browsers, but the password is sent in clear text. Use this only if you can protect the communication with SSL encryption.

- **Digest authentication** This authentication method was introduced as a feature of HTTP 1.1, so it might not be supported by all browsers. It sends a hashed value instead of a clear-text password, making it more secure than basic authentication. This method requires a Windows 2000 Domain Controller. You have to store a clear-text version of the password on the Domain Controller used to validate the password, so the Domain Controller must be secured from physical and network intrusions. If no Windows 2000 Domain Controller is available, this option will be unavailable, as seen in the Authentication Methods dialog box shown later in this chapter.

- **Integrated Windows (NTLM) authentication** This is method available only with Internet Explorer. It's the most secure method because it never sends the user name or password over the network. Use this method if you require your clients to use Internet Explorer to access your application. Note also that Integrated Windows-based authentication will not work over an HTTP proxy connection, which might make it impossible for clients on a corporate network using a proxy to log in to an application over the Internet. It also requires each person who logs on to your site to have an NT account either on the Web server or on a domain controller trusted by the Web server.

If more than one authentication type check box is selected, Digest and Integrated Windows-based authentication will always take precedence over basic authentication.

After IIS has authenticated the user, it passes the authenticated identity to ASP.NET, which can then use that information to allow or deny access to resources within the application. See "Authorizing Users and Roles" on page 177 for more information about this type of authorization.

Change the authentication method used by IIS

1   Open Internet Services Manager.

2   Right-click the site, virtual directory, or file for which you want to modify the authentication method, and then click Properties.

3   In the Anonymous Access And Authentication Control area of the Directory Security tab (or the File Security tab for files), click the Edit button. This will open the Authentication Methods dialog box.

4   In the Authentication Methods dialog box, clear the Anonymous Access check box. Then select the check box for the desired authentication method, shown as it appears on Windows XP in the following illustration. (Windows 2000 is slightly different, requiring an additional button click to get to the user name and password.)

5   Click OK to close the Authentication Methods dialog box, and then click OK to close the Properties dialog box for the resource you selected in step 2.

Configure Windows-based authentication for ASP.NET

1   Open the Web.config file for the Chapter_06 application in Visual Studio .NET.

2   Modify the <authentication> element as follows. (Note: you can set the authentication method only at the application or server level. Attempting to add the <authentication> element to a Web.config in a subdirectory that is not configured as an IIS application will result in an error.)

```
<authentication mode="Windows" />
```

3   If desired, you can have ASP.NET impersonate the logged-in user (so that resource requests are made in the security context of the logged-in user) by adding the <identity> element as follows somewhere inside the <system.web> opening and closing tags (see "Using Impersonation" later in this chapter for more information about impersonation):

```
<identity impersonate="true">
```

4   Save the Web.config file.

After you have set the authentication mode to Windows, set the authorization method in the Web.config file to protect the desired resources.

Using Passport Authentication

Passport authentication uses the centralized Passport authentication service provided by Microsoft. Passport authentication gives users a single login to use with any Passport-enabled site. To use Passport authentication with ASP.NET, you must download and install the Passport SDK, which is available at *http://www.passport.com/business*. ASP.NET provides a wrapper around the Passport authentication service, so you can use it simply by setting the appropriate value for the Web.config <authentication> element.

Configure ASP.NET to use Passport authentication

1   Open the Web.config file for the application in Visual Studio .NET.

2   Modify the <authentication> element as follows:

```
<authentication mode="Passport" />
```

3   If desired, you can set up an internal redirect URL for Passport authentication by adding a <passport> child element as follows. This will cause users who have not authenticated to be redirected to the specified internal URL rather than the default Passport login site.

```
<authentication mode="Passport">
    <passport redirectUrl="<URL>">
</authentication>
```

4   Save the Web.config file.

> **note**
>
> On several machines during testing, at the end of the installation process for the Passport SDK we received a "Page Not Found" error as the SDK setup opened a browser window. In some cases, waiting a few seconds and pressing the refresh button allowed us to continue. Problems with the Passport SDK can be resolved through the Passport support links (such as *https://www.netservicesmanager.com/wizard/support.html*).

Security in ASP.NET

6

> **note**
>
> To download and install the Passport SDK and use Passport authentication on your site, you will need to register on *http://www.microsoft.com /netservices/passport* and pay a license fee.

Using Forms-based Authentication

Forms-based authentication enables developers to easily implement "roll-your-own" security in their applications. Whereas in classic ASP you would need to add an include file or component to every page to look for an authentication cookie and then redirect to a login page if the cookie didn't exist, ASP.NET Forms-based authentication takes care of all this for you.

All you need to do is create the login page, tell ASP.NET where to find it (through settings in Web.config), and set the desired authorization restrictions. In your login page, you can verify the user name and password credentials entered by the user against a database, Windows 2000 Active Directory, or another credential store of your choice, such as an XML file. After you've verified the user's credentials, you can use the methods exposed by the FormsAuthentication class to set or remove an authentication cookie, redirect the user to the original page they requested, or renew the authentication cookie.

> **caution**
>
> In Forms-based authentication, the user name and password are sent as clear text. To ensure the security of this information, you should always use an SSL-enabled connection for your login page.

In the following example, we'll create a login page and a page to display the user name of the currently logged-in user. We will also add the necessary elements and attributes to Web.config, including authentication credentials against which we'll authenticate requests.

Create a login page

1   Open Visual C# .NET, and create a new project named Chapter_06.

2   Add a new Web Form. Name the form *Login.aspx*.

3   Use the Web Form toolbox palette to add four *Label* controls, two *Textbox* controls, a *CheckBox* control, and a *Button* control to the page. The result should look like the following illustration. Note the glyphs in the upper

left corner of each control. This is an indication that the controls are server controls (as opposed to standard HTML elements that are simply rendered by the client).

4 Set the *Text* property of the first *Label* control to **Username:**, set the *Text* property of the second *Label* control to **Password:**, set the *Text* property of the third *Label* control to **Persist Cookie?**, set the *TextMode* property of the second *Textbox* control to **Password**, set the *Text* property of the *Button* control to **Login**, and then set the *Text* property of the fourth *Label* control to be blank. The result should look like the following illustration:

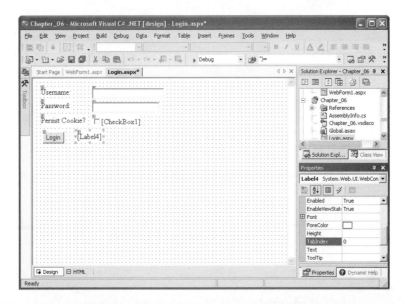

5   Double-click the *Button* control in the designer. This will open up the code-behind module for the page, and add the *Button_Click* event handler.

6   Add the following *using* line to the top of the code-behind module, before the existing class declaration for the *Login* class. This will enable you to use the methods of the *FormsAuthentication* class without explicitly naming the *System.Web.Security* namespace each time.

```
using System.Web.Security;
public Class Login
{
    // class code
```

7   Add the following code to the *Button_Click* handler. (The completed code-behind module should look similar to the illustration that follows the code.)

```
if ( FormsAuthentication.Authenticate(TextBox1.Text,
TextBox2.Text) )
{
    FormsAuthentication.RedirectFromLoginPage(TextBox1.Text,
CheckBox1.Checked);
}
else
{
    Label4.Text = "Incorrect username or password!";
}
```

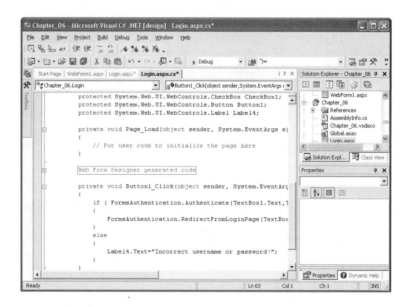

8   On the File menu, click Save All.

Configure Forms-based authentication

1 Open the Web.config file for the Chapter_06 project by double-clicking it in Solution Explorer.

2 Modify the <authentication> and <authorization> elements of Web.config as follows, replacing *<username>* with the desired user name, and *<password>* with a hashed password of your choice. (A helper page for hashing passwords named *HashPwd.aspx* is included with the practice files for this chapter.) In the Web.Config file included with the application, the password is set to the hashed value of the literal string "password" (without the quotes, of course).

```
<authentication mode="Forms">
    <forms name="formsauth" loginUrl="login.aspx"
        protection="All" timeout="60">
        <credentials>
            <user name="<username>" password="<password>"/>
        </credentials>
    </forms>
</authentication>

<authorization>
    <deny users="?" />
</authorization>
```

The modified file should look like the following illustration:

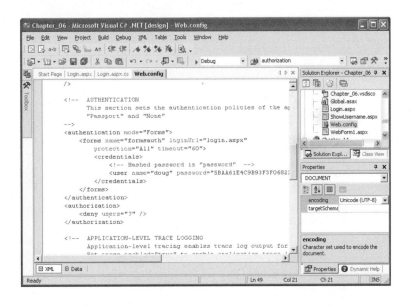

note

By default, you will need to know the password to use any page on the site because of the way it is secured. To avoid this and enable you to use the *hashpwd.aspx* page, I added the following section to the Web.Config file just below the closing *<system.web>* tag:

```
<location path="hashpwd.aspx">
    <system.web>
            <authorization>
                    <allow users="?" />
            </authorization>
    </system.web>
</location>
```

This section allows the *hashpwd.aspx* file to be accessed by even unauthenticated users. The *<location>* tag is described more fully in "Authorizing Users and Roles," later in this chapter.

3   Save Web.config. The application is now configured to use Forms-based authentication and refuse all requests from anonymous users.

Create a page to display the user name

1   Add a new Web Form to the Chapter_06 project. Name the form **ShowUsername.aspx**.

2   Add a *Label* control and a *Button* control to the page. The result should look like the following illustration:

3   Change the *Text* property of the *Button* control to **Logout**.

4   Double-click the *Button* control in the designer. This will open up the code-behind module for the page and add the *Button_Click* event handler.

5   Add the following line to the top of the code-behind module before the class declaration. This will enable you to use the methods of the *FormsAuthentication* class without explicitly naming the *System.Web.Security* namespace each time.

```
using System.Web.Security;
```

6   Add the following code to the *Button_Click* handler. The call to the *Signout* method of the *FormsAuthentication* helper class removes the Forms-based authentication cookie, while the *Response.Redirect* call ensures that the user is redirected to the login page.

```
FormsAuthentication.Signout();
Response.Redirect("ShowUsername.aspx");
```

7   Replace the comment in the *Page_Load* event handler with the following code:

```
Label1.Text = "Username is: " + User.Identity.Name;
```

8   Save the page and code-behind module. The completed code-behind module should look similar to the following illustration:

Build and test the project

1 To build the project, on the Build menu, click Build Chapter_06.

2 Right-click ShowUsername.aspx, click Browse With, click Microsoft Internet Explorer, and then click the Browse button. You should be automatically redirected to the login page, as shown in the following illustration. Note the *ReturnUrl* query string argument, which contains the path to the page you originally requested.

3 Enter the user name and password (unhashed) you configured in Web.config, and then click Login. If you select the Persist Cookie? check box, the Forms-based authentication cookie will be a persistent cookie rather than session cookie. Assuming the credentials you enter match those in Web.config, you will be redirected to ShowUsername.aspx, as shown in the following illustration. Otherwise, an error message will be displayed.

4 Click the Logout button. You will be redirected to the login page.

tip

For the sake of simplicity, we left the ID properties of the controls in the preceding example at their defaults (*Label1*, *Button1*, and so on). In a real application, it is recommended to give controls more meaningful names, such as *PasswordBox*, *LoginButton*, and the like.

note

In this example Web.config file, the URL for the login page is specified with the *loginUrl* attribute of the <forms> element. (For more information about all the attributes of the <forms> element, see Appendix B.) However, if you leave this attribute out, ASP.NET supplies a name *login.aspx* (which happens to be the same as in the example) as the default.

ASP.NET also supplies a default value of *default.aspx* for the redirect page when *FormsAuthentication.RedirectFromLoginPage* is called with no *RedirectUrl* query string argument. So in the preceding example, if you call the login page directly and authenticate successfully, ASP.NET will attempt to redirect you to default.aspx. If there's no such page, you'll get a "page not found" error.

Using Authorization

After you've authenticated the user making the request, the next step is to authorize the request. Authorization means deciding whether to permit the user to access the requested resource.

Authorization in ASP.NET takes two major forms: authorization against NTFS Access Control Lists (ACLs) and URL-based authorization.

Using NTFS ACLs for Authorization

ACL-based authorization is useful when you're using Windows-based authentication in ASP.NET. With ACL-based authorization, you use tools such as the Properties dialog box to set the list of users or groups that are allowed to access a resource, and see what rights (read, write, execute, and so on) each user has. The primary advantage of using ACL-based authorization with Windows-based authentication is that it does not require writing any security-specific code in your ASP.NET application. All security settings can be taken care of administratively.

When a request for a resource (such as an ASP.NET page) comes in, IIS authenticates the request, using whichever method (basic, digest, or integrated Windows) has been configured for the application. IIS passes the identity of the logged-in user (or the configured anonymouse user account, if anonymous access is enabled) to ASP.NET, which then impersonates the user to check the ACL for the requested resource to see if the user has the required permission. If so, ASP.NET fulfills the request.

Configure ACL-based authorization

1 Configure your ASP.NET application to use Windows-based authentication and impersonate the logged-in user by adding the following sections to the application's Web.config file, inside the opening and closing <system.web> tags. Save the file after making the changes.

```
<authentication mode="Windows" />
<identity impersonate="true" />
```

2 In Windows Explorer, right-click a file or folder in your application's physical directory to which you want to restrict access, and click Properties. To modify the security settings, you must be logged in as an administrator or use an account with ownership rights on the resource to be configured.

3 Click the Security tab and add or remove users or groups as desired. Note that you should remove the Everyone group if it is present. If you want ASP.NET to be able to access a resource when not impersonating another user, the ASPNET account should be given access to the resource. When you're finished applying permissions, click OK to close the dialog box.

4 Browse to the protected resource. You might be prompted to log in using your Windows user name and password if you are not already logged in as a user with access to the folder. If you enter credentials for one of the accounts you configured in step 3, you should be able to access the resource.

Using URL-Based Authorization

URL-based authorization, which is new in ASP.NET, enables you to grant or deny access to resources in your application based on their URL (thus the name) using the <authorization> element. Unlike the <authentication> element, which cannot be used in or applied to a subdirectory of an application, the <authorization> element can be applied to subdirectories and even individual files, either by creating Web.config files in the subdirectories or by using the *path* attribute of the <location> element to specify the URL for the resource to be protected. URL-based authentication also enables you to specify the HTTP method for which a particular rule applies.

Authorizing Users and Roles

The most basic form of ASP.NET URL-based authorization looks like this:

```
<configuration>
   <system.web>
      <authorization>
         <allow users="Andrew" />
         <deny users="*" />
      </authorization>
   </system.web>
</configuration>
```

When the <authorization> element just shown is added to the Web.config for an application, it enables the user, Andrew, to access resources in the application's root directory and in any subdirectories that do not have conflicting <authorization> permissions set. The <authorization> element also denies access to all other users. The *users* attribute of the <allow> and <deny> elements enables you to specify comma-separated lists of users to be allowed or denied access to the URL being protected. (Note that if no path is specified, ASP.NET will apply the settings to the directory in which the Web.config containing the settings resides, as well as its children.) ASP.NET provides the following two wildcards for allowing and denying access:

- **Asterisk (*)** Use this wildcard to allow or deny all users.
- **Question mark (?)** Use this wildcard to allow or deny anonymous users.

You can also specify a comma-separated list of roles (equivalent to NT groups) to allow or deny access by adding the roles attribute to an <allow> or <deny> element:

```
<allow roles="Administrators, Users">
```

Note that authorization settings for child directories override those of the parent, unless the parent settings are locked down using the optional *allowOverride* attribute of the <location> element. To prevent the preceding authentication settings from being overridden, you would modify the Web.config file as follows:

```
<configuration>
   <location allowOverride="false">
      <system.web>
         <authorization>
            <allow users="Andrew" />
            <deny users="*" />
         </authorization>
      </system.web>
   </location>
</configuration>
```

Note that the <location> element also has a *path* attribute that enables you to specify the path to which the settings contained between the <location> tags apply. This can be a very convenient way to specify the authorization settings for multiple files or directories in an application from a single Web.config file, which enables the developer or administrator to decide which settings can be overridden by child Web.config files. This is an especially useful feature in shared server or shared hosting situations. A server administrator can place master permissions in the Machine.config file for the server and use the <location> element to prevent these permissions from being overridden.

Allowing or Denying Specific HTTP Methods

In addition to the *users* attribute, the <allow> and <deny> elements also expose a *verbs* attribute, which enables you to specify the HTTP verb type to allow or deny for the specified user(s) or role(s). Extending the preceding example, you could prevent all users from making *POST* requests while still allowing them other access by modifying your Web.config file as follows:

```
<configuration>
   <location allowOverride="false">
      <system.web>
         <authorization>
            <allow users="Andrew" />
            <deny verbs="POST" users="*" />
         </authorization>
      </system.web>
   </location>
</configuration>
```

Limiting the request types to those necessary for a page or pages in your application can be an important way to prevent hackers from compromising your site. If a hacker is unable to make a *POST* request, it is that much more difficult for him to take advantage of a vulnerability that requires sending data in an HTTP POST request. You can restrict HTTP verb access for a page or set of pages by adding the *path* attribute to the <location> element, as described in "Authorizing Users and Roles" earlier in this chapter.

Using Impersonation

Impersonation is the process by which ASP.NET takes on the security context of the user making the request. This allows ASP.NET (and components called by ASP.NET) to gain access to resources that the user is authorized to access.

In classic ASP, impersonation was used by default. If the user making the request had not been authenticated by IIS using basic or NTLM authentication, ASP requests ran with the security context of the IUSR_MACHINENAME built-in account. In ASP.NET, impersonation must be turned on explicitly by using the *impersonation* attribute of the <identity> element. Without impersonation, ASP.NET runs as the built-in ASPNET account. (You can use the <processModel> configuration section to configure ASP.NET to run as a different account that has more privileges, such as the SYSTEM built-in account, although this carries some increased security risks due to the higher level of privilege of the SYSTEM account.)

For example, you might want to take advantage of impersonation when you use trusted connections with SQL Server. Trusted connections use Windows security to connect to a SQL Server database without the need for a SQL Server user name and password. As discussed earlier in this chapter, one of the challenges facing ASP.NET developers is deciding where to store database login information to reduce the risk of it being compromised. With trusted connections, this is not a problem because the login information is never stored by the application.

Enable trusted connections to SQL server

1   Configure your application to use Windows-based authentication, as described in "Using Windows-Based Authentication" earlier in this chapter.

2   Add the <identity> element to your configuration file to make ASP.NET impersonate the identity of the client making the request.

```
<identity impersonate="true">
```

3   Add the desired Windows accounts to the SQL Server security database.

4   In the connection string used to connect to the database, specify Trusted_Connection=yes. The full connection string would look something like the following:

```
"server=(local)\VSdotNET;database=pubs;Trusted_Connection=yes"
```

5   Using one of the accounts that you added to the SQL Server security database, log in to the ASP.NET application. You should be able to access the data on the SQL Server database.

> **note**
>
> If you cannot use Windows-based authentication in your ASP.NET application, you might still be able to take advantage of trusted connections by configuring the default ASPNET account (used to run the ASP.NET worker processes) as a SQL Server login account. Keep in mind, though, that this will allow anyone who can access any ASP.NET application to access the database according to the SQL Server permissions you set up for the ASPNET account. The process of setting up the ASPNET account as a SQL Server login is described in Chapter 9.

Understanding Code Access Security

Another new security feature in ASP.NET is code access security. A full discussion of code access security is beyond the scope of this book, but here's an overview.

Code access security is Microsoft's answer to the challenge of preventing untrusted code from performing actions on your system that might result in the damage or compromise of data. It enables ASP.NET developers and/or server administrators to specify the level of trust a given application should have, using the <securityPolicy> and <trust> elements in Web.config. (See Appendix B for more information about these elements.) ASP.NET comes preconfigured with a set of code access security templates that are mapped to trust levels in Machine.config. Depending on the level of trust specified in the <trust> element, the proper set of code access security permissions are applied to the application. This can include such permissions as whether the application can read from parts of the file system outside its Web space, write to its file space, access reads only, or only execute code.

Like the <location> element that allows the lockdown of configuration settings at a machine level, code access security and the templates used to apply its permissions are ideal in shared server environments in which you want to allow users to create their own ASP.NET applications but want to be able to choose which actions can be taken by code written by different users.

Security Resources

The following are some URLs to keep handy when securing your application.

- *http://www.microsoft.com/technet/security*   This is the starting point for finding security-related information for Windows, IIS, and other Microsoft products. There is a host of good information about improving the security of your servers and applications to be found here.

- *http://www.microsoft.com/technet/security/iis5chk.asp*   This is the Secure Internet Information Services 5 Checklist. Prepared by Michael Howard of the Windows 2000 and IIS security teams, this document provides recommendations and best practices for securing IIS 5.

- *http://www.microsoft.com/technet/treeview/default.asp?url=/technet /itsolutions/security/tools/tools.asp*   This is a list of security tools available through the Microsoft Technet Web site.

- *http://nsa2.www.conxion.com/win2k/download.htm*   This is the download site for the Windows 2000 Security Recommendation Guides prepared by the National Security Agency (NSA).

- *http://www.microsoft.com/technet/treeview/default.asp?url=/technet /columns/security/10imlaws.asp*   This is the 10 Immutable Laws of Security, a list of the many ways to lose control of your computer.

- *http://www.microsoft.com/technet/treeview/default.asp?url=/technet /columns/security/10salaws.asp*   This is the 10 Immutable Laws of Security Administration, a list of sage advice for those who have the onerous task of securing systems under their control.

Quick Reference

To	Do this
Remove unused components	Open the Control Panel, double-click the Add/Remove Programs icon, and then click the Add/Remove Windows Components button.
Create a Windows 2000 security template	Open the Security Templates MMC snap-in, right-click the folder for the new template, and click New Template.
Apply a security template	Open the Security Configuration and Analysis MMC snap-in. To import the desired template, right-click the Security Configuration And Analysis node, and click Import Template. To apply the imported template, right-click the Security Configuration And Analysis node, and click Configure Computer Now.
Change the blank *sa* password of a default install of MSDE	Use the *osql* command-line utility to run the *sp_password* stored procedure. You can also add logins, remove logins, and perform many other tasks with *osql* and the system stored procedures.
Enable logging for a Web site	Open the Internet Services Manager, navigate to the site you want to configure, right-click it, and then click Properties. In the Properties dialog box for the site, click the Web Site tab and ensure that the Enable Logging check box is selected.
Enable SSL communications for a site	Use the Web Server Certificate Wizard to create a certificate request (or follow the procedures recommended by the certification authority of your choice). After you have received and installed your certificate, open the Internet Services Manager, navigate to the site to be configured for SSL, and access the Properties dialog box for the site. On the Directory Security tab, click the Server Certificate button and use the Assign an existing certificate option in the Web Server Certificate Wizard to assign the newly installed certificate to the site. You can require SSL communications by using the Edit button on the Directory Security tab.
Enable ASP.NET to use Windows-based authentication	Set the mode attribute of the <authentication> element in Web.config to *Windows*.
Enable ASP.NET to use Passport authentication	Set the mode attribute of the <authentication> element in Web.config to *Passport*. Install the Passport SDK and follow the instructions to configure.

To	Do this
Enable ASP.NET to use Forms-based authentication	Set the *mode* attribute of the <authentication> element in Web.config to *Forms*. Add the <forms> element with the desired attributes, such as *loginURL* and *timeout*.
Lock down authorization settings	Wrap the *<authentication>* tags in a <location> element pair with the *allowOverride* attribute set to *false*.

PART 3

ASP.NET
Web Forms

Creating Web Forms

In this chapter, you will learn how to

✔ *Create Web Forms pages.*

✔ *Make the parts of a Web Form work together.*

✔ *Create and utilize User Controls.*

✔ *Handle page and control events.*

In previous chapters, you've seen examples of ASP.NET pages—some simple and some complicated. The simplest ASP.NET page consists of plain HTML and is named with the .aspx extension. Although that's perfectly valid, it's also missing a lot of what comprises ASP.NET pages and what makes them Web Forms.

Web Forms go beyond what classic ASP pages offered, adding new directives, new re-usability options in the form of user controls and server controls, and a new server-side data-binding syntax. This chapter will explore how a page is put together and how you can use these new features in your Web Forms.

Anatomy of an ASP.NET Web Form

The following listing is an example of a relatively simple Web Forms page.

```
<%-- Example of the @ Page directive --%>
<%@ Page Language="c#" ClassName="Hello" %>
<html>
<head>
   <script runat="server">
       // this is a script code declaration block
       private string name = "Doug";
       public string Name
```

```
        {
           get
           {
              return name;
           }
           set
           {
              name = value;
           }
        }
        public void SayHello()
        {
           Label1.Text = "Hello, " + name + "!";
        }
        public void Page_Load(object sender, System.EventArgs e)
        {
           if ( IsPostBack )
           {
              if ( NameTextBox.Text != "" )
              {
                 Name = NameTextBox.Text;
              }
              SayHello();
           }
        }
     </script>
  </head>
  <body>
     <!-- this is a server side form -->
     <form runat="server">
        <!-- a Server Control -->
        <asp:Label id="NameLabel" runat="server">Name: </asp:Label>
        <!-- a Server Control -->
        <asp:textbox id="NameTextBox" runat="server"/>
        <!-- a Server Control -->
        <asp:button id="NameButton" text="Submit" runat="server"/>
     </form>
     <!-- a Server Control -->
     <asp:Label id=Label1 runat="server"/>
  </body>
</html>
```

This example contains a directive, HTML markup, a *<script>* code declaration block, a server-side form, and several server controls. The following sections describe all these elements, as well as other elements that can be used in a Web Form page.

Understanding Page Elements

The preceding listing shows examples of many of the elements that can be used in an ASP.NET Web Form. Those elements include server-side comments, the @ *Page* directive, static HTML, a server-side *<script>* code-declaration block containing both event handlers and methods, and several ASP.NET server controls. Table 7-1 describes the elements that can be used in an ASP.NET page.

Table 7-1. ASP.NET Page Elements	
Element	**Description**
Static HTML tags	These standard HTML elements are treated by ASP.NET as literal controls that are rendered to the client browser as represented in the source file.
HTML comments	HTML comments allow descriptive text to be added to a page. This text is sent to the client but not rendered by the browser. For example, this is an HTML comment: *<!—HTML Comment —>*.
Directives	Directives, such as @ *Page*, provide the ASP.NET runtime with information about how to process the page. Using directives, you can control ASP.NET features like session state, wiring up of events, output caching, the language used in the page's script blocks, importing namespaces, and registering custom controls for use within a page.
Server-side code	Code can be contained in either server-side *<script>* code declaration blocks or <% %> render blocks. See "Writing Code in Web Forms," later in this chapter, for information about using code declaration and render blocks. ASP.NET supports server-side code in any language that targets the runtime. Unlike ASP, you can use only a single server side language on a page.
Event handlers	Event handlers are procedures in *<script>* code declaration blocks that handle page or server control events, such as *Page_Load* or *control_Click* events. Most ASP.NET code should be written in or called from event handlers, rather than being written in render blocks.
<script> code declaration blocks	These blocks are used to contain page-level procedures and to declare variables that are global to the page. Executable code, other than global variable declarations in code declaration blocks, must be contained within a procedure declaration. Server-side code declaration blocks must have the *runat="server"* attribute, as shown in the previous listing.

continued

Table 7-1. ASP.NET Page Elements *(continued)*	
Element	**Description**
<% %> render blocks	These blocks are used to contain executable code not contained within procedures. Overuse of render blocks can result in code that is difficult to read and maintain.
Client-side *<script>* blocks	These blocks are used to contain script code to be executed on the client, usually in response to a client-side event. Choice of language (set by the *language* attribute) is dictated by the languages supported by the target browser. JavaScript is the most common choice for cross-browser compatibility in client scripts.
Server-side comments	Server-side comments allow descriptive text to be added to a page. Unlike HTML comments, this text is not sent to the client. The syntax is as follows: <%-- --%>
User controls	These are custom controls that are defined declaratively in files with the .ascx extension. They provide a simple and straightforward mechanism for reuse of UI and UI-related code and can contain most of the same elements as Web Forms pages.
ASP.NET server controls	This set of built-in controls provides ASP.NET developers with a programming model that mimics that of Microsoft Visual Basic. Controls are added to a page, and programmers write code to handle events raised by users' interaction with the controls at runtime. ASP.NET provides two sets of built-in controls: the HTML controls, which provide a 1-to-1 mapping of server-side controls for most HTML elements, and the Web controls, which provide a set of controls that are very similar to the Visual Basic UI controls.
Custom server controls	Custom server controls are another mechanism for code reuse in ASP.NET. They're defined in class files (.cs or .vb files) and are precompiled into managed assemblies before use.

Understanding Page Lifetime

The goal of the ASP.NET Web Forms programming model is to provide an experience similar to that of a Visual Basic, rich client, event-driven application, in which user actions, such as selecting an item from a list or clicking a button, cause server-side code to be executed. This is accomplished through *postbacks*.

The first time an ASP.NET Web Forms page is executed, the code contained within the page (and any code-behind class associated with the page) is compiled into a class that inherits from the Page base class. The following illustration shows the relationship between the page, its code-behind class (if any), and the compiled assembly. After the code is compiled, the class is executed, the resulting HTML is rendered to the browser, and the class is removed from memory.

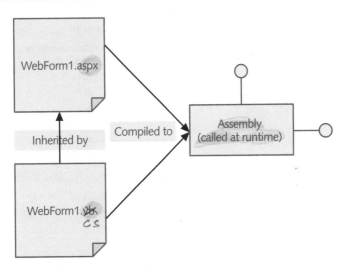

Each ASP.NET Web Forms page contains a server-side *<form>* tag that directs the page to post back to itself when the user submits the form. Many ASP.NET server controls also render JavaScript to the client, allowing actions such as selecting an item in a drop-down list to cause a postback. The ASP.NET runtime also renders a hidden form field that allows the page to maintain its state between requests.

The postback and hidden form field are key because when the client is interacting with the page, there is no code running on the server at all. The postback and hidden form field allow the page to be reconstituted on the server and code to be executed in response to the event raised by the user action and any changes to the form fields. After the page has been processed and the output rendered to the browser, the page and its controls are again discarded. The steps in this process are as follows:

1   The user requests the page from the browser.

2   The page and controls are loaded and initialized.

3   If the page request is the result of a postback, the control state is loaded from the viewstate (hidden form field), and any changes submitted by the user are applied. (Note that both the original values in the viewstate and the updated values are available to server-side code.)

4   Page event handlers and event handlers for events triggered by user actions are executed.

5   Control state is saved to viewstate (hidden form field).

6   HTML output from the page is rendered to the browser.

7   The page and controls are unloaded.

It's important to note that although most server controls save their state to viewstate automatically, the same is not true for properties that you define in your pages, or for user controls or custom server controls. You'll learn how to use viewstate for storing custom control state in Chapter 10.

Using Directives

If you've developed a classic ASP page, you've worked with directives. There were few directives in classic ASP, but they were important. Most prominent were the @ *Language* directive and the *#Include* directive. The @ *Language* directive, which appeared at the top of every classic ASP page, told the ASP runtime which language engine to use in interpreting script found in <% %> render blocks in the page. The *#Include* directive told the ASP interpreter to include a particular file inline with the current ASP page.

Directives are simply ways for developers to declaratively determine how certain aspects of a program will operate. In classic ASP, this was somewhat limited. In fact, there were only the following four @ directives in classic ASP, in addition to the @ *Language* directive:

- @ *Codepage*   Used in globalization to set the code page for an ASP page
- @ *EnableSessionState*   Used to disable session state for a page
- @ *LCID*   Used to set the locale identifier for a page
- @ *Transaction*   Used to specify whether and how the page participates in COM+ transactions

ASP.NET greatly expands the use of directives, adding a number of useful directives for everything from controlling page behavior and configuration to caching page output. In addition, @ directives in ASP.NET have attributes, which increase their power and flexibility. The classic ASP directives just listed are represented in ASP.NET as attributes of the @ *Page* directive, which is described in the next section.

@ Page

The @ *Page* directive, which is allowed in .aspx files only, defines page-specific attributes that are used by ASP.NET language compilers and the runtime to determine how the page will behave. The default values for a few of these attributes are set in the *Pages* configuration section in Machine.config. Some of the attributes, including *AutoEventWireup*, are set or overridden in pages created by Visual Studio .NET. The attributes available for the @ *Page* directive are listed in the Table 7-2.

Table 7-2. @ *Page* Attributes		
Attribute	**Values**	**Purpose**
AspCompat	*true/false*	Provides compatibility with COM components created with Visual Basic 6.0 (or earlier) by forcing the page to be run in an STA (Single Threaded Apartment). Also provides the component with access to unmanaged instances of the ASP intrinsics (Session, Application, Request, and so on). This setting will likely degrade performance, so use it only when necessary. Default is *false*.
AutoEvent Wireup	*true/false* Default is set in the *<pages>* section of Machine.config or Web.config.	Determines whether or not handlers for events such as *Page_Load* are set up automatically. See "Event Handling," later in this chapter, for more information. Default is *true*.
Buffer	*true/false*	Default is set in the *<pages>* section of Machine.config or Web.config. Determines whether rendered output is buffered before being sent to the client or is sent as it is rendered. Default is *true*.
ClassName	Any valid class name.	Determines the name of the page generated by dynamically compiling the page. This attribute works with or without *Codebehind*, and with either the *Src* or *Codebehind* attributes. The default behavior if this attribute is omitted is for the page name to be in the form *filename_aspx*.
ClientTarget	Any valid *UserAgent* string.	Available values are set in the *<clientTarget>* section of Machine.config or Web.config. Determines the target browser for which server controls should render output. The User Agent string should be one recognized by the server controls being used.
Codebehind	File name of code-behind class.	Used in Visual Studio .NET to locate code-behind classes to be compiled during a build operation. It is not used by the ASP.NET runtime.

(continued)

Table 7-2.	@ *Page* Attributes (continued)	
Attribute	**Values**	**Purpose**
CodePage	Any valid code page value.	Same as in classic ASP.
Compiler Options	String containing valid compiler options.	Allows developers to pass compiler options for the page to the compiler. For Visual Basic .NET and C#, this can be any valid sequence of command-line switches for the compiler.
ContentType	Any valid MIME type (such as *text/html* or *application /vnd.ms-excel*).	Sets the MIME type for the page output. This attribute is useful when returning binary content (such as images) to the client.
Culture	Any valid culture string (such as *en-US* for US English).	Determines the culture setting for the page.
Debug	*true/false*	Default is set by the *debug* attribute of the *<compilation>* section of Machine.config or Web.config. Determines whether pages are compiled with debug symbols or without. This setting affects performance, so production applications should have this set to *false*. The default is *false*.
Description	Any string.	Provides a text description of the page. This attribute is ignored by the ASP.NET runtime.
Enable SessionState	*true/false/ readonly*	Default is set in the *<pages>* section of Machine.config or Web.config. Determines whether a request to the page will initiate a new session, and whether or not the page can access or modify data stored in an existing session. Default is *true*.
Enable ViewState	*true/false*	Default is set in the *<pages>* section of Machine.config or Web.config. Determines whether or not viewstate is enabled for the page. *ViewState* allows server controls to save their current state from request to request. Default is *true*.

Attribute	Values	Purpose
EnableView StateMac	*true/false*	Default is set in the *<pages>* section of Machine.config or Web.config. Determines whether ASP.NET runs a Machine Authentication Check (MAC) on the content of the hidden form field that is used to store viewstate to ensure that it has not been altered on the client. Default is *false*.
ErrorPage	Any valid URL.	Specifies a page to which the client is redirected if there is an unhandled exception in the page.
Explicit	*true/false*	Default is set in the *<compilation>* section of Machine.config or Web.config. Determines whether code written in Visual Basic is subject to the *Option Explicit* rule when compiled. Default is *true*.
Inherits	Any class derived from the *Page* class. Format is *namespacename .classname* or *classname*.	Specifies a code-behind class for the page. Any code contained in the page is combined with the code in the code-behind class into a single class.
Language	Any valid string for an installed .NET language (such as *vb/visualbasic, c# cs/csharp,* and so on)	Default is set in the *<compilation>* section of Machine.config or Web.config. Specifies the language compiler to be used to compile the page. Default is *vb*.
LCID	Any valid locale identifier.	Same as classic ASP.
Response Encoding	Any valid encoding string. Default is set in the *<globalization>* section of Machine.config or Web.config.	Used in globalization to set the character encoding for the HTTP response. Default is *utf-8*.
Src	File name of code-behind class	Specifies the name of a code-behind class file to be compiled dynamically at runtime.

(continued)

Table 7-2. @ *Page* Attributes *(continued)*		
Attribute	**Values**	**Purpose**
Strict	*true/false*	Determines whether code written in Visual Basic is subject to the *Option Strict* rule when compiled. Default is *false*.
Trace	*true/false*	Default is set in the *<trace>* section of Machine.config or Web.config. Determines whether the page includes trace output. Default is *false*.
TraceMode	*SortByTime/ SortByCategory*	Default is set in the *<trace>* section of Machine.config or Web.config. Determines how the trace output is sorted when tracing is enabled. Default is *SortByTime*.
Transaction	One of the following: *NotSupported Supported Required RequiresNew*	Determines whether and how the page will participate in COM+ transactions. Default is *NotSupported*.
Warning Level	*0 – 4*	Specifies the warning level at which the compiler should abort page compilation. Lower numbers allow compilation to continue through warnings of greater severity. Levels 2–4 apply to C# only.

@ *Page* Examples

In this section, we'll take a look at a couple of examples of using the @ *Page* directive. The first example will show how to enable debugging of ASP.NET pages, and the second will show how to enable page-level tracing.

Enabling Debug Information

By default, ASP.NET pages created as a part of a Visual Studio .NET Web application project are compiled with debug symbols. Having debug symbols available is good during development because it offers much richer error information than was available in classic ASP, as shown in the following illustration:

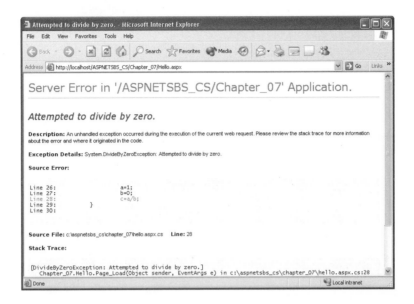

This functionality, however, exacts a performance penalty so you should turn this option off when you deploy your application. There are two specific places where debug symbols are enabled in Visual Studio .NET: in Web.config (which enables debug symbols for .aspx pages) and in the Configuration Manager properties for the project/solution (which enables debug symbols for code-behind classes and other compiled classes in the project). The following procedures describe how to turn off debug symbols for each.

Disable debug symbols in Web.config

1   Open the Web.config for the desired project in Visual Studio .NET.

2   Change the *debug* attribute of the <compilation> element to **false**.

```
<compilation defaultLanguage="c#" debug="false" />
```

3   Save and close the file. Now if you encounter an unhandled error in code contained within the .aspx page, ASP.NET will provide you with an error page without the specific error information made possible by the use of debug symbols, as shown in the illustration on the following page.

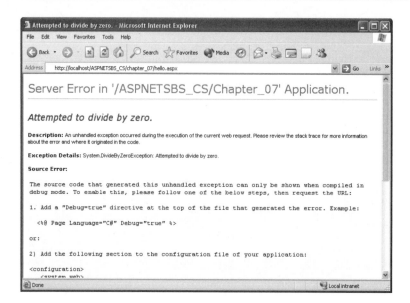

Disable debug symbols using the Configuration Manager

1   Right-click the solution containing the desired project in Solution Explorer, and click Configuration Manager. The dialog box similar to the following illustration appears:

2   To disable debug symbols for a single project, click that project in the dialog box, and click Release in the Configuration drop-down list, as shown in the following illustration:

3   To disable debug symbols for all projects, in the Active Solution Configuration drop-down list, click Release, as shown in the following illustration:

4   Click the Close button.

Enabling Tracing

By default, the *trace* functionality is not enabled for ASP.NET pages. As with the *debug* attribute, disabling tracing is good for performance because there is overhead associated with tracing. Tracing enables you to view information about the current request, including the collections (cookies, forms, headers, querystrings, and server variables) associated with the request. Here's how to enable tracing on a page-by-page basis.

Enable tracing

1 Open the desired page in Visual Studio .NET.

2 If not already in HTML view, click on the HTML tag at the bottom of the design screen. Add the *trace* attribute to the @ *Page* directive, with a value of *true*.

```
<%@ Page trace="true" %>
```

3 Save the file. When you request the file from a browser, you'll be able to see the trace information appended to the page output, as shown in the following illustration.

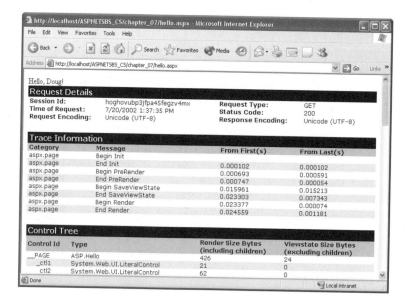

For more information on tracing and its uses in debugging ASP.NET applications, refer to Chapter 14.

tip

In addition to manually adding (or modifying) the attributes of the @ *Page* directive, you can also use the Properties pane in Visual Studio .NET to set the *Debug* or *Trace* properties of the DOCUMENT object to enable or disable these features on a per-page basis.

@ Control

The @ *Control* directive, which is allowed in .ascx files only, performs the same function as the @ *Page* directive. However, instead of setting attributes for pages, it sets the attributes for user controls, which are reusable snippets of code named with the .ascx file extension. The attributes exposed by the @ *Control* directive are a subset of those exposed by the @ *Page* directive, and their purpose and values are the same as in the @ *Page* Attributes table beginning on page 193. The attributes available for the @ *Control* directive are as follows:

- *AutoEventWireup*
- *ClassName*
- *Codebehind*
- *CompilerOptions*
- *Debug*
- *Description*
- *EnableViewState*
- *Explicit*
- *Inherits*
- *Language*
- *Strict*
- *Src*
- *WarningLevel*

@ Import

The @ *Import* directive is used to import either a Microsoft .NET Framework namespace or a custom namespace into a page. Importing a namespace enables you to write code against the members of that namespace without explicitly specifying the namespace each time. The @ *Import* directive has only one attribute, *Namespace*, which specifies the namespace to import. Each @ *Import* directive can have only one *Namespace* attribute, so you must use a separate @ *Import* directive for each namespace you wish to import. For example, to use the .NET Framework *SmtpMail* and *MailMessage* classes to send e-mail from an ASP.NET page, you would need to add the *System.Web.Mail* namespace to your page, as follows:

```
<%@ Import namespace="System.Web.Mail" %>
```

Then to create an instance of the *MailMessage* class, you would use the following:

```
Dim myMail As New MailMessage
```

Without the @ *Import* directive, you would need to use the following:

```
Dim myMail As New System.Web.Mail.MailMessage
```

@ Implements

The @ *Implements* directive is used to implement a defined interface from within an ASP.NET page. An interface provides an abstract definition of a set of methods and properties. When you implement an interface, you commit to supporting the methods and properties defined by the interface, and you must create matching method and property definitions in your .aspx file, using *<script>* blocks. The @ *Implements* directive can't be used to implement interfaces in a code-behind file. It has one attribute, *interface*, which specifies the interface being implemented.

@ Register

The @ *Register* directive is used with both user controls and custom server controls to register them for use within a page. The @ *Register* directive's attributes are listed in Table 7-3.

Table 7-3. @ Register Attributes		
Attribute	**Values**	**Purpose**
Assembly	Any valid assembly name. The assembly name should not contain a file extension.	Specifies the precompiled assembly for a custom server control. Used with the *Namespace* and *TagPrefix* attributes. The assembly named needs to be available to the application, either by being placed in the bin subdirectory of the application or by being installed into the global assembly cache.
Namespace	Any valid namespace name.	Specifies the namespace to be associated with the tag prefix specified by the *TagPrefix* attribute.
Src	Any valid path to a user control (.ascx) file	Accepts either relative or absolute URLs. Specifies the location of a user control associated with a *TagName/TagPrefix* pair.

Attribute	Values	Purpose
TagName	Any string (must be valid for XML).	Specifies an alias for a user control to be used in implementing the user control within the page. Must be used with the *TagPrefix* attribute.
TagPrefix	Any string (must be valid for XML).	Specifies an alias for a tag prefix for a user control or custom server control to be used in implementing the control within the page. If used without the *TagName* attribute, as with a custom server control, the tag name is the same as the class name defined in the server control assembly specified by the *Assembly* and *Namespace* attributes.

For examples of the use of the @ *Register* directive, see "Creating and Using User Controls" and "Using Server Controls," later in this chapter.

@ Assembly

The @ *Assembly* directive is used to link an assembly into a page at compilation time. This enables developers to use all the classes, methods, and so forth exposed by the assembly as if they were part of the page. The @ *Assembly* directive's attributes are listed in Table 7-4. Only one of the *Name* and *Src* attributes of the @ *Assembly* directive can be used at a time.

Table 7-4. *@ Assembly* Attributes		
Attribute	**Values**	**Purpose**
Name	Any valid assembly name.	Specifies the name of a compiled assembly to be linked to when the page is compiled.
Src	Any valid path to a class source file (.vb, .cs, and so on).	Specifies the path to a source file to be dynamically compiled and linked to the current page.

Note that it is not necessary to use the @ *Assembly* directive to link in assemblies residing in the bin subdirectory of your application. These assemblies are automatically linked in by default, based on the *<assemblies>* subsection of the *<compilation>* section of the Machine.config configuration file, which contains the following tag:

```
<add assembly="*"/>
```

This specifies that ASP.NET should link in any assemblies in the bin subdirectory. Note also that any other assemblies specified by an *<add>* tag in the *<assemblies>* subsection do not require linking with the @ *Assembly* directive.

@ OutputCache

The @ *OutputCache* directive is used to specify that the rendered output of the page or user control in which it appears should be cached. It also specifies the attributes that determine the duration of caching, the location of the cached output, and the attributes that determine when a client will receive freshly rendered content rather than the cached content. Output caching in user controls can be especially useful when some of the content in a page is relatively static but other content is frequently updated, making it a poor candidate for caching. In a case like this, you could move the static content into a user control and use the @ *OutputCache* directive to cache its content, while leaving the rest of the page to be dynamically generated with each request.

The @ *OutputCache* directive's attributes are listed in Table 7-5.

Table 7-5. @ OutputCache Attributes		
Attribute	**Value**	**Purpose**
Duration	The number of seconds. (Required.)	Specifies the time, in seconds, for the page or control to be cached.
Location	One of the following: *Any Client Downstream None Server* (Required.)	Specifies the location where cached output should be stored.
VaryByCustom	Any valid text string.	Specifies a custom string by which to vary the output cache. If *browser* is used, output caching will vary based on the browser name and major version. If you want to vary by HTTP request data other than the requesting browser, you will need to override the GetVaryByCustomString method of the HttpApplication class in Global.asax to implement your custom string.

Attribute	Value	Purpose
VaryByHeader	A list of valid HTTP headers, separated by semicolons.	Specifies one or more HTTP headers to be used to vary the output cache. When a request is received with a value for the specified HTTP header(s) that does not match that of any of the cached pages, a new version of the page will be rendered and cached. This attribute cannot be used with user controls.
VaryByParam	A list of querystring keys or form field names, separated by semicolons, or one of the following: *none* * (Required.)	Specifies one or more names of either querystring keys passed with a *GET* request, or form field names passed with a *POST* request to be used to vary the output cache. When a request is received with a value for one of the specified parameters that does not match that of any of the cached pages, a new version of the page will be rendered and cached. If the value of this attribute is set to *None*, the output cache will not vary based on *GET* and *POST* parameters. If the value is set to *, the output cache will vary by all *GET* and *POST* parameters.
VaryByControl	A list of properties exposed by a user control, separated by semicolons.	Specifies one or more properties exposed by a user control to be used to vary the output cache. When a request is received with a value that does not match the specified property of any of the cached pages, a new version of the page will be rendered and cached. This attribute can only be used for output caching with user controls, not with ASP.NET pages.

Enabling Output Caching

For pages or user controls whose content does not change frequently, output caching can provide a simple and powerful way to improve the performance of your application. With output caching enabled, requests that match the parameters of the cached pages will be served from the cache, which is much faster than rendering the page again. Use these steps to enable output caching on a Web Forms page.

Enable output caching

1   Open the desired Web Forms page in Visual Studio .NET.

2   Add the @ *OutputCache* directive with the required *Duration*, *Location*, and *VaryByParam* attributes. This directive should go at the top of the .aspx page, just below the @ *Page* directive.

```
<%@ OutputCache duration="60" location="Any" VaryByParam="*" %>
```

3   Save the file. With these values for the attributes, the output of the page will be cached for 60 seconds. Any *GET/POST* requests with parameters that do not match an existing cached version of the page will be served a freshly rendered version of the page, which will then be cached.

For more information about output caching and using the ASP.NET cache engine to store arbitrary data, refer to Chapter 12.

@ *Reference*

The @ *Reference* directive enables you to dynamically load user controls by referencing the file name of the desired control and then using the Page.LoadControl method to load the control at runtime. The @ *Reference* directive directs the ASP.NET runtime to compile and link the specified control to the page in which it is declared. You'll see an example of the @ *Reference* directive later in this chapter.

The *Page* Class

The *Page* class provides much of the functionality of an ASP.NET page. Pages can take advantage of this functionality because every page derives from the *Page* class and inherits all the methods and properties that it exposes. Some of the more notable members of the *Page* class, which resides in the *System.Web.UI* namespace, are included in the following list.

■   The ASP Intrinsic objects (*Application*, *Session*, *Request*, *Response*, *Server*, and *Context*) are implemented in ASP.NET as class instances, which are exposed as properties of the page object. For example, the *Server* functionality is provided by a class called *HttpServerUtility*. Because the instance of *HttpServerUtility* is exposed as the *Server* property of the *Page* class, you can call its methods (*Server.Transfer*, for example) just as you could in classic ASP.

■   The *Controls* collection provides access to the collection of controls defined for the page. As you'll see later in this chapter, you can use this collection to add or modify controls on a page.

- The *IsPostBack* property enables you to determine whether the current request is a *GET* request or a *POST* request resulting from the current page being posted back to itself. This property is very useful for deciding what to do when loading a Web Forms page, as you'll see later in this chapter.

- The *User* property provides access to information about the currently logged-in user.

- The *Cache* property provides access to the ASP.NET cache engine, allowing data to be cached for later retrieval.

- The *FindControl* method enables you to locate a control contained in the page's *Controls* collection by specifying its *ID* property.

- The *ViewState* property provides access to a state dictionary (based on the *StateBag* class) that enables you to store information in Key/Value pairs. This information is passed with each request as a hidden HTML form field.

- The *ClearChildViewState* method enables you to delete all viewstate information for any child controls on the page. This is useful if you want these controls to maintain their state most of the time, but want to clear the state programmatically under specific circumstances.

Many other properties and methods are exposed by the *Page* class. A substantial number of these are inherited from the *Control* class, from which the *Page* class is derived, or the *Object* class, from which the *Control* class (and ultimately, every other class) is derived. This is an example of how inheritance enables you to build a very rich object model.

There are two methods by which an ASP.NET page is inherited from the *Page* class. The first is adding the @ *Page* directive to an .aspx file, which automatically makes all the properties and methods of the *Page* class available to any code written in the page. The second method, which is discussed in more detail later in this chapter, is inheriting from the *Page* class in a code-behind class that is associated with the page by either the *Src* or *Inherits* attribute. This not only makes all the members of the *Page* class available to the code-behind class, but it also allows ASP.NET to combine the code in the Web Form's .aspx file with the code in the code-behind class file into a single compiled class at compile time. This single compiled class contains all the methods and properties exposed by the *Page* class, as well as any methods and properties implemented by your code.

Any of the members of the *Page* class can be called within code in a page without explicitly using the page name. For example, to write text to the browser using the *Write* method of the *Response* object, you would use the code on the next page.

```
<%
    Response.Write("Hello, World!");
%>
```

You could also use

```
<%
    Page.Response.Write("Hello, World!");
%>
```

But it is not necessary to add the *Page* property because the *Response* property and the other Page members are exposed directly.

Writing Code in Web Forms

One of the strengths of classic ASP was that it gave you a lot of flexibility in writing your code. You could write your code inline with the HTML markup as a part of <% %> render blocks. You could write your code in subroutines in render blocks. And you could write your code in *<script>* declaration blocks, either as arbitrary code or as subroutines.

Although this flexibility made it very easy to create ASP pages, it was also a major weakness of classic ASP because it allowed for sloppy coding. It was far too easy to write unmanageable spaghetti code with some code inline, some code in subroutines, and so on. In addition, although code in render blocks in classic ASP was executed in a linear fashion, arbitrary code (code not contained in a subroutine) in a *<script>* block was not. This often caused confusion because sometimes this code was executed out of sequence with what developers expected.

ASP.NET solves these problems by imposing limitations on what types of code can be written, and where. Although many of the examples in this book use the default technique of writing UI-specific code in a code-behind module (rather than in the Web Forms page itself), it's worth looking at these limitations for those times when you want to work without code behind. As with classic ASP, there are still two ways to write code within a Web Forms page: *<script>* blocks and <% %> render blocks.

Using *<script>* Code Declaration Blocks

As mentioned, in classic ASP, you could write pretty much any code you wanted (property and method definitions, arbitrary code, and so on.) in a *<script>* block using the *runat="server"* attribute. The problem was that you couldn't be sure when any arbitrary code in the *<script>* block would execute, relative to the code in the rest of the page. For this reason, ASP.NET does not allow you to use arbitrary code within *<script>* blocks, which are now referred to as code declaration blocks, to emphasize their purpose of declaring properties and methods.

So if you want to call Response.Write within a code declaration block, you need to wrap that call within a method declaration. The following code will work:

```
<script language="c#" runat="server">
   public void SayHello()
   {
      Response.Write("Hello, World!");
   }
</script>
```

The following code will cause an error:

```
<script language="c#" runat="server">
      Response.Write("Hello, World!");
</script>
```

Likewise, you can declare a local member variable in a declaration block, but you cannot assign a value to it outside of a defined method. So the following code will work:

```
<script language="c#" runat="server">
   string Name;
   public void SetName()
   {
      Name = "Andrew";
   }
</script>
```

But the following will cause an error:

```
<script language="c#" runat="server">
   string Name;
   Name = "Doug";
</script>
```

There is one exception to the variable assignment rule. You can initialize the value of a variable by assigning a value as part of the variable declaration, as follows:

```
<script language="c#" runat="server">
   string Name = "Doug";
</script>
```

The *language* attribute of the *<script>* block is optional. If it is omitted, the value will default to the language specified by the @ *Page* directive's *language* attribute. If no *language* attribute has been specified for the @ *Page* directive, the value will default to *VB*. Thus, you specify a language attribute to ensure that your C# code will compile correctly.

Using ASP <% %> Code Render Blocks

Like *<script>* blocks, <% %> render blocks in classic ASP were pretty much "anything goes." In many cases, this led to sloppy programming habits and hard-to-maintain code. ASP.NET solves these problems by not allowing anything other than inline code and expressions in render blocks. This means that you can no longer place method definitions in a render block. So the following code will cause a compiler error:

```
<%
public void SayHello()
{
    Response.Write("Hello, World!");
}
%>
Whereas the following code will work fine:
<%
    Response.Write("Hello, World!");
%>
```

Compatibility with Classic ASP

Clearly, one of the issues that arises from these changes is that a good deal of code written in classic ASP will not be compatible with the restrictions on the use of code declaration and render blocks. For this reason, it is a good idea to examine any classic ASP code that you are considering migrating to ASP.NET for these incompatibilities, and address them before making the migration (and discovering too late that the code won't work). Of course, because you have decided to use C# rather than VB.NET, any conversion will be more involved than simply restructuring code. That said, a conversion from VBScript to C# is often a mechanical affair. Having ASP code structured properly (with code in script blocks set up inside functions) will make even the conversion from VBScript to C# easier.

Creating and Using User Controls

User controls are a new feature of ASP.NET that provides a simple and fast method for reusing your presentation code. User controls can also dramatically increase performance when used in conjunction with the @ *OutputCache* directive described previously. They are sometimes referred to as *declarative* controls (as opposed to server controls, which are *compiled* controls).

At their simplest, user controls consist of HTML markup and/or ASP.NET code persisted in a file with the .ascx file extension. As you saw earlier in this chapter, developers of user controls can also add the @ *Control* directive to specify aspects of how the user control will behave. Unlike Web Forms pages, user controls cannot be called directly. Instead, they must be used in an existing page.

User controls can contain most, but not all, of the same elements that can be used in Web Forms pages. For example, user controls should not contain *<html>*, *<body>*, or *<form>* elements because presumably they already exist in the page in which the user control is used. It's also a good idea to at least add the @ *Control* directive, along with its *ClassName* attribute, as follows:

```
<%@ Control ClassName="MyClass" %>
```

Adding the *ClassName* attribute allows the user control to be strongly typed when added to a page programmatically (as opposed to declaratively).

Creating a user control is fairly straightforward. In the following example, you'll create a user control that calculates compounding interest. (Don't worry about the math...that's provided as part of the example.)

Create a user control

1   Create a new Web Application project in Visual Studio .NET. Name the project Chapter_07. (If you've installed the practice files, make sure to create the project in a location other than *http://localhost/aspnetsbs_cs/Chapter_07* to avoid conflicts).

2   Add a user control to the project by right-clicking the project in Solution Explorer, pointing to Add, and clicking Add Web User Control on the shortcut menu. Name the user control Compound.ascx.

3   Add six Label controls, three *TextBox* controls, a *DropDownList* control, and a *Button* control to the user control design surface. When finished, the control should look like the following illustration. Because user controls start out in FlowLayout mode by default, you'll need to press the Enter

key to move a control to a new line. It's important that the controls be named/numbered in the order in which they appear on the page (that is, the first label is Label1, the second, Label2, and so on) so that the code in later steps will work.

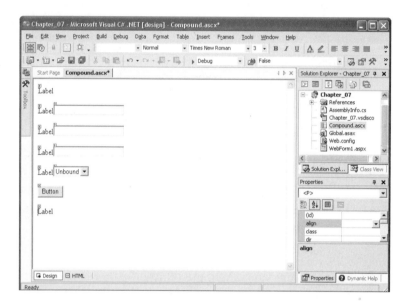

4 Set the properties of the controls as follows:

Control	Property	Value
Label1	Text	**Compound Interest Calculator**
Label1	Font-Bold	**True**
Label1	Font-Size	**Large**
Label2	Text	**Principal ($):**
Label3	Text	**Rate (%):**
Label4	Text	**Years:**
Label5	Text	**Compounding Frequency:**
Button1	Text	**Calculate**
Label6	Text	(leave blank)

5 Click the *DropDownList* control, click the *Items* property, and then click the ellipsis (...) button to open the Collection Editor. Add four items, with the following text and values, and then click OK:

Item	Text	Value
0	**Annually**	1
1	**Quarterly**	4
2	**Monthly**	12
3	**Daily**	365

6 When you have finished modifying the properties, the design view of Compound.ascx should look like the following illustration:

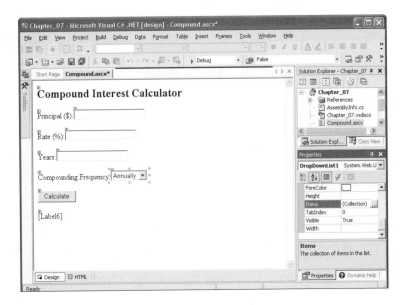

7 Next double-click the Calculate button. This will switch to the code-behind for the user control, and add the *Button1_Click* event handler. Add the following code, which calls the function to calculate the compounded interest, to the event handler. (Note that the following code is a single line but uses the Visual Basic line continuation character for readability.)

```
Label6.Text="Final Balance: " +
    CalculateBalance(Convert.ToInt32(TextBox1.Text),
    (Convert.ToDouble(TextBox2.Text) / 100.0),
    Convert.ToInt32(TextBox3.Text),
    Convert.ToInt16(
        DropDownList1.SelectedItem.Value)).ToString();
```

8 Immediately following the closing curly brace of the *Button1_Click* event handler, add the code on the next page, which defines the function for calculating the compound interest.

```
private string CalculateBalance(int Principal,
    double Rate, int Years,
    int Period)
{
    double result;
    double NumToBeRaised = (1 + Rate / Period);
    result=Principal * System.Math.Pow(NumToBeRaised,
            (Years * Period));
    return(result.ToString("C"));
}
```

9   Save the control and code-behind module, and then build the Chapter_07 project.

This control takes a dollar amount representing the principal to be invested (or borrowed), an interest rate, a period in years, and a compounding frequency, and uses these values to calculate the ending balance. This control encapsulates all the controls and methods necessary for doing the calculation, so the only way to access them is through the user interface defined by the control. It is also possible to expose the controls and/or their values publicly, so they can be manipulated at runtime from the containing page.

To use this control, you need to add it to a Web Forms page. There are two ways to do this: declaratively and programmatically. The declarative method is simpler, but the programmatic method gives you better runtime control.

Adding a User Control to a Page Declaratively

To use a user control in a Web Forms page, make the control available to the page, and then implement the control on the page. As described in "Using Directives," earlier in this chapter, user controls can be made available to a page using either the @ *Register* directive or the @ *Reference* directive, depending on whether you are adding the control declaratively or programmatically. If you want to add the control declaratively, use the @ *Register* directive to set up the tag syntax for the control. Fortunately, the Visual Studio .NET environment makes this a simple matter of drag and drop.

Add a control to a Web Form declaratively

1   If it is not already open, open the Chapter_07 project created in the previous example.

2   Add a new Web Forms page to the project, and name it **CompoundContainer.aspx**.

3 Drag the Compound.ascx user control from Solution Explorer to the design surface of CompoundContainer.aspx. The result should look like the following illustration:

4 Save the CompoundContainer.aspx file, and then browse it using Internet Explorer by right-clicking the file in Solution Explorer, clicking Browse With, and then clicking Internet Explorer in the list. Enter amounts for the principal, rate, and years, choose a compounding frequency, and then click Calculate. The result should look similar to the following illustration.

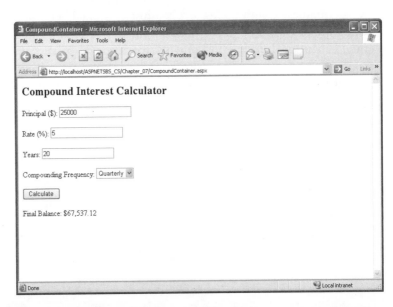

If you look at the HTML view for CompoundContainer.aspx, you'll see that Visual Studio .NET takes care of adding both @ *Register* directive that makes the user control available to the page, and the tag that represents the user control. This greatly simplifies the process of adding a user control to the page, and should probably be your preferred method for adding user controls in Visual Studio .NET. You can, however, also add a user control to the page programmatically, as you'll see in the next section.

Adding a User Control to a Page Programmatically

The steps for adding a control to a page programmatically are somewhat similar, but a bit more involved than adding a control declaratively. You still need to make the control available to the page. For controls that are to be added programmatically, you can do this with either the @ *Register* directive, as in the previous example, or the @ *Reference* directive. Because the @ *Register* directive is more commonly used for declarative controls, use the @ *Reference* directive.

Add an @ *Reference* directive

1   Add a new Web Form to the Chapter_07 project. Name the file CompoundProgrammatic.aspx.

2   Switch to HTML view, and add the following code to the page, just below the @ *Page* directive:

```
<%@ Reference Control="Compound.ascx" %>
```

3   Save the file, but don't close it.

The @ *Reference* directive tells ASP.NET to compile and link the user control Compound.ascx with the page when it is compiled. This makes the control available to be added to the page. Because you're not going add a tag within the HTML markup for the control's output, take advantage of a special server control called the *Placeholder* control. As the name suggests, this enables you to put a placeholder in the HTML markup to which you can add controls later. In this way, you can decide precisely where you want the output from the control to appear.

Add the *Placeholder* control

1   Add a PlaceHolder of the HelloReference.aspx page: *CompoundProgrammatic*

```
<form id="CompoundProgrammatic" method="post"
runat="server">
    <asp:PlaceHolder ID="CompoundHolder" Runat="server"/>
</form>
```

2   Save the file, but don't close it yet.

Finally we need to add the control to the page and to the *Controls* collection of the *Placeholder* control, which will place the output of the control where we want it. Then the control will take care of the rest, just as in the previous example.

Add a user control to a page programmatically

1   Switch to Design view, and double-click an empty area of the page. This will open the code-behind module for the page and place the cursor in the *Page_Load* event handler. Add the following code to the event handler:

```
Control CalcCompound = LoadControl("Compound.ascx");
CompoundHolder.Controls.Add(CalcCompound);
```

2   Save the page and code-behind module, and then build the Chapter_07 project.

3   Browse CompoundProgrammatic.aspx, using the Browse With dialog box. The output of the page should be the same as in the previous illustration.

Comparing User Controls to Include Files

User controls perform a similar function to server-side includes in classic ASP, but they're considerably more powerful because of the level of integration with the page model. A user control can have its own controls, and it can save the viewstate of its controls or its own viewstate. This allows the user control to maintain its state across multiple calls without any effort on the part of the page containing the user control. User controls can expose both properties and methods, making them easy to understand for developers who are used to components.

Include files are still available in ASP.NET, mainly for backward compatibility with classic ASP. For new applications, it makes more sense to use user controls, given their advantages.

Event Handling

One of the biggest differences between classic ASP and ASP.NET is the execution model. In classic ASP, pages were executed in a top-to-bottom fashion. That is, with the exception of detours to execute functions defined in the page, classic ASP pages were procedural rather than event-driven, like Visual Basic programs.

ASP.NET changes that by bringing event-driven programming to Web development through server controls and postbacks. At runtime, the code in a Web Form, as well as in any code-behind class associated with that Web Form, is compiled into an assembly. When executed, the code in that assembly fires events that you can handle, both those exposed by the Page class and those that are fired by server controls that have been added to the page.

Page Processing Stages

A Web Forms page goes through the following processing stages:

- *Init*   Page and control settings are initialized as necessary for the request.
- *LoadViewStat*   Server control state that was saved to viewstate in an earlier request is restored.
- *LoadPostData*   Any data returned in server control form fields is processed and the relevant control properties are updated.
- *Load*   Controls are created and loaded, and control state matches the data entered by the client.
- *RaisePostDataChangedEven*   Events are raised in response to changes in control data from the previous request to the current request.
- *RaisePostBackEvent*   The event that caused the postback is handled, and the appropriate server-side events are raised.
- *PreRender*   Any changes that need to be made prior to rendering the page are processed. Any processing after this point will not be rendered to the page.
- *SaveViewStat*   Server control state is saved back to the page's viewstate prior to tearing down the controls.
- *Render*   Control and page output is rendered to the client.
- *UnLoad*   The page and its constituent controls are removed from memory on the server.

Of these stages, you can add page-level event handlers for the *Init*, *Load*, *PreRender*, and *UnLoad* events. These handlers are typically named *Page_Init*, *Page_Load*, *Page_PreRender*, and *Page_UnLoad*, respectively. For other stages, such as the *LoadViewState*, *SaveViewState*, and *Render* stages, you can override the appropriate method to customize the processing of these stages. Overriding these methods is discussed in Chapter 10.

Some events, such as those fired by the page, are fired automatically as certain stages of page processing occur. Others, such as those associated with server controls, are actually triggered on the client (such as a user clicking a button server control) but are fired and handled on the server when the page is posted back to the server. Because the page is reloaded and the control state is restored with each postback, to the client it appears as though the page is there throughout the client's interaction with it, and the application appears to operate much like a Visual Basic form-based application.

Handling Page Events

Each stage in the processing of a Web Forms page fires an event that enables you to perform processing of your own during that stage. Although you might not have realized it, you've already learned how to take advantage of these event handlers in your own pages. When you double-click an empty area of a Web Form in Design view, the IDE opens the code-behind module for the Web Form and places the cursor in the *Page_Load* event handler, which is added to the code-behind module when the Web Form (and its associated code-behind module) is added to the project. By default, Visual Studio .NET also adds a handler for the *Page_Init* event to the code-behind module, but this event handler is hidden using the *# Region...#End Region* keywords. You can expand the hidden area by clicking the plus sign on the left margin. The following illustration shows the code contained within the *Web Forms Designer Generated Code* region, in CompoundProgrammatic.aspx.cs:

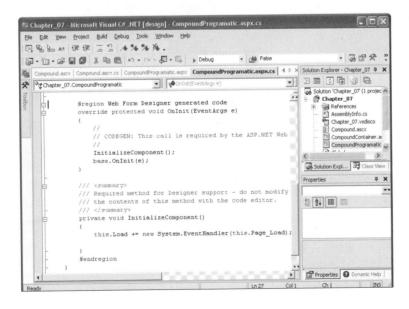

You can handle other page events, such as the *Page_Unload* event, by adding the appropriate handler code to the code-behind module, as shown in the following code fragment.:

```
private void Page_UnLoad(object sender,
    System.EventArgs e)
{
    // Event handling code
}
```

Of course, you can also handle events if you're not using code-behind by adding the appropriate event handler to a server-side script block within the .aspx page:

```
<script runat="server">
    public void Page_Load(object sender, System.EventArgs e)
    {
        // Event handling code
    }
</script>
```

important

The preceding code assumes that the *AutoEventWireup* attribute of the page has been set to *true*. For pages created outside of Visual Studio .NET, you won't need to set this manually, because *true* is the default setting that is inherited from the *<pages>* configuration section in Machine.config. However, pages created in Visual Studio .NET have the *AutoEventWireup* attribute in their *@ Page* directive set to *false*. This means that all event handlers in these pages must be manually wired to the events that they are to handle. You'll learn more about manually setting event handlers in Chapter 8.

Handling Control Events

As with events exposed by the *Page* class, you've already seen many examples of handling control events in this and other chapters. Handling the default event for a given control is as simple as double-clicking the control in Visual Studio .NET's Design view. Visual Studio .NET then takes care of adding the appropriate event handler to the code-behind module for the page, and wiring it up using the Handles keyword. For example, if you were to double-click the *DropDownList* control in the Compound.ascx control in Design view, Visual Studio .NET would add the following code to Compound.aspx.cs:

```
private void DropDownList1_SelectedIndexChanged(object sender,
    System.EventArgs e)
{

}
```

You can add handlers for other events associated with a control using similar syntax. When writing the event handler in code-behind, it doesn't matter what you name the event handling procedure, as long as you properly add the event handler, like Visual Studio .NET does when it adds the *Page_Load* handler to the *InitializeComponent* event handler, as in this example:

```
this.Load += new System.EventHandler(this.Page_Load);
```

Still, it's a good idea to stick with the naming convention of *ControlName_EventName*, because this makes it easy to tell at a glance the control and event that a given procedure is handling.

Handling control events in pages that do not use code-behind is fairly straightforward. There are two steps. First add an event handler procedure to a server-side script block in the page\. The second step is to map the event raised by the control to the event handler using an attribute on the control tag.

For example, if you wanted to handle the Click event of a *Button* control named Button1, you would add the following code to the *<script>* block in ServerControls.aspx:

```
public void Button1_Click(object Sender,System.EventArgs e)
{
    // Event handler code
}
```

And then you would add the following attribute to the *Button1* server control tag:

```
<asp:Button id="Button1" onClick="Button1_Click" runat="server"/>
```

Again, it is not required that the event handler procedure be named with the *ControlName_EventName* naming convention, but using this convention will make your code easier to read.

Handling Page Errors

Although using structured exception handling can be useful for catching exceptions that are expected (see "Ways to Handle Exceptional Situations" in Chapter 4), there are times when you want to handle errors at the page level. This is possible through a special event handler called *Page_Error*.

The *Page_Error* event is raised whenever a page encounters an unhandled exception. Within the *Page_Error* event handler, you can examine the exception that occurred using the Server.GetLastError method and take appropriate action or display a friendly message to the user.

Page Runtime Structure

As discussed earlier, at runtime ASP.NET combines the code in the page and any associated code-behind class into a single class, and then it compiles that class and executes it on the server. In the process, ASP.NET builds a control tree containing all the controls on the page, including *LiteralControl* server controls for each section of HTML text.

important

When compiling a page, ASP.NET automatically creates controls that represent the HTML markup in the page, using the *LiteralControl* server control class. This allows the HTML markup to be easily manipulated at runtime, and greater flexibility in adding controls at runtime. If the page contains <% %> render blocks, however, ASP.NET will not create controls to encapsulate the HTML markup. If you want to be able to manipulate the markup as *LiteralControls*, don't use <% %> render blocks.

At the top of the control tree is the control that represents the page, which has the ID __PAGE. Beneath that are any child controls that belong to the page's Controls collection. Each child control, depending on the type of control, might in turn have its own Controls collection containing child controls, and so on. This structure makes it much easier to find and manipulate controls at runtime.

View the page control tree

The easiest way to view the control tree for a page is to turn on tracing for the page. To view the control tree for the ServerControls.aspx page you created earlier, follow these steps:

1   Open Hello.aspx (included in the source archive for this chapter) in a text editor.

2   Add the *Trace* attribute to the @ *Page* directive and set its value to *true*. The completed directive is as follows:

```
<%@ Page Language="c#" ClassName="Hello" Trace="true" %>
```

3   Save the file and browse the page. The control tree section of the ServerControls.aspx trace output is shown in the following illustration. Notice that where a control has been given an explicit ID through its *id* tag attribute, that ID is used in the control tree.

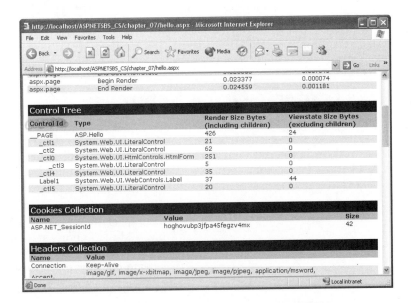

Adding and Manipulating Controls at Runtime

Thanks to the control tree built by ASP.NET at runtime, you can easily add, remove, or manipulate controls at runtime, even if you don't know the name of a control. For example, you can use the *Add* method of the page's *Controls* collection to add a new control to the page at runtime.

```
TextBox MyTextBox = new TextBox();
Page.Controls.Add(MyTextBox);
```

If you want to place the new control at a particular position in the control tree, you can use the *AddAt* method instead.

```
TextBox MyTextBox = new TextBox();
Page.Controls.AddAt(2, MyTextBox);
```

To remove a control by name, you can use the *Remove* method.

```
Page.Controls.Remove(MyTextBox);
```

And to remove a control by index, you can use *RemoveAt*.

```
Page.Controls.RemoveAt(2);
```

To locate a particular control by ID, you can use the *FindControl* method of the page or control containing the control you're looking for.

```
MyControl = Page.FindControl("MyTextBox");
```

Note that because *FindControl* returns an object of type Control (rather than of the specific type of control used), you will need to cast to the appropriate control type before using properties or methods that are specific to that control type.

Chapter 7 Quick Reference

To	Do this
Modify the runtime behavior of an ASP.NET Web Form	Add the @ *Page* directive to the page and set the desired attributes.
Use classes by name without explicitly specifying their namespace	In a Web Form, add the @ *Import* directive, with the *Namespace* attribute specifying the namespace to import. In a C# code-behind file, add the Imports statement with the desired namespace.
Make a user control or custom server control available for use on a Web Form	Drag the user control from Solution Explorer to the design surface of a Web Form.
Enable output caching	Add the @ *OutputCache* directive to the page, and set the desired attributes.
Create a user control	Right-click the project in Solution Explorer, point to Add, and click Add Web User Control. Add the desired controls to the user control, write any code necessary, and then save the files and build the project.
Write server-side functions in a Web Forms page	Create a *<script>* block with the *runat="server"* attribute and place the functions within it.
Handle page-level events	Add an event handler with the appropriate signature (such as *Page_eventname*) to the code-behind module for the page (or server *<script>* block for pages that do not use code-behind).

Using Server Controls

In this chapter, you will learn how to

✔ *Use the two main types of server controls: HTML controls and Web controls.*

✔ *Use specialized Web controls, such as the Calendar control and the Validation server controls.*

✔ *Manipulate server controls programmatically at runtime.*

✔ *Handle server control events.*

Chapter 7 looked at how Web Forms pages are constructed, including some simple uses of server controls. This chapter will take an in-depth look at using server controls in your application.

Types of Controls

As discussed briefly in the previous chapter, the built-in server controls in ASP.NET are divided into two groups, HTML controls and Web controls, each of which is contained in its own namespace. In this section, we will discuss the available controls in each group and show examples of when and how to use each type of control. We will also discuss some of the specialized Web controls, including the *Calendar* and *AdRotator* controls, as well as the *Validation* server controls.

HTML Controls

The HTML controls map 1-to-1 with the standard HTML elements. However, some HTML elements don't map directly to a specific HTML control. You use an HTML control instead of just coding HTML because you can easily manipulate the look and functionality of the page at runtime by changing the control's attributes programmatically.

The HTML controls reside in the *System.Web.UI.HtmlControls* namespace, which is available to Web Forms pages automatically. The HTML elements for which there is direct mapping are shown in Table 8-1.

HTML element	Control type	Purpose
<a>	*HtmlAnchor*	This element allows programmatic access to the HTML anchor element and exposes the *ServerClick* event.
<button>	*HtmlButton*	This element allows programmatic access to the HTML button element and exposes the *ServerClick* event. It is defined in the HTML 4.0 spec and is supported only by Internet Explorer 4.0 and higher.
<form>	*HtmlForm*	This element allows programmatic access to the HTML form element and acts as a container for other server controls. Any controls that need to participate in postbacks should be contained within an *HtmlForm* control.
<img>	*HtmlImage*	This element allows programmatic access to the HTML image element.
<input type="button"> *<input type="submit">* *<input type="reset">*	*HtmlInputButton*	This element allows programmatic access to the HTML input element for the *button*, *submit*, and *reset* input types and exposes the *ServerClick* event.
<input type="checkbox">	*HtmlInputCheckBox*	This element allows programmatic access to the HTML input element for the *checkbox* input type and exposes the *ServerChange* event.
<input type="file">	*HtmlInputFile*	This element allows programmatic access to the HTML input element for the *file* input type.
<input type="hidden">	*HtmlInputHidden*	This element allows programmatic access to the HTML input element for the *hidden* input type and exposes the *ServerChange* event.

Table 8-1.   Mapping HTML Elements to HTML Controls

HTML element	Control type	Purpose
<input type="image">	*HtmlInputImage*	This element allows programmatic access to the HTML input element for the *image* input type and exposes the *ServerClick* event.
<input type="radio">	*HtmlInputRadioButton*	This element allows programmatic access to the HTML input element for the *radio* input type.
<input type="text"> *<input type="password">*	*HtmlInputText*	This element allows programmatic access to the HTML input element for the *text* and *password* input types and exposes the *ServerClick* event.
<select>	*HtmlSelect*	This element allows programmatic access to the HTML select element and exposes the *ServerChange* event.
<table>	*HtmlTable*	This element allows programmatic access to the HTML table element. Note that some table subelements (such as *<col>*, *<tbody>*, *<thead>*, and *<tfoot>*) are not supported by the *HtmlTable* control.
<td> and *<th>*	*HtmlTableCell*	This element allows programmatic access to HTML table cell elements.
<tr>	*HtmlTableRow*	This element allows programmatic access to HTML table row elements.
<textarea>	*HtmlTextArea*	This element allows programmatic access to the HTML text area element and exposes the *ServerChange* event.
<body>, *<div>*,	*HtmlGenericControl*	This element allows *<span>*, *<font>*, etc. programmatic access to any HTML element not specifically represented by its own HTML control class.

Each HTML control class is derived from the generic *HtmlControl* class. This class provides methods and properties common to all HTML controls, such as the *Attributes* collection, which provides a collection of name/value pairs for any attributes contained in the tag definition for the control (such as *id="myControl"* or *border="1"*). The individual control classes then expose additional methods and properties that are specific to the HTML element that they represent. For example, the *HtmlAnchor* control exposes an *Href* property that enables you to programmatically modify the URL to which the anchor tag is linked. The *HtmlAnchor* control also exposes a *Target* property, which enables you to modify the target of the anchor tag.

tip
Because the HTML controls do not expose a strongly typed control equivalent for every HTML element, you can use the *Attributes* collection to add tag attributes to any HTML control programmatically. This enables you to programmatically set tag attributes that are not exposed as properties by the HTML control classes:

```
HtmlInputText myTB = New HtmlInputText();
myTB.Attributes["onBlur"] = "javascript:alert('Lost focus!');";
```

Many of the HTML controls also expose events to which you can respond (above and beyond the standard events inherited from *HtmlControl*). There are two events exposed by HTML controls, *ServerClick* and *ServerChange*.

note
Unlike the server controls in the *Web control* namespace, which only handle server-side events, HTML controls can handle both server-side events and any client-side events that exist for the HTML element to which they map. For example, the *HtmlInputButton* control supports both the server-side *ServerClick* event and the client-side *Click* event.

To handle both events, use the following tag declaration, which enables you to perform actions on the client before the page is posted back to the server, if desired:

```
<input type="submit" onclick="client_handler"
    onserverclick="server_handler" runat="server"/>
```

Because of their close mapping to individual HTML elements, HTML controls provide the fastest and easiest path for moving from static HTML to the power of ASP.NET server controls.

note

In Web Forms pages, there are three basic rules of the game when it comes to case sensitivity:

■ Namespaces and class names are case sensitive. For example, namespaces imported using the @ *Import* directive will cause an error if the correct case is not used. This is a common cause of errors when you are just getting started with ASP.NET.

■ Tag names and attributes are not case sensitive. This also applies to server control properties expressed as tag attributes.

■ Control names used in <script> blocks or in code-behind classes might be case sensitive, depending on whether the language you're using is case sensitive. C# is case-sensitive, for example, so using the incorrect case for a control name or property in C# code can lead to errors.

When you're working with a case-sensitive language such as C#, or when you receive errors such as "The Namespace or type *<namespace>* for the Import 'System.*<namespace>*' cannot be found," it's usually a good idea to check for incorrect case in control, class, or namespace names.

HTML Control Examples

To demonstrate the simplicity and power of HTML controls, let's take a look at some examples. Let's say you have the following static HTML page:

```
<html>
<body>
<font>Hello, World!</font>
</body>
</html>
```

By simply adding the *runat="server"* attribute and an *id* attribute to the *<body>* and *<font>* elements, you can turn these elements into *HtmlGenericControls*.

```
<html>
<body id="Body" runat="server">
<font id="HelloFont" runat="server">Hello, World!</font>
</body>
</html>
```

After you've converted the elements to HTML controls, it is fairly simple to manipulate them in server-side code.

```
<html>
<head>
<script language="c#" runat="server">
   public void Page_Load(object sender, EventArgs e)
   {
       Body.Attributes["bgcolor"] = "Red";
       HelloFont.Attributes["size"] = "7";
       HelloFont.Attributes["color"] = "Blue";
   }
</script>
</head>
<body id="Body" runat="server">
<font id="HelloFont" runat="server">Hello, World!</font>
</body>
</html>
```

If you save and run this code, the output should look like the following illustration.

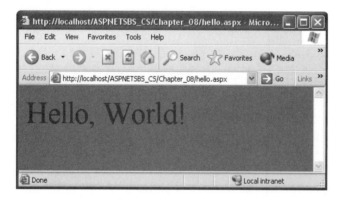

HTML controls are useful for dynamically adding and removing HTML table rows or *<select>* items. In the following example, you'll see how to dynamically add and remove items in a drop-down list created by an *HtmlSelect* control.

Add items to a drop-down list dynamically

1   Create a new project in Microsoft Visual Studio .NET. Name the project **Chapter_08**. (To avoid conflicting with the practice files, if installed, this project should not be created under *http://localhost/aspnetsbs_cs*).

2   Add a new Web Form to the project and name it **HtmlSelect.aspx**.

3   Switch to HTML view and add the following HTML markup to the page, between the <form> and </form> tags:

```
What's your favorite ice cream?<br/>
<select id="IceCream" size="1">
    <option>Chocolate</option>
    <option>Strawberry</option>
    <option>Vanilla</option>
</select>
<input id="Enter" type="button" value="Enter">
<h3><span id="Fave"></span></h3>
```

4   Switch back to Design view. The page should look similar to the following illustration:

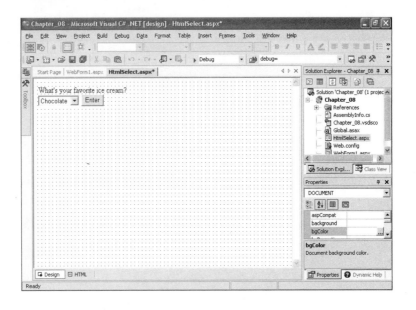

Using Server Controls   8

5   Right-click the drop-down list representing the <select> element, and click
Run As Server Control. Repeat for the button element. Note the glyphs
that Visual Studio .NET adds to these elements, indicating that they are
now server controls. The glyphs are shown in the following illustration:

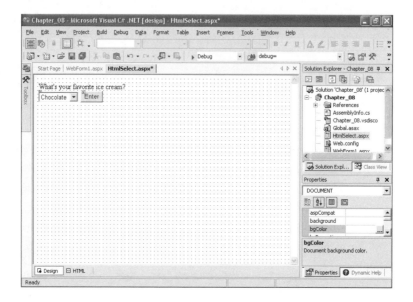

Because the <span> element has no representation in Design view,
you'll need to add the runat="server" attribute to this element manually.

6   Switch to HTML view, and then add the runat="server" attribute to the
<span> elements to transform it into a server control.

7   Switch back to Design view and double-click an open area of the page. This
will open the code-behind module for the page and place the cursor in the
Page_Load event handler. Add the following code, which adds two items
to the *HtmlSelect* control and removes one, to the *Page_Load* event handler:

```
if ( !(Page.IsPostBack) )
{
    this.IceCream.Items.Add("Pistachio");
    this.IceCream.Items.Add("Rocky Road");
    // We don't like Strawberry
    this.IceCream.Items.Remove("Strawberry");
}
```

8   Using the tabs at the top of the editor window, switch back to
HtmlSelect.aspx. Double-click the Enter button. This will add the
Enter_ServerClick event handler to the code-behind module and switch

you back to the code-behind module. Add the following code to the *Enter_ServerClick* event handler:

```
Fave.InnerHtml = "Your favorite is " + IceCream.Value + "!";
```

9 Save the page and code-behind module, build the project, and then browse the page. The output should look similar to the following illustration:

10 Click Rocky Road in the drop-down list, and then click the Enter button. The output should look similar to the following illustration:

Web Controls

Web controls are truly the gem in the crown of ASP.NET. These server controls give you an unprecedented level of productivity by providing a rich, event-driven programming model, similar to that of Visual Basic. The Web controls reside in the *System.Web.UI.WebControls* namespace, which is available to all Web Forms pages automatically.

The Web controls run the gamut of functionality, from simple controls like the *Button*, *TextBox*, and *Label* controls, to the richer *ListBox* and *DropDownList* controls, to the even richer *Calendar* and *AdRotator* controls. There are even special controls that are especially designed for data binding, including the *DataGrid*, *DataList*, and *Repeater* controls. You'll see examples of these types of controls in later sections.

> **note**
>
> Although the *System.Web.UI.WebControls* and *System.Web.UI.HtmlControls* namespaces are available to Web Forms pages automatically, the same is not true of code-behind pages associated with Web Forms pages. If you want to use controls in either of these namespaces without using the fully qualified class name, you need to add the appropriate *Imports* statement to your code-behind class to import the namespace. Fortunately for those using Visual Studio, this is taken care of at the project level for Microsoft Visual C# .NET projects. To see the list of namespaces imported by default in a Visual C# .NET project, look at the top of any of the .cs files, where the using statements are placed.

Server Controls

As you saw in the last chapter, adding server controls to a page is fairly easy. There are two different ways to add controls to a page, declaratively and programmatically. Either way enables you to set properties of the control as desired, and either one can be used to place a control where you want it on the page.

Adding Controls Declaratively

The ASP.NET HTML controls use essentially the same syntax as standard HTML elements, with the exception of the *runat* attribute, which is always set to *server*. Web controls also use a tag-based syntax but are prefaced with *asp:*. Therefore, you'd declare an *HtmlInputButton* server control with the following syntax:

```
<input id="Enter" type="button" value="Enter"
    OnServerClick="Enter_Click" runat="server">
```

You would declare an ASP.NET *Button* server control with the following syntax:

```
<asp:button id="Enter" Text="Enter" OnClick="Enter_Click"
    runat="server" />
```

Notice that in the second example, a / character is added before the closing > character. This is required when you do not use a complete closing tag. Here's an example of when you'd use a closing tag:

```
<asp:label id="myLabel" runat="server">Hi there!</asp:label>
```

You enclose the literal text *Hi there!* between an opening and closing tag. The literal text becomes the *Text* property of the *Label* control. The *Label* control, which renders as a *<span>* on the client side, is one of a number of controls that enable you to enclose literal text for the *Text* property (or some other property of the control) between the opening and closing tags. Other controls include the *Literal*, *Panel*, *PlaceHolder*, and *TextBox* controls.

Choosing the Right Control

Because there are two distinct sets of server controls to choose from, you might wonder how to choose the right control for a given application. In general, if you are interested in handling client-side events or are converting HTML elements to server controls, you should look at the HTML controls. If you're familiar with the Visual Basic programming model, the Web controls provide a model that maps very closely to that model. The Web controls also provide additional functionality, such as validation, and provide a strong basis for customization.

Using Server Controls

8

You could also accomplish the same result by using a single-tag syntax.

```
<asp:label id="myLabel" text="Hi there!" runat="server"/>
```

When you add a control to the page declaratively, you are doing two things: giving the control enough information to be created and initialized properly, and setting the properties for the control. The first part is accomplished by the *asp:* prefix and the tag *(control)* name, plus the *id* and *runat* attributes. Only the prefix/tagname and *runat* attribute are required to create a server control, but the *id* attribute is required if you want to refer to the control in server-side code.

After you've provided this minimum information, you can set additional properties by adding attributes to the tag declaration corresponding to the property you want to set. For example, if you wanted to set the *Visible* property of a *Label* control to *false* (to set up a message declaratively and show it by making it visible later in server-side code), you would modify the declaration as follows:

```
<asp:label id="myLabel" text="Hi there!" visible="false"
    runat="server"/>
```

Some of the more feature-filled controls, such as the *DataGrid* control, use a combination of attributes in the main tag definition and subtags that declare additional controls or set properties (such as the *ItemStyle* and *AlternatingItemStyle* tags that can be used with the *DataGrid* or *DataList* controls) to define the properties for the control. You'll see examples of these in this chapter 9.

Adding and Manipulating Controls Programmatically

Although adding controls to the page declaratively is probably the most straightforward approach, you can also add controls to the page and manipulate them programmatically. This gives you greater control because you can choose how and if to add controls at runtime.

Adding a control programmatically is as simple as declaring a new instance of the control class and adding it to the page's *Controls* collection, as follows:

```
Label myLabel = New Label();
// You can also just use Controls, but the Page reference makes it
// clear what you intend, which is always a good idea.
Page.Controls.Add(myLabel);
myLabel.Text = "Hi there!";
```

The code just shown creates the *Label* control and sets its text property to *Hi there!*. There's just one problem. As written, the code adds the control to the end of the page's *Controls* collection, which is actually after the closing *<body>* and *<html>* tags, which ASP.NET treats as *Literal* controls on the server. The code that is sent to the browser is shown here:

```
<html>
<head>
</head>
<body>
</body>
</html>
<span>Hi there!</span>
```

Although this output will still be rendered in most browsers, it's not ideal because it's incorrect HTML syntax. This presents even more of a problem when you are dealing with both declaratively and programmatically created controls. Creating controls out of order can produce unintended results. So what do you do?

One option is to call the *AddAt* method of the *Controls* collection instead of *Add*. *AddAt* takes two arguments: an integer representing the location in the collection where the control should be added, and the name of the control to add.

```
Page.Controls.AddAt(3, myLabel);
```

The only problem is that to render the control where you want it in the page, you have to know exactly where the control should appear in the collection. This is not always practical.

An easier way to ensure that programmatically created controls appear where you want them to is to use a *PlaceHolder* control to locate the control in the page. The *PlaceHolder* control has no UI of its own. All the content within a *PlaceHolder* control is rendered based on the controls in its *Controls* collection. To make sure the control in the previous example is displayed within the body of the HTML document sent to the browser, you can use the following code:

```
<%@ Page Language="c#" %>
<html>
<head>
<script runat="server">
    private void Page_Load(object sender,System.EventArgs e)
    {
        System.Web.UI.WebControls.Label myLabel;
        myLabel = new System.Web.UI.WebControls.Label();
```

```
        myPH.Controls.Add(myLabel);
        myLabel.Text = "Hi there!";
    }
</script>
</head>
<body>
    <asp:placeholder id="myPH" runat="server" />
</body>
</html>
This produces the following HTML output:
<html>
<head>
</head>
<body>
    <span>Hi there!</span>
</body>
</html>
```

Multiple controls can be added to the same placeholder, and multiple placeholders can be used in the same page.

Adding Controls with Visual Studio .NET

Of course, the easiest way to add ASP.NET server controls to a Web Forms page (and to discover all the properties available for a control) is to use the Visual Studio .NET Toolbox to add a control to the page. The Web Forms tab of the Toolbox is shown in the following illustration.

Add server controls using Visual Studio .NET

1   Open Visual Studio .NET and open the Chapter_08 project created earlier in this chapter, Chapter_08.sln.

2   Add a new Web Form to the project. Name the file **DropDownList.aspx**.

3   Open the Toolbox by moving the mouse pointer over the Toolbox tab in the IDE, and if necessary, clicking the Web Forms tab of the Toolbox.

To add a control to the page, you can simply double-click the desired server control. The control will be inserted into the page at the location of the cursor if the page is in FlowLayout mode, or at the top-left corner of the page if the page is in GridLayout mode. In GridLayout mode, you can also select a control from the Toolbox and draw it on the form as you would a Visual Basic–style control. In either FlowLayout or GridLayout mode, you can also drag and drop controls from the Toolbox onto the page at the desired location.

4   Using one of the techniques just described, add two Label controls, a DropDownList control, and a Button control to the page. After the controls have been added, the page arranges the controls so that they look similar to the following illustration.

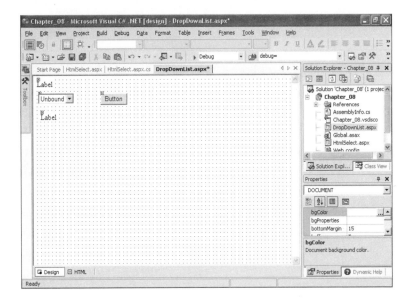

5 Set the properties of the added controls as follows:

Control	Property	Value
Label1	Text	What's your favorite ice cream?
Button1	Text	Enter
Label2	Text	(blank)
	Font-Bold	True
	Font-Size	Larger

6 Click *DropDownList1* in the designer window, and then select its Items property in the Properties pane. Click the ellipsis button (...) to open the collection editor and edit the Items property.

7 Using the Add button, add three items to the collection, and set their *Text* and *Value* properties to Chocolate, Strawberry, and Vanilla, respectively. In Visual C# .NET, if you enter a value for *Text* and do not enter anything in the *Value* field, *Value* defaults to what is entered as the *Text*. The result should look similar to the following illustration. When you are done adding items, click OK.

8 Double-click an open area of the page. This will open the code-behind module for the page and place the cursor in the *Page_Load* event handler. Add the following code to the *Page_Load* event handler. The code adds two items to the *DropDownList* control and removes one. This code is almost the same as used in the HTML controls example, only the control name has been changed:

```
if ( !(Page.IsPostBack) )
{
    this.DropDownList1.Items.Add("Pistachio");
    this. DropDownList1.Items.Add("Rocky Road");
    // We don't like Strawberry
    this. DropDownList1.Items.Remove("Strawberry");
}
```

9 Using the tabs at the top of the editor window, switch back to DropDownList.aspx. Double-click the Button1 button. This will add the *Button1_Click* event handler to the code-behind module and switch back to the code-behind module. Add the following code to the *Button1_Click* event handler:

```
Label2.Text = "Your favorite is " + DropDownList1.SelectedItem.Value + "!";
```

10 Save the page and code-behind module, build the project, and then browse the page. The output should look similar to the following illustration:

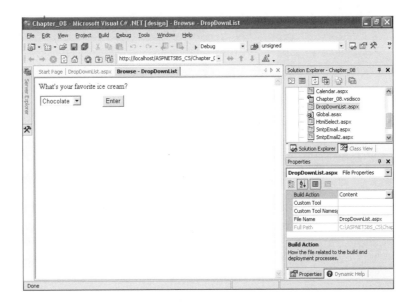

11 Select Rocky Road from the drop-down list, then click the Enter button. The output should look similar to the following illustration:

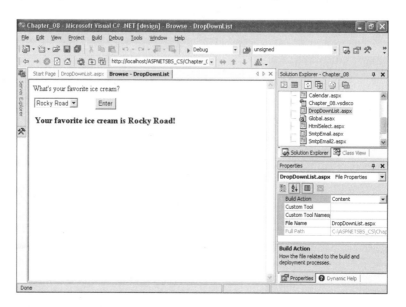

Applying Styles to Controls

After you've added your controls to the page, you'll probably want to make changes to how those controls are displayed. For example, you might want to make the text of a *Label* control red. Simply set the *ForeColor* property of the control to *Red* in the HTML view of an ASPX file, as follows:

```
<asp:label id="myLabel" forecolor="red" runat="server">
    Hi there!
</asp:label>
```

But what if you want to do something more complicated? Although controls such as *Label* expose properties like *ForeColor* and *BackColor*, there are times when this will not be sufficient. Let's say you want to apply a Cascading Style Sheet (CSS) class defined elsewhere (either in a *Style* block at the top of the page or in a linked style sheet) to a server control. Or maybe you just want to use CSS styles directly in your control tag. For these occasions, the *CssClass* and *Style* properties defined in the *WebControl* base class (and inherited by all *WebControl* classes) come in handy. With the *CssClass* property, you can set up a CSS class such as the following:

```
<style type="text/css">
.mylabel { font-size:24pt; font-weight:bold; color:red; }
```

```
</style>
```
You can use this to format your control as follows:
```
<asp:label id="myLabel" cssclass="mylabel" runat="server">
   Hi there!
</asp:label>
```
This technique works fine for linked style sheets as well.
The *Style* property can be used to specify CSS styles directly as follows:
```
<asp:label id="myLabel"
   style="font-size:24pt; font-weight:bold; color:red;"
   runat="server">
   Hi there!
</asp:label>
```

Note that whether you set the color of a *Label* control with the *ForeColor* property or use the *CssClass* or *Style* properties declaratively, the result is rendered as a class or style attribute on the resulting *<span>* tag, which is the client-side representation of the *WebControl* control.

> ## note
>
> Although you can set most control properties declaratively by using the property name as an attribute of the tag used to declare the control, some compound properties (properties that are represented by another class) require that you use a slightly different attribute syntax.
>
> A good example of this is the *Font* property (defined in the *WebControl* base class), which returns an instance of the *FontInfo* class. To modify the font of a control that inherits from *WebControl* (such as the *Label* control), use attributes in the form *font-<propertyname>*, as follows:
>
> ```
> <asp:label id="myLabel" font-name="arial"
>    runat="server>
> ```
>
> You can also access these properties programmatically, using the form *<controlname>.Font.<propertyname>*, as follows:
>
> ```
> myLabel.Font.Name = "Arial"
> ```

Finally, you can also apply styles to your controls based on the client-side representation of the control. As noted, *Label* controls are rendered on the client as *<span>* tags, so if you define a style that applies to all *<span>* elements, your *Label* controls will also use this style. As long as you know the client-side representation of a particular control (which you can get by viewing the source of the page from the browser), you can create a style sheet to format that control.

Additional Web Controls

Web controls are quite easy to use and provide a great deal of flexibility. So far, you've used only simple examples. This section will look at a few more complex examples to demonstrate the use of various Web controls. The first example will show you how to use server controls to set up a form for sending e-mail from an ASP.NET Web Form through Simple Mail Transport Protocol (SMTP). The second example will show you how to use *Panel* controls to simulate a wizard-style multipage interface within a single Web Forms page.

Sending Mail

A common task for many Web applications is sending e-mail to customers or visitors. Often, this e-mail is generated automatically, without the need for specific data entry. But site operators might also want a way to send a quick e-mail through the site. Web controls, in combination with the .NET *SmtpMail* and *MailMessage* classes, can make it quick and easy to add this functionality to a Web application.

> **note**
>
> The following example assumes that you have access to an SMTP server from which to send your e-mail. Windows 2000, Windows XP Professional, and Windows .NET Server come with an SMTP service that is part of the services provided by IIS. The SMTP service is relatively easy to install and configure. Details for setting up the SMTP service can be found at *http://msdn.microsoft.com/library/en-us/dnduwon/html/d5smtp.asp*.

Add e-mail sending to a Web application

1   If it is not already open, open the Chapter_08 project, named Chapter_08.sln, created earlier in this chapter, and then add a new Web Form to the project. Name the Web Form SmtpEmail.aspx.

2   Using the Visual Studio .NET Table editor (on the Table menu, point to Insert, and then click Table), add an HTML table to the page to ensure that your controls line up nicely on the page. Specify that the table should have six rows and two columns, as shown in the following illustration. Click OK to insert the table.

paste

Using Server Controls

3   Add a *Label* control and a *TextBox* control to each of the first five rows of the
table, as shown in the following illustration. Note that in addition to dragging
controls from the Toolbox to the page, you can create new controls by clicking an existing control of the desired type (such as a *Label* control), right-
clicking the control, clicking Copy on the shortcut menu, clicking the location
where a new control should be added, and pressing Ctrl+V. This has the
advantage of creating a copy of the existing controls with identical properties
to those of the original control (with the exception of the *ID* property).

4   Add a *Button* control and an *HtmlInputButton* control with the type set to
reset to the last row of the table. To add the HTML Reset button, switch to
the HTML tab of the Toolbox, drag the Reset Button to the appropriate table
cell, right-click the Reset Button, and click **Run As Server Control** on the
shortcut menu. Using an *HtmlInputButton* as a reset button enables you
to reset the form fields on the client without a round trip to the server and
manipulate the control on the server side as well, as you'll do in a later step.

5   Set the properties of the added controls as follows:

Control	Property	Value
Label1	Text	To:
Label2	Text	CC:
Label3	Text	BCC:
Label4	Text	Subject:
Label5	Text	Body:
TextBox5	TextMode	MultiLine
	Columns	60
	Rows	10
Button1	Text	Send

When finished, the page should look like the following illustration:

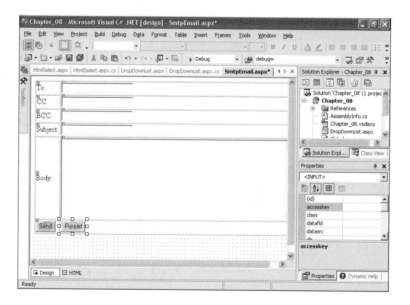

6   Now that you've completed the UI, you need to add code to send the mail when the Send button is clicked. Double-click the Send button, which will open the code-behind module for the page, insert a *Click* handler for the button, and then add the following code, which creates an instance of the *MailMessage* class, sets the necessary properties, and then sends the message using the *Send* method of the *SmtpMail* class. (Because the *Send* method is a *Static* method, it is not necessary to create an instance of *SmtpMail* to use the method.) After the mail has been sent, the code hides all the form controls by setting the *Visible* property for each control to *false*, and adds a *HyperLink* control to link back to the original page to send another e-mail, if desired. Note that you need to set *Mail.From* to a valid e-mail address and change *SmtpMail.SmtpServer* to the name of an available server running SMTP if the local machine is not running an SMTP service:

```
// Create MailMessage instance, set properties and send.
MailMessage Mail = new MailMessage();
Mail.To = TextBox1.Text;
Mail.Cc = TextBox2.Text;
Mail.Bcc = TextBox3.Text;
Mail.Subject = TextBox4.Text;
Mail.Body = TextBox5.Text;
// Set the property below to a valid email address
Mail.From = "doug@accessmicrosystems.com";
SmtpMail.SmtpServer = "mail.accessmicrosystems.com";
SmtpMail.Send(Mail);
// Use the first label to display status
Label1.Text = "Mail Sent";
// Hide the rest of the controls
TextBox1.Visible = false;
Label2.Visible = false;
TextBox2.Visible = false;
Label3.Visible = false;
TextBox3.Visible = false;
Label4.Visible = false;
TextBox4.Visible = false;
Label5.Visible = false;
TextBox5.Visible = false;
Button1.Visible = false;
Reset1.Visible = false;
// Add a Hyperlink control to allow sending another email
HyperLink Link = new HyperLink();
```

```
Link.Text = "Click here to send another email.";
Link.NavigateUrl = "SmtpEmail.aspx";
// This line is only necessary if the page is in GridLayout
mode
Link.Attributes["Style"] = "LEFT: 8px; POSITION: absolute; "
+
    "TOP: 50px";
Page.Controls.Add(Link);
```

7   For the previous code to work, you need to add a *using* directive to import the System.Web.Mail namespace so you can refer to its classes without using the namespace name each time. This directive should go at the top of the code-behind module, before the class definition:

```
using System.Web.Mail;
```

8   Save the page and code-behind module, and then build the project. Browse the page by right-clicking SmtpEmail.aspx in Solution Explorer, clicking Browse With, and then clicking Internet Explorer. Click the Browse button. The output should look something like the following illustration. After you've sent an email, the link should take you back to the original page.

This example shows how simple it can be to send e-mail using server controls on a Web Form, but it does have a shortcoming. It takes a fair amount of code to hide all the controls after you've sent the e-mail. You can fix this by adding another *Label* control outside the table and then turning the table into an

HtmlTable control by adding the *runat="server"* attribute. You can then hide all the controls in the table by setting the *Visible* property of *HtmlTable* to *false*. The full code for this example, named SmtpEmail2.aspx, can be found in the practice files for this chapter.

Registration Wizard

Another common need in Web applications is providing users with an easy way to register. Registration enables you to provide personalized services, saved shopping carts, and other valuable services for your visitors. To make this as simple as possible, you might want to use a multipage format similar to a Windows Wizard interface. This type of interface will be immediately familiar to Windows users. The following listing shows the code for a simple registration wizard implemented as an ASP.NET Web Form. This listing also shows how you can use a single-page structure for controls and code, as opposed to the code-behind structure of Visual Studio .NET. Unlike Web Forms created in Visual Studio .NET, the code in the listing does not need to be precompiled. However, because the code is included in the page (which must be deployed to the Web server on which it will run), anyone with file access to the Web server can read the code (assuming they have the correct permissions). By contrast, using code-behind modules enables you to deploy just the .aspx files and compiled assembly (or assemblies) without deploying the code-behind modules that contain the UI-related code.

RegWiz.aspx

```
<%@ Page Language="c#" %>
<html>
<head>
<script  runat="server">
   private void Page_Load(object sender,System.EventArgs e)
   {
      if ( !(IsPostBack) )
      {
         Step1.Font.Bold = true;
      }
   }
   private void Next_Click(object sender, System.EventArgs e)
   {
      switch (((Button)sender).Parent.ID)
      {
         case "Page1":
            Page1.Visible = false;
```

```csharp
                Step1.Font.Bold = false;
                Page2.Visible = true;
                Step2.Font.Bold = true;
                break;
            case "Page2":
                Page2.Visible = false;
                Step2.Font.Bold = false;
                Page3.Visible = true;
                Step3.Font.Bold = true;
                ReviewFName.Text += FirstName.Text;
                ReviewMName.Text += MiddleName.Text;
                ReviewLName.Text += LastName.Text;
                ReviewEmail.Text += Email.Text;
                ReviewAddress.Text += Address.Text;
                ReviewCity.Text += City.Text;
                ReviewState.Text += State.Text;
                ReviewZip.Text += Zip.Text;
                break;
        }
    }
    private void Previous_Click(object sender, System.EventArgs e)
    {
        switch (((Button)sender).Parent.ID)
        {
            case "Page2":
                Page2.Visible = false;
                Step2.Font.Bold = false;
                Page1.Visible = true;
                Step1.Font.Bold = true;
                break;
            case "Page3":
                Page3.Visible = false;
                Step3.Font.Bold = false;
                Page2.Visible = true;
                Step2.Font.Bold = true;
                break;
        }
    }
</script>
<style type="text/css">
div
{
```

```
              background:silver;
              width:400px;
              border:2px outset;
              margin:5px;
              padding:5px;
       }
       </style>
       </head>
       <body>
          <form runat="server">
             <asp:label id="RegWiz" text="Registration Wizard"
                font-bold="true" font-size="16" font-name="verdana"
                runat="server"/>
             <br/>
             <asp:label id="Step1" text="Step 1: Enter Personal Info"
                font-name="verdana" runat="server"/>
             <br/>
             <asp:label id="Step2" text="Step 2: Enter Address Info"
                font-name="verdana" runat="server"/>
             <br/>
             <asp:label id="Step3" text="Step 3: Review"
                font-name="verdana"
                runat="server"/>
             <br/>
             <asp:panel id="Page1" runat="server">
                <table align="center">
                   <tr>
                      <td>
                         <asp:label id="FirstNameLabel" text="First Name:"
                            runat="server"/>
                      </td>
                      <td>
                         <asp:textbox id="FirstName" runat="server"/>
                      </td>
                   </tr>
                   <tr>
                      <td>
                         <asp:label id="MiddleNameLabel" text="Middle Name:"
                            runat="server"/>
                      </td>
                      <td>
                         <asp:textbox id="MiddleName" runat="server"/>
```

```
              </td>
          </tr>
          <tr>
              <td>
                  <asp:label id="LastNameLabel" text="Last Name:"
                      runat="server"/>
              </td>
              <td>
                  <asp:textbox id="LastName" runat="server"/>
              </td>
          </tr>
          <tr>
              <td>
                  <asp:label id="EmailLabel" text="Email:"
                      runat="server"/>
              </td>
              <td>
                  <asp:textbox id="Email" runat="server"/>
              </td>
          </tr>
          <tr>
              <td colspan="2" align="center">
                  <asp:button id="P1Previous" Text="Previous"
                      enabled="false" onclick="Previous_Click"
                      runat="server"/>
                  <asp:button id="P1Next" Text="Next"
                      onclick="Next_Click" runat="server"/>
                  <input id="P1Reset" type="reset" runat="server"/>
              </td>
          </tr>
      </table>
  </asp:panel>
  <asp:panel id="Page2" visible="false" runat="server">
      <table align="center">
          <tr>
              <td>
                  <asp:label id="AddressLabel" text="Street Address:"
                      runat="server"/>
              </td>
              <td>
                  <asp:textbox id="Address" runat="server"/>
              </td>
```

```
    </tr>
    <tr>
      <td>
        <asp:label id="CityLabel" text="City:"
            runat="server"/>
      </td>
      <td>
        <asp:textbox id="City" runat="server"/>
      </td>
    </tr>
    <tr>
      <td>
        <asp:label id="StateLabel" text="State:"
            runat="server"/>
      </td>
      <td>
        <asp:textbox id="State" runat="server"/>
      </td>
    </tr>
    <tr>
      <td>
        <asp:label id="ZipLabel" text="Zip Code:"
            runat="server"/>
      </td>
      <td>
        <asp:textbox id="Zip" runat="server"/>
      </td>
    </tr>
    <tr>
      <td colspan="2" align="center">
        <asp:button id="P2Previous" Text="Previous"
            onclick="Previous_Click" runat="server"/>
        <asp:button id="P2Next" Text="Next"
            onclick="Next_Click" runat="server"/>
        <input id="P2Reset" type="reset" runat="server"/>
      </td>
    </tr>
  </table>
</asp:panel>
<asp:panel id="Page3" visible="false" runat="server">
  <table align="center">
    <tr>
```

```
            <td colspan="2">
                <asp:label id="ReviewFName" text="First Name: "
                    runat="server"/>
            </td>
        </tr>
        <tr>
            <td colspan="2">
                <asp:label id="ReviewMName" text="Middle Name: "
                    runat="server"/>
            </td>
        </tr>
        <tr>
            <td colspan="2">
                <asp:label id="ReviewLName" text="Last Name: "
                    runat="server"/>
            </td>
        </tr>
        <tr>
            <td colspan="2">
                <asp:label id="ReviewEmail" text="Email: "
                    runat="server"/>
            </td>
        </tr>
        <tr>
            <td colspan="2">
                <asp:label id="ReviewAddress" text="Address: "
                    runat="server"/>
            </td>
        </tr>
        <tr>
            <td colspan="2">
                <asp:label id="ReviewCity" text="City: "
                    runat="server"/>
            </td>
        </tr>
        <tr>
            <td colspan="2">
                <asp:label id="ReviewState" text="State: "
                    runat="server"/>
            </td>
        </tr>
```

```
        <tr>
          <td colspan="2">
            <asp:label id="ReviewZip" text="Zip: "
                runat="server"/>
          </td>
        </tr>
        <tr>
          <td colspan="2">
            <asp:button id="P3Previous" Text="Previous"
                onclick="Previous_Click" runat="server"/>
            <asp:button id="P3Next" Text="Next" enabled="false"
                onclick="Next_Click" runat="server"/>
            <input id="P3Reset" type="reset" disabled="true"
                runat="server"/>
          </td>
          </td>
        </tr>
      </table>
    </asp:panel>
  </form>
</body>
</html>
```

The keys to the functionality of the registration wizard are the three *Panel* controls and the *Next_Click* and *Previous_Click* event handlers. The *Panel* controls contain *Label*, *TextBox*, and *Button* Web controls (as well as an *HtmlInputButton* control for resetting the form fields), which are formatted using standard HTML table elements. When the user clicks the Next button or the Previous button (depending on which one is enabled for that page), the event handlers hide the currently visible panel, show the next (or previous) panel, and update the *Label* controls that tell the user which step in the process they are on currently. Because the *sender* parameter passed into the button event handlers is passed in as an object, it must be cast to the correct type (in this case, a *Button*) to get the *ID* of the *Parent*.

Because ASP.NET takes care of maintaining the state of the controls from request to request (using ViewState), it is simple to display the data entered by the user on the third panel by simply accessing the *Text* property of the *TextBox* controls on the other panels. Notice that the caption text of the controls on the third panel is set declaratively in the tag, and the text that the user entered is appended to this text programmatically in the event handler using the &+= operator. The first page of the registration wizard is shown in the illustration on the next page.

note

The *<style>* block that you defined takes care of formatting the *Panel* controls by defining the desired style for the *<div>* HTML element. Note that because the *Panel* control is rendered as a *<div>* on Internet Explorer and as a *<table>* element on Netscape and other non–Internet Explorer browsers, you might need to find another way to do the formatting if you want cross-browser compatibility.

One way to accomplish this is through browser sniffing. The *Request* object exposed by the *Page* class has a *Browser* property that provides information on the browser making the current request. By querying the *Browser* property (and its subproperties), you can perform a simple *if* statement that links to one style sheet if the browser is IE, and to another style sheet if it is another browser.

Specialty Controls

In addition to the standard suite of Web controls that provide functionality much like that of the Visual Basic GUI controls, ASP.NET offers a set of richer specialty controls that reside in the *System.Web.UI.WebControls* namespace. Currently, these include the *AdRotator*, *Calendar*, and *Xml* controls. This section will describe the purposes of these controls and show some examples.

AdRotator

The *AdRotator* control is used to display a random selection from a collection of banner advertisements specified in an XML-based advertisement file. The advertisement file contains an *<Ad>* node for each specified advertisement. This node contains nodes that configure the path to the image to display for the ad, the URL to navigate to when the ad is clicked, the text to be displayed if the image is not available, the percentage of time the ad should come up in rotation, and any keyword associated with the ad. (Keywords can be used to filter ads, allowing the use of a single advertisement file with multiple *AdRotator* controls and providing each control with different content.)

> ## note
> The random selection for the *AdRotator* control will be identical for any *AdRotators* on the page that have identical attributes. You can take advantage of this by using the *AdRotator* control to display a random selection of header and footer information.

Use the *AdRotator* control

1   If it is not already open, open the Chapter_08 project created earlier in this chapter, and then add a new Web Form to the project. Name the Web Form **AdRotator.aspx**.

2   Change the *pageLayout* property from GridLayout to **FlowLayout**.

3   Switch to HTML view, add three *Label* controls and two *AdRotator* controls between the <form> tags using the attributes shown in the following code, and then save AdRotator.aspx:

```
<asp:label id="title" font-name="Verdana" font-size="18"
    text="AdRotator Example" runat="server"/>
<br/><br/>
<asp:label id="Dev" font-name="Verdana" font-size="16"
    text="Ad 1" runat="server"/>
<br/>
<asp:AdRotator id="AdRotDev" target="_blank" runat="server"
    advertisementfile="Ads.xml" keywordfilter="Developers"/>
<br/><br/>
<asp:label id="User" font-name="Verdana" font-size="16"
    text="Ad 2" runat="server"/>
<br/>
<asp:AdRotator id="AdRotUsr" target="_blank" runat="server"
    advertisementfile="Ads.xml" keywordfilter="Users"/>
```

4   Create a new XML file by right-clicking the Chapter_08 project in Solution Explorer, pointing to Add, Add New Item, and then clicking XML File as shown in the following illustration. Name the file Ads.xml and click Open.

5   Add the following XML to the file, and then save Ads.xml:

```xml
<Advertisements>
    <Ad>
        <ImageUrl>images/image1.gif</ImageUrl>
        <NavigateUrl>http://www.microsoft.com</NavigateUrl>
        <AlternateText>Microsoft Main Site</AlternateText>
        <Impressions>60</Impressions>
        <Keyword>Users</Keyword>
    </Ad>
    <Ad>
        <ImageUrl>images/image2.gif</ImageUrl>
        <NavigateUrl>http://msdn.microsoft.com/net</NavigateUrl>
        <AlternateText>Microsoft .NET on MSDN</AlternateText>
        <Impressions>80</Impressions>
        <Keyword>Developers</Keyword>
    </Ad>
    <Ad>
        <ImageUrl>images/image3.gif</ImageUrl>
        <NavigateUrl>http://www.microsoft.com</NavigateUrl>
        <AlternateText>Microsoft Main Site</AlternateText>
        <Impressions>40</Impressions>
```

```
        <Keyword>Users</Keyword>
    </Ad>
    <Ad>
        <ImageUrl>images/image4.gif</ImageUrl>
        <NavigateUrl>http://msdn.microsoft.com/net</NavigateUrl>
        <AlternateText>Microsoft .NET on MSDN</AlternateText>
        <Impressions>20</Impressions>
        <Keyword>Developers</Keyword>
    </Ad>
</Advertisements>
```

6   Create a new folder in the project called images by right clicking on the
        project root and selecting Add and then New Folder from the shortcut
        menu, and copy the images contained in the images directory of the
        practice files for Chapter 8 to the new folder.

7   Save and build the project, and then browse AdRotator.aspx. The output
        should look similar to the following illustration. If you refresh the page,
        you should see the ads change randomly, based on the weightings set
        in the XML file.

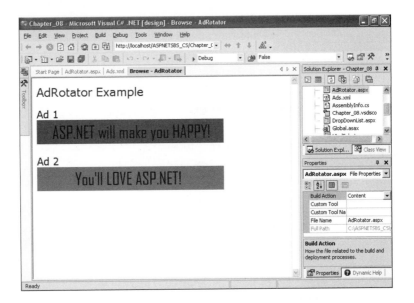

Calendar

The *Calendar* control is one of the richest and most flexible of the specialized
controls, providing nearly 30 properties for controlling the appearance of
the calendar. The *Calendar* control enables you to provide a calendar-based
interface for choosing dates or for viewing date-related data.

For example, you could query date data for a series of events or appointments and then use a *Calendar* control to display them by adding the dates to the calendar's *SelectedDates* collection. When a user clicks a date on the calendar, you could display information about the event on that date.

You could also allow users to specify one or more dates for data entry by providing a *Calendar* control for them to click. The *Calendar* control supports selection of both single dates and date ranges (by week or month). Using a *Calendar* control for date entry instead of a text box can help prevent errors in converting the date entered by the user into a *Date* data type for storage or manipulation.

Use the *Calendar* control

1   If it is not already open, open the Chapter_08 project created earlier in this chapter, and then add a new Web Form to the project. Name the Web Form **Calendar.aspx**.

2   Change the *pageLayout* property from GridLayout to **FlowLayout**.

3   Switch to HTML view, and then add three Label controls, two RadioButton controls, two Textbox controls, and a Calendar control between the <form> tags. Note that the *GroupName* property is used to make the radio buttons mutually exclusive.

```
<asp:label id="title" text="Calendar Example"
    font-name="Verdana" font-size="18" runat="server"/>
<br/>
<asp:calendar id="Calendar1" runat="server"/>
<br/>
<asp:radiobutton id="StartRadio" text="Start Date"
    groupname="Chooser" runat="server"/>
<asp:radiobutton id="EndRadio" text="End Date"
    groupname="Chooser" runat="server"/>
<br/>
<asp:label id="StartDateLabel" text="Start Date" runat="server"/
>
<asp:textbox id="StartDate" runat="server"/>
<br/>
<asp:label id="EndDateLabel" text="End Date" runat="server"/
>
<asp:textbox id="EndDate" runat="server"/>
```

4   Save the page, build the project, and then browse the page. The output should look similar to the following illustration:

5 Looks good so far, but now you need to relate clicking on a date in the calendar to setting the text in the text boxes. First click on the Calendar.aspx tab if it's not already selected, and switch back to Design view, and then double-click the *Calendar* control. This will switch to the code-behind module for Calendar.aspx and add the *Calendar1_SelectionChanged* event handler. Add the following code to the event handler:

```
{
    if ( StartRadio.Checked==true )
    {
        StartDate.Text =
Calendar1.SelectedDate.ToShortDateString();
    }
    else
    {

EndDate.Text = Calendar1.SelectedDate.ToShortDateString();
    }
}
```

6 To initialize the controls, add the following code to the *Page_Load* event handler in the code-behind module:

```
If ( !(IsPostBack) )
{
        StartRadio.Checked=True;
    Calendar1.SelectedDate=DateTime.Now;
```

Using Server Controls

8

```
StartDate.Text=Calendar1.SelectedDate.ToShortDateString()
Calendar1.TodaysDate=Calendar1.SelectedDate;
}
```

7   Save the page and code-behind module, then build the project, and browse Calendar.aspx. At this point, you should be able to use the calendar to set the value of both text boxes. Which text box is set depends on which radio button is selected.

8   The calendar is fairly plain, so let's use some of the available properties to liven it up a bit. Switch back to Calendar.aspx (switching back to HTML view, if required) and modify the <asp:calendar> tag to match the following code. Notice that you need to add a closing </asp:calendar> tag so you can use the child <titlestyle> tag to set attributes of the calendar's *TitleStyle* property.

```
<asp:calendar id="Calendar1"
    backcolor="lightgray"
    borderstyle="groove"
    borderwidth="5"
    bordercolor="blue"
    runat="server">
    <titlestyle backcolor="blue" forecolor="silver"
        font-bold="true"/>
</asp:calendar>
```

9   Save and browse the page again. (You don't need to re-build the project because you only changed the .aspx file.) The output should look similar to the following illustration:

Xml

The *Xml* control is a specialty control that enables you to display XML code in Web Forms pages. This is important because raw XML within an ASP.NET Web Form will not be displayed predictably. The *Xml* control can read XML from a string, from a provided URL, or from an object of type *System.Xml.XmlDocument*.

In addition to simply displaying XML from a given source, the *Xml* control can apply an XSL *Transform* document to the XML to perform formatting on the document. The XSL Transform can come from a URL or it can be provided by an object of type *System.Xml.Xsl.XslTransform*. The files Xml.aspx and Xml.xslt, included with the practice files for this chapter, show how you can use the Xml control to display the contents of the Ads.xml document in an HTML table.

Validation Controls

Another specialized set of controls that reside in the *System.Web.UI.WebControls* namespace are the *Validation* controls, which perform various kinds of validation on other controls.

You can use *Validation* controls to do the following:

- Ensure that required fields are filled in
- Ensure that data entered by the user falls within a given range
- Ensure that data entered by the user matches a specific pattern
- Compare the values of two controls for a given condition (equality, greater than, and so on) or compare the value of a control to a specified value
- Ensure that all controls on a page are valid before submitting the page

Shared Members

There are a number of important properties and methods that all *Validation* controls share. These properties and methods are inherited from the *BaseValidator* class and include the following:

- *ControlToValidate*   This property sets or retrieves a value of type *String* that specifies the input control to validate.
- *Display*   This property sets or retrieves a value that determines how the error message for a *Validation* control will be displayed. The value must be one of the values specified by the *ValidatorDisplay* enumeration. The default is *Static*.

- **EnableClientScript** This property sets or retrieves a boolean value that determines whether client-side validation will be performed. Server-side validation is always performed with the *Validation* controls, regardless of this setting. The default is *true*.

- **Enabled** This property sets or retrieves a boolean value that determines whether the control is enabled. The default is *true*.

- **ErrorMessage** This property sets or retrieves a value of type *String* that specifies the error message to be displayed if the input from the user is not valid.

- **ForeColor** This property sets or retrieves a value of type *Color* that represents the color of the error message specified in the *ErrorMessage* property. The default is *Color.Red*.

- **IsValid** This property sets or retrieves a boolean value that signifies whether the control specified by the *ControlToValidate* property passes validation.

- **Validate** This method causes the control on which it is called to perform validation, and it updates the *IsValid* property with the result.

The following table lists the *Validation* controls available in ASP.NET.

Table 8-2. *Validation* Controls Types		
Control Type	**Purpose**	**Important members**
CompareValidator	This control performs validation of a user-entered field with either a constant or another user-entered field. The *ControlToCompare* and *ValueToCompare* properties are mutually exclusive. If both are set, the *ControlToCompare* property takes precedence.	*ControlToCompare* This property sets or retrieves a value of type *String* containing the name of the control whose value will be compared to the value of the control specified by the *ControlToValidate* property. *Operator* This property sets or retrieves a value that represents the type of comparison to be performed. The value must be one of the values specified by the *ValidationCompareOperator* enumeration. The default is *Equal*. *ValueToCompare* This property sets or retrieves a value of type *String* containing a constant value to which the value of the control specified by the *ControlToValidate* property will be compared.

Control Type	Purpose	Important members
CustomValidator	This control performs customized validation based on developer-specified logic.	*ServerValidate* This event is raised when server-side validation is to be performed. Map the *OnServerValidate* method in the *Validation* control tag to the desired server-side event handler to perform custom validation. *ClientValidationFunction* This property sets or retrieves a value of type *String* containing the name of a client-side function with which to perform client-side validation, if desired.
RangeValidator	This control performs validation of a user-entered field to ensure that the value entered is within a specified range.	*MaximumValue* This property sets or retrieves a value of type *String* containing the maximum value of the range to validate against. *MinimumValue* This property sets or retrieves a value of type *String* containing the minimum value of the range to validate against.
RegularExpressionValidator	This control performs validation of a user-entered field to ensure that the value entered matches a specified pattern.	*ValidationExpression* This property sets or retrieves a value of type *String* containing the regular expression to validate against.
RequiredFieldValidator	This control performs validation of a user-entered field to ensure that a value is entered for the specified field.	*InitialValue* This property sets or retrieves a value of type *String* containing the initial value of the range to validate against. The default is an empty string. If this property is set to a string value, validation will fail for the control only if the user-entered value matches the value of this property.

(continued)

Using Server Controls

8

Table 8-2. *Validation* Controls Types *(continued)*		
Control Type	**Purpose**	**Important members**
ValidationSummary	This control provides a summary of validation errors in a given Web Form, either in the Web Form page, a message box, or both.	*DisplayMode* This property sets or retrieves a value that determines the way the control will be displayed. The value must be one of the values specified by the *ValidationSummaryDisplayMode* enumeration. The default is *BulletList*. *HeaderText* This property sets or retrieves a value of type *String* containing the header text to be displayed for the validation summary. *ShowMessageBox* This property sets or retrieves a boolean value that determines whether the validation summary is displayed in a client-side message box. The default is *false*. This property has no effect if the *EnableClientScript* property is set to *false*. *ShowSummary* This property sets or retrieves a boolean value that determines whether the validation summary is displayed in the Web Form page. The default is *true*.

Validating Required Fields

To see how the *Validation* controls operate, let's return to one of the earlier examples, the Web Form named SmtpEmail.aspx. One of the problems that you might have had with the page was that if it was submitted without a To, CC, or BCC address, it would throw an exception. You can prevent this problem by requiring at least one To address.

Require data entry with the *RequiredFieldValidator* control

1   Open the file SmtpEmail.aspx created earlier in this chapter.

2 Add a *RequiredFieldValidator* control to the same table cell as the *TextBox1* textbox control and set its properties as follows:

Control	Property	Value
RequiredFieldValidator1	ControlToValidate	TextBox1
	Display	Dynamic
	ErrorMessage	Required!

3 Save the page, and browse it with Internet Explorer using the Browse With option. (Because you have only changed the .aspx file, the project does not need to be rebuilt.) If you do not enter a To address, the output will look something like the following illustration, and you will not be able to submit the page.

In addition to using the *RequiredFieldValidator* to ensure that an e-mail address is entered, you can add a *RegularExpressionValidator* to each of the address fields to ensure that the data entered by the user matches the pattern for a valid e-mail address. This prevents delivery errors due to malformed e-mail addresses and helps prevent the mail server's resources from being wasted attempting to deliver such mail.

Validating by Comparison

Another of the previous examples with the potential for trouble is the *Calendar* control example. As coded in the example, the *Calendar* control can be used to set a start date that is later than the end date. Clearly, if you're storing these dates or using them to drive some programmatic logic, this is not something you want to allow. Fortunately, the *CompareValidator* control can help prevent this problem, as illustrated by the following example.

Use the *CompareValidator* control

1   Open the file Calendar.aspx created earlier in this chapter, switching to design mode, if required.

2   Add a *CompareValidator* control below the *EndDate TextBox* control, and set its properties as follows:

Control	Property	Value
CompareValidator1	ControlToValidate	StartDate
	ControlToCompare	EndDate
	Type	Date
	Operator	LessThan
	Display	Dynamic
	ErrorMessage	Start Date must be before End Date!

3   Right-click an empty area of the page, click View Code on the shortcut menu to switch to the code-behind module, and then add a line of code to the *Calendar1_SelectionChanged* event handler to cause the *Validation* control to validate each time the event handler is fired. The *Page.Validate* call should go between the curly brace ({) at the bottom of the *else* clause and the curly brace (}) at the end of the method.

```
Page.Validate();
```

4   Save the file and code-behind module, and then rebuild the project. Browse the page, and set the end date to a date earlier than the start date. The validation error message will appear, as shown in the following illustration. Additionally, the *IsValid* property of the page will be set to *false*. You can test this property before saving the date values to ensure that they are valid.

Validation controls can also improve the security of your application. For example, you can use the *RegularExpressionValidator* control to ensure that passwords entered by users (such as when establishing account information) meet minimum length and complexity requirements. This can make it more difficult for the bad guys to crack your application.

Data-Bound Controls

One of the most significant advances in ASP.NET is in the area of data binding. The *System.Web.UI.WebControls* namespace contains a set of data-bound controls that offer substantial functionality and flexibility without the necessity of tying front-end UI logic into back-end database logic, as was the case with the data-bound Design-Time Controls available in classic ASP through the Visual InterDev 6.0 development environment. The data-bound controls also enable you to provide data binding regardless of the browser that your clients are using. This is because the controls run on the server and return plain HTML to the client, unlike some of the data-binding techniques that were possible with Internet Explorer versions 4.0 and later.

Another major improvement is that the data-bound controls can use a variety of sources, not just data from a database. Data-bound controls in ASP.NET can be bound to data from an array, an ADO.NET DataSet, a DataView, or any data source that implements the ICollection or IList interfaces. The data-bound controls include the *DataGrid*, *DataList*, and *Repeater* controls. Chapter 9 will discuss these controls in detail.

Other Controls

In addition to the HTML controls and Web controls that come with the Microsoft .NET Framework, there are some additional controls that are currently available as separate downloads. These are the ASP.NET Mobile controls and the Internet Explorer Web controls.

ASP.NET Mobile Controls

The ASP.NET Mobile controls are currently available as the Microsoft .NET Mobile Internet Toolkit. These controls are designed to tailor their output to handheld devices, such as cell phones, PocketPCs, and other mobile devices. The Mobile Internet Toolkit is currently available *at http://download.microsoft.com /download/VisualStudioNET/Install/1.0/NT45XP/EN-US/MobileIT.exe.* More information about the Mobile Web Toolkit can be found at *http://msdn.microsoft.com/vstudio/nextgen/technology/mobilewebforms.asp.* At the time of this writing, it's unclear whether these controls will ship with the .NET Framework in the future or continue to be a separate download.

Internet Explorer Web Controls

The Internet Explorer Web controls are a set of ASP.NET server controls that take advantage of advanced features of Internet Explorer 5.5 or later, while still providing cross-browser compatibility by rendering HTML 3.2 output for down- level browsers. The controls include the following:

- *MultiPage*   Used with the *TabStrip* control to provide sophisticated tabbed interfaces in ASP.NET
- *TabStrip*   Provides a tabbed interface for navigation
- *Toolbar*   Provides toolbar functionality for ASP.NET Web Forms pages
- *TreeView*   Provides the ability to display and navigate hierarchical structures or data can be used for site navigation, or to provide a Web-based Explorer-style interface

The Internet Explorer Web controls can be downloaded from *http://msdn.microsoft.com/downloads/samples/internet/ ASP_DOT_NET_ServerControls/WebControls/default.asp.* You can read more about the Internet Explorer Web controls and their use at *http://msdn.microsoft.com/workshop/webcontrols/overview/overview.asp.*

Chapter 8 Quick Reference

To	Do This
Create a control that can handle both client-side and server-side events	Use an HTML control by right-clicking the control in Design view and clicking Run As Server Control (or by adding an *id* attribute and the *runat="server"* attribute to the desired HTML element). Note that the element must support the desired client-side event. You can then add attributes to map the events to the appropriate client-side and server-side event handlers.
Show or hide an ASP.NET server control	Modify the *Visible* property of the control.
Add or modify an HTML attribute to an HTML control or Web control that is not exposed as a property of the control	Add or modify the attribute by its name using the *Attributes* collection of the control: *MyControl.Attributes["Attribute"]*. Note that all attributes, including those exposed as properties on a control, are available through the *Attributes* collection.
Apply styles to a control	Set the *Style* or *CssClass* (Web controls only) of the control to the desired CSS style or class string.
Validate user input	Add a *Validator* server control to the page and set its *ControlToValidate* property to the ID of the control the user will use to enter input. The type of control to use depends on what you want to validate.

9

Accessing and Binding Data

In this chapter, you will learn how to

✔ *Connect to a database using ADO.NET.*

✔ *Use ASP.NET data-bound controls to display and edit data.*

✔ *Use the* DataGrid, DataList *and* Repeater *control.*

In the previous two chapters, you learned about creating Web Forms and taking advantage of ASP.NET server controls in your Web Forms applications. With that overview of these two important technologies under your belt, let's look at data access. The ability to store and access data is central to most Web applications, and this is an area that classic ASP made very simple for developers through the ActiveX Data Objects (ADO) COM components. The Microsoft .NET platform provides a set of classes called ADO.NET that is the logical successor to ADO, although the underlying object model has undergone significant changes. ASP.NET, meanwhile, exposes a set of data-bound controls (which were touched on briefly in Chapter 8) that integrate seamlessly with ADO.NET to provide data-binding services.

important

ADO.NET is a large enough topic to merit a book of its own, so at best this chapter will provide an overview. You're strongly encouraged to use the available resources, such as the ASP.NET and HowTo QuickStart tutorials (installed with the Microsoft .NET Framework SDK samples), which have numerous ADO.NET examples. Other resources include the .NET Framework SDK and Microsoft Visual Studio .NET documentation, and of course other books, such as the Microsoft Press title *Building Web Solutions with ASP.NET and ADO.NET* by Dino Esposito, a noted expert on ADO and ADO.NET.

Understanding ADO.NET

In classic ASP, the most common way to access data was through ADO. Developers used ADO Connection objects to connect to a database, and ADO Command and Recordset objects to retrieve, manipulate, and update data. When designing applications, particularly those with high scalability requirements or those whose back-end datasource might change at some point, developers needed to be careful not to tie their front-end presentation code into their back-end database. If they did, they'd end up having to rewrite everything if there were a change in the back-end database.

The ADO.NET class architecture is factored somewhat differently from classic ADO. ADO.NET classes are separated into two major categories: datasource-specific and non-datasource-specific.

Understanding .NET Data Providers

Classes that are specific to a particular datasource are said to work with a specific .NET Data Provider. A .NET Data Provider is a set of classes that allow managed code to interact with a specific datasource to retrieve, update, and manipulate data. ADO.NET comes with two .NET Data Providers: the SQL Server .NET Data Provider, which provide optimized access to SQL Server databases, and the OLE DB .NET Data Provider, which enables you to connect to any datasource for which you have an OLE DB Provider installed.

important

The OLE DB .NET Data Provider does not support the OLE DB 2.5 interfaces. This means that the Microsoft OLE DB Provider for Exchange and the Microsoft OLE DB Provider for Internet Publishing cannot be used with the OLE DB .NET Data Provider. Additionally, the OLE DB .NET Data Provider is incompatible with the OLE DB Provider for ODBC. At the time of this writing, Microsoft was providing a downloadable .NET Data Provider for ODBC at *http: //msdn.microsoft.com/downloads/sample.asp?url=/msdn-files/027/001 /668/msdncompositedoc.xml*.

The following illustration shows the major classes of the SQL Server .NET Data Provider and how they relate to one another:

The *SqlConnection* class is used to establish a connection to a SQL Server database. Unlike the *ADO Connection* object, the *SqlConnection* class (or its OLE DB equivalent, the *OleDbConnection* class) cannot be used to execute SQL statements against a datasource. The *SqlConnection* class is used solely for opening connections, setting or retrieving properties of a connection, or handling connection-related events. You'll learn how to use the *SqlConnection* class to connect to a database later in this chapter.

The *SqlCommand* class is used to execute SQL statements or stored procedures against a SQL Server database. The *SqlCommand* class (and its OLE DB equivalent, the *OleDbCommand* class) can execute statements or stored procedures that do not return values, or that return single values, XML, or DataReaders.

The *SqlDataReader* class provides forward-only, read-only access to a set of rows returned from a SQL Server database. DataReaders (including both the SqlDataReader and OleDbDataReader) provide lightweight, high-performance access to read-only data and are the best choice for accessing data to be displayed in ASP.NET.

The *SqlDataAdapter* class is used as a bridge between the *DataSet* class and SQL Server. The *SqlDataAdapter* class can be used to create a DataSet from a given SQL statement or stored procedure represented by a *SqlCommand* instance, update the back-end SQL Server database based on the contents of a DataSet, or insert rows into or delete rows from a SQL Server database. The *OleDbAdapter* class performs the same tasks for OLE DB datasources.

important

You might have noticed that in the discussion of the classes that make up the SQL Server .NET Data Provider, the names of the classes start with Sql rather than SQL. This is because the names of the classes in the .NET Framework use Pascal casing (after the style of the Pascal language), in which only the first character of each distinct word in a given class is capitalized.

This is important because class and namespace names are case sensitive in a language such as C#. Using the incorrect case name (for example, SQLConnection instead of SqlConnection) will result in a compiler error. So if you get an error complaining that the type isn't defined or the namespace doesn't exist, there's a pretty good chance that you're dealing with a capitalization problem.

Understanding DataSets

The main class not specific to a datasource is the *DataSet* class. This is essentially an in-memory representation of one or more tables of data. This data can be read from an XML file or stream, or might be the result of a query against a datasource.

One important thing about the *DataSet* class is that it doesn't know anything about the datasource from which it receives its data other than what that data is and sometimes the types of the data columns. (See the section about typed

DataSets later in this chapter.) The following illustration shows the major classes associated with the *DataSet* class and how they relate to one another. Note that the Rows, Columns, and Constraints objects are properties of the *DataTable* class.

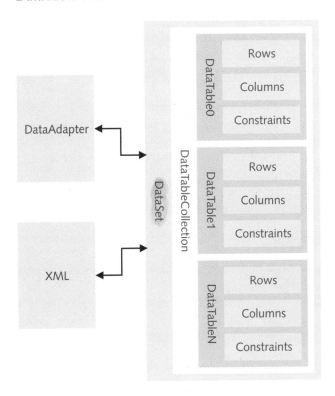

The fact that a DataSet knows nothing about the source of its data means that it's abstracted from the back-end datasource. This is important because it means that if you pass a DataSet from a component used for data retrieval to your Web Forms page to be used for data-binding, it doesn't matter to your Web Forms page where the data comes from as long as the DataSet structure remains the same. The back-end database can be changed without necessitating any changes in the Web Forms page. This makes it much easier to maintain a Web application.

DataSets contain a collection of tables, each of which contains a collection of rows, a collection of columns, and a collection of constraints. You can use these collections to get information about the objects contained within them, as well as to access and update individual data values. The DataSet can also contain a collection of relationships between the tables it contains, allowing hierarchical data to be represented. You'll learn about the *DataSet* class and related classes in detail later in this chapter.

> **note**
>
> Unlike classic ADO, in which XML support was added after the initial object model had been created, XML support has been designed into the ADO.NET model from the ground up. Classes such as SqlCommand, OleDbCommand, and DataSet have built-in support for reading and writing XML data. DataSets in particular can be built from or saved as XML, making them ideal for transporting data between tiers in a multi-tier application or for temporarily storing data to disk for later retrieval.

Creating and Opening Connections

The first step in accessing data from a database is, of course, creating the connection. ADO.NET provides two classes for creating connections to a database: *SqlConnection* and *OleDbConnection*. Which one you use depends on the type of database you will be connecting to and the needs of your application.

SqlConnection

For applications that use SQL Server as the back-end database and are unlikely to change to a different database in the future, the *SqlConnection* class is the appropriate choice. This class is optimized for the best performance when connecting to a SQL Server database. The *SqlConnection* class will also provide superior performance when accessing data in an MSDE database because MSDE uses the same database engine and protocols as SQL Server.

Creating a *SqlConnection* class is simple and can be done in one line of code.

```
SqlConnection mySqlConn=new SqlConnection(ConnectionString);
```

This creates a connection called mySqlConn to the SQL Server specified by the ConnectionString passed to the constructor of the *SqlConnection* class. Opening the connection is as simple as calling the following:

```
mySqlConn.Open();
```

Closing the connection is just as easy:

```
mySqlConn.Close();
```

important

As with classic ADO, it is very important that you close any connection you open when you are finished with it. Connections are not closed automatically when they go out of scope. Open connections are not returned to the connection pool where they would be available to other clients. This can prevent your application from effectively handling larger numbers of users without unacceptable performance degradation.

In addition to setting the connection string by passing it to the constructor of the *SqlConnection* instance, you can create the *SqlConnection* instance with no constructor argument and set the connection string later through the *ConnectionString* property.

The connection string for *SqlConnection* consists of key/value pairs separated by semicolons. Values can be delimited by either single or double quotes, but both cannot be used for the same value (for example, key='value's' should be key="value's"). All spaces, except those appearing in quotes, are ignored.

important

When you're creating connection strings dynamically based on user input, make sure to validate user input so that additional keys are not intentionally added to the connection string by the user. For example, a user could add the database key to his or her password in an attempt to connect to a different database. Because the last key with the same name will be used to set the value for a connection string, failure to validate input can result in inappropriate access.

Table 9-1 on the next page lists the valid keys for a *SqlConnection* connection string.

Table 9-1. *SqlConnection* Connection String Keys	
Key	**Description**
Application Name	This is the name of the application from which the connection is being made.
AttachDBFilename	This is the file name and full path to the primary file of an attachable database. This key requires the Database key to specify the database name.
Connect Timeout or *Connection Timeout*	This is the number of seconds before an attempted connection is aborted and an error is raised. The default is 15.
Connection Lifetime	This is the time in seconds that a pooled connection should remain alive. When a connection is returned to the connection pool, it is destroyed if the current time is more than this many seconds past its creation time. The default is 0, meaning that the connection will not be destroyed.
Connection Reset	This is a Boolean value that determines whether the connection state is reset when a connection is retrieved from the pool. If set to *false*, the connection state will not be reset, which saves a trip to the server. But the programmer must then manually take any steps necessary to ensure that the connection state is appropriate for the application's use. The default is *true*.
Current Language	This is the SQL Server language name.
Data Source or *Server* or *Address* or *Addr* or *Network Address*	This is the server name or network address of the SQL Server instance to which the connection will be made.
Enlist	This key determines whether the connection is automatically enlisted in the creator's current transaction context. The default is *true*.
Initial Catalog or *Database*	This is the name of the database to which the connection will be made.
Integrated Security or *Trusted Connection*	This key determines whether the connection uses the Windows authentication credentials of the caller to authenticate against SQL Server. Setting this to *true* alleviates the need for authenticating a user ID and password, which means that you don't need to worry about storing these values. The default is *false*.

Key	Description
Max Pool Size	This key determines the maximum number of connections to be pooled. The default is 100.
Min Pool Size	This key determines the minimum number of connections that should be in the pool. The default is 0.
Network Library or *Net*	This key specifies the network library to use when connecting to the specified SQL Server. The default is dbmssocn, which specifies the TCP/IP sockets library. Other valid values are dbnmpntw Named pipes dbmsrpcn Multiprotocol dbmsadsn Apple Talk dbmsgnet VIA dbmsipcn Shared memory dbmsspxn IPX/SPX The server must have the appropriate DLL for the specified network library.
Packet Size	This key specifies the number of bytes per network packet to use in communicating with SQL Server. The default is 8192.
Password or *Pwd*	This key specifies the password to use to log into the SQL Server database.
Persist Security Info	If this key is set to *false*, this key prevents sensitive information, such as passwords, from being returned as a part of the connection if the connection is open. The default is *false*.
Pooling	This key determines whether pooling is enabled for this connection. When set to *true*, a requested connection will be pulled from the appropriate pool. If no connections are available from the pool, the requested connection is created and then returned to the pool when closed. The default is *true*.
User ID	This is the name of the SQL Server user account with which to log into the server.
Workstation ID	This is the name of the machine connecting to SQL Server. The default is the local machine name.

OleDbConnection

For applications that need to query databases other than SQL Server, such as Access or Oracle, the *OleDbConnection* class is the appropriate choice. This class uses a standard OLE DB Provider string to connect to any OLE DB datasource through the OLE DB Provider for that datasource.

Creating an OleDbConnection is simple and can be done in one line of code.

```
OleDbConnection myOleDbConn =
new OleDbConnection(ConnectionString);
```

This creates a connection called myOleDbConn to the database specified by the ConnectionString passed to the constructor of the OleDbConnection class. The ConnectionString argument is a standard OLE DB Provider string. The following, from the MSDN .NET Framework Class Library Reference, shows some examples of OLE DB Provider strings for connecting to Oracle, MS Access, and SQL Server datasources, respectively:

```
Provider=MSDAORA; Data Source=ORACLE8i7; User ID=OLEDB;
    Password=OLEDB;
```

```
Provider=Microsoft.Jet.OLEDB.4.0;
    Data Source=c:\bin\LocalAccess40.mdb;
```

```
Provider=SQLOLEDB;Data Source=MySQLServer;Integrated Security=SSPI;
```

The Provider= clause is required. You can also use other clauses supported by the particular OLE DB Provider to set other properties for the Provider. For example, the Initial Catalog= clause is used by the SQL Server OLE DB Provider to indicate the database against which queries will be run.

You open the connection by calling the following:

```
myOleDbConn.Open();
```

And you close it by calling the following:

```
myOleDbConn.Close();
```

---

note
You cannot use the OLE DB Provider for ODBC with the OLE DB .NET Data Provider. You can download a separate .NET Data Provider for ODBC from http://msdn.microsoft.com/downloads/.

Later in this chapter, you'll see examples of using connections to perform data access.

Using Trusted Connections

As mentioned in Chapter 6, ASP.NET is configured by default to use the un-privileged ASPNET account to run ASP.NET worker processes. This means that unlike in beta versions of ASP.NET, you must now use one of the following two techniques to use a trusted connection.

■ Use Windows authentication and impersonation to connect to the database using the credentials of the logged-in user.

■ Set up the ASPNET account as a SQL Server login.

In this section, you'll learn how to use the latter technique to enable the use of trusted connections without the need for Windows authentication.

important

Setting up the ASPNET account in SQL Server will allow any ASP.NET application on the Web server to access the database with whatever privileges have been granted to the ASPNET account. For this reason, this technique should be used only on development systems or production systems on which you are in control of all ASP.NET applications. This technique should generally not be considered for shared server applications.

note

You can run the following command to actually install the Pubs database, if for some reason it is not already present. (Note that it should be entered as a single line.)

```
osql -E -S <domain name>\VSDOTNET -i
"c:\Program Files\Microsoft Visual Studio .Net\FrameworkSDK
\Samples\Setup\instpubs.sql
```

To set up the ASPNET account to access the Pubs SQL Server sample database using SQL Enterprise Manager, follow these steps:

1   Open SQL Enterprise Manager by clicking Start, All Programs (or Programs in Windows 2000), Microsoft SQL Server, Enterprise Manager.

2   Expand the tree and locate the desired SQL Server or MSDE instance. Expand this instance and locate the Security node.

3   Expand the Security node, right-click the Logins node, and then click New Login on the shortcut menu.

4   On the General tab, click the desired domain (or local machine name) in the Domain drop-down list, and then click the elipsis (...) button next to the Name text box.

5   Click the account named ASPNET (aspnet_wp account), click Add, and then click OK.

6   Change the Database default to *pubs*. Click the Database Access tab.

7   On the Database Access tab, scroll to the pubs database, select the Permit check box, and then add the db_datareader and db_datawriter roles to the ASPNET login account by selecting the check boxes for these roles.

8   Click OK. You can now use a trusted connection to read from and write to the pubs sample database.

To set up the ASPNET account to access the Pubs sample database in the VSdotNET MSDE database using the oSql command-line tool, follow these steps:

1   Start the oSql command-line utility by entering the following at a command prompt. (If using a SQL Server database other than a local version of the VSdotNET MSDE instance, enter that server or instance name as the -S parameter.) You should see a 1> prompt if the command completes successfully.

```
oSql -S(local)\VSdotNET -E
```

2   Call the sp_grantlogin system stored procedure to grant login access to the ASPNET account. The syntax should look like the following, with <domain> replaced by your domain or local machine name. The *go* command entered at the 2> prompt tells oSql to execute the stored procedure.

```
1> sp_grantlogin '<domain>\ASPNET'
2> go
```

3   Call the sp_defaultdb system stored procedure to change the default database for the ASPNET account to *pubs*. The syntax should look like the following, with <domain> replaced by your domain or local machine name.

```
1> sp_defaultdb '<domain>\ASPNET', 'pubs'
2> go
```

4   Call the sp_adduser system stored procedure to add the ASPNET login account to the pubs database, passing the db_datareader argument to add the account to the db_datareader role. The syntax should look like the following, with <domain> replaced by your domain or local machine name.

```
1> sp_adduser '<domain>\ASPNET', 'ASPNET', 'db_datareader'
2> go
```

5   If desired, call the sp_addrolemember system stored procedure to add the ASPNET account to the db_datawriter role. In this step, ASPNET is the user name added to the pubs database in the previous step. The syntax should look like the following:

```
1> sp_addrolemember 'db_datawriter', 'ASPNET'
2> go
```

6   Type **exit** and press the Enter key to exit the oSql utility.

After you've set up the ASPNET account as described, you should be able to access the desired database using a trusted connection, as shown in the connection strings used in the samples later in this chapter.

Reading and Updating Data with Commands

The Command classes, SqlCommand and OleDbCommand, are the ADO.NET equivalents of the ADO Command object. These classes can be used to retrieve read-only data through a DataReader (you'll see examples of this later in this chapter); execute Insert, Update, Delete, and other statements that don't return records; retrieve aggregate results; and retrieve an XML representation of data. *SqlCommands* and *OleDbCommands* can also be used in conjunction with a related DataReader to populate a DataSet with data or update a back-end database with updated data from a DataSet. The *SqlCommand* and the *OleDbCommand* classes can work with either SQL statements or stored procedures (for datasources that support them).

SqlCommand

The *SqlCommand* class is the appropriate class to use when you want to run commands against a SQL Server. Here are the steps to follow when using a *SqlCommand* object. Each step outlines one or more ways to initialize or use the *SqlCommand* class.

1   Create the *SqlCommand* object. Note that the constructor of the SqlCommand is overloaded, so you can save steps by passing arguments (such as the query for the Command and/or the *SqlConnection* object to use for the command) to its constructor, rather than setting the properties after the object is created.

```
// Default constructor
SqlCommand mySqlCmd = new SqlCommand();

//Passing in a query
string SQL  = "SELECT au_id FROM authors";
SqlCommand mySqlCmd2 = new SqlCommand(SQL);

//Passing in a query and a connection
SqlConnection mySqlConn = new
SqlConnection("datasource=localhost\
VSdotNET;database=pubs;integratedsecurity=true");
string SQL = "SELECT au_id FROM authors";
SqlCommand mySqlCmd3 = new SqlCommand(SQL, mySqlConn);

//Passing in a query, a connection, and a transaction
SqlConnection mySqlConn = new
SqlConnection("datasource=localhost\
VSdotNET;database=pubs;integratedsecurity=true");
SqlTransaction mySqlTrans = mySqlConn.BeginTransaction();
string SQL = "SELECT au_id FROM authors";
SqlCommand mySqlCmd4 =
new SqlCommand(SQL, mySqlConn, mySqlTrans);
```

2   If you haven't set them in the constructor, set the *CommandText* property to the desired SQL query or stored procedure name, and the *Connection* property to an open SqlConnection object.

```
mySqlCommand.CommandText = "SELECT au_id FROM authors";
// Assumes that mySqlConn has already been created and opened
mySqlCommand.Connection = mySqlConn;
```

3   Call one of the following four methods that execute the command:

```
//Use ExecuteNonQuery to execute an INSERT, UPDATE or
//DELETE query where that query type has been set using the
//CommandText property
mySqlCmd.ExecuteNonQuery();

//Use ExecuteReader to execute a SELECT command and
//return a datareader
SqlDataReader mySqlReader = mySqlCmd.ExecuteReader

//Use ExecuteScalar to execute a command and return the
value of
//the first column of the first row. Any additional results
//are ignored.
Object Result;
Result = mySqlCmd.ExecuteScalar();

//Use ExecuteXmlReader to execute a SELECT command and
//fill a DataSet using the returned XmlReader
string SQL = "SELECT * FROM authors FOR XML AUTO, XMLDATA";
SqlCommand mySqlCmd = new SqlCommand(SQL, mySqlConn);
DataSet myDS = new DataSet();
MyDS.ReadXml(mySqlCmd.ExecuteXmlReader(),
XmlReadMode.Fragment);
```

4   Make sure to close the connection when you're finished with it.

The following example walks you through creating the code necessary to retrieve the contents of the Authors table of the Pubs sample SQL Server database as XML, and to display that data in a Web Forms page.

note

The data access samples in this book are written to run against the MSDE sample database included with Microsoft Visual C# .NET. For information about installing MSDE, see Appendix C. If you want to run the data access samples against a SQL Server database other than the VSdotNET MSDE database, or if you are unable to use a trusted connection to SQL Server or MSDE, you must modify the connection string in the examples to match the appropriate server name and logon credentials.

Display XML data in a Web page

1   Open Visual Studio and create a new project called Chapter_09. On the File menu, click Save WebForm1.aspx As and name the default Web Page created by Visual Studio **ExecuteXmlReader.aspx**.

2   Make ExecuteXmlReader.aspx the start page by right-clicking it in Solution Explorer, and clicking Set As Start Page on the shortcut menu.

3   Copy the file Authors.xsl from the source archive file into the folder where the project was just created.

4   Add an *Xml* component from the Toolbox onto the form. Use the Properties pane to change the ID to XmlDisplay. Set the TransformSource to **Authors.xsl**

5   Switch to the source Code Editor by pressing F7 or clicking Code on the View menu.

6   Add the following *uses* clause to the top of the source file:

```
uses System.Data.SqlClient;
```

7   Scroll down to the *Page_Load* event handler and add the following code:

```
string ConnStr;
// You may want to adjust this string…
ConnStr = "data source=(local)\\VSdotNET;" +
    "database=pubs;integrated security=true";
// Create and open the connection
SqlConnection MySqlConn = new SqlConnection(ConnStr);
MySqlConn.Open();
try
{
    string SQL = "SELECT * FROM authors FOR XML AUTO,
XMLDATA";
    SqlCommand mySqlCmd = new SqlCommand(SQL, MySqlConn);
    DataSet MyDS = new DataSet();
    // Fill the DataSet, using the XML read from MSDE/SQL
Server
    MyDS.ReadXml(mySqlCmd.ExecuteXmlReader(),
XmlReadMode.Fragment);
    XmlDisplay.DocumentContent = MyDS.GetXml();
}
finally
{
    MySqlConn.Close();
}
```

8 To save the solution on the File menu, click Save All.

9 To build the application, on the Build menu, click Build Chapter_09.

10 To run the application, press F5 or click Start on the Debug menu. The resulting screen should look like the following illustration:

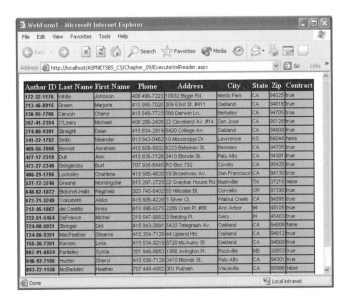

This example creates and opens a SqlConnection to the Pubs database, creates a SQL query string to retrieve the contents of the Authors table as XML, and creates a new SqlCommand, passing in the SQL query and the SqlConnection. Then it creates a DataSet and uses the *ExecuteXmlReader* method of the SqlCommand to pass an XmlReader to the DataSet's *ReadXml* method, which allows the DataSet to populate itself from the XmlReader. Finally, the code sets the *DocumentContent* property of the declared *Xml* server control to the result of the *GetXml* method of the DataSet. The *Xml* control uses the XSL Transformation document authors.xsl to format the Xml content displayed by the *Xml* control.

note

The code shown in Step 7 in the previous example shows an important pattern when using database connections. Immediately after the call to *Open*, you enter a *try* block. In the *finally* section, you close the connection. This ensures that the connection is closed no matter what happens in the code after the call to *Open*.

The following listing shows the content of authors.xsl.

```xml
<xsl:stylesheet version='1.0'
   xmlns:xsl='http://www.w3.org/1999/XSL/Transform'>
   <xsl:template match="/">
   <style>
      .header{font-weight:bold;color:white;background-color:black;}
      .value{font-family:arial;font-size:.7em;background
       -color:silver}
   </style>
   <table border="1" cellspacing="0" cellpadding="1"
      bordercolor="black">
      <tr class="header">
         <th>Author ID</th>
         <th>Last Name</th>
         <th>First Name</th>
         <th>Phone</th>
         <th>Address</th>
         <th>City</th>
         <th>State</th>
         <th>Zip</th>
         <th>Contract</th>
      </tr>
   <xsl:for-each select='Schema1/authors'>
      <tr>
         <td nowrap="true" class="value">
            <b>
               <xsl:value-of select='@au_id' />
            </b>
         </td>
         <td nowrap="true" class="value">
            <xsl:value-of select='@au_lname' />
         </td>
         <td nowrap="true" class="value">
            <xsl:value-of select='@au_fname' />
         </td>
```

```
            <td nowrap="true" class="value">
               <xsl:value-of select='@phone' />
            </td>
            <td nowrap="true" class="value">
               <xsl:value-of select='@address' />
            </td>
            <td nowrap="true" class="value">
               <xsl:value-of select='@city' />
            </td>
            <td nowrap="true" class="value">
               <xsl:value-of select='@state' />
            </td>
            <td nowrap="true" class="value">
               <xsl:value-of select='@zip' />
            </td>
            <td nowrap="true" class="value">
               <xsl:value-of select='@contract' />
            </td>
         </tr>
      </xsl:for-each>
      </table>
      </xsl:template>
</xsl:stylesheet>
```

OleDbCommand

For most purposes, using the *OleDbCommand* class is effectively the same as using the *SqlCommand* class. Instead of connecting with the *SqlConnection* class, you can use the *OleDbConnection* class. One significant difference, however, is that the *OleDbCommand* class does not have an *ExecuteXmlReader* method.

Here's how to use an *OleDbCommand* to execute an aggregate query against the Northwind Microsoft Access sample database and return a result. (This example assumes that you have the Northwind.mdb database installed locally.)

note
Northwind.mdb is a standard example database included with Microsoft Access. If sample Access databases are installed as part of Microsoft Office, Northwind.mcb will be located in the \Program Files\Microsoft Office\Office \Samples folder on the drive where Microsoft Office is installed.

Accessing and Binding Data

9

1   Create and open an *OleDbCommand* with the appropriate connection string for connecting to the Northwind database, where <filepath> is the path to Northwind.mdb on your machine.

```
string ConnStr;
ConnStr = "Provider=Microsoft.Jet.OLEDB.4.0;" +
"Data Source=<filepath>\northwind.mdb;";
OleDbConnection myOleDbConn = new OleDbConnection(ConnStr);
myOleDbConn.Open();
```

2   Create a variable to contain the SQL query. (Note that the query can also be passed as a literal string to the constructor of the *OleDbCommand* class.)

```
string SQL  = "SELECT Count(*) FROM products";
```

3   Create an *OleDbCommand* object, passing the SQL query and the connection object to the constructor.

```
OleDbCommand myOleDbCmd =
new OleDbCommand(SQL, myOleDbConn);
```

4   Create a variable to receive the return value from the command. This variable is declared as type Object because that is the return type of the *ExecuteScalar* method of the *OleDbCommand* object.

```
object Result;
```

5   Call the *ExecuteScalar* method of the *OleDbCommand* object and use the returned value. Note that the value must be cast to the correct type before using it because the returned type is Object. This is especially important if you need to use methods of a particular type that are not implemented by Object.

```
Result = myOleDbCmd.ExecuteScalar();
Value.Text += (string)Result;
```

The following example shows how you would use the objects in the OleDb namespace to display the returned result in a Web Forms page.

1   In Visual Studio .NET open the project created in the previous example, Chapter_09. Right-click the root of the project in Solution Explorer. On the shortcut menu, point to Add and click Add Web Form.

2 Name the new Web Form **ExecuteScalar.aspx**.

3 Make ExecuteScalar.aspx the start page by right-clicking it in Solution Explorer and clicking Set As Start Page on the shortcut menu.

4 Add a label to the form by dragging a label from the Toolbox to the form. Use the Properties pane to change the ID of the label to **Value**.

5 Switch to code view by pressing the F7 key or clicking Code on the View menu.

6 Add the following *using* clause to the *using* clauses at the top of the file:

```
using System.Data.OleDb;
```

7 Scroll down to the *Page_Load* event handler and add the following code, replacing <filepath> with the path where Northwind.mdb exists:

```
string ConnStr;
string SQL;
ConnStr="Provider=Microsoft.Jet.OLEDB.4.0;" +
    @"Data Source=<filepath>\Northwind.mdb;";
OleDbConnection MyOleDbConn =
    new OleDbConnection(ConnStr);
MyOleDbConn.Open();
try
{
    SQL="SELECT Count(*) FROM products";
    OleDbCommand MyOleDbCommand =
    new OleDbCommand(SQL,MyOleDbConn);
    object Result;
    Result=MyOleDbCommand.ExecuteScalar();
    Value.Text="The Count is: " + Result.ToString();
}
finally
{
    MyOleDbConn.Close();
}
```

8 To save the solution, on the File menu, click Save All.

9 To build the application, on the Build menu, click Build Chapter_09.

10   To run the application, press F5 or on the Debug menu, click Start. The resulting screen should look like the following illustration:

note

Although the previous example uses Microsoft Access to demonstrate the ability of the OleDbCommand object to connect to non-SQL Server databases, you shouldn't use Access for ASP.NET applications. For initial prototyping and development, or for applications with minimal scalability requirements (5–10 concurrent users or fewer), MSDE is the better choice.

MSDE is a SQL Server–compatible database that is available with a number of Microsoft products, including SQL Server, Microsoft Office, and Visual Studio. A version of MSDE also comes with Visual C# .NET Standard, as well as with the .NET Framework SDK, and it's installed with and used to run the SDK samples, if you choose to install them. (Please refer to Chapter 6 for important guidance about installing sample applications.) MSDE is built on the same database engine as SQL Server but it's tuned for approximately five concurrent users.

The advantage of using MSDE is that all your development tasks are identical to developing against SQL Server without the licensing expense of a full-blown SQL Server. (The license to use and distribute MSDE is included in the afore-mentioned products. Check the end-user license agreement to ensure that your use is within the terms of the agreement.) And if your application's scalability needs to grow, you can simply move your database to SQL Server for increased performance and scalability, with no code or data changes required.

In addition to using SQL text queries, you can also use stored procedures as the basis of a *SqlCommand* or *OleDbCommand* object. This is as simple as setting the *CommandText* property of the object to the name of the stored procedure that you want to execute, and then setting the *CommandType* to *CommandType.StoredProcedure*. If you're familiar with the execution of stored procedures under classic ADO, this isn't so different from what you would have done with the ADO Command object.

Calling Stored Procedures with Parameters

Calling stored procedures with input or output parameters is a little more involved, but it's still pretty straightforward. You simply create parameters (either SqlParameter or OleDbParameter objects); set the appropriate properties, such as ParameterName, Direction, type (SqlType or OleDbType), and Value; and then add the parameter object to the Parameters collection of the Command object. The following example shows the code required to execute the byroyalty stored procedure in the Pubs sample SQL Server database. It returns a SqlDataReader, which is then bound to an ASP.NET DataGrid control. (You'll learn more about data binding later in this chapter.)

Read data using a stored procedure and *SqlDataReader*

1   In Visual Studio, open the project created in the previous example, Chapter_09. Right-click the root of the project in Solution Explorer, and on the shortcut menu, point to Add, and click Add Web Form. Name the form **ExecuteReader.aspx**.

2   Make ExecuteReader.aspx the start page by right-clicking it in Solution Explorer and clicking Set As Start Page on the shortcut menu.

3   Drag a DataGrid from the Toolbox it on the form. Use the Properties pane to change the ID of the DataGrid1 to **MyGrid**.

4   Switch to code view by pressing the F7 key or clicking Code on the View menu.

5   Add the following *using* clause to the *using* clauses at the top of the file:

    ```
    using System.Data.SqlClient;
    ```

6   Scroll down to the *Page_Load* event handler and add the following code:

    ```
    string ConnStr;
    string SQL;
    ConnStr=@"Data Source=(local)\VSdotNET;" +
        "database=pubs;integrated security=true";
    SqlConnection MySqlConn=new SqlConnection(ConnStr);
    MySqlConn.Open();
    try
    {
        SQL="byroyalty";
        SqlCommand MySqlCmd=new SqlCommand(SQL,MySqlConn);
    ```

```
    MySqlCmd.CommandType=CommandType.StoredProcedure;
    SqlParameter MySqlParam=new
     SqlParameter("@percentage",SqlDbType.Int);
    MySqlParam.Value=40;
    MySqlCmd.Parameters.Add(MySqlParam);
    SqlDataReader Reader;
    Reader=MySqlCmd.ExecuteReader();
    MyGrid.DataSource=Reader;
    MyGrid.DataBind();
}
finally
{
    MySqlConn.Close();
}
```

7   To save the solution, on the File menu, click Save All.

8   To build the application, on the Build menu, click Build Chapter_09.

9   To run the application, press F5 or on the Debug menu, click Start. The resulting screen should look like the following illustration:

The previous example creates and opens a connection to the Pubs database, creates a SqlCommand, sets its *CommandType* to *CommandType.StoredProcedure*, and then creates a *SqlParameter*, passing the parameter name and datatype to the parameter's constructor.

important

Unlike ADO, when specifying a parameter name to ADO.NET, you must use the exact name the stored procedure expects, including the *at* symbol (@).

The code then sets the value of the parameter, adds it to the *Parameters* collection of the SqlCommand, and executes the command. The resulting SqlDataReader is then bound to a *DataGrid* control, which displays the results.

Using DataSets

DataSets are one of the two main ways of working with data in ADO.NET. (The other is DataReaders, which you've been using and will learn about in more detail later in this chapter.) DataSets provide a database-independent, in-memory representation of data. Unlike most other objects we have looked at in which there is one version in the *SqlClient* namespace and a similar object in the *OleDb* namespace, there is a single *DataSet* class. DataSet is found in the *System.Data* namespace. This data can be used for display or to update a back-end database through the appropriate DataAdapter. A DataSet can also read data from and write data to an XML file or a *Stream* object.

DataSets can be constructed and manipulated programmatically by adding, modifying, or deleting DataTables, DataColumns, and DataRows in the DataSet. You can also use such DataSets to update a back-end database (assuming that the schema of the tables you've constructed is compatible) by calling the Update method of the DataSet.

You can work with typed DataSets to make your code easier to read and your ADO.NET code less error-prone. Also, you can use a DataView to filter the contents of a DataSet for use in display (such as for data-binding) or calculations.

Using DataAdapters

DataAdapters enable you to get data from a back-end database into a DataSet, and update a back-end database from a DataSet. There are two DataAdapters that are installed with the .NET Framework, the *SqlDataAdapter* and the *OleDbDataAdapter*. Each of these DataAdapters uses the appropriate *Connection* class and *Command* classes to either retrieve or update data.

The *Fill* method of the *SqlDataAdapter* and *OleDbAdapter* classes can be used to populate a DataSet with results from a back-end database, using the *Command* object specified by the *SelectCommand* property of the DataAdapter. The following code creates and opens a connection to the database specified by the *ConnStr* argument. Then it creates a new SqlDataAdapter and sets its *SelectCommand* property to a newly created *SqlCommand* object that uses the query specified by the *SQL* argument. Finally the code creates a new DataSet, populates it using the *Fill* method of the SqlDataAdapter, and closes the connection.

```
SqlConnection mySqlConn = new SqlConnection(ConnStr);
mySqlConn.Open();
SqlDataAdapter mySqlAdapter = new SqlDataAdapter();
mySqlAdapter.SelectCommand = new SqlCommand(SQL, mySqlConn);
DataSet myDS = new DataSet();
mySqlAdapter.Fill(myDS);
mySqlConn.Close();
```

At this point, the data in the DataSet can be updated or deleted, new rows can be added, or the entire DataSet can be passed to another component because it no longer has a connection to the back-end database.

Reading XML Data

In addition to populating a DataSet from a database using a DataAdapter, you can also read the data for a DataSet from an XML file or stream using the ReadXml method of the DataSet. Because you can also save a DataSet as XML using the *WriteXml* method, the two techniques together can be a convenient way of serializing and deserializing the data in a DataSet. The ExecuteXmlReader.aspx example earlier in the chapter shows an example of using the ReadXml method to populate a DataSet with XML data retrieved from SQL Server using the FOR XML AUTO query syntax.

Using DataTables, DataColumns, and DataRows

Another way of populating a DataSet is to create its tables, columns, and rows programmatically. This enables you to create a DataSet without connecting to a back-end database. Assuming that the schema of the created table(s) matches your database (which is handled in the following code by reading in an XSD schema file, shown in the listing AddTitle.xsd later in the chapter, created from the Pubs Titles table), you can then connect to the database and update it based on the row(s) you've added to the DataSet programmatically.

The following example shows how to create a program that adds a new row to the Titles table of the Pubs sample SQL Server database. Note that the *SelectCommand* property of the SqlDataAdapter is set by passing the SQL string variable to the constructor of the SqlDataAdapter. This is necessary to allow the

UpdateCommand (the command that is called when the *Update* method of the *SqlDataAdapter* is called) to be built automatically, using the *SqlCommandBuilder* object.

> **note**
>
> Depending on which version of the .NET Framework you've installed, you might need to add the path to the folder containing the Visual Basic .NET compiler to your PATH environment variable for the preceding command to work. The procedure for locating and adding this path to the PATH environment variable is detailed in the "Installing the Sample Files" section at the beginning of this book.

Add a new row to a table

1   In Visual Studio, open the project created in the previous example, Chapter_09. Right-click the root of the project in Solution Explorer, and on the shortcut menu, point to Add, and click Add Web Form. Name the form **AddTitle.aspx**.

2   Make AddTitle.aspx the start page by right-clicking it in Solution Explorer and clicking Set As Start Page on the shortcut menu.

3   Copy AddTitles.xsd from the Source Archive to the folder where the project resides.

4   Unlike previous examples, this example will use an HTML table to format the screen. To conveniently do this, it is best to change the layout of the page from GridLayout to FlowLayout. Right click anywhere on the page, and click Properties on the shortcut menu. In the Document Property Pages dialog box, change the page layout from GridLayout to FlowLayout in the drop-down list, and click OK.

5   Rather than add components through the design interface, in this example, copy the following HTML from the example in the Source archive and paste it into your page. The HTML code sets up a table to be used to display captions and text boxes. Change to HTML mode by clicking the HTML tab at the bottom of the design window. Insert the following HTML between the beginning and ending form tags:

```
<h3>Inserting a Title</h3>
<table width="300">
 <tr>
  <td colspan="2" bgcolor="silver">Add a New Title:</td>
 </tr>
 <tr>
  <td nowrap>Title ID: </td>
```

```
  <td>
   <asp:textbox id="title_id" text="XX0000" runat="server"/>
  </td>
  </tr>
 <tr>
  <td nowrap>Title: </td>
  <td>
   <asp:textbox id="title" text="The Tao of ASP.NET"
    runat="server"/>
  </td>
 </tr>
 <tr nowrap>
  <td>Type: </td>
  <td>
   <asp:textbox id="type" text="popular_comp"
    runat="server"/>
  </td>
 </tr>
 <tr>
  <td>Publisher ID: </td>
  <td>
    <asp:textbox id="pub_id" text="1389" runat="server"/>
  </td>
 </tr>
 <tr>
  <td>Price: </td>
  <td>
   <asp:textbox id="price" text="39.99" runat="server"/>
  </td>
 </tr>
 <tr>
  <td>Advance: </td>
  <td>
   <asp:textbox id="advance" text="2000" runat="server"/>
  </td>
 </tr>
 <tr>
  <td>Royalty: </td>
  <td>
   <asp:textbox id="royalty" text="5" runat="server"/>
  </td>
 </tr>
```

```
<tr>
 <td nowrap>Year-to-Date Sales: </td>
 <td>
  <asp:textbox id="ytd_sales" text="0" runat="server"/>
 </td>
</tr>
<tr>
 <td>Notes: </td>
 <td>
   <asp:textbox id="notes" textmode="multiline"
    text="Philosophy and Code...a perfect mix."
    rows="3" columns="30" runat="server"/>
 </td>
</tr>
<tr>
 <td nowrap>Publication Date: </td>
 <td>
   <asp:textbox id="pubdate" text="12/01/01"
    runat="server"/>
 </td>
</tr>
<tr>
 <td></td>
 <td style="padding-top:15">
   <asp:button text="Add Title" runat="server"/>
 </td>
</tr>
<tr>
 <td colspan="2">
   <asp:datagrid id="titlegrid" runat="server"
    BorderColor="#999999"
    BorderStyle="None"
    BorderWidth="1px"
    BackColor="White"
    CellPadding="3"
    GridLines="Vertical">
   <SelectedItemStyle Font-Bold="True"
    ForeColor="White" BackColor="#008A8C">
   </SelectedItemStyle>
   <AlternatingItemStyle BackColor="#DCDCDC">
   </AlternatingItemStyle>
   <ItemStyle ForeColor="Black"
```

```
      BackColor="#EEEEEE">
      </ItemStyle>
      <HeaderStyle Font-Bold="True"
       ForeColor="White" BackColor="#000084">
      </HeaderStyle>
      <FooterStyle ForeColor="Black"
       BackColor="#CCCCCC">
      </FooterStyle>
      <PagerStyle HorizontalAlign="Center"
       ForeColor="Black" BackColor="#999999"
       Mode="NumericPages">
      </PagerStyle>
      </asp:datagrid>
    </td>
  </tr>
</table>
```

After inserting this code, switch back to design mode by clicking the Design tab at the bottom of the design window. In the designer, the screen should look something like the following illustration:

6   Switch to the Code Editor by pressing F7 or clicking Code on the View menu. At the top of the file, add the following *using* clause:

```
using System.Data.SqlClient;
```

7 Scroll down to the Page_Load event handler and add the following code:

```
DataSet MyDS = new DataSet();
DataTable TitleTable;
DataRow TitleRow;
string ConnStr;
ConnStr=@"server=(local)\VSdotNET;database=pubs;" +
    "Trusted_Connection=yes";
string SQL;
SQL="SELECT * FROM Titles";
SqlConnection MySqlConn=
    new SqlConnection(ConnStr);
SqlDataAdapter MySqlAdapter=
    new SqlDataAdapter(SQL,ConnStr);
SqlCommandBuilder MySqlCB=
    new SqlCommandBuilder(MySqlAdapter);

MyDS.ReadXmlSchema(
    Server.MapPath("AddTitle.xsd"));

if ( this.IsPostBack )
{
    TitleTable=MyDS.Tables[0];
    TitleRow=TitleTable.NewRow();

    TitleRow["title_id"]=title_id.Text;
    TitleRow["title"]=title.Text;
    TitleRow["type"]=type.Text;
    TitleRow["pub_id"]=pub_id.Text;
    TitleRow["price"]=double.Parse(price.Text);
    TitleRow["advance"]=double.Parse(advance.Text);
    TitleRow["royalty"]=int.Parse(royalty.Text);
    TitleRow["ytd_sales"]=int.Parse(ytd_sales.Text);
    TitleRow["notes"]=notes.Text;
    TitleRow["pubdate"]=DateTime.Parse(pubdate.Text);
    TitleTable.Rows.Add(TitleRow);

    MySqlAdapter.Update(MyDS);

    titlegrid.DataSource=MyDS.Tables[0].DefaultView;
    titlegrid.DataBind();
}
```

Accessing and Binding Data

9

8   To save the solution, on the File menu, click Save All.

9   To build the application, on the Build menu, click Build Chapter_09.

10   To run the application, press F5 or on the Debug menu, click Start. Click the Add Title button. When the page posts back, scroll down to the bottom of the screen. The resulting screen should look like the following illustration:

Setting Up Relationships

Because DataSets can contain multiple tables of data, it makes sense that you would want the DataSet to contain information about the relationships between these tables. This would enable you to treat them as true relational data, as well as maintain any hierarchy and foreign key relationships inherent in the data. The DataSet class fulfills this need with its Relations collection, which contains a collection of *DataRelation* objects, each of which describes a parent/child relationship between two matching columns in different tables in the DataSet.

DataRelation objects can be added to a DataSet programmatically or inferred from a supplied XSD schema.

Accessing Values

Values in a DataSet are accessed by referring to the DataTables and DataRows containing the data. The DataTables are available through the Tables collection of the DataSet, and you can reference a particular table either by index (zero-based) or by table name (key) as follows:

```
DataTable MyTable  = myDS.Tables[0];
DataTable MyTable  = myDS.Tables["tablename"];
```

You can also iterate over the DataTableCollection (returned by the *Tables* property of the DataSet), DataRowCollection (returned by the *Rows* property of a DataTable), or the DataColumnCollection (returned by the *Columns* property of a DataTable). The code in the following example iterates over all the tables in a DataSet and all the rows in each table. Then it displays the value of each column in the row, using an ASP.NET Literal control as a placeholder for the text.

Iterate through a *DataTableCollection*

1 In Visual Studio, open the project created in the previous example, Chapter_09. Right-click the root of the project in Solution Explorer, and on the shortcut menu, point to Add, and click Add Web Form. Name the form **DisplayDataSetItems.aspx**.

2 Make DisplayDataSetItems.aspx the start page by right-clicking it in Solution Explorer and clicking Set As Start Page on the shortcut menu.

3 Add an ASP.NET Literal server control. Drag the literal control from the Toolbox to the form. Use the Properties pane to change the ID of the Literal1 control to **Value**.

4 Switch to the Code Editor by pressing F7 or clicking Code on the View menu. At the top of the file, add the following *using* clause:

```
using System.Data.SqlClient;
```

5 To fill the DataSet, scroll down to the *Page_Load* event handler and add the following code:

```
DataSet MyDS=new DataSet();
string ConnStr;
string SQL;
ConnStr=@"server=(local)\VSdotNET;database=pubs;" +
    "Trusted_Connection=yes";
SQL="SELECT * FROM Titles " +
    "SELECT * FROM Publishers ";
SqlConnection MySqlConn=new SqlConnection(ConnStr);
SqlDataAdapter MySqlAdapter=new SqlDataAdapter(SQL,ConnStr);

MySqlAdapter.Fill(MyDS);
```

Most of this should look somewhat familiar by now. One difference is that the SQL command contains two distinct SELECT statements. This is to cause two tables to be retrieved into the DataSet.

6 Iterate through the DataTables, DataRows and DataColumns. Just below the code added in the previous step, add the following code:

```
// Get each DataTable in the DataTable Collection
// and display each row value by appending it to
// the Text property of the Literal control.

foreach ( DataTable CurrentTable in MyDS.Tables )
{
    Value.Text+="Table: " +
        CurrentTable.TableName.ToString() + "<br/>";
    Value.Text+=
                    "----------------<br/>";
    foreach ( DataRow CurrentRow in CurrentTable.Rows )
    {
        Value.Text+="<br/>   ";
        foreach ( DataColumn CurrentColumn in
CurrentTable.Columns )
        {
            if ( CurrentRow[CurrentColumn]!=null )
            {
                if ( CurrentRow[CurrentColumn]!=DBNull.Value )
                {
                Value.Text+=CurrentRow[CurrentColumn].ToString();
                }
                else
                {
                    Value.Text+="NULL";
                }
                Value.Text+="<br/>   ";
            }
        }
    }
}
```

7 To save the solution, on the File menu, click Save All.

8 To build the application, on the Build menu, click Build Chapter_09.

9   To run the application, press F5 or on the Debug menu, click Start. The resulting screen should look like the following illustration:

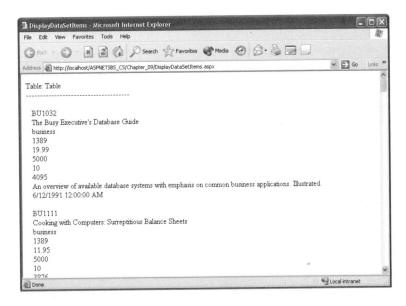

Scroll toward the bottom of the screen and you should see the transition between displaying titles and publishers, as shown in the following illustration:

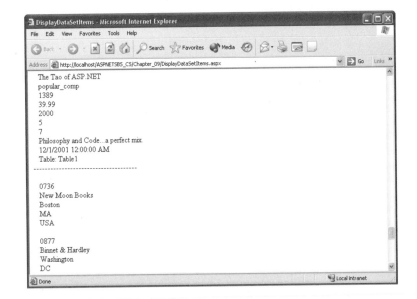

Updating DataSets

After you've populated a DataSet with data, either by using a DataAdapter or by calling the *ReadXml* method of the DataSet, you might want to update that data. You can edit an individual value by specifying the table, row, and column of the item you want to edit and supplying a new value.

```
myDS.Tables[0].Rows[0].Columns[2] = "popular_comp";
```

But what if you edit several values and then realize that you want to roll back one or more of the changes? Fortunately, the DataSet provides robust support for accepting and rejecting changes in the data by maintaining multiple versions of the data for each row. Each row contains the following versions.

- **Original**   This contains the data originally loaded into the row.
- **Default**   This contains the default values for the row (specified by the *DefaultValue* property of the row's columns). If no defaults have been specified, this contains the same data as the Original version.
- **Current**   This contains updated data for any columns that have been updated, and the same data as the Original version for columns that have not been updated.
- **Proposed**   After calling *BeginEdit* on a row and before calling the *EndEdit* or *CancelEdit* methods of the DataRow, the Proposed version contains changes to data that have not yet been applied to the Current version. If *CancelEdit* is called, the Proposed version is deleted. If *EndEdit* is called, the changes in the Proposed version are applied to the Current version.

You can determine whether changes have been made to an item in a row by comparing the item's Original or Default version with the Current version.

```
if ( CurrentRow[1, DataRowVersion.Current] ==
   CurrentRow[1, DataRowversion.Proposed] )
{
   // Take appropriate action
}
```

You can accept or reject changes to data on a row-by-row basis.

```
if ( CurrentRow[0, DataRowVersion.Current] == "" )
// Blank field not allowed
{
   CurrentRow.RejectChanges();
}
else
{
   CurrentRow.AcceptChanges();
}
```

You can check the current state of a row by checking the row's *RowState* property.

```
string CurrentState;
CurrentState = CurrentRow.RowState;
if ( CurrentState == DataRowState.Modified )
{
   // Take appropriate action
}
```

There are five possible row states.

- **Added**   This is a row that has been added to the table prior to *AcceptChanges* being called. Once *AcceptChanges* is called, this row's RowState will be set to *Unchanged*.

- **Deleted**   This is a row whose *Delete* method has been called.

- **Detached**   This is a newly created row that has not yet been added to a DataRowCollection, or a row that has been removed from a DataRowCollection but not destroyed.

- **Modified**   This is a row whose data has changed but whose *AcceptChanges* method has not been called.

- **Unchanged**   This is a row whose data has not changed since the last call to *AcceptChanges*.

After you've called *AcceptChanges* on the DataSet, you call the *Update* method of the DataAdapter used to load data into the DataSet to update the underlying database with the new values.

Typed DataSets

One of the coolest new features of ADO.NET is the ability to create strongly typed DataSets. Typed DataSets are special classes that are generated by the xsd.exe command line utility and are descendents of the *DataSet* class. They use an XSD schema to create additional public properties and methods that enable you to access the columns of the DataSet's tables directly by name, rather than having to use either an index or a late-bound key. This can improve runtime performance and reduce the likelihood of errors in coding against the DataSet.

There are two ways to create Typed DataSets. One way is by using Visual Studio .NET. There is also a manual way for people who find the auto-generated code more than they need, or who want finer control. First lets look at the manual procedure.

Creating a typed DataSet manually for the AddTitles example that was shown earlier requires just a few steps. The following example assumes you've already created an XSD schema for the table or tables in the DataSet, which you can do with the *WriteXmlSchema* method of a DataSet that's been loaded with data from the table or tables:

Create a typed DataSet manually

1   Open a command prompt at the location of the XSD schema file.

2   Create the class for the typed DataSet using the xsd.exe utility. The xsd.exe utility will be in the \Program Files\Microsoft Visual Studio .NET \FrameworkSDK\Bin folder. You might want to add this folder to your path. The /d option specifies that we want to create a DataSet, the /l option sets the language as VB, and the /n option specifies that the class should use the namespace AddTitle. AddTitle.xsd is the name of your XSD schema file, which is shown in the AddTitle.xsd listing.

```
xsd.exe /d /l:cs AddTitle.xsd /n:AddTitle
```

3   Compile the class using the csc.exe command-line compiler. The /t option specifies that you want to compile as a library component (DLL), the /r options specify assemblies that you need to reference, and the /out option directs the compiler to save the compiled assembly in the bin subdirectory of the current directory.

```
csc.exe /t:library AddTitle.cs /r:System.dll
/r:System.Data.Dll /r:System.Xml.Dll
/out:bin/AddTitle.dll
```

AddTitle.xsd

```xml
<?xml version="1.0" standalone="yes"?>
<xsd:schema id="TitleDataSet" targetNamespace="http://
www.aspnetb.com.ns" xmlns="" xmlns:xsd="http://www.w3.org/2001/
XMLSchema" xmlns:msdata="urn:schemas-microsoft-com:xml-msdata">
 <xsd:element name="TitleDataSet" msdata:IsDataSet="true">
  <xsd:complexType>
   <xsd:choice maxOccurs="unbounded">
    <xsd:element name="Titles">
    <xsd:complexType>
    <xsd:sequence>
    <xsd:element name="title_id" type="xsd:string" minOccurs="0" />
    <xsd:element name="title" type="xsd:string" minOccurs="0" />
    <xsd:element name="type" type="xsd:string" minOccurs="0" />
    <xsd:element name="pub_id" type="xsd:string" minOccurs="0" />
    <xsd:element name="price" type="xsd:decimal" minOccurs="0" />
    <xsd:element name="advance" type="xsd:decimal" minOccurs="0" />
    <xsd:element name="royalty" type="xsd:int" minOccurs="0" />
    <xsd:element name="ytd_sales" type="xsd:int" minOccurs="0" />
    <xsd:element name="notes" type="xsd:string" minOccurs="0" />
    <xsd:element name="pubdate" type="xsd:dateTime" minOccurs="0" />
    </xsd:sequence>
    </xsd:complexType>
    </xsd:element>
   </xsd:choice>
  </xsd:complexType>
 </xsd:element>
</xsd:schema>
```

You can also create a Typed DataSet using Visual Studio .NET. The following steps walk you through doing just that on a new form modeled after *AddTitle.aspx*, a previous example.

Create and use a typed DataSet in Visual Studio

1 In Visual Studio, open the project created in the previous example, Chapter_09. Right-click the root of the project in Solution Explorer, and on the resulting shortcut menu, point to Add, and click Add Web Form. Name the form **AddTitle_TypedDS.aspx**.

Accessing and Binding Data

9

2   Make AddTitle_TypedDS.aspx the start page by right-clicking it in Solution Explorer and clicking Set As Start Page on the shortcut menu.

3   Make sure you are in Design mode and copy the HTML code from the AddTitle.aspx example but change the heading from "Inserting a Title" to "**Inserting a Title with a Typed DataSet.**" Insert the code in the same place in the file.

4   Drag a SqlDataAdapter from the Toolbox to the form, and the DataAdapter Configuration Wizard will appear:

5   Click Next. You will be prompted to select or create a connection. Create one by clicking the New Connection button. In the Select Or Enter A Server Name drop-down list, click the (local)\VSdotNET instance of SQL Server. In the Select The Database On The Server drop-down list, click Pubs. The Data Link Properties dialog box should look like the following illustration (presuming you are logged into a Windows account that has rights to connect to SQL Server):

6 Click OK in the Data Link Properties dialog box, and then click Next. The Choose A Query Type page of the wizard will appear (as shown in the following illustration). Select the Use SQL Statements option.

7   Click Next. In the Generate SQL Statements dialog box, you can generate the Select statement you want to use. Although you can type in commands (for instance, SELECT * FROM Titles), if you click the Query Builder button, a screen will appear that enables you to select tables. Click the Titles table in the list, and click the Add button. Click Close to close the Add Table dialog box, and the Query Builder will appear. You can select the * (All Columns) check box to select all columns, or you can click the columns individually. Selecting the specific columns you want can often be more efficient. In this example, select each column individually, as shown in the following illustration:

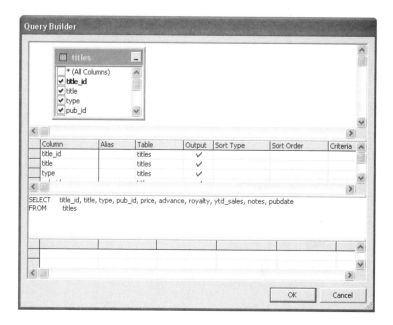

8   Click OK in the Query Builder, and then click Next in the Generate SQL Statements dialog box.

9   Click Finish in the final page of the DataAdapter Configuration Wizard, as shown in the following illustration:

10   A new pane should appear at the bottom of the main editing window in Visual Studio .NET. It will have two components, named *sqlDataAdapter1* and *sqlConnection1*. Use the Properties pane to change the names to **daTitles** and **cnPubs**, respectively. When renamed, the screen should look like the following illustration:

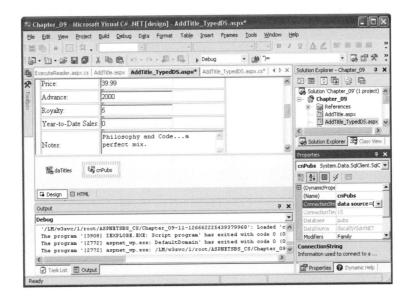

11   Click the daTitles component, and on the Data menu, click Generate
DataSet. The Generate DataSet dialog box, as shown in the following
illustration, will appear. The default name for the types DataSet will be
DataSet1. Change the name to **TitleDataSet**. Click OK.

12   Switch to the Code Editor by pressing F7, or clicking Code on the View
menu. At the top of the file, add the following *using* clause:

```
using System.Data.SqlClient;
```

13   Add the following code to the *Page_Load* event handler:

```
if ( this.IsPostBack )
{
  this.cnPubs.Open();
  try
  {
    TitleDataSet.titlesRow MyTitleRow;
    MyTitleRow=titleDataSet1.titles.NewtitlesRow();
    MyTitleRow.title_id=title_id.Text;
    MyTitleRow.title=title.Text;
    MyTitleRow.type=type.Text;
```

```
MyTitleRow.pub_id=pub_id.Text;
MyTitleRow.price=decimal.Parse(price.Text);
MyTitleRow.advance=decimal.Parse(advance.Text);
MyTitleRow.royalty=int.Parse(royalty.Text);
MyTitleRow.ytd_sales=int.Parse(ytd_sales.Text);
MyTitleRow.notes=notes.Text;
MyTitleRow.pubdate=DateTime.Parse(pubdate.Text);
titleDataSet1.titles.AddtitlesRow(MyTitleRow);
this.daTitles.Update(this.titleDataSet1);

titlegrid.DataSource=this.titleDataSet1.Tables[0];
titlegrid.DataBind();
}
finally
{
  this.cnPubs.Close();
}
}
```

14   To save the solution, on the File menu, click Save All.

15   To build the application, on the Build menu, click Build Chapter_09.

16   To run the application, press F5 or on the Debug menu, click Start. Change the Title ID so that you do not try to insert a duplicate into the table. Click the Add Title button. When the page posts back, scroll down to the bottom of the screen. The resulting screen should look almost exactly like the previous AddTitles.aspx example, with a different heading.

Now when you create the DataSet, you create an instance of TitleDataSet instead of DataSet. Looking at the code that Visual Studio .NET adds to the form, you will see the following declaration:

```
protected Chapter_09.TitleDataSet titleDataSet1;
```

Similarly, you use strong types for the table and row. This is the code that you added to the Page_Load event handler, for example:

```
TitleDataSet.titlesRow MyTitleRow;
```

When you use typed DataSets with Visual Studio .NET, you automatically get IntelliSense code completion for all the members of the TitleDataSet. This makes coding against a typed DataSet much easier and considerably less error-prone.

Accessing and Binding Data

The following illustration shows how easy it is to pick the correct field from a typed DataSet using IntelliSense.

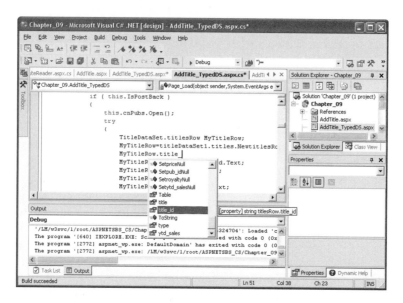

One other thing worth noting is that unlike the previous AddTitles.aspx example, when filling in the price and advance in the Typed DataSet example, rather than using *double.Parse*, you need to use *decimal.Parse*. Using *double.Parse* would actually require an explicit cast to decimal, so using decimal.Parse just makes more sense. Having programmed the previous example, you might have never even known that price and advance were decimal rather then double. In most cases, there is no practical difference between casting the return of *double.Parse* to a decimal, but clearly parsing to the correct type directly is more efficient. Another advantage of Typed DataSets!

Using DataViews

The *DataView* class provides a means for sorting, searching, editing, filtering, and navigating DataTables. DataViews can also be data-bound, as you'll see in later examples. Data binding allows ASP.NET server controls to display bound data automatically, even when multiple rows or columns of data are contained in the datasource. This greatly simplifies the display of data in ASP.NET. You can access an unfiltered view of the data in a table in a DataSet as follows:

```
DataView MyDV;
MyDV = MyDS.Tables[0].DefaultView;
```

After you have a reference to the DataView, you can filter it by adding an expression to the *RowFilter* property.

```
MyDV.RowFilter = "type='business'";
```

Search the DataView using the Find method.

```
int RowNum  = MyDV.Find("BU1032");
```

Sort the DataView by adding an expression to the *Sort* property.

```
MyDV.Sort = "type, title_id DESC";
```

You've already seen some basic examples of binding to a DataView. You'll look at data binding in more detail later in this chapter.

Reading Data with DataReaders

DataSets are great when you need really rich control over your data—updates, rollbacks, reading and writing schemas, and so on. But when all you need to do is display some data quickly and efficiently, the DataSet (and the DataAdapter used to fill it) has a fair amount of overhead that you might not want to incur. Enter the DataReader.

A DataReader provides the equivalent of a forward-only, read-only cursor on your data. It is both faster and more lightweight than a DataSet, making it ideal when you need to retrieve a set of rows and iterate over them just once (to display them, for example). Unlike DataSets, you can also data-bind directly to DataReaders, without the need for a DataView.

SqlDataReader

SqlDataReader is the class to use when accessing data from a SQL Server database. You create this class by calling the *ExecuteReader* method on a *SqlCommand* object.

```
SqlDataReader MySqlDR  = MySqlCmd.ExecuteReader();
```

To access the rows in a *SqlDataReader* instance, you call the *Read* method of the instance, usually in a loop.

```
while ( MySqlDR.Read() )
{
    Response.Write(MySqlDR.Item[0]);
}
```

After you're finished with the *SqlDataReader*, you should always call its *Close* method, as well as calling the *Close* method on the associated *Connection* object.

```
MySqlDR.Close();
```

> **note**
>
> To avoid having to explicitly close the connection associated with the command used to create either a *SqlDataReader* or an *OleDbDataReader*, pass the *CommandBehavior.CloseConnection* argument to the *ExecuteReader* method of the connection.
>
> ```
> mySqlDR = mySqlCmd.ExecuteReader(CommandBehavior.CloseConnection)
> ```
>
> The associated connection will be closed automatically when the *Close* method of the DataReader is called. This makes it all the more important to always remember to call Close on your DataReaders!

OleDbDataReader

Creating and using an *OleDbDataReader* is essentially the same as for the *SqlDataReader*, with one notable exception. The *OleDbDataReader* can handle hierarchical recordsets retrieved using the MSDataShape OLE DB Provider. When an *OleDbDataReader* is created based on an *OleDbCommand* that returns a hierarchical recordset, the OLE DB chapter is returned as a column in the *OleDbDataReader*. The value of the column is an *OleDbDataReader* representing the child records.

Data Binding

One exciting advance in the move from classic ASP to ASP.NET is the availability of server-side data binding. Data binding is the process of declaratively tying elements of the UI for a page (such as controls) to data in an underlying datastore. Data binding on the client has been available in Internet Explorer for a number of years, but it requires all your users to use the same browser; if they don't, you need to do a massive amount of testing to ensure compatibility with different browser versions. Server-side data binding solves this problem by binding and rendering data on the server and returning cross-browser-compatible HTML.

ASP.NET enables you to bind against a variety of sources, including properties and method call results, arrays and collections, and DataReaders and DataViews. Typically, binding is done either declaratively, by using the <%#expression%> syntax, or by programmatically setting the *DataSource* property of a control to the desired datasource. The data is bound by calling the *DataBind* method, either at the Page level (which binds all controls on the page) or on the control being bound (which binds the control and any child controls). The *DataBind* method causes the control and its children to evaluate any data-binding expression(s) associated with the control and assign the resulting values to the appropriate control attribute. Data binding allows controls like the *DataGrid* control, which can handle multiple rows and columns, to iterate over and format the data specified by their *DataSource* property for display.

Simple Data Binding

The simplest type of data-binding uses the <%#expression%> syntax to replace the <%#expression%> construct with the value represented by the expression. This is different than, for instance, the ASP <%=expression%> syntax. The substitution takes place only when DataBind() is called. For example, follow these steps to create a simple page that binds to a page-level property.

Bind data at the page level

1 In Visual Studio, open the project created in the previous example, Chapter_09. Right-click the root of the project in Solution Explorer, and on the shortcut menu, point to Add, and click Add Web Form. Name the form **SimpleDataBinding.aspx**.

2 Make SimpleDataBinding.aspx the start page by right-clicking it in Solution Explorer and clicking Set As Start Page on the shortcut menu.

3 Add a Textbox, a button, and a label to the Web form. Use the Properties pane to change the ID of the label to **lblHello**, and Visible to False. Change the text of the label to **Hello, <%# Name %>!**. Change the ID of the text box to **txtHello**. Change the ID of the button to **btnSubmit** and the text of the button to **Submit**. The resulting screen should look something like the following illustration.

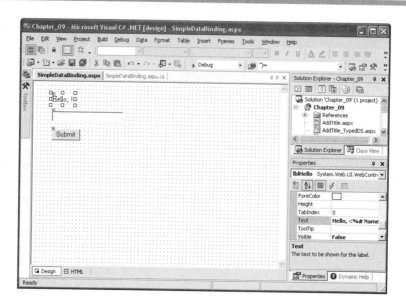

4   Double-click the button. An event handler called *btnSubmit_Click* will appear in the Code Editor. Add the following code to the event handler:

```
Name=txtHello.Text;
lblHello.Visible=true;
DataBind();
```

5   Outside of any function but inside the *SimpleDataBinding* class, add the following declaration for a string called Name:

```
protected string Name;
```

6   To save the solution, on the File menu, click Save All.

7   To build the application, on the Build menu, click Build Chapter_09.

8   To run the application, press F5 or on the Debug menu, click Start. Enter your name in the text box, and click Submit. The resulting screen should look like the following illustration:

Binding to Controls

The same syntax can be used to bind to controls. For example, you can bind the selected item of a *DropDownList* control to the *Text* property of an ASP.NET *Label* control using the code shown in the following example.

Bind data to a *Label* control

1 In Visual Studio, open the project created in the previous example, Chapter_09. Right-click the root of the project in Solution Explorer, and on the shortcut menu, point to Add, and click Add Web Form. Name the form **ControlBinding.aspx**.

2 Make ControlBinding.aspx the start page by right-clicking it in Solution Explorer and clicking Set As Start Page on the shortcut menu.

3 Add a label, a drop-down list, and a button to the form. Use the Properties pane to change the ID of the label to **lblFlavor**, and *Visible* to **False**. Change the text of the label to **Favorite Ice Cream: <%# MyList.SelectedItem.Text %>!** Change the ID of the drop-down list to **MyList**. Change the ID of the button to **btnSubmit** and the text of the button to **Submit**. Arrange components so that the resulting screen looks something like the following illustration:

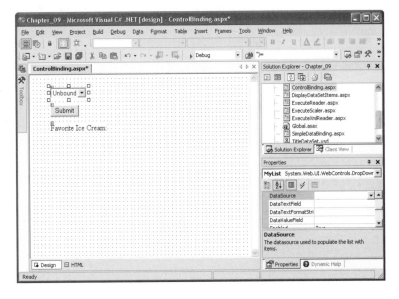

4 Switch to the Code Editor by pressing F7 or clicking Code on the view menu.

5 Add the following code to the *Page_Load event* handler:

```
if ( this.IsPostBack!=true )
{
    MyArrayList=new ArrayList();
    MyArrayList.Add("Chocolate");
    MyArrayList.Add("Vanilla");
    MyArrayList.Add("Strawberry");
    MyList.DataSource=MyArrayList;
    MyList.DataBind();
}
else
{
    this.lblFlavor.Visible=true;
}
this.DataBind();
```

6 Outside of any function but inside the *ControlBinding* class, add a declaration for an ArrayList called *MyArrayList*:

```
protected ArrayList MyArrayList;
```

7 To save the solution, on the File menu, click Save All.

8 To build the application, on the Build menu, click Build Chapter_09.

9 To run the application, press F5 or on the Debug menu, click Start. Click a flavor in the drop-down list, and click Submit. The resulting screen should look like the following illustration:

Using *DataBinder.Eval*

DataBinder.Eval is a static method that is used to evaluate a data-binding expression at runtime. This can simplify the process of casting various datatypes to be displayed as text. The basic syntax of *DataBinder.Eval* is

```
<%# DataBinder.Eval(Container, EvalExpression, FormatExpression) %>
```

Container is the object that contains the expression to be evaluated (for *DataGrid*, *DataList*, or *Repeater* controls, this is always *Container.DataItem*), *EvalExpression* is the full name of the property or item to be evaluated, and *FormatExpression* is a string formatting expression (such as {0:c}) to be used to format the string result. Note that if no format expression argument is passed, *DataBinder.Eval* will return an object instead of a string.

> **note**
>
> Because *DataBinder.Eval* uses late binding and reflection (which allows managed code to interrogate other managed code at runtime), it might be significantly slower than the other data-binding techniques. For this reason, you should only use DataBinder.Eval when you need to, such as for performing string formatting on numeric data.

Using the *DataBound* Controls

Chapter 8 looked at the ASP.NET server controls and mentioned briefly one very important group of controls. The *DataBound* controls, which include the *DataGrid* control (and its constituent controls), the *DataList* control, and the *Repeater* control, enable you to set a datasource programmatically. Then they iterate over that datasource and display the data based on formatting that you define, either through properties of the control or by adding template definitions. The neat thing about this is that you define the formatting for a single row and the data-bound controls take care of applying that formatting to all rows of data.

Choosing which control to use rests largely on the format you want your data to be in and how much control you want over the formatting of the data. The *DataGrid* control is the simplest to use and displays data in a table format. The *DataList* control is a little more involved in terms of implementation but it provides a greater degree of control over formatting through the use of templates. Finally, for the control freak in all of us, the *Repeater* control, which has no built-in formatting of its own, provides ultimate control over formatting through templates.

Using *DataGrids*

The *DataGrid* control presents bound data in a tabular format and provides a number of properties that you can use to format the data. This control can automatically generate all columns in the table from the datasource, or you can use specialized column controls to provide additional functionality or formatting for a given column or columns.

At its simplest, there are three basic steps to using a *DataGrid* control.

1   Add the DataGrid to the page.

2   Set the *DataSource* property of the DataGrid to an appropriate datasource. This datasource can be defined in the page, or you can call a method in an external object to supply the data.

3   Call the *DataBind* method of the control to automatically bind the data to the control. You can also call the *DataBind* method of the *Page* object, which will bind (or rebind) all the data-bound controls on the page by calling *DataBind* on each control in turn.

Let's look at an example. In "HTML Controls" in Chapter 8, there is an example that used a drop-down list to list flavors of ice cream. Suppose you want to show similar information in a table format. The problem with this approach is that the data is explicitly added to the control in the code (or declaratively by adding items to the control in its tag declaration). Thus, any time the data changes, you have to explicitly change the code that creates the control. Additionally, because the creation of the data and the creation of the control are tightly coupled, it's not possible to reuse this data, either elsewhere on the page or elsewhere in the application.

So in this first example, you'll create the data you want to use in a custom procedure in a <script> block, and then call that procedure to populate the datasource of your *DataGrid* control. Start with a very simple DataGrid that has no formatting whatsoever.

Bind an array to a DataGrid

1   In Visual Studio, open the project created in the previous example, Chapter_09. Right-click the root of the project in Solution Explorer, and on the shortcut menu, point to Add, and click Add Web Form. Name the form **DataGrid.aspx**.

2   Make DataGrid.aspx the start page by right-clicking it in Solution Explorer, and clicking Set As Start Page on the shortcut menu.

3 Drag a *Label* control and a *DataGrid* control from the Toolbox to the form. Change the ID DataGrid1 to MyGrid. Change the ID of the label to **Title**, and set the font and text as shown in the Properties pane in the following illustration:

4 Switch to the Code Editor by pressing F7 or clicking Code on the View menu.

5 Add the following function inside the class *DataGrid* class:

```
private ICollection CreateData()
{
    ArrayList DataArray=new ArrayList();

    DataArray.Add("Chocolate");
    DataArray.Add("Vanilla");
    DataArray.Add("Strawberry");
    DataArray.Add("Pistachio");
    DataArray.Add("Rocky Road");

    return DataArray;
}
```

6   Add the following code to the *Page_Load* event handler:

```
MyGrid.DataSource=CreateData();
MyGrid.DataBind();
```

7   To save the solution, on the File menu, click Save All.

8   To build the application, on the Build menu, click Build Chapter_09.

9   To run the application, press F5 or on the Debug menu, click Start. The resulting screen should look like the following illustration:

Although this is a very simple example, you used two lines of code (setting the DataSource and calling *DataBind*) to accomplish what would have taken considerably more code in classic ASP. Now let's jazz things up a bit by editing live data with multiple columns per row in a grid.

Bind live data to a DataGrid

1   In Visual Studio, open the project created in the previous example, Chapter_09. Right-click the root of the project in Solution Explorer, and on the shortcut menu, point to Add and click Add Web Form. Name the form **DataGridEdit.aspx**.

2   Make DataGridEdit.aspx the start page by right-clicking it in Solution Explorer and clicking Set As Start Page on the shortcut menu.

3   Add a *DataGrid* control to the form by dragging it from the Toolbox to the form. Change the *ID* DataGrid1 to **MyGrid**.

4   Switch to the Code Editor by pressing F7 or clicking Code on the View menu.

5   Add the following *using* clause to the top of the source file:

```
using System.Data.SqlClient;
```

6   Add the following method inside the *DataGridEdit* class:

```
private void BindData(string SortBy)
{
  string ConnStr;
  ConnStr=@"server=(local)\VSdotNET;database=pubs;" +
    "Trusted_Connection=yes";
  string SQL;
  SQL="SELECT * FROM Publishers";
  if ( SortBy!=null && SortBy!="" )
  {
    SQL+=" ORDER BY " + SortBy;
  }
  SqlConnection MySqlConn=
   new SqlConnection(ConnStr);
  SqlCommand MySqlCmd=new SqlCommand(SQL,MySqlConn);
  MySqlConn.Open();
  try
  {
    MyGrid.DataSource=MySqlCmd.ExecuteReader();
    MyGrid.DataBind();
  }
  finally
  {
    MySqlConn.Close();
  }
}
```

7   Add the following code to the *Page_Load* event handler:

```
if ( this.IsPostBack!=true )
{
    BindData("");
}
```

8   To save the solution, on the File menu, click Save All.

9   To build the application, on the Build menu, click Build Chapter_09.

10   To run the application, press F5 or on the Debug menu, click Start. The resulting screen should look like the following illustration:

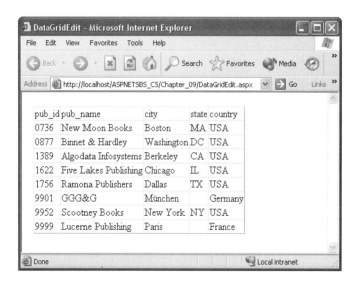

But wait! There's more. In addition to autogenerating columns from the bound data, DataGrids also support creating columns declaratively. This gives you greater control over both the formatting and the behavior of individual columns. For example, you can use a *BoundColumn* control to provide customized header text for a column or to apply special formatting to the bound text in each row. You can also use a *ButtonColumn* control to display a command button in each row of a column, an *EditButtonColumn* control to provide in-place editing for a row, and a *HyperlinkColumn* control to provide a hyperlink for each row of the grid with the text caption, the URL, or both being data-bound. Finally, you can use a *TemplateColumn* control to apply complex formatting to each row of a specific column. In addition to manually creating and modifying the various controls within the grid, you can use Visual Studio .NET to control the behavior and look of the DataGrid. Let's see how we can improve this example's appearance using the Visual Studio .NET tools.

Use Visual Studio .NET to format a DataGrid

1   In Visual Studio, open the project created in the previous example, Chapter_09. Continue working on DataGridEdit.aspx.

2   Click the *DataGrid* control. Toward the bottom of the Properties pane, you will see two links to tools specially designed to control the *DataGrid* control.

3 Click the Auto Format link, and the Auto Format dialog box will appear. Click Professional 1 in the Select A Scheme list, as shown in the following illustration:

4 Choosing the scheme in the Auto Format dialog box changes the HTML declaration for the DataGrid from a very simple declaration to something like the following code. Using schemes helps you quickly create a consistent look for all your grids.

```
<asp:DataGrid id="MyGrid"
   style="Z-INDEX: 101; LEFT: 19px; POSITION: absolute; TOP:
   22px" runat="server"
   BorderColor="#999999" BorderStyle="None" BorderWidth="1px"
   BackColor="White" CellPadding="3" GridLines="Vertical">
   <SelectedItemStyle Font-Bold="True" ForeColor="White"
   BackColor="#008A8C">
```

```
      </SelectedItemStyle>
    <AlternatingItemStyle BackColor="#DCDCDC">
      </AlternatingItemStyle>
    <ItemStyle ForeColor="Black" BackColor="#EEEEEE">
      </ItemStyle>
    <HeaderStyle Font-Bold="True" ForeColor="White"
    BackColor="#000084">
      </HeaderStyle>
    <FooterStyle ForeColor="Black" BackColor="#CCCCCC">
      </FooterStyle>
    <PagerStyle HorizontalAlign="Center" ForeColor="Black"
      BackColor="#999999" Mode="NumericPages">
      </PagerStyle>
  </asp:DataGrid>
```

5   Click the Property Builder link at the bottom of the Properties pane.
The MyGrid Properties dialog box appears:

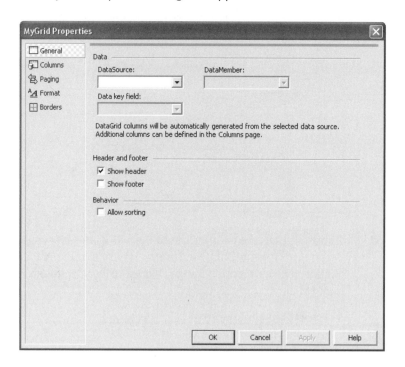

6 Click Columns in the left side of the dialog box. Clear the Create Columns Automatically At Run Time check box. Add columns to allow each field to have friendlier names. Use the header text and data fields in the following table and eventually the dialog box will look like the next illustration.

Header text	Data field
Publisher ID	pub_id
Publisher Name	pub_name
City	city
State	state
Country	country

7   Click Paging on the left side, and the dialog box changes to something like the following illustration. The data here does not warrant paging, so leave it as it stands.

8   Click Format on the left side, and click Header in the Objects box. In the Horizontal Alignment drop-down list, click Center. This will change the horizontal alignment of all titles in the header. Double click Columns to expand the list of Columns, and then double click Columns[0] Publisher ID to expand the Publisher ID column. Change Horizontal Alignment to Center. This will change the alignment of the items displayed as the Publisher ID. This is what the dialog box looks like:

9   Click the Apply button, and click OK to close the dialog box.

10 To save the solution, on the File menu, click Save All.

11 To build the application, on the Build menu, click Build Chapter_09.

12 To run the application, press F5 or on the Debug menu, click Start.
        The resulting screen should look like the following illustration:

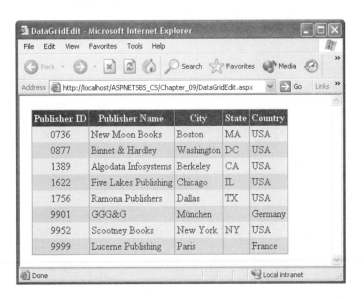

This looks much better, but there is still more we can do to improve this example. We might want to add the ability to sort by one or more of the columns.

Sort a DataGrid

1　In Visual Studio, open the project created in the previous example, Chapter_09. Double-click the project in Solution Explorer. Continue working on DataGridEdit.aspx.

2　Click the Property Builder link, and the MyGrid Properties dialog box will appear. With General selected in the left pane of the window, check the last checkbox in the right pane that is labeled Allow sorting. Click Columns on the left side of the dialog box, and set the Sort Expression for each column to the name of the field on which the column is based. Click Apply or OK to exit the dialog box. For instance, the Publisher ID column should look like this illustration:

3 Click the DataGrid, and click the lightning bolt in the Properties pane to show the events available in the grid. Double-click the field to the right of SortCommand. The Code Editor will appear inside *MyGrid_SortCommand*. This method is passed an object representing the sender, and a *DataGridSortCommandEventArgs* that contains information to be used in processing the sort request. Add the following code:

```
SortExpression=e.SortExpression.ToString();
BindData(e.SortExpression.ToString());
```

4 Add the following declaration inside the *DataGridEdit* Class, above the *BindData* method:

```
private string SortExpression;
```

5 To save the solution, on the File menu, click Save All.

6 To build the application, on the Build menu, click Build Chapter_09.

7 To run the application, press F5 or on the Debug menu, click Start. The resulting screen should look like the following illustration:

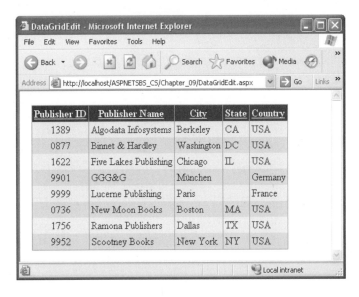

You can run this example and click any of the column headers to sort the data by the selected column. Because you specify the exact sort expression, you can actually make the sort more complex, perhaps sorting by State and City when you click the State header. Next you might want to allow editing to take place. The following example shows how editing can be added.

Edit and delete data in a DataGrid

1   In Visual Studio, open the project created in the previous example, Chapter_09. Continue working on DataGridEdit.aspx.

2   Click the DataGrid, and click the link to the Property Builder. Click Columns on the left side of the dialog box, and click Button Column label to expand the types of buttons. Add Edit, Update,Cancel and Delete to the selected columns. Rearrange the columns so that the Edit, Update, Cancel button is first and Delete is second, as shown in the following illustration. Click OK.

3   With the DataGrid selected, change the DataKeyField in the Properties pane to pub_id. The DataKeyField is used to control what field is used as the primary key for editing, which enables you to identify the selected record.

4 Click the lightning bolt in the Properties pane, and double-click the field next to EditCommand. The Code Editor will appear inside the *MyGrid_EditCommand* event handler. This handler is passed an object representing the sender, and a *DataGridCommandEventArgs* object. We set the EditItemIndex to the index passed in as a member of the *DataGridCommandEventArgs* object. Insert the following code:

```
MyGrid.EditItemIndex=e.Item.ItemIndex;
BindData(SortExpression);
```

5 Click the DataGridEdit.aspx tab and double-click the field next to CancelCommand. The Code editor will appear inside the *MyGrid_CancelCommand* event handler. This handler is passed an object representing the sender, and a *DataGridCommandEventArgs* object. By setting the EditItemIndex to -1, we let the grid know that no row should be selected as an edit row. Insert the following code:

```
MyGrid.EditItemIndex=-1;
BindData(SortExpression);
```

6 Click the DataGridEdit.aspx tab, and double-click the field next to UpdateCommand. The Code Editor will appear inside the *MyGrid_UpdateCommand* event handler. This handler is passed an object representing the sender, and a *DataGridCommandEventArgs* object. The following code uses a simple SQL statement to do the actual update in the database. Finally, the *EditItemIndex* is reset to -1 and data is rebound by calling *BindData*. Insert the following code:

```
string ConnStr;
string SQL;
TextBox pub_id,pub_name,city,state,country;
ConnStr=@"server=(local)\VSdotNET;database=pubs;" +
    "Trusted_Connection=yes";
SqlConnection MySqlConn=
    new SqlConnection(ConnStr);
pub_id=(TextBox)e.Item.Cells[2].Controls[0];
pub_name=(TextBox)e.Item.Cells[3].Controls[0];
city=(TextBox)e.Item.Cells[4].Controls[0];
state=(TextBox)e.Item.Cells[5].Controls[0];
country=(TextBox)e.Item.Cells[6].Controls[0];
```

```
SQL="UPDATE Publishers SET "+
    "pub_name='" + pub_name.Text + "'," +
    "city='" + city.Text + "', " +
    "state='" + state.Text + "', " +
    "country='" + country.Text + "' " +
    " WHERE pub_id='" + pub_id.Text + "' ";
MySqlConn.Open();
try
{
    SqlCommand MySqlCmd=new SqlCommand(SQL,MySqlConn);
    MySqlCmd.ExecuteNonQuery();
}
finally
{
    MySqlConn.Close();
    MyGrid.EditItemIndex=-1;
    BindData(SortExpression);
}
```

7   Go back to DataGridEdit.aspx and double-click the field next
to DeleteCommand. The Code Editor will appear inside the
MyGrid_DeleteCommand event handler. This handler is passed an
object representing the sender, and a *DataGridCommandEventArgs* object.
The following code uses a simple SQL statement to do the actual delete
in the database. Insert the following code:

```
string key;
string ConnStr;
string SQL;

ConnStr=@"server=(local)\VSdotNET;database=pubs;" +
    "Trusted_Connection=yes";
SqlConnection MySqlConn=
    new SqlConnection(ConnStr);
key=MyGrid.DataKeys[(int)e.Item.ItemIndex].ToString();
SQL="DELETE FROM Publishers "+
    " WHERE pub_id='" + key + "' ";
MySqlConn.Open();
try
```

```
{
    SqlCommand MySqlCmd=new SqlCommand(SQL,MySqlConn);
    MySqlCmd.ExecuteNonQuery();
}
finally
{
    MySqlConn.Close();
    MyGrid.EditItemIndex=-1;
    BindData(SortExpression);
}
}
```

8 To save the solution, on the File menu, click Save All.

9 To build the application, on the Build menu, click Build Chapter_09.

10 To run the application, press F5 or on the Debug menu, click Start. Click the Edit link for one of the items. The resulting screen should look like the following illustration:

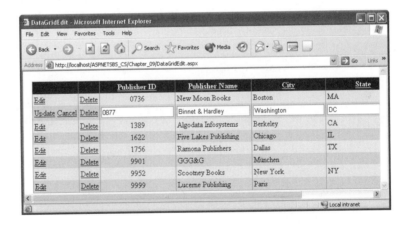

important

In-place editing in a DataGrid is not always the best way to provide editing. Alternatively, especially when there are a number of columns, you could insert a link column to an edit form or even use the EditCommand to link to a different view of the data for editing.

Using DataLists

DataLists provide an excellent mix of built-in functionality and control over display formatting. Unlike the *DataGrid* control, in which the rows are displayed one after the other in a table format, the DataList can display its items in multiple columns and can display rows horizontally or vertically.

Follow these steps to display information from the Titles table of the Pubs SQL Server sample database.

Bind to a *DataList* control

1   In Visual Studio, open the project created in the previous example, Chapter_09. Right-click the root of the project in Solution Explorer, and on the shortcut menu, point to Add, and click Add Web Form. Name the form **TitlesDataList1.aspx**.

2   Make TitlesDataList1.aspx the start page by right-clicking it in Solution Explorer and clicking Set As Start Page on the shortcut menu.

3   Drag a label and a data list from the Toolbox onto the form. Change the *Text* of the label to **Binding to a DataList control** and change the *Font-Name* to **Verdana** and the *Font*-Size to **Large**. Change the *ID* of the data list to **TitleList**, *RepeatColumns* to **3**, and *GridLines* to **Both**.

4   Although Visual Studio .NET has a Property Builder for *DataList* controls, sometimes it is better to manually create the code to be displayed for each row in the DataList. In this case, you will start with a simple bit of code for the Item Template, but it will become more complex as the example becomes more complex. To do this, move into HTML mode by clicking the HTML tab at the bottom of the design window. Find the *asp:DataList* opening tag, and between the opening and closing *asp:DataList* tags, insert the following code:

```
<ItemTemplate>
 <h5><%# DataBinder.Eval(Container.DataItem,"title")%></h5>
 <br/>
</ItemTemplate>
```

5 Switch to the Code Editor by pressing F7 or clicking Code on the View menu.

6 Add the following code to the *using* clauses at the top of the code file:

```
using System.Data.SqlClient;
```

7 Scroll down to the *Page_Load* event handler. In this example, you will use a DataAdapter and a DataSet to fill the DataList. Insert the following code:

```
string ConnStr;
DataSet MyDS=new DataSet();
ConnStr=@"server=(local)\VSdotNET;database=pubs;" +
   "Trusted_Connection=yes";
string SQL;
SQL="SELECT * FROM Titles ORDER BY Title";
SqlConnection MySqlConn=
   new SqlConnection(ConnStr);
SqlDataAdapter MySqlAdapter=
   new SqlDataAdapter(SQL,MySqlConn);
MySqlConn.Open();
try
{
   MySqlAdapter.Fill(MyDS);
   TitleList.DataSource=MyDS.Tables[0].DefaultView;
   TitleList.DataBind();
}
finally
{
   MySqlConn.Close();
}
```

8 To save the solution, on the File menu, click Save All.

9 To build the application, on the Build menu, click Build Chapter_09.

10   To run the application, press F5 or click Start on the Debug menu. The resulting screen should look like the following illustration:

Clearly, this layout isn't too pleasing visually, so let's spice it up a bit.

Add fancy formatting to a DataList

1   In Visual Studio, open the project created in the previous example, Chapter_09. Double-click on TitlesDataList1.aspx to open it.

2   Save TitlesDataList1.aspx as TitlesDataList2.aspx. Make sure you are in TitlesDataList1.aspx file in Visual Studio, and then on the File menu, click Save TitlesDataList1.aspx As. Enter **TitlesDataList2.aspx** as the new file name, and click Save. Switch to HTML mode by clicking the HTML tab at the bottom of the design window. Change the HTML Title (inside opening and closing Title tags) to **TitlesDataList2**. Delete everything between the opening and closing <ItemTemplate> tags and insert this code between the opening and closing <ItemTemplate> tags. (Note that the first table row uses a format string containing the path to an image file with a place-holder for the title_id to bind the title_id for each item to its graphic. This path must point to somewhere that is a virtual directory, or under a virtual directory set up in IIS. The path in the example will be present if you have installed the ASP.NET Quickstarts programs.)

```
<table>
 <tr>
  <td rowspan="4">
   <img align="top"
     src='<%# DataBinder.Eval(Container.DataItem, "title_id",
       "/quickstart/aspplus/images/title-{0}.gif") %>' >
  </td>
 </tr>
 <tr>
  <td>
   <em>Title: </em>
  </td>
  <td nowrap>
   <%# DataBinder.Eval(Container.DataItem, "title")%>
   <br/>
  </td>
 </tr>
 <tr>
  <td>
   <em>Price: </em>
  </td>
  <td nowrap>
   <%# DataBinder.Eval(Container.DataItem, "price", "{0:c}")%>
   <br/>
  </td>
 </tr>
 <tr>
  <td>
   <em>Category: </em>
  </td>
  <td nowrap>
   <%# DataBinder.Eval(Container.DataItem, "type")%>
   <br/>
  </td>
 </tr>
</table>
```

3   To save the solution, on the File menu, click Save All.

4   To build the application, on the Build menu, click Build Chapter_09.

5   To run the application, press F5 or on the Debug menu, click Start. The resulting screen should look like the following illustration:

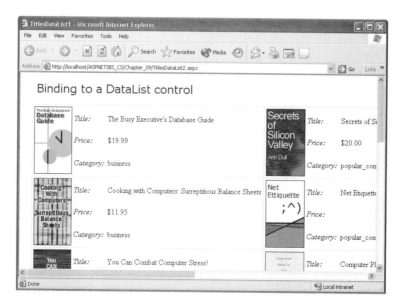

The <ItemTemplate> is only one of the templates that can be used with the *DataList* control, but they all work similarly. Other templates you can define include the following:

- **AlternatingItemTemplate**   Sets the formatting for alternating items
- **EditItemTemplate**   Formats the fields used when an item in the data list is switched to Edit mode
- **FooterTemplate**   Sets formatting for the footer of the data list
- **HeaderTemplate**   Sets formatting for the header of the data list
- **SelectedItemTemplate**   Sets the formatting for the item in the data list that has been selected by the user
- **SeparatorTemplate**   Sets the format of the divider between items in the data list

Like a data grid, a data list can be set up for in-place editing of values. This requires adding a *LinkButton* or *Button* control to the ItemTemplate with the *CommandName* set to edit; implementing an *EditItemTemplate*; setting up the event handlers for the *EditCommand*, *DeleteCommand*, *CancelCommand*, and *UpdateCommand* events; and mapping the event handlers to the events. When the Edit button for an item is clicked, the event handler should set the *EditItemIndex* to the number of the item that was clicked, which can be retrieved from the *DataListCommandEventArgs* passed to the event handler. The *EditItemTemplate* should include *LinkButton* or *Button* controls for the *DeleteCommand*, *CancelCommand*, and *UpdateCommand*, and event handlers should be added for each.

Using Repeaters

The *Repeater* control lets you go "hog-wild" with templates. If you can write it in HTML and/or server controls, you can put it into a template.

important

Because of the way that you add HTML code to a Repeater, it is possible to create a perfectly valid page that will not display properly in the Visual Studio .NET Designer window.

The following example shows how the previous example can be updated to work with a Repeater instead of a data list. It adds a *HeaderTemplate* and a *SeparatorTemplate* to further improve the look of the page.

Use a *Repeater* control with headers and separators

1   In Visual Studio, open the project created in the previous example, Chapter_09. Right-click the root of the project in Solution Explorer, and on the shortcut menu, point to Add and click Add Web Form. Name the form **TitlesRepeater.aspx**.

2   Make TitlesRepeater.aspx the start page by right-clicking it in Solution Explorer, and clicking Set As Start Page on the shortcut menu.

3   When using a *Repeater* control, you will want to use FlowLayout rather than the default, GridLayout. The *Repeater* control does not allow for placement using the grid layout and will move to the upper left corner of the page even in GridLayout mode. Change to FlowLayout by right-clicking the page, clicking Properties on the shortcut menu, and then setting the page layout to FlowLayout.

4   Drag a label and a DataList from the Toolbox to the form. Change the text of the label to **Binding to a Repeater control**. Change the font size to **Larger**, and the font nme to **Verdana**. Change the ID of the Repeater to **MyRepeater**.

5   Although Visual Studio .NET has a Property Builder for *Repeater* controls, sometimes it is better to manually create the code to be displayed for each row in the Repeater. In this case, you will start with a simple bit of code for the Item Template, but it will become more complex as the example becomes more complex. To do this, move into HTML mode by clicking the HTML tab at the bottom of the design window. Find the *asp:Repeater* opening tag, and between the opening and closing *asp:Repeater* tags, insert the following code:

```
<ItemTemplate>
    <table>
        <tr>
            <td rowspan="4">
                <img align="top"
                src='<%# DataBinder.Eval(Container.DataItem,
                "title_id", "/quickstart/aspplus/images
                /title-{0}.gif") %>' >
            </td>
        </tr>
        <tr>
            <td>
                <em>Title: </em>
            </td>
            <td nowrap>
            <%# DataBinder.Eval(Container.DataItem, "title")%>
                <br/>
            </td>
        </tr>
        <tr>
            <td>
                <em>Price: </em>
```

```
        </td>
        <td nowrap>
        <%# DataBinder.Eval(Container.DataItem, "price",
            "{0:c}")%>
            <br/>
          </td>
      </tr>
      <tr>
        <td>
          <em>Category: </em>
        </td>
        <td nowrap>
        <%# DataBinder.Eval(Container.DataItem, "type")%>
            <br/>
          </td>
      </tr>
    </table>
</ItemTemplate>
<HeaderTemplate>
    <h4 style="background-color:silver;">Titles</h4>
</HeaderTemplate>
<SeparatorTemplate>
    <hr>
</SeparatorTemplate>
```

6　Switch to the Code Editor by pressing F7 or clicking Code on the View menu.

7　Add the following code to the *using* clauses at the top of the code file:

```
using System.Data.SqlClient;
```

8　Scroll down to the *Page_Load* event handler. In this example, you will use a DataAdapter and a DataSet to fill the DataList. This code is identical to the code in the previous example except that a Repeater is data bound rather than a DataList. Insert the following code:

```
string ConnStr;
DataSet MyDS=new DataSet();
ConnStr=@"server=(local)\VSdotNET;database=pubs;" +
    "Trusted_Connection=yes";
string SQL;
SQL="SELECT * FROM Titles";
SqlConnection MySqlConn=
```

```
    new SqlConnection(ConnStr);
SqlDataAdapter MySqlAdapter=
    new SqlDataAdapter(SQL,MySqlConn);
MySqlConn.Open();
try
{
    MySqlAdapter.Fill(MyDS);
    MyRepeater.DataSource=MyDS.Tables[0].DefaultView;
    MyRepeater.DataBind();
}
finally
{
    MySqlConn.Close();
}
```

9   To save the solution, on the File menu, click Save All.

10   To build the application, on the Build menu, click Build Chapter_09.

11   To run the application, press F5 or click Start on the Debug menu.
        The resulting screen should look like the following illustration:

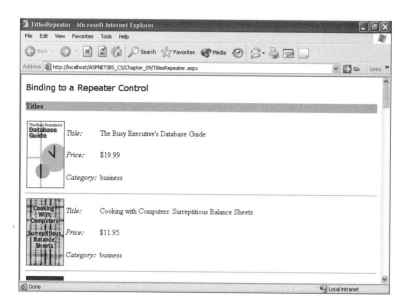

Remember that for the images to be displayed, the ASP.NET QuickStart samples
must be installed.

All templates available to the DataList control can be used with the Repeater control, and editing is handled the same with a Repeater as with a DataList.

Chapter 9 Quick Reference

To	Do this
Connect to a SQL Server database	Create and open an instance of the SqlConnection class from the System.Data.SqlClient namespace.
Connect to an OLE DB datasource	Create and open an instance of the OleDbConnection class from the System.Data.OleDb namespace.
Execute SELECT, UPDATE, INSERT, or DELETE statements against a database	Create an instance of the SqlCommand or OleDbCommand class, and call one of its Execute methods.
Use an in-memory cache of hierarchical data	Create an instance of the DataSet class from the System.Data namespace. Populate the DataSet by calling the Fill method of the SqlDataAdapter or OleDbDataAdapter class.
Display read-only data in a bound control	Bind the control to a SqlDataReader or an OleDbDataReader. Be sure to pass the CommandBehavior.CloseConnection argument to the ExecuteReader method when creating the DataReader.
Bind data to a control	Set the *DataSource* property of the control to the DataReader, data view, or other datasource, and then call the DataBind method of the control (or call the page's DataBind method).
Edit bound data in a data grid	Add an Edit, Update, Cancel button column using the Property Builder, and add event handlers for Edit, Update and Cancel in code.
Delete bound data in a data grid	Add a Delete button column using the Property Builder, and add a Delete event handler in code.
Display bound data in multiple columns	Use a DataList control and set the RepeatColumns attribute to the number of columns desired.
Display bound data with the greatest possible flexibility	Use a Repeater control, and manually add HTML code along with data binding directives.

PART 4

Beyond
The Basics

10

Creating Custom Server Controls

In this chapter, you will learn how to

✔ *Choose a base class for your control.*

✔ *Create a namespace for your control(s).*

✔ *Register and use your control in a page.*

✔ *Extend and aggregate existing controls.*

✔ *Maintain state in custom server controls.*

✔ *Handle postbacks.*

Having spent the last two chapters studying ASP.NET server controls, ADO.NET, and data binding, by now you're probably thinking, "These server controls sure are cool; I wish I could create my own." Well, wish no longer! In this chapter, you'll learn how to create custom ASP.NET server controls.

There are nearly as many reasons for developing custom server controls as there are developers, but generally they fall into three categories: reuse, specialization, and maintenance.

Creating custom server controls makes *reuse* easy. You can wrap a bunch of related functionality and UI elements into a control and then reuse that control where you need that functionality. For example, you can create a server control that encapsulates all the fields and validation logic necessary for user registration. Then instead of rewriting that code any time you need a user registration screen, you simply add your control to the page instead.

Specialization refers to taking an existing functionality, such as a server control, and adding your own customized functionality to it. Specialization in ASP.NET server controls is typically done through inheritance. You specialize in inheritance by inheriting from a class that provides most of the functionality you want, and then adding additional functions or overriding existing ones and adding your own implementation of those functions. The TextBoxPlus control sample later in this chapter provides an example of specialization.

Finally, custom ASP.NET server controls simplify the *maintenance* of your applications. After a server control has been developed and tested, it can be reused reliably in many places. If you find a bug in your control, it can be fixed in a single place (the source class for your control), and all you need to do to distribute the fix is replace the assembly containing the fixed control. This is a major improvement over reuse through include files, or having no reuse at all.

Creating Your First Control

Creating custom server controls with ASP.NET is fairly straightforward. A custom ASP.NET server control is any class that inherits from the *Control* class of the *System.Web.UI* namespace or one that inherits from any of the controls derived from Control. Choosing the control from which to derive your custom control is largely a matter of how much functionality you want to build into your control. You'll learn how to choose a control to inherit from later in this section.

All server controls that send output directly to the browser do so by overriding the *Render* method of the control from which they're derived. Controls that are derived from a control with its own UI rendering (such as the *TextBox* server control) should also call the *Render* method on the base class to have the base control render its own output. Note that the location in your code at which you call the *Render* method of the base class is important. That's where the rendered output of the base control will appear. The *Render* method of the sample file TextBoxPlus.cs on this book's companion Web site demonstrates this concept.

In addition to sending output to the browser directly through the *Render* method, some custom controls (in particular, compositional controls) send output to the browser indirectly by overriding the *CreateChildControls* method of the base *Control* class, which is used to add controls to a custom control at runtime. Some also call the *RenderChildren* method, which causes all the child controls of a given control to execute their *Render* methods.

tip

Although there is no inherent difference in the resulting HTML on the browser between rendering controls using the *Render* method and composing controls using the *CreateChildControls* method, there are differences in terms of performance and ease of programming. Using composition is somewhat easier for the developer, and it does not require any knowledge of HTML. Rendering offers better performance and reduced overhead, but you do need to know HTML to take advantage of it. Additionally, if you want to create a control that contains two distinct server controls (such as a text box with a built in validation control) a composite control is really the only way to go.

Creating a Namespace

Each custom control must belong to a namespace because the @ *Register* directive, which makes custom controls available for use in a page, has a *Namespace* attribute that is used to locate the control class to instantiate at runtime.

You create a namespace using the namespace keyword. In C#, you use the namespace keyword and a bracketed block of code following it to define the scope of the namespace.

```
namespace myNS
{
    // Class definitions, etc. go inside the namespace
}
```

Note that if you are creating your custom control using Visual Studio .NET, the IDE will create the namespace for you automatically.

important

Although Microsoft Visual Studio .NET creates a namespace for each new project automatically, this is implemented differently depending on the language you choose. For example, in a Visual C# project, the namespace keyword is added to class files and code-behind files automatically. In a Microsoft Visual Basic .NET Web application, the namespace for the project is defined by the Root Namespace option set in the Project Properties dialog box for the project. This means that although you will not actually see the namespace keyword in your class files, a namespace will be created when the class is compiled during the build process for the project.

In both languages, the default name for the namespace is the name of the project.

Creating a Class

Each custom server control is defined in a class. You can have more than one class defined in a single namespace within a file, but the class is what defines the boundary of the control. You can put multiple controls within a single file, if you want. When you compile this file, all the classes (and the controls they represent) are compiled into a single assembly. Having multiple related controls can make deploying your controls simpler.

You define classes in Visual Basic .NET with the class keyword. Similar to namespaces, classes in Visual Basic .NET are defined with a class keyword and a section of code enclosed in brackets that together define the scope of the class.

```
class myControl
{
    // Variables, procedures, etc.
}
```

As with namespaces, Visual Studio .NET automatically takes care of creating a class for you when you create a new Web Control Library project. This default Web control class, which inherits from the *WebControl* class in the *System.Web.UI.WebControls* namespace, contains a property declaration for a default *Text* property, as well as an overridden *Render* method that renders the contents of the *Text* property to the browser. These default members are provided to give you a head start on creating your own control functionality.

> ### important
>
> The Standard Edition of Visual Basic .NET, included with this Deluxe Learning Edition package, does not support the Web Control Library project type. You can, however, add a *Web Custom Control* to a Web Project, as you'll see in our first example. If you want to create a stand-alone assembly for your custom control for reuse in other projects, you can simply remove the default Web Form (WebForm1.aspx) from the Web Project and then add one or more *Web Custom Control* classes to the project for the control or controls you want to create.

Inheriting from a Base Class

One of the most important steps in creating a custom server control is choosing the class from which your control will inherit. This can be a more difficult decision than you might think because there are so many choices.

You need to consider both how the control will be used and who will use it. Because one of the reasons for creating custom controls is to reuse controls that have most (but not quite all) of the functionality you need, you might be tempted to simply jump right into inheriting a very rich control and get the most bang for your buck. You should keep in mind that any public property, method, or event exposed by the base control will be exposed by a derived control automatically. If you don't plan for this, your control might do something unexpected, or you might unwittingly introduce bugs when someone uses the control in a way that you didn't anticipate.

This might not be a problem if you are creating the control for your own use. If you plan to share it with others, however, remember that people can be very creative in finding ways to break software, and developers are more creative than most. By making a lot of public methods that you didn't write available, you increase the chances that another developer will break your code. To avoid this problem, you should generally inherit from the class that provides the fewest public members while still providing the desired functionality.

For example, if you want basic UI plumbing code but don't want the additional functionality of a *TextBox* or *Label* control, you can inherit from the *WebControl* class, which implements such basic UI features as the *BackColor* and *ForeColor* properties, and the *ApplyStyle* method. As noted earlier, this is the default for a *Web Custom Control* class added with Visual Studio .NET. If you don't need the UI plumbing, you can inherit from the *Control* class, which has no UI-related members. Of course, this means that you have to implement all UI-related code yourself.

Rendering Output from a Control

The final step in the implementation of a control is rendering its output. To do this, you override the *Render* method of the base class. Remember that as with choosing a base class to inherit from, this step is handled for you automatically when you add a *Web Custom Control* class to a Visual Studio .NET project.

```
protected override void Render(HtmlTextWriter output)
{
    // custom rendering code
}
```

As mentioned earlier, you can call the *Render* method of the base class to send its rendered output to the browser as well. This is useful mainly for controls that inherit from classes, such as the *TextBox* class, that define their own UI. Note that the call to the *Render* method of the base class can appear anywhere within the *Render* method of the derived control, enabling you to determine where in your custom control the rendered output of the base class will appear. The base keyword in the following snippet provides access to the members of the class from which the current class is inherited.

```
protected override void Render(HtmlTextWriter output)
{
    // custom rendering code
    base.Render(output)
    // additional custom rendering code, if desired
}
```

Note that because the ASP.NET runtime calls the overridden *Render* method automatically when the containing page is requested, passing in the necessary *HtmlTextWriter* instance, you can simply pass that instance as the argument to the *Render* method in the base class.

Building Your First Control in Visual Studio .NET

After you understand the basics of writing a control, the next step is actually writing one. There are several ways to create a control. You can use the tools provided with the .NET SDK and create the control in Notepad or a similar editor or you can use Visual Studio .NET. Depending on the version of Visual Studio .NET you are using, there are two ways to create your controls. If you are using the Professional version or greater, you can create a separate Web Control Library project to house your Web control. If you are using the Standard or Deluxe Learning Edition, you can only create Web controls as part of an ASP.NET Web Application project. In the examples that follow, the controls will be built using the latter method, which can be done in all versions of Visual Studio .NET.

In this first example, you'll create a control that adds a built-in label to a simple TextBox control.

Create an enhanced *TextBox* control

1   Open Visual Studio .NET and create a new ASP.NET Web Application project. Name the project **Chapter_10_Controls**. (If you're using the Professional Edition or above, you should use the Web Control Library project type instead.) If you are using the Standard or Deluxe Learning Edition, when the project creation has completed, delete WebForm1.aspx from the project by right-clicking the file in Solution Explorer and clicking Delete. Use the same techniques to delete Global.asax, Web.Config, and Chapter_10_Controls.vsdisco.

> **note**
>
> This example uses the ASP.NET Web Application project type to contain the custom controls because the Standard edition of Microsoft Visual C# .NET does not include the Web Control Library project type. You can use the ASP.NET Web Application project type because its output, a class library assembly (or DLL), is the same as the output of the Web Control Library. The major difference is that the ASP.NET Web Application project sets up an IIS Application folder for the project, from which the projects pages can be browsed. Ideally, you should always use the Web Control Library project type (if available) to avoid creating an unnecessary IIS Application folder.

2 Right-click the project in Solution Explorer, click Add, and then click Add Component. The dialog box that appears has quite a few likely sounding options (including Component Class), however, you should select the Web Custom Control entry toward the bottom of the list of options. Name the control **TextBoxPlus.cs** as shown in the following illustration:

The default class added by Visual Studio .NET is a completely functional, though otherwise uninteresting, example control. It inherits from the *WebControl* class, and contains a string property named *Text*. The *Render* method simply writes the *Text* property to the HTML stream being written. After being compiled, the control will reside in the *Chapter_10_Controls* namespace. Visual Studio .NET also automatically adds metadata attributes to the class to provide design-time support for the control. You'll learn about these attributes later in this chapter.

3   To customize the control, change the class that the control inherits from to the *TextBox* class (which also resides in the *System.Web.UI.WebControls* namespace) to reuse its functionality. Change the *Inherits* statement that immediately follows the class declaration from:

```
public class TextBoxPlus : System.Web.UI.WebControls.WebControl
```

to

```
public class TextBoxPlus : System.Web.UI.WebControls.TextBox
```

4   Because we are not using the *Text* property provided by default, change all occurrences of the word Text (which is the public name of the property) to **LabelText**, and all occurrences of *text* (which is the name of the private instance variable that contains the value of the property) to **labelText**. Note that these are differentiated by case of the first letter of the variable names because C# is case sensitive. The *LabelText* property will enable users of the control to set the text to be displayed with the text box.

5   To add a call to render the base control, add the following line within the *Render* method immediately after the call to output.Write:

```
base.Render(output);
```

This will cause the output of the base *TextBox* control to be rendered immediately following the text of the *LabelText* property. The complete code for the class is as follows (the attributes have been removed for clarity):

```
public class TextBoxPlus : System.Web.UI.WebControls.TextBox
{
  private string labelText;

  public string LabelText
  {
    get
    {
      return labelText;
    }
    set
    {
      labelText = value;
    }
  }

  /// <summary>
```

```
/// Render this control to the output parameter specified.
/// </summary>
/// <param name="output"> The HTML writer to write out to
    </param> protected override void Render(HtmlTextWriter
    output)
{
    output.Write(LabelText);
    base.Render(output);
}
}
}
}
```

6   Save the class file, and build the project. The control is now ready for use.

The next step is to actually use the control. To make it as easy as possible to use the control, you can add your custom control to the Visual Studio .NET Toolbox.

Add a custom Web control to the Toolbox

1   Create a new ASP.NET Web Application project. Name the project **Chapter_10**. The IDE should automatically load WebForm1.aspx when the project is created.

2   Right-click inside the Toolbox, and click Customize Toolbox on the shortcut menu. The dialog box shown in the following illustration will appear:

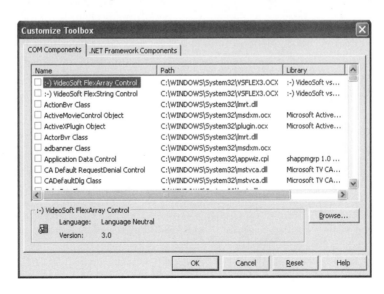

3   Click the .NET Framework Components tab, and then click the Browse button. In the Open dialog box, navigate to the bin folder under the Chapter_10_Controls project folder, select Chapter_10_Controls.dll, and then click the Open button. You will be returned to the previous dialog box with the *TextBoxPlus* control highlighted, as shown in the following illustration:

4   Click OK to close the Customize Toolbox dialog box. The *TextBoxPlus* control will be added to the Web Forms tab of the Toolbox.

Of course, adding the control to the Toolbox is only part of the process. Next you'll learn how to use the custom control on a Web Forms page.

Add a custom server control to a Web Form

1   In the Properties pane, change the *pageLayout* property of the WebForm1.aspx to **FlowLayout**.

2   If it's not already open, open the Toolbox, click the Web Forms tab, and then scroll to the bottom of the tab. You should see the *TextBoxPlus* control at the bottom of the list, as shown in the following illustration:

3   Double-click the *TextBoxPlus* control. This will add a copy of the control to
       WebForm1.aspx. Select the control, and use the Properties pane to change
       the *LabelText* property to **Name:**. The page with the control should look
       like the following illustration:

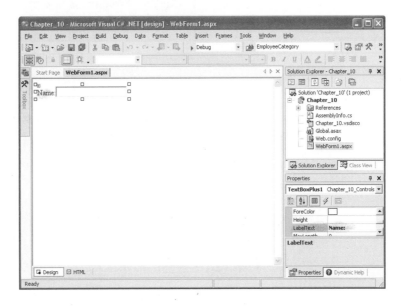

4   Save WebForm1.aspx, and then build the project.

5   Right-click WebForm1.aspx, click Browse With, click Microsoft Internet Explorer, and then click the Browse button. The output should look similar to the following illustration:

Although Visual Studio .NET makes it easy to add a control to a page, there is no magic involved. All the things that Visual Studio .NET does while adding a component can be done without Visual Studio .NET. It is important to understand some of the things that Visual Studio .NET is doing. When a control is added by double-clicking the control or dragging it from the Toolbox to the page, an @ *Register* directive is added at the top of the .aspx file, just below the @ *Page* directive. In this example, the @ *Register* directive is like the following line:

```
<%@ Register TagPrefix="cc1" Namespace="Chapter_10_Controls"
    Assembly="Chapter_10_Controls" %>
```

> **note**
>
> The default *TagPrefix* used by Visual Studio .NET is cc1, cc2 and so on. You can manually change the *TagPrefix* and then change the beginning namespace part of the opening and closing tag from cc1: to whatever you would like to use. Alternatively, you can use the *TagPrefix* attribute in the control to specify a *TagPrefix* to be used when the control is dropped onto a form in Visual Studio .NET. The following line should be added just above the opening of the namespace:
>
> ```
> <assembly:TagPrefix("TextBoxPlus","MyControls")>
> ```
>
> Using this line, *TextBoxPlus* would have a *TagPrefix* of MyControls rather than cc1.

Additionally, the tag to create the control is added wherever the control has been dropped (or at the cursor location, in the case of double-clicking the control in the Toolbox):

```
<cc1:TextBoxPlus id="TextBoxPlus1" runat="server"
LabelText="Name:"></cc1:TextBoxPlus>
```

Private vs. Shared Assemblies

By default, all the custom assemblies you create are private and are made available to a Web application by placing them in the bin directory of the application, where they are loaded by ASP.NET automatically. Assemblies can also be shared across all clients on a machine by placing them in the Global Assembly Cache (GAC). Barring any security configuration in the assembly that prevents it, assemblies in the GAC can be used by any managed application on that machine.

Private assemblies enable you to limit the use of an assembly to the application in whose bin subdirectory the assembly resides. Shared assemblies enable you to reuse your assemblies in multiple applications without needing to maintain a copy of an assembly for each application that uses it.

To install an assembly into the GAC, you need to give the assembly a strong name (and sign it with a public key, which you can generate with the sn.exe .NET Framework utility). Then add it to the GAC either by using the gacutil.exe .NET Framework utility or by dragging the assembly into the %windir%\assembly folder, which will add the assembly to the GAC automatically. Note that when deploying assemblies to the GAC for production applications, Microsoft recommends using Microsoft Windows Installer 2.0 to install the assembly to the GAC, which provides rollback protection, as well as automated uninstall. The Web Setup project type, available in Visual Studio .NET Professional and above, will create a Windows Installer package for your Web application to which you can add a Global Assembly Cache folder containing any controls you wish to install in the GAC.

The GAC supports versioning of assemblies, so you can install multiple versions of the same assembly by setting its *AssemblyVersionAttribute* attribute. Clients can then specify which version of an assembly to load at runtime. This attribute is added to the AssemblyInfo.vb (or AssemblyInfo.cs, for C# projects) file automatically by Visual Studio .NET, with the value *1.0.**, which automatically increments the build number of the assembly each time the project is built.

Adding Custom Controls Programmatically

In addition to adding the control to the page declaratively as shown earlier, you can add custom controls to the page programmatically, just as you can with the standard ASP.NET server controls. Adding controls programmatically does not require the @ *Register* directive. If you created the control in a project separate from the project in which it will be used, you might want to add an *Imports* directive to the code-behind class to avoid the need to use the fully qualified name to refer to the controls in your assembly.

Add a control programmatically

1   If it's not already open, open the Chapter_10 project created earlier.

2   Add a new Web Form to the project. Name the form **AddControl.aspx**, and change its *pageLayout* property to **FlowLayout**.

3   Double-click anywhere on the page and you will see the *Page_Load* event handler in the code-behind module for AddControl.aspx. Add the following code to the event handler:

```
Chapter_10_Controls.TextBoxPlus TBP
    =new Chapter_10_Controls.TextBoxPlus();
TBP.LabelText="Programmatic Control Label: ";
this.Controls.Add(TBP);
```

4   Save the changes, and then build the project. Right-click AddControl.aspx and on the shortcut menu, click Browse With. Select Microsoft Internet Explorer, and then click the Browse button.

The result will be an error informing you that " Control '_ctl0' of type 'TextBoxPlus' must be placed inside a form tag with runat=server." The reason for this error is that the *Add* method of the *Controls* collection actually places the added control at the end of the controls collection. In this case, that means the control is placed after the last HTML tag in the page (which is represented in the Controls collection as an ASP.NET Literal control). Because the *TextBox* control from which *TextBoxPlus* is derived must be placed between the <form runat="server"> and </form> tags, this code generates an exception. There are a couple of solutions for this. First you could use the *AddAt* method rather than the *Add* method to add the control to the Controls collection. *AddAt* takes an additional parameter: an index into the array of controls. This is not an ideal solution because you need to know which index to use. A better solution is adding an ASP.NET Placeholder control.

5   Switch back to AddControl.aspx by clicking its tab in the editor, or double clicking AddControl.aspx in Solution Explorer. Drag a *PlaceHolder* control from the Toolbox onto the page.

6 Switch back to the *Page_Load* event handler by double-clicking anywhere on the page. Change the following line:

```
this.Controls.Add(TBP);
```

to:

```
PlaceHolder1.Controls.Add(TBP);
```

Because dragging the *PlaceHolder* control onto the page inserted it between the <form runat="server"> and </form> tags, adding the *TextBoxPlus* control to the placeholder's *Controls* collection ensures that the control will be rendered in the desired location (and one that won't generate an exception).

7 Save the changes, and then build the project. Browse AddControl.aspx, and the output should look similar to the following illustration:

Adding Functionality

As cool as it might be to create and consume a custom server control in a very few lines of code (including both the control and the Web Forms page that consumes it), it provides minimal functionality. Clearly, to be truly useful, you need to add to the control.

The next several sections will look at how to add properties and methods to a control, create, raise and handle events, handle postbacks, maintain state in a control, and create templated controls. By the end of this section, you'll be able to add a significant amount of functionality to what is now a very simple control.

Adding Properties and Methods

To make the control more functional, you're going to provide a property that determines the type of data entered into the text box. You'll also define a method to format text entered into the text box based on this property.

Add a property

1   Open the project Chapter_10_Controls if it is not already open, and then open TextBoxPlus.cs.

2   Add the following code to the top of the file, just below the ~~Imports~~ *using* statements. The code creates an enumeration that defines the allowable values of the property you're going to add.

```
public enum TextTypes
{
  CurrencyText,
  DecimalText,
  PlainText
}
```

3   Copy the *labelText* variable definition and paste a copy below the original. Change the name of the copy to **textType**, and change the type from String to **TextTypes**. This will restrict the allowable values for this property to those defined by the TextType enumeration.

4   Copy the *LabelText* property procedure and paste a copy below the original. Change the *DefaultValue* attribute of this property to **PlainText**, and then Modify the property procedure so that it looks like the following code:

```
[Bindable(true),
Category("Appearance"),
DefaultValue("PlainText")]
public TextTypes TextType
{
  get
  {
    return textType;
  }
  set
  {
    textType = value;
  }
}
```

5   Save the file, but don't close it yet.

Add a method

1 Add the following code directly below the closing curly brace of the *Render* method. Using the *FormatCurrency* and *Format* methods ensures that the currency and decimal formatting will work for multiple locales, based on the *LCID* attribute of the @ *Page* directive.

```
protected void FormatText()
{
  switch(textType)
  {
    case TextTypes.CurrencyText:
      this.Text=(double.Parse(this.Text)).ToString("C");
      break;
    case TextTypes.DecimalText:
      this.Text=(Convert.ToInt32(this.Text)).ToString("F");
      break;
  }
}
```

2 Add the following code to the *Render* method, before the call to *base.Render*. Checking the *IsPostBack* method prevents the *Text* property from being formatted at design-time because the *Render* method of the control is called at design-time each time a property of the control is altered, to display the design-time rendering of the control.

```
if ( Page.IsPostBack )
{
  if ( textType!=TextTypes.PlainText )
  {
    this.FormatText();
  }
}
```

3 Save the class file and rebuild the project.

4 Close the Chapter_10_Controls project, and open the Chapter_10 project. Add a new Web Form to the project, and name it **TBP_Client.aspx**.

5 Change the *pageLayout* property of the page to **FlowLayout**.

6 Using the Toolbox, add an instance of the *TextBoxPlus* control to the page, and then add a *Button* control to the page.

7 Set the *TextType* property of the *TextBoxPlus* control to **CurrencyText**, and the *LabelText* property to **Enter a whole number:**.

8   Save TBP_Client.aspx, build the project, and then browse the page. The output should look similar to the following illustration:

9   Enter **250** in the text box, and click the button. The resulting output should look similar to the following illustration:

If you add the *LCID* attribute to the @ *Page* directive and set its value to that of a country other than the United States (such as 2057 for the United Kingdom), the output of the *TextBoxPlus* control will automatically reflect the change, with no changes to the control necessary.

Creating More Advanced Controls

As you have seen in the previous sections, ASP.NET makes it very easy to create useful controls by inheriting from an existing control and then adding properties and methods to create a specialized version of that control. But the fun doesn't stop there. You can override control methods to allow your control to participate in the postback process, and create custom events for your control. In this section, you'll learn about these techniques, including how to build a registration and login control that implements them.

Handling Postbacks

As discussed previously, a *postback* is the process by which a Web Forms page submits an HTTP POST request to itself in response to some user action, such as clicking a button. The postback itself is initiated by a control that causes the HTML form to be submitted, such as a client-side button element, the *Button* server control, or a server control that emits JavaScript code to submit the page, such as the *DropDownList* control (note that the *DropDownList* control only emits JavaScript code for posting back the page if its *AutoPostBack* property is set to *True*). In this section, we'll focus on the processing of postbacks, which occurs on the server after the postback has been initiated by the user's action. At some point, it is likely that you will want to develop a control that handles postback data and/or events. In this section, you'll learn how to handle both.

There are three phases in the execution of an ASP.NET Web Forms page during which you have the opportunity to work with postback information: the LoadPostData phase, the RaisePostDataChangedEvent phase, and the RaisePostBackEvent phase. To work with the associated data or events, you override the associated method for the desired phase. To override the methods, you need to implement the *IPostBackDataHandler* interface, the *IPostBackEventHandler* interface, or both. *IPostBackDataHandler* defines the *LoadPostData* method and the *RaisePostDataChangedEvent* method. *IPostBackEventHandler* defines the *RaisePostBackEvent* method.

Here's a summary of what the postback methods are typically used for:

Method	Purpose
LoadPostData	Loads data posted in form fields into local variables for later processing. Returns a Boolean indicating whether form values have changed since the last postback.
RaisePostBackDataChangedEvent	Called if LoadPostData returns *true*. It is used to respond to changes in posted data.
RaisePostBackEvent	Processes data posted back from form fields, and raises any related events from the control.

note

You implement interfaces in the fashion specified by the language you're using. As shown earlier, interfaces are implemented in Visual Basic .NET using the implements keyword. Unlike inheritance, which only allows inheriting from a single base class, you can implement as many interfaces as you'd like. Separate each interface name with a comma, as follows:

```
class <className> : IPostBackDataHandler, IPostBackEventHandler
```

You'll see examples of how to work with postback data in the registration and login control example in the next section.

Creating, Raising, and Handling Events

Another important aspect of creating a custom server control is dealing with events. While the event model in ASP.NET is designed to closely emulate event handling in a desktop application, such as a Visual Basic forms-based application, there are some significant differences in the models.

The most significant difference is that control events are raised and handled only on the server. Only after a Web Forms page has been posted back to the server can the state of each control be examined and appropriate events raised and handled.

Another difference is that custom ASP.NET server controls do not directly handle client events, such as clicks, mouseovers, and key presses because these events occur on the client (although controls can emit client-side code to handle such events). To communicate an event that occurs on the client to the server, the page must be posted back to the server.

There are three parts to dealing with custom events in a custom server control: creating the event, raising the event, and handling the event. (Handling the event is typically done outside the control, but the plumbing for making it work is set up in the control.)

Creating and Raising Events

Events in ASP.NET use two important objects: *EventHandler* and *EventArgs*. *EventHandler* is a delegate used as the basis for creating a new event, whereas the *EventArgs* class is used to pass data with an event or to signify that no event data was passed.

You create events using the event keyword as follows:

```
public event EventHandler OnEvent
```

EventHandler is the name of the event handler. Notice that the event is declared as type event.

---

note

The *EventHandler* delegate is the basis for all event handler delegates. A delegate defines the signature for the event—that is, it specifies the arguments that an event handler for that event must accept—and acts as a type-safe function pointer to link the event to its event handler routine. The signature for *EventHandler* is as follows:

```
public delegate void EventHandler(object sender, EventArgs e);
```

This means that any event defined using the *EventHandler* delegate must accept both an *Object* and an *EventArgs* argument:

```
void Control_Event(object sender, EventArgs e)
{
    // event handling code
}
```

You can create your own events that pass data to their event handlers by creating a custom class derived from *EventArgs*, and then creating a new delegate for your event that specifies your custom class instead of *EventArgs* as one of its arguments.

Next you raise the event (based on the criteria you set up within your control to determine if the event should be called) using the *RaiseEvents* keyword as follows:

```
public  void RaisePostBackEvent(string eventArgument)
{
    if ( EventName != null )
    {
        EventName(this, EventArgs.Empty)
    }
}
```

This code is executed when the *RaisePostBackEvent* method is called during page execution. It tests whether the *EventName* delegate is not null, and if it is not, it raises the *EventName* event, which is typically handled outside of the control.

Handling Custom Events

After you've created the event and the code to raise the event, you (or the developer consuming the event) will need to write code to handle the event. This consists of two steps: creating an event handler and wiring the event to it. Although event handlers were discussed in Chapter 7, it's worth reviewing these steps here.

An event handler is a page-level procedure that typically accepts two arguments: the source of the event and an *EventArgs* instance (or an instance of a class derived from *EventArgs*) representing any data passed with the event. An event handler for the *EventName* event would look like the following:

```
void ControlName_EventName(object source , EventArgs e)
{
  // Event handling code
}
```

In this code, *ControlName* represents the name of the control in which the event is defined, and *EventName* represents the name of the event. This syntax is not required, but it's the naming convention typically followed for event handlers. You can call your event handlers whatever you want, but following the *ControlName_EventName* naming standard will make your code easier to read and maintain. A good example of this is the *Page_Load* event handler found in the code-behind module for every new Web Form created in Visual Studio .NET. Because the *Page* class is derived from the *Control base* class, it exposes the *Load* event defined by the base class. Because *Page_Load* is the most common event for adding logic to a Web Form, the template for a Web Form in Visual Studio .NET creates the handler for you by default.

To wire the event handler to your control, you need to do one of two things, depending on whether you're dealing with a declarative control or a control added programmatically. For declarative controls (those defined using a tag in the .aspx file), add an *OnEventName* attribute to the tag in which you declare the control, with the value set to the name of the event handler routine:

```
<ASPNETSBS:MyControl id="MC1" OnEventName="MC1_EventName"
    runat="server">
```

The good news is that Visual Studio provides support for handling and wiring up events, including custom events through the code editor and IntelliSense statement completion, as you'll see in a full implementation of these principles after the discussion of handling postbacks.

Overriding Inherited Events

In addition to creating custom events from scratch, you can override events that are defined on the base control from which your control is derived. The standard events that are defined by the *control* class are as follows:

- *Init* Initialize settings for the current request.
- *Load* Perform actions that need to be performed for each request after child controls have been created and initialized.
- *DataBinding* Perform actions needed to evaluate data-binding expressions associated with a control.
- *PreRender* Perform any modifications to the control or data necessary before rendering the control.
- *UnLoad* Perform clean-up tasks before the control is removed from memory.

To override an event exposed by an inherited class, override its associated *OnEventName* method. For example, to override the *PreRender* event, you would use the following code in your control (note that the *OnPreRender* method takes only one argument, of type *EventArgs*):

```
protected override void OnPreRender(EventArgs e)
{
  // Event handling code
  base.OnPreRender(e);
}
```

Event Execution Order

When you're handling events, it's important to understand that the standard control events and methods occur in a consistent order, including events and methods related to postbacks. This is important because if you write code in an event handler that occurs before the objects manipulated by that code have been created and initialized, the results will be unpredictable at best. One of the most common problems relating to event execution order is when you add controls to the page programmatically. If you add those controls in the *Page_Load* event handler, the controls will not maintain their ViewState during postbacks because the *LoadViewState* event, which takes care of re-populating the state of controls on the page, occurs *before* the

(continued)

continued

Load event. Because the controls have not yet been created when the *LoadViewState* event is fired, the state for controls created in *Page_Load* is discarded. If you want controls added programmatically to maintain *ViewState*, you should add those controls in the *Page_Init* event handler instead.

The following is the order of the standard events and methods for controls.

- *Initialize*   During this phase, the *Init* event is raised.

- *LoadViewState*   During this phase, controls that use *ViewState* are populated with data from the hidden __VIEWSTATE field submitted with the request. The *LoadViewState* method can be overridden to customize this process.

- *LoadPostData*   During this phase, data posted back with the request is evaluated and appropriate action is taken. Override the *LoadPostData* method to write code for this phase.

- *Load*   During this phase, the *Load* event is raised.

- *RaisePostDataChangedEvent*   During this phase, change events are raised in response to differences between the current state of a control's members and the values submitted with the request. Override the *RaisePostDataChangedEvent* method to write code for this phase.

- *RaisePostBackEvent*   During this phase, event handlers for server-side events are called. Override the *RaisePostBackEvent* method to write code for this phase.

- *PreRender*   During this phase, any modifications necessary before rendering are made. Changes made after this phase will not be saved to *ViewState*.

- *SaveViewState*   During this phase, controls that use *ViewState* save their data to the hidden __VIEWSTATE field. The *ViewState* method can be overridden to customize this process.

- *Render*   During this phase, the control and its children are rendered to the browser.

- *Dispose*   During this phase, any clean-up of expensive resources such as file handles, database connections, and so on, is performed. Override the *Dispose* method to write code for this phase.

When overriding methods for inherited events (*Init*, *Load*, *PreRender*, and so on), it's usually a good idea to call the base implementation of the event's method from within your overridden version. This ensures that any handlers associated with those events are called. The syntax for calling the base handler is as follows:

```
protected override void OnLoad(EventArgs e )
    // Event handling code
    base.OnLoad(e);
}
```

Creating Registration and Login Controls

To demonstrate event handling and postback handling, you're going to build a control that can handle user registration and logins. This control will integrate with ASP.NET Forms authentication and can be used to prevent content in your application from being viewed or downloaded by users who have not registered on your site. (Note that any content you want to protect must be registered to ASP.NET in the IIS App Mappings.)

The control will have two modes: Login, and Register. In Login mode, the control will render two text boxes, one for the user name and another for the password, a Submit button, and a Reset button. In Register Mode, the control will render three text boxes, one for the user name, one for the password, and one for the user to confirm their password. The control will expose four custom events, *AuthSuccess*, *AuthFailure*, *RegSuccess*, and *RegFailure*, which the client can use to determine whether the user entered the correct credentials, or whether there was a problem with the user's registration information. To raise these events, you'll use some of the postback methods that were described earlier. This example is more involved than others you've seen previously, so we'll break it up into sections to make it easier to follow.

Create the basic control

1   Open the Chapter_10_Controls project, and add a new Web Custom Control class to the project. Name the class **RegLogin.cs**.

2   Add the following using statements to the top of the file.

```
using System.Collections.Specialized;
using System.Data;
using System.Web.Security;
using System.Web;
```

3   Change the class that the control inherits from *System.Web.UI.WebControl* to *Control* (attributes omitted for clarity).

```
public class RegLogin : System.Web.UI.Control
{
```

4   Delete the *DefaultProperty("Text")* attribute that precedes the class definition because we won't be using a *Text* property in the control. The attribute should look like the following line:

```
[ToolboxData("<{0}:RegLogin runat=server></{0}:RegLogin>")] _
```

5   Save RegLogin.cs.

Now that you've got the control class created, let's continue by adding member variables for storing the user name, password, and other important information for the control, including a *Mode* property that will use an Enumeration as its type.

Add member variables and properties

1   Just below the class declaration, add private *String* variables for the user name, password, password confirmation, and status message (which will contain read-only information about the status of the control). You can delete the text member variable that was created when you created the control class because we won't be using it.

```
private string userName;
   private string password;
   private string passwordConfirm;
   private string statusMessage;
```

2   Add a Boolean member variable called **displayRegLink**. This variable will be used to determine whether to display a hyperlink that will enable the user to switch the control to Register mode. The default is false.

```
private bool displayRegLink = false;
```

3   Between the using statements and the class definition, add the following code, which creates an enum for the mode member variable.

```
public enum RegLoginModes
{
    Register,
    Login
}
```

An enumeration enables you to specify the valid values for a given property or argument that uses the enumeration as its type. The enumeration is also used by Visual Studio .NET to provide IntelliSense statement completion for members of that type. Enumerations can make working with variables and properties less error-prone by limiting input to only valid values.

4   Add a new member variable called **mode**, with the type *RegLoginMode*. Set the value of the member to **RegLoginMode.Login**:

```
private RegLoginMode mode = RegLoginMode.Login;
```

5   Modify the default *Text* property (which was added automatically when the file was created) from this:

```
[Bindable(true),
  Category("Appearance"),
  DefaultValue("")]
public string Text
{
  get
  {
    return text;
  }

  set
  {
    text = value;
  }
}
```

to look like the following:

```
[Bindable(false), Browsable(false)] _
  public string StatusMessage
  {
    get
    {
      return _statusMessage;
    }
  }
```

This exposes *statusMessage* as a public property, so that the consuming page can read it. The property has only a get because it is used only to communicate information from the control to the page. Because the property value cannot be set, we add the *Bindable* and *Browsable* attributes to the property declaration and set the value of each to *false*. This prevents the property from being available for databinding and from showing up in the property browser.

6   Save RegLogin.cs

The next part of the process is displaying a UI for the control. As with the *TextBoxPlus* control, you'll do this by overriding the *Render* method. But in this case, the actual rendering will be passed off to specialized methods for the two modes: *Login* and *Register*. Two different rendering techniques will be demonstrated.

The first rendering technique, which will be used for rendering the login UI, will make use of the methods and properties exposed by the *HtmlTextWriter* class, an instance of which is passed to the *Render* method by the ASP.NET runtime. These include the *WriteLine*, *WriteBeginTag*, *WriteEndTag*, and *WriteAttribute* methods, which enable you to construct HTML elements programmatically, piece-by-piece, as well as the *DefaultTabString* and *SelfClosingTagEnd* properties. Using these methods and properties enables you to render code that will be more readable (hence, easier to troubleshoot) on the client end of the request, without having to remember a language-specific escape character for tabs or linefeeds. The code produced using this technique is a little heftier than that produced using the second technique.

The second rendering technique, which will be used for rendering the registration UI, will make use of the *StringBuilder* utility class in the *System.Text* namespace. The *StringBuilder* class should be used whenever you need to do a significant number (generally five or more) of string concatenations. Because string concatenation results in a new *String* object being created based on the string(s) and/or literals being concatenated, it can carry significant performance overhead. Using a *StringBuilder* can significantly improve performance by enabling you to manipulate string data without having to create and allocate space for a new *String* object with each manipulation. With this technique, we create a *StringBuilder* instance, and call its *Append* method to add to the output string. Unlike the technique using the *HtmlTextWriter* class, this technique requires using constants like "\t" (for Tab) and "\n" (newline) for formatting the rendered code.

Create the user interface

1   Because the default Web Custom Control code already has an override for the *Render* method of the *Control* class, simply modify the existing method to look like the following:

```
protected override void Render(HtmlTextWriter output)
{
  switch (mode)
  {
    case RegLoginMode.Register:
      DisplayRegUI(output);
      break;
    case RegLoginMode.Login:
```

```
        DisplayLoginUI(output);
        break;
  }

}
```

Note that you use the mode member variable to decide which UI to display. If the control is in *Login* mode (the default), the login UI will be displayed. If the control is in *Register* mode, the registration UI will be displayed. Note also that both UI rendering functions (which you'll add next) accept the *HtmlTextWriter* instance passed into the *Render* method as an argument. This will be used in these functions to render output to the browser.

2   Create two private methods with void return type, DisplayRegUI, and DisplayLoginUI:

```
private void DisplayLoginUI(HtmlTextWriter output)
{

}


private void DisplayRegUI(HtmlTextWriter output)
{

}
```

3   Add the following code to DisplayLoginUI. This code uses methods and properties exposed by the *HtmlTextWriter* class to write out the desired HTML output, in this case, an HTML table for formatting, with two text boxes for input, as well as an HTML button for posting back the control's contents, and a reset button.

```
output.WriteLine(HtmlTextWriter.DefaultTabString +
    "<table>");
output.WriteLine(HtmlTextWriter.DefaultTabString +
    HtmlTextWriter.DefaultTabString + "<tr>");
output.WriteLine(HtmlTextWriter.DefaultTabString +
    HtmlTextWriter.DefaultTabString +
    HtmlTextWriter.DefaultTabString + "<td>");
output.WriteLine(HtmlTextWriter.DefaultTabString +
    HtmlTextWriter.DefaultTabString +
    HtmlTextWriter.DefaultTabString +
    HtmlTextWriter.DefaultTabString + "Username: ");
output.WriteLine(HtmlTextWriter.DefaultTabString +
    HtmlTextWriter.DefaultTabString +
    HtmlTextWriter.DefaultTabString + "</td>");
```

```
            output.WriteLine(HtmlTextWriter.DefaultTabString +
                HtmlTextWriter.DefaultTabString +
                HtmlTextWriter.DefaultTabString + "<td>");
            output.Write(HtmlTextWriter.DefaultTabString +
                HtmlTextWriter.DefaultTabString +
                HtmlTextWriter.DefaultTabString +
                HtmlTextWriter.DefaultTabString);
            output.WriteBeginTag("input");
            output.WriteAttribute("name", this.UniqueID);
            output.WriteAttribute("type", "text");
            output.WriteAttribute("value", userName);
            output.WriteLineNoTabs(HtmlTextWriter.SelfClosingTagEnd);
            output.WriteLine(HtmlTextWriter.DefaultTabString +
                HtmlTextWriter.DefaultTabString +
                HtmlTextWriter.DefaultTabString + "</td>");
            output.WriteLine(HtmlTextWriter.DefaultTabString +
                HtmlTextWriter.DefaultTabString + "</tr>");
            output.WriteLine(HtmlTextWriter.DefaultTabString +
                HtmlTextWriter.DefaultTabString + "<tr>");
            output.WriteLine(HtmlTextWriter.DefaultTabString +
                HtmlTextWriter.DefaultTabString +
                HtmlTextWriter.DefaultTabString + "<td>");
            output.WriteLine(HtmlTextWriter.DefaultTabString +
                HtmlTextWriter.DefaultTabString +
                HtmlTextWriter.DefaultTabString +
                HtmlTextWriter.DefaultTabString + "Password: ");
            output.WriteLine(HtmlTextWriter.DefaultTabString +
                HtmlTextWriter.DefaultTabString +
                HtmlTextWriter.DefaultTabString + "</td>");
            output.WriteLine(HtmlTextWriter.DefaultTabString +
                HtmlTextWriter.DefaultTabString +
                HtmlTextWriter.DefaultTabString + "<td>");
            output.Write(HtmlTextWriter.DefaultTabString +
                HtmlTextWriter.DefaultTabString +
                HtmlTextWriter.DefaultTabString +
                HtmlTextWriter.DefaultTabString);
            output.WriteBeginTag("input");
            output.WriteAttribute("name", this.UniqueID);
            output.WriteAttribute("type", "password");
            output.WriteLineNoTabs(HtmlTextWriter.SelfClosingTagEnd);
            output.WriteLine(HtmlTextWriter.DefaultTabString +
                HtmlTextWriter.DefaultTabString +
                HtmlTextWriter.DefaultTabString + "</td>");
```

```
output.WriteLine(HtmlTextWriter.DefaultTabString +
    HtmlTextWriter.DefaultTabString + "</tr>");
output.WriteLine(HtmlTextWriter.DefaultTabString +
    HtmlTextWriter.DefaultTabString + "<tr>");
output.WriteLine(HtmlTextWriter.DefaultTabString +
    HtmlTextWriter.DefaultTabString +
    HtmlTextWriter.DefaultTabString + "<td>");
output.Write(HtmlTextWriter.DefaultTabString +
    HtmlTextWriter.DefaultTabString +
    HtmlTextWriter.DefaultTabString +
    HtmlTextWriter.DefaultTabString);
output.WriteBeginTag("input");
output.WriteAttribute("name", this.UniqueID);
output.WriteAttribute("type", "button");
output.WriteAttribute("value", "Submit");
output.WriteAttribute("OnClick", "javascript:" +
    Page.GetPostBackEventReference(this, "Login"));
output.WriteLineNoTabs(HtmlTextWriter.SelfClosingTagEnd);
output.WriteLine(HtmlTextWriter.DefaultTabString +
    HtmlTextWriter.DefaultTabString +
    HtmlTextWriter.DefaultTabString + "</td>");
output.WriteLine(HtmlTextWriter.DefaultTabString +
    HtmlTextWriter.DefaultTabString +
    HtmlTextWriter.DefaultTabString + "<td>");
output.Write(HtmlTextWriter.DefaultTabString +
    HtmlTextWriter.DefaultTabString +
    HtmlTextWriter.DefaultTabString +
    HtmlTextWriter.DefaultTabString);
output.WriteBeginTag("input");
output.WriteAttribute("name", this.UniqueID);
output.WriteAttribute("type", "reset");
output.WriteLineNoTabs(HtmlTextWriter.SelfClosingTagEnd);
output.WriteLine(HtmlTextWriter.DefaultTabString +
    HtmlTextWriter.DefaultTabString +
    HtmlTextWriter.DefaultTabString + "</td>");
output.WriteLine(HtmlTextWriter.DefaultTabString +
    HtmlTextWriter.DefaultTabString + "</tr>");
if ( displayRegLink == true )
{
    output.WriteLine(HtmlTextWriter.DefaultTabString +
        HtmlTextWriter.DefaultTabString + "<tr>");
    output.WriteLine(HtmlTextWriter.DefaultTabString +
        HtmlTextWriter.DefaultTabString +
```

```
                    HtmlTextWriter.DefaultTabString + "<td colspan='2'>");
            output.WriteBeginTag("a");
            output.WriteAttribute("name", "RegLink"");
            output.WriteAttribute("href", "javascript:" +
                Page.GetPostBackEventReference(this, "DisplayRegUI"));
            output.Write(HtmlTextWriter.TagRightChar);
            output.Write("Register");
            output.WriteEndTag("a");
            output.WriteLine(HtmlTextWriter.DefaultTabString +
                HtmlTextWriter.DefaultTabString +
                HtmlTextWriter.DefaultTabString + "</td>");
            output.WriteLine(HtmlTextWriter.DefaultTabString +
                HtmlTextWriter.DefaultTabString + "</tr>");
    }
    output.WriteLine(HtmlTextWriter.DefaultTabString +
        "</table>");
    }
```

Note the call to *GetPostBackEventReference* in the code for rendering the submit button. This allows a value (*"Login"*) to be passed when the page is posted back, so that the code that processes the postback knows which button was clicked. Note also the *if* statement that checks the value of the *displayRegUI* member variable. If the value of this variable is *true*, a hyperlink will be rendered to allow the user to switch to registration mode.

4   Add the following code to *DisplayLoginUI*. This code creates a *StringBuilder*, concatenates the HTML output, and then writes the contents of the *StringBuilder* to the browser.

```
//Create StringBuilder for concatenating output string
System.Text.StringBuilder SBOut = new
System.Text.StringBuilder();;

SBOut.Append("\t" + "<table>" + "\n");
SBOut.Append("\t" + "\t" + "<tr>" + "\n");
SBOut.Append("\t" + "\t" + "\t" + "<td>" + "\n"");
SBOut.Append("\t" + "\t" + "\t" + "Username: " + "\n");
SBOut.Append("\t" + "\t" + "\t" + "</td>" + "\n");
SBOut.Append("\t" + "\t" + "\t" + "<td>" + "\n");
SBOut.Append("\t" + "\t" + "\t" + "<input type='text' " +
    "name='" + this.UniqueID + "' value='" +
    this.userName + "'/>" + "\n");
SBOut.Append("\t" + "\t" + "\t" + "</td>" + "\n");
SBOut.Append("\t" + "\t" + "</tr>" + "\n");
```

```
SBOut.Append("\t" + "\t" + "<tr>" + "\n");
SBOut.Append("\t" + "\t" + "\t" + "<td>" + "\n");
SBOut.Append("\t" + "\t" + "\t" + "Password: " + "\n");
SBOut.Append("\t" + "\t" + "\t" + "</td>" + "\n");
SBOut.Append("\t" + "\t" + "\t" + "<td>" + "\n");
SBOut.Append("\t" + "\t" + "\t" + "<input type='password' " +
    "name='" + this.UniqueID + "'/>" + "\n");
SBOut.Append("\t" + "\t" + "\t" + "</td>" + "\n");
SBOut.Append("\t" + "\t" + "\t" + "</tr>" + "\n");
SBOut.Append("\t" + "\t" + "\t" + "<td>" + "\n");
SBOut.Append("\t" + "\t" + "\t" + "Confirm Password: " +
"\n");
SBOut.Append("\t" + "\t" + "\t" + "</td>" + "\n");
SBOut.Append("\t" + "\t" + "\t" + "<td>" + "\n");
SBOut.Append("\t" + "\t" + "\t" + "<input type='password' " +
    "name='" + this.UniqueID + "'/>" + "\n");
SBOut.Append("\t" + "\t" + "\t" + "</td>" + "\n");
SBOut.Append("\t" + "\t" + "</tr>" + "\n");
SBOut.Append("\t" + "\t" + "<tr>" + "\n");
SBOut.Append("\t" + "\t" + "\t" + "<td>" + "\n");
SBOut.Append("\t" + "\t" + "\t" + "<input type='button' " +
    "value='Submit' OnClick=\"jscript:" +
    Page.GetPostBackEventReference(this, "Register") +
    "\">" + "\n");
SBOut.Append("\t" + "\t" + "\t" + "</td>" + "\n");
SBOut.Append("\t" + "\t" + "\t" + "<td>" + "\n");
SBOut.Append("\t" + "\t" + "\t" + "<input type='reset'/>" +
"\n");
SBOut.Append("\t" + "\t" + "\t" + "</td>" + "\n");
SBOut.Append("\t" + "\t" + "</tr>" + "\n");
SBOut.Append("\t" + "</table>" + "\n");
// Send the output to the browser.
output.Write(SBOut);
```

Note that as with the *DisplayLoginUI* method, a call to *GetPostBackEventReference* is used to generate the code necessary for initiating the postback, including indicating which button was clicked (in this case, *Register*).

5   Save RegLogin.cs.

At this point, if you were to build the Chapter_10_Controls project and add the control to a page, it would render the login UI and could postback the data in its form fields, but that's about it. To take things further, you'll need to add postback handling and custom event code.

Handle Postbacks and Events

1 Define events for success and failure of both authentication and registration, using the base *EventHandler* delegate as the basis for the events. Place the event declarations just below the member variable declarations you added earlier:

```
public event EventHandler AuthSuccess;
public event EventHandler AuthFailure;
public event EventHandler RegSuccess;
public event EventHandler RegFailure;
```

2 Directly below the *inherits* keyword, add *Implements* statement to implement the *IPostBackDataHandler* and *IPostBackEventHandler* interfaces.

```
public class RegLogin : System.Web.UI.Control,
        IPostBackDataHandler,
        IPostBackEventHandler
```

3 Implement the *LoadPostData* method defined in the *IPostBackDataHandler* interface to load the posted values into the local variables. The return value of this function determines whether the *RaisePostDataChangedEvent* method is called on this control. Add the method at the bottom of the class, as shown in the following illustration:

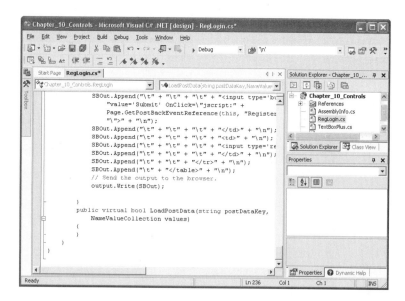

4 Add the following code to the *LoadPostData* method:

```
string[] newValues  = values[postDataKey].Split(',');
bool Result = false;

switch (Page.Request.Form["__EVENTARGUMENT"])
{
case "DisplayRegUI":
   mode = RegLoginMode.Register;
   break;
case "Login":
   Result = LoadLoginPostData(newValues);
   break;
case "Register":
   mode = RegLoginMode.Register;
   Result = LoadRegisterPostData(newValues);
   break;
}
return Result;
```

The code takes the collection of form field values posted from the form and places them into the string array *newValues*. It then declares a Boolean variable for the return value of the *LoadPostData* method. Next it uses the *__EVENTARGUMENT* form field, which is automatically sent with each postback (thanks to our use of *GetPostBackEventReference*), to decide how to process the loaded data (or in the case of the value *DisplayRegUI*, to display the registration UI, and forego further processing).

5 After adding the code in Step 4, if you try to compile the code, you will notice that there are two errors because these are calls to two methods you haven't added yet, *LoadLoginPostData* and *LoadRegisterPostData*. Add declarations for these methods below the *LoadPostData* method:

```
private bool LoadLoginPostData(string[] newValues)
{
}
private bool LoadRegisterPostData(string[] newValues)
{
}
```

6   Add the following code to *LoadLoginPostData*:

```
string newUserName="";
string newPassword="";

// Get the username
newUserName=newValues[0];
// ...and the password
newPassword=newValues[1];

// return true if the values have changed
//   since last postback
if ( newUserName!=userName ||
   newPassword!=password )
{
   userName=newUserName;
   password=newPassword;
   return true;
}
else
{
   return false;
}
```

The code retrieves the user name and password entered by the user, checks to see if they've changed since the last postback, and then loads them into local variables for later processing. If the values have changed since the last postback, the code returns *True*, which will cause the *PostBackDataChangedEvent* method to be called later in the processing of the request.

7   Add the following code to *LoadRegisterPostData*:

```
// Get the user name
userName=newValues[0];
// ...and the password
password=newValues[1];
// ...and the password confirmation
passwordConfirm=newValues[2];

// We don't expect the data to change from
//   request to request here, so we just
//   return false
return false;
}
```

8 Implement the *RaisePostDataChangedEvent* method. Although this control does not make use of this method, you are still required to implement it because it is defined as part of the *IPostBackDataHandler* interface. The method is declared as in the following code:

```
public virtual void RaisePostDataChangedEvent()
{
    // No implementation...required to implement
    //   interface
}
```

9 Implement the *RaisePostBackEvent* method by adding the following method to the end of the class:

```
public void RaisePostBackEvent(string eventArgument) _
{

}
```

10 Add the following code to *RaisePostBackEvent*:

```
switch (mode)
{
case RegLoginMode.Register:
  if ( eventArgument!= "DisplayRegUI" )
  {
   if ( !(SaveCredentials(userName, password, passwordConfirm)) )
   {
    if ( RegFailure!=null )
    {
     RegFailure(this, EventArgs.Empty);
    }
    mode = RegLoginMode.Register;
   }
   else
   {
    if ( RegSuccess!=null )
    {
     RegSuccess(this, EventArgs.Empty);
    }
    mode = RegLoginMode.Login;
   }
  }
  break;

case RegLoginMode.Login:
```

```
// If login is not valid, raise the AuthFailed event
//  and display the link for registration.
if ( !(VerifyCredentials(userName,password)) )
{
 if ( AuthFailure!=null )
 {
  AuthFailure(this, EventArgs.Empty);
 }
}
else
{
 if ( AuthSuccess!=null )
 {
  AuthSuccess(this, EventArgs.Empty);
 }
 FormsAuthentication.SetAuthCookie(_userName, false);
}
break;
}
```

The code uses the mode variable to decide how to process the data that was loaded in the *LoadPostData* method, calling either *VerifyCredentials* or *SaveCredentials*. You'll add both of these methods in the next section. If the authentication or registration succeeds, the appropriate success event is raised. Likewise, if the authentication or registration processing fails, the appropriate failure event is raised. Note that if authentication succeeds, the code also calls the *FormsAuthentication.SetAuthCookie* method, passing in the user name of the current user.

11   Save RegLogin.cs.

Now it's time to get down to the nitty gritty: verifying and saving user credentials. The technique the control will use to store credentials is a simple XML file. The XML file, which will be automatically created by the control the first time the control is used, will contain the date a user registered, his or her user name, and an MD5 hashed value representing the password. Saving new registration information will be performed by the *SaveCredentials* method. Verifying the user's credentials against existing credentials will be performed by the *VerifyCredentials* method. Finally, the control will use a *CreateBlankUsersFile* utility method to create the initial XML file.

warning

You should not use this control for restricting access to critical information. This control is designed to limit only anonymous browsing of content. Because the control will allow users to register on their own, it provides a means of limiting only who can access content on your site. Note that you could further restrict access to content by adding a field to the XML file for whether the user is approved or enabled. By setting this field to *false* by default, you would be able to choose whether someone who registered could access content *before* they can log in.

Save and validate user credentials as XML

1   Add the following code to RegLogin.cs, after the *RaisePostBackEvent* method:

```
private bool SaveCredentials(string Username,
    string Password, string PasswordConfirm)
{
  DataSet LoginDS = new DataSet();
  LoginDS.ReadXml(Page.Server.MapPath("Users.xml"));
  if ( !(
     LoginDS.Tables[0].Select("username='"" + Username +
"'").Length > 0 ))
   {
     if ( password != "" &&
        password == passwordConfirm )
     {
        DataRow NewLogin = LoginDS.Tables[0].NewRow();
        NewLogin["username"] = userName;
        NewLogin["password"] =
   FormsAuthentication.HashPasswordForStoringInConfigFile(password,
   "MD5");
        NewLogin["registerDate"] =
DateTime.Today.ToShortDateString();
        LoginDS.Tables[0].Rows.Add(NewLogin);
        LoginDS.WriteXml(Page.Server.MapPath("Users.xml"));
        statusMessage = "Registration succeeded. Please log
in.";
        return true;
     }
     else
```

```
        {
            statusMessage = "No password entered " +
                "or passwords do not match. Please re-enter.";
            return false;
        }
    }
    else
    {
        statusMessage = "An identical username exists. Please
choose another.";
        return false;
    }
}
```

The *SaveCredentials* method uses the *ReadXml* method of the *DataSet* class to read the current Users.xml file, and checks to see if there's already a user in the file with the same name as that entered by the user in the registration form. If not, the method then checks to make sure that both the password and confirmation password values are identical. If they are, the method creates a new row from the dataset, stores the user name and a hashed version of the password, adds the row to the dataset, and uses the DataSet's *WriteXml* method to save the updated table to the file. After all this succeeds, it sets the *statusMessage* property to indicate that registration succeeded, and returns *true* (which causes the *RegSuccess* event to be raised). If the user name already exists or if the passwords don't match, the *statusMessage* property is set to an appropriate message, and the method returns *false* (causing the *RegFailure* event to be raised).

2   Add the following code to RegLogin.cs, after the *SaveCredentials* method:

```
private bool VerifyCredentials(string Username,
    string Password )
{
    DataSet LoginDS = new DataSet();
    try
    {
        LoginDS.ReadXml(Page.Server.MapPath("Users.xml"));
    }
    catch ( System.IO.FileNotFoundException )
    {
        CreateBlankUsersFile();
        LoginDS.ReadXml(Page.Server.MapPath("Users.xml"));
    }
```

```
  if ( LoginDS.Tables[0].Select("username='" + Username +
"'").Length > 0 )
  {
    DataRow[] LoginRow =
       LoginDS.Tables[0].Select("username='" + Username +
"'");
    if ( LoginRow[0]["password"].ToString() ==
FormsAuthentication.HashPasswordForStoringInConfigFile(Password,
"MD5") )
    {
      statusMessage = "Credentials Validated.";
      return true;
    }
    else
    {
      statusMessage = "Invalid Password.";
      return false;
    }
  }
  else
  {
    statusMessage = "Username not found. Have you regis-
tered?";
    displayRegLink = true;
    return false;
  }
}
```

The *VerifyCredentials* method also uses the *ReadXml* method to fill the
dataset from Users.xml. Unlike *SaveCredentials*, however, the code in
VerifyCredentials is wrapped in a *Try...Catch* block. This is because
VerifyCredentials will always be called first, and if a *FileNotFoundException*
is thrown, the *CreateBlankUsersFile* method is called to create the Users.xml
file. After the dataset has been filled, the code selects the row that matches
the provided user name, if it exists, and checks the stored password hash
against the hashed version of the password entered by the user. If the
passwords match, the *statusMessage* property is set to indicate success,
and the method returns *True* (which results in the *AuthSuccess* event
being raised). If either the user name does not exist in the XML file or the
passwords do not match, the *statusMessage* property is set to indicate
these problems, and the method returns *False* (resulting in the *AuthFailure*
method being raised).

> **note**
>
> One variable in the code added above is worth noting.
>
> ```
> LoginRow[0]["password"].ToString()
> ```
>
> Looking at the .NET Framework reference for the *DataRow* class, you might be tempted to use the item property to get at the password element, like this fragment:
>
> ```
> LoginRow[0].Item["password"].ToString()
> ```
>
> In C#, Item is the indexer for the class, and so .Item is not only not required, but not allowed!

3   Add the following code to RegLogin.cs, after the *VerifyCredentials* method:

```
public void CreateBlankUsersFile()
{
   System.IO.StreamWriter NewXml =
    System.IO.File.CreateText(Page.Server.MapPath("Users.xml"));

   NewXml.WriteLine("<users>");
   NewXml.WriteLine("  <!-- user field describes a single user -
->");
   NewXml.WriteLine("  <user>");
   NewXml.WriteLine("  <!-- date field contains the registration
date -->");
   NewXml.WriteLine("     <registerDate>" +
    DateTime.Today.ToShortDateString() + "</registerDate>");
   NewXml.WriteLine("     <!-- username field -->");
   NewXml.WriteLine("     <username>TempUser</username>");
   NewXml.WriteLine("     <!-- password field contains MD5 hash
value -->");
   NewXml.WriteLine("     <password>" +
 FormsAuthentication.HashPasswordForStoringInConfigFile("password",
"MD5") +
    "</password>");
   NewXml.WriteLine("  </user>");
   NewXml.WriteLine("</users>");
   NewXml.Close();
}
```

The *CreateBlankUsersFile* method allows the control to create its own storage file without requiring the intervention of the user. The method uses a

StreamWriter to create and write to a text file. When finished writing the default elements, the method closes the *StreamWriter*.

> **tip**
> Because the file is created by the ASP.NET process, by default it will have full permissions granted to the ASPNET user account under which ASP.NET is run, as well as to the SYSTEM account and the Administrators group. However, the Users group will have only Read & Execute and Read permissions on the file. This means that unless you are logged on as an Administrator, you will not be able to manually edit the Users.xml file.

4   Save RegLogin.cs, and build the Chapter_10_Controls project.

If you entered all the code correctly, the project should build correctly, and the control will be ready to use. If you have any problems, you can check your code against the finished example that is available with the practice files for this chapter.

The last part of the process is using the control in a page. To use the control, you'll need to create a new Web Forms page, create the control (either declaratively or programmatically), and set up handlers for its exposed events. You'll also need to configure your application to use Forms Authentication, create a sample page to be protected by Forms Authentication, and configure your application to prevent browsing of the Users.xml file created by the control.

Configure for Forms Authentication

1   Open the Chapter_10 project and then open the Web.config file in that project.

2   Modify the *<authentication>* configuration element to look like the following:

```
<authentication mode="Forms">
  <forms
    loginUrl="Login.aspx"
    protection="All">
  </forms>
</authentication>
```

This forces any requests for content that requires authentication to be redirected to Login.aspx if an authentication cookie is not present. It also specifies that the cookie is both encrypted and subject to validation to protect its contents.

Custom Controls

10

3   Add a <location> section with an *<authorization>* configuration element that looks like the following. This code should go between the opening <configuration> tag and the opening <system.web> tag:

```
<location path="ProtectMe.aspx">
 <system.web>
  <authorization>
   <deny users="?"/>
  </authorization>
 </system.web>
</location>
```

This section disallows any requests for the file ProtectMe.aspx (which you'll add to the project shortly) by users who have not been authenticated. Thanks to the <authentication> section, such requests will be redirected to Login.aspx (which you'll also add to the project shortly, and which will make use of the *RegLogin* control).

4   Save Web.config, but don't close it yet.

These steps will effectively protect the file ProtectMe.aspx from unauthorized access (after you've created it, anyway), but they leave out something very important: protecting the XML file that will contain the user information. By default, XML files are browseable from within a Web application. All someone needs to know is the name of the file, and they can view its contents. Although the *RegLogin* control does make use of MD5 hashing to protect passwords, its still a good idea to prevent browsing of the Users.xml file. The next set of steps will show you how to do this.

Secure Users.xml

1   Open the Web.config file for the Chapter_10 project, if it's not already open.

2   Add the following section between the <system.web> and </system.web> tags:

```
<httpHandlers>
   <add verb="*" path="Users.xml"
type="System.Web.HttpForbiddenHandler"/>
</httpHandlers>
```

This will prevent any requests for a file named Users.xml within the scope of the application from being fulfilled by passing the request to the *HttpForbiddenHandler HttpHandler* class. This is the same technique used by ASP.NET to protect the global.asax, web.config, and other non-browseable files.

3   Save and close Web.config.

4   Open the Internet Information Services administration tool, drill down to the Chapter_10 project application, right-click the application icon, and click Properties. The Properties dialog box for the Chapter_10 application will be displayed, as shown in the following illustration:

5   Click the Configuration button. The Application Configuration dialog box will be displayed, as shown in the following illustration:

6 On the Mappings tab, which is selected by default, click the Add button. The Add/Edit Application Extension Mapping dialog box will be displayed, as shown in the following illustration:

7 Click the Browse button, click Dynamic Link Libraries (*.dll) in the Files Of Type drop-down list, browse to the location of aspnet_isapi.dll (by default *%windir%*\Microsoft.NET\Framework*%version%*), click it, and click the Open button.

8 When you are returned to the Add/Edit Application Extension Mapping dialog box, click the Executable text box. This step is required in Microsoft Windows XP to enable the OK button, as described in Microsoft Knowledge Base article Q317948.

9 In the Extension: text box, type **.xml**. Note that the leading period is required.

10 Click the OK button to add the mapping. After the mapping has been added, the Application Configuration dialog box will look similar to the following illustration:

11 Click the OK button to close the Application Configuration dialog box, and then Click OK again to close the Properties dialog box. Now anyone attempting to view Users.xml (presuming the file actually exists) will see the message shown in the following illustration:

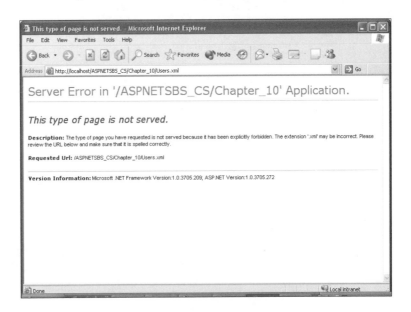

Note that if you want to protect any file named Users.xml in any application on the machine, you should add the *<add>* element in step 2 to machine.config, rather than Web.config, add the mapping of the .xml extension to the ASP.NET ISAPI process using the Master Properties in IIS, and apply the changes to all Web sites when prompted. Keep in mind that there is some overhead in having ASP.NET process all requests for .xml files, so you should only do this on a machine-wide basis if you intend to use the *RegLogin* control across many applications or sites on a machine.

important

It's worth reiterating at this point that although this example uses hashed passwords, and you've added protection for the Users.xml file, this example should only be used for protecting content from casual anonymous browsing. If you have content for which security is critical, you should consider storing user credentials in a more secure location, such as a database, and implement SSL encryption for the login page to ensure that user names and passwords aren't captured in transit.

Create a page to protect

1   Add a new Web Form to the Chapter_10 project. Name the file **ProtectMe.aspx**.

2   Add a label and a button to the page, and set the button's *Text* property to **Log Out**, as shown in the following illustration:

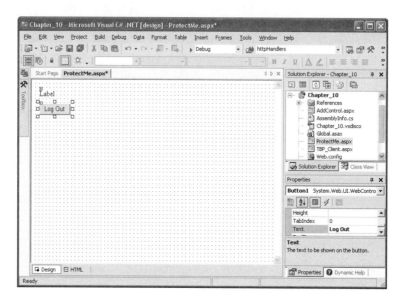

3   Double-click the button, and then add the following code to the *Button1_Click event* handler:

```
FormsAuthentication.SignOut();
Response.Redirect(Request.RawUrl);
```

This code will remove the authentication cookie and then redirect the request to the same page, which will result in the user being redirected to the login page.

4   Add the following using clause at the top of the file, along with the other using clauses:

```
using System.Web.Security;
```

5   Add the following code, which displays the user name of the currently logged-in user, to the *Page_Load* event handler:

```
Label1.Text = "Logged in as " + User.Identity.Name + ".";
```

6   Save and close both the code-behind module and the Web Form.

Now you're finally ready to create your login page. In this next procedure, you'll create a login page, add the *RegLogin* control to the Visual Studio .NET Toolbox, add the control to the page, and add the necessary event handlers to handle the control's events.

Use the *RegLogin* control

1   Add a new Web Form to the Chapter_10 project. Name the file **Login.aspx**.

2   With Login.aspx open in Design view, expand the Toolbox, right-click the Web Forms tab, and click Customize Toolbox on the shortcut menu.

3   In the Customize Toolbox dialog box, click the .NET Framework Components tab, and then click the Browse button.

4   Browse to the location of the Chapter_10_Controls assembly (the /bin directory of the Chapter_10_Controls project), select the assembly, and click the Open button.

5   Click the OK button to add the *RegLogin* control to the Toolbox.

6   Double-click the *RegLogin* control icon to add it to the page. At this point, the page should look similar to the following illustration:

7 Add a *Label* control below the *RegLogin* control, and set its *Visible* property to *False*. Leave a little space vertically between the *RegLogin* control and the *Label* control.

8 Right-click an empty area of the page, and click View Code on the shortcut menu.

9 Below the declarations for *RegLogin1* and *Label1*, add a declaration for a bool named **DoRedirect**. (You'll use this later when handling the *AuthSuccess* event handler.)

```
private bool DoRedirect = false;
```

10 In the *Page_Load* event handler, add the following line:

```
Label1.Visible=false;
```

11 Go back to the Design view of Login.aspx. Click *RegLogin1*, and click the lightning bolt on the Properties pane to show events. Double-click *AuthSuccess* in the list of events. This will add an event handler for the *AuthSuccess* event and bring you back to Code view, as shown in the following illustration:

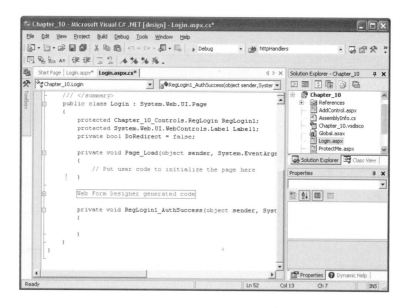

12 Add the following code to the *AuthSuccess* event handler:

```
if ( Request.QueryString["ReturnUrl"]!=null )_
{
   DoRedirect = true;
}
```

This will signal that the page should redirect the user to the page they originally requested (you'll add the code for this in a few steps). Because the *RegLogin* control automatically sets the Forms authentication cookie when authentication succeeds, this request will be successful.

13 Using the same technique as in Step 11, add the *AuthFailure* event handler, and then add the following code to it:

```
Label1.ForeColor = System.Drawing.Color.Red;
Label1.Text = RegLogin1.StatusMessage;
Label1.Visible = true;
```

14 Using the same technique as in Step 11, add the *RegSuccess* event handler, and then add the following code to it:

```
Label1.ForeColor = System.Drawing.Color.Green;
Label1.Text = RegLogin1.StatusMessage;
Label1.Visible = true;
```

15 Using the same technique as in Step 11, add the *RegFailure* event handler, and then add the following code to it:

```
Label1.ForeColor = System.Drawing.Color.Red;
Label1.Text = RegLogin1.StatusMessage;
Label1.Visible = true;
```

16 Using the same technique as in Step 11, add the *PreRender* event handler. Add the following code, which redirects the user if *DoRedirect* is *true*:

```
if ( DoRedirect )
{
    Response.Redirect(Request.QueryString["ReturnUrl"]);
}
```

17 Save the Web Form and code-behind, and then build the Chapter_10 project.

Now that you've finished your login page, you'll test it by attempting to access ProtectMe.aspx, which is protected from anonymous access by the <location> section you added to Web.config earlier.

Test the page

1   Browse ProtectMe.aspx with Internet Explorer by right-clicking it in Solution Explorer, clicking Browse With, clicking Microsoft Internet Explorer, and then clicking the Browse button. The initial output should look like the following illustration:

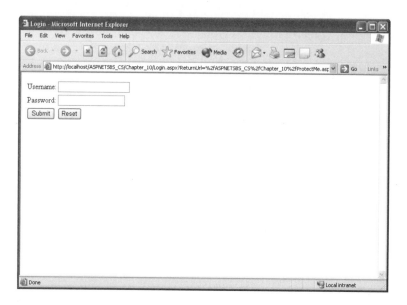

2   Without entering a user name or password, click the Submit button. The output shown should look like the following illustration:

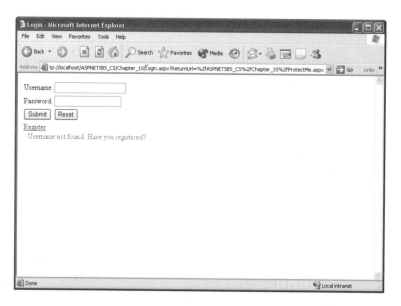

At this point, if it did not already exist, the Users.xml file has been created by the control.

3 Click the Register link. The output shown should look like the following illustration:

4 Enter **NewUser** for the user name and **password** (case sensitive) in the Password and Confirm Password fields, and then click Submit. The output shown should look like the following illustration:

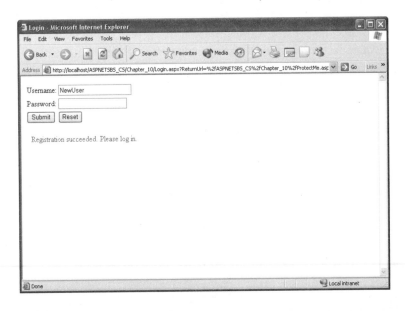

5   Enter **password** (case sensitive) in the Password field, and then click Submit. You will be redirected to ProtectMe.aspx, and the output shown should look like the following illustration:

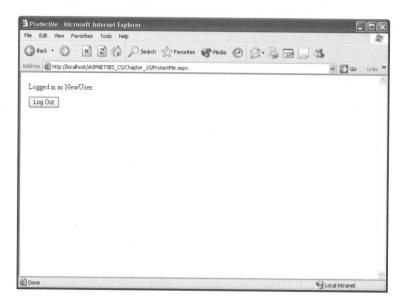

6   Click the Log Out button. You will be redirected to Login.aspx.

7   Experiment with the registration interface, such as entering an existing user name or omitting the passwords, and see how the control responds.

Maintaining State

In the previous examples, data used by the controls has been stored in local variables. For many controls, this can work just fine. But unless you explicitly retrieve submitted values and repopulate the member controls with these values, as you did in the *LoadPostData* method of the previous example, the member controls will be blank when the page is posted back to the server and the results are returned. In many cases, you might want to maintain the state of the constituent controls of your custom server control without having to explicitly write code to test for new values and repopulate the member controls with each postback.

To solve this problem, ASP.NET provides a state-management facility called *ViewState*. This is provided by an instance of the *StateBag* class of the *System.Web.UI* namespace. You store data in *ViewState* as key/value pairs, which makes working with it quite similar to working with session state. To add a value to *ViewState* or modify an existing value, you can simply specify the item's key and assign a value as follows:

```
// C#
ViewState["MyKey"] = MyValue;
```

> **note**
>
> To use *ViewState*, controls must be contained within a <form> block with the runat="server" attribute set.

Note that you can also add items to *ViewState* using the *Add* method of the *StateBag* class, and remove them using the *Remove* method. You can clear all *ViewState* values with the *Clear* method.

> **note**
>
> Using *ViewState* has both performance and security implications because all the information stored in *ViewState* is round-tripped to the client as a base64 encoded string. The size of the *ViewState* hidden field can become quite large with controls that contain a lot of data, which can have a negative impact on performance. You might want to disable *ViewState* for these controls by setting their *EnableViewState* property to *false*.
>
> Because the *ViewState* field is sent as a text string, you should never use *ViewState* to store information such as connection strings, server file paths, credit card information, or other sensitive data. Remember that after the *ViewState* has been sent to the client, it would be fairly simple for a hacker to decode the string and retrieve any data contained within. Don't count on base64 encoding to protect sensitive data sent to the client.
>
> Finally, the *ViewState* of controls is saved between the firing of the *PreRender* and *Render* events, so any changes to control state that you want to save in *ViewState* must be made during the *PreRender* event. Changes made to control state after the *PreRender* event will not be saved to *ViewState*.

Retrieving values from *ViewState* is a bit more involved. Because the *Item* property of the *StateBag* class returns an object, you will need to cast the object to the proper type before performing any type-specific actions on it or passing it to another procedure that expects a particular type. The syntax for retrieving a string value is as follows:

```
string MyString;
MyString = ViewState["MyKey"].ToString();
```

The simplest way to automate the process of saving control state to *ViewState* is to substitute *ViewState* items for the local member variables for storing the values of properties of the control.

Creating Custom Controls Through Composition

The previous examples in this chapter overrode the *Render* method of the *Control* class to render its custom output, and called the *Render* method of the base class to reuse its UI. This method works fine, but it's difficult to make use of the functionality of more than one pre-existing control using this technique.

Compositional controls use a different technique to create the user interface for a custom control out of a number of preexisting or custom controls. A compositional control overrides the *CreateChildControls* method exposed by the *Control* class, and in that method, it programmatically instantiates and sets properties of the constituent controls that make up the user interface for the custom server control. Compositional controls should also implement the *INamingContainer* interface, which provides a new naming scope for the constituent controls to ensure that their names are unique within the page.

Most often, you'll want to inherit from the *Control* class for custom controls that use composition, rather than from a more functional class. Because most of the functionality in a compositional control is provided by its constituent controls, you expose a minimum of functionality from the base class. Exposing less functionality from the base class can help avoid unexpected behavior in your control from superfluous base class members. For example, a control that inherits from *WebControl* exposes a number of UI related members, such as *BackColor*, *BorderColor*, *Height* and *Width* members that might not be desirable in your custom control.

Overriding *CreateChildControls*

The *CreateChildControls* method is substituted for the *Render* method in compositional controls. A sample *CreateChildControls* method is as follows:

```
protected override void CreateChildControls()
{
```

```
Label MyLabel = new Label()1
MyLabel.Text = "Label: ";
Me.Controls.Add(MyLabel);
MyText = new TextBox();
this.Controls.Add(MyText);
Button MyButton = new Button();
MyButton.Text = "Submit";
this.Controls.Add(MyButton);
}
```

It is not necessary in a compositional server control to call the *Render* method, because all the individual controls added to the *Controls* collection will take care of rendering themselves during the Render stage of page processing.

If you want to manipulate controls after they've been added to the *Controls* collection, you can access them either by their numeric index, as shown in the following code snippet, or by calling the *FindControl* method of the *Control* class and passing in the ID of the control you want to manipulate.

```
TextBox MyText  = (TextBox)Controls[1];
```

Implementing *INamingContainer*

Compositional controls should always implement the *INamingContainer* interface. This interface does not contain any property or method declarations. It simply creates a new naming scope for the current control to ensure that the names of child controls are unique within the page. As with any interface in Visual Basic .NET, inheriting the *INamingContainer* interface is done using the implements keyword, which appears as part of the class definition, on the line immediately following the *Inherits* statement for the class (if you include an *Imports* statement for the *System.Web.UI* namespace, you can omit the namespace in the *Inherits* and *Implements* statements shown here):

```
public class CompControl : System.Web.UI.Control,
    System.Web.UI.INamingContainer
{
  // class code
}
```

In the following code listing, which replicates the functionality of the *TextBoxPlus* control, you'll see examples of both overriding the *CreateChildControls* method and implementing *INamingContainer*. The .cs file for this control, as well as a Web Form that uses the compositional version of the control, are available in the practice files for this chapter.

TextBoxPlus_Comp.cs

```csharp
using System;
using System.Web.UI;
using System.Web.UI.WebControls;
using System.ComponentModel;

namespace Chapter_10_Controls
{
  /// <summary>
  /// Summary description for TextBoxPlus_Comp.
  /// </summary>
  [DefaultProperty("Text"),
  ToolboxData("<{0}:TextBoxPlus_Comp runat=server></
{0}:TextBoxPlus_Comp>")]
  public class TextBoxPlus_Comp :
System.Web.UI.WebControls.WebControl
  {
    private TextTypes textType;
    private Label label;
    private TextBox textBox;

    [Bindable(true), Category("Appearance"), DefaultValue("Label")]
    public string LabelText
    {
      get
      {
        EnsureChildControls();
        return label.Text;
      }

      set
      {
        EnsureChildControls();
        label.Text = value;
      }
    }

    [Bindable(true), Category("Appearance"),
DefaultValue("PlainText")]
    public TextTypes TextType
    {
      get
```

```
    {
      EnsureChildControls();
      return textType;
    }

    set
    {
      EnsureChildControls();
      textType = value;
    }
}

[Bindable(true), Category("Appearance"), DefaultValue(" ")]
public string Text
{
  get
  {
    EnsureChildControls();
    return textBox.Text;
  }

  set
  {
    EnsureChildControls();
    textBox.Text = value;
  }
}

protected override void CreateChildControls()
{
  label = new Label();
  this.Controls.Add(label);

  textBox = new TextBox();
  this.Controls.Add(textBox);
}

protected override void OnPreRender(System.EventArgs e)
{
  if ( Page.IsPostBack )
  {
    if ( textType != TextTypes.PlainText )
    {
```

```
        FormatText();
      }
    }
  }

  protected void FormatText()
  {
    EnsureChildControls();
    switch(textType)
    {
    case TextTypes.CurrencyText:
      this.Text=(double.Parse(this.Text)).ToString("C");
      break;
    case TextTypes.DecimalText:
      this.Text=(Convert.ToInt32(this.Text)).ToString("F");
      break;
    }
  }
  }
}
```

Chapter 10 Quick Reference

To	Do this
Inherit from a base class	In C#, insert a colon (:) and then list the class to be inherited after the class name.
Render output from a control	Override the *Render* method of the control class from which the custom control is derived. To take advantage of the rendered output of controls like *TextBox* and *Label*, call the *Render* method of the base class when you are finished rendering custom output.
Handle postbacks	Implement the *IPostBackDataHandler* and/or *IPostBackEventHandler* interfaces, and implement the methods defined by the interfaces.
Maintain state in a custom control	Store state in and retrieve state from the ViewState object in your property procedures.

11

Creating and Using Web Services

In this chapter, you will learn how to

✔ *Determine when to use a Web service.*

✔ *Create a Web service.*

✔ *Advertise and locate a Web service.*

✔ *Consume a Web service.*

Previous chapters have focused on the creation of ASP.NET Web Forms, the technologies that make ASP.NET development possible, and those that make it very simple and quick to create robust, feature-rich Web applications. Another important and useful part of ASP.NET is XML-based Web services.

Today, Web services are not a very well-understood technology. This is partly because of inaccurate and superficial reporting from the media, which describes Web services as everything from subscription software to a proprietary plot by Microsoft to take over the Internet. These stories might sound great in print, but they are based on misunderstandings and ignorance of this potentially revolutionary technology.

Understanding XML-Based Web Services

For many years, developers have sought ways to reuse the products of their work and combine the disparate systems that their organizations already invested in into a cohesive whole. This quest has been fraught with difficulties, ranging from disparate platforms and systems with no common standard for communication to security measures that prevent potential clients outside a corporate network from using existing functionality.

Early on, Remote Procedure Calls (RPC) were used as a way to allow one machine to use the functionality of a remote machine. RPC involved calling a function on a client machine and passing parameter information to the server, which in turn passed result and status information back to the client. Although RPC worked, it required at least one developer who understood the somewhat arcane world of Interface Definition Language (IDL). Distributed COM (DCOM) offered a somewhat simpler solution, but both RPC and DCOM required opening normally unopened ports in corporate firewalls, and the binary nature of the communications between client and server (also known as the *wire format*) caused problems when, for instance, integer sizes or internal byte ordering differed from machine to machine. Even with two Microsoft Windows machines communicating using DCOM, configuration problems caused many veteran programmers to give up on DCOM.

Some of the solutions for these difficulties have included creating custom Web front-ends for existing functionality, and using proprietary communications and/or packaging technologies to bridge the gap between systems. The former solution worked well in some situations, but the organization hosting the application had to create and maintain a UI for the functionality, as well as create a front-end for any additional functionality added later. Moreover, this UI might not meet the needs of their existing or future clients. The use of proprietary communications or bridging software typically meant greater expense, reliance on a single vendor, and dependence on that vendor's maintenance and upgrades. XML-based Web services address both of these issues squarely, allowing programmatic functionality to be exposed without the need for a custom Web-based UI and proprietary bridging software.

Web services are discrete units of programmatic functionality exposed to clients through standardized communication protocols and data formats, namely HTTP and XML. These protocols and formats are both well understood and widely accepted. (Although XML is still a relatively immature technology, it has rapidly gained acceptance in the industry due to its promise as a bridging technology.)

By communicating over HTTP, Web services overcome the problem of communicating across the Internet and corporate firewalls without resorting to proprietary solutions that require additional communications ports to be opened to external access. Because Web services use XML to format requests and responses, Web services can be exposed from and consumed by any platform that can format and parse an XML message. This allows XML-based Web services to bring together disparate pieces of functionality, whether existing or new, or internal or external to an organization, into a coherent whole. The following illustration shows how XML-based Web services can bring together a variety of applications and platforms. Note that because XML Web services can communicate over standard protocols such as HTTP, they can work over firewalls. In addition to the interactions shown, server-to-server Web services calls are also possible.

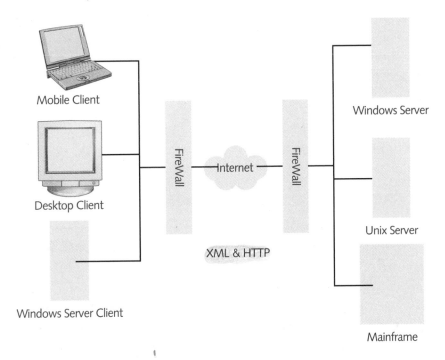

Web services are accessed by calling into a listener that is able to provide a contract to describe the Web service, process incoming requests or pass them on to other application logic, and pass any responses back to the client. The following illustration shows how a Web service application can be layered. It is also possible to use Web services to access legacy logic as well as new application logic, or wrap legacy logic for access by a Web service.

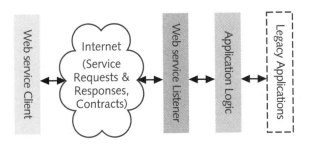

SOAP and Web Services

The SOAP protocol is a key enabler of XML-based Web services as a strategy for application integration and Internet-based software services. SOAP, which stands for Simple Object Access Protocol, is an XML-based messaging protocol that is being standardized by the World Wide Web Consortium (W3C) and has wide support from a variety of vendors. The SOAP specification provides a mandatory format for SOAP messages (referred to as *SOAP envelopes*), as well as optional standards for data encoding, request/response processing, and binding of SOAP messages to HTTP.

SOAP and XML-based Web services are beyond the scope of this book. Fortunately, one of the advantages of the ASP.NET programming model is that it abstracts the complexity of SOAP messaging from the development of Web services.

Additional Needs for Web Services

As mentioned earlier in this chapter, a Web service is simply a way to provide discrete units of application functionality over standard Web protocols, using a standardized message format. To be truly useful, however, Web services also need to provide the following:

- A contract that specifies the parameters and datatypes it expects, as well as the return types (if any) that it sends to callers.
- A means of locating the Web services offered by a given server or application, and the descriptions of those services.

The next several sections will examine creating, advertising, locating, and consuming Web services from the standpoint of an ASP.NET Web developer.

Creating a Web Service

In ASP.NET, the complexities of SOAP messaging and HTTP transport are abstracted from developers, so creating XML-based Web services is actually quite simple. This abstraction is enabled through attributes that tell the common language runtime to treat a specified class and its methods as Web services. Based on these attributes, the runtime provides all the plumbing necessary to expose the class and methods as Web services, a contract that clients can use to determine how to call the Web service, and the return types to expect from it.

Declaring a Web Service

Web services in ASP.NET are defined in files with the .asmx file extension. The actual code for an ASP.NET Web service can reside either in the .asmx file or in a precompiled class. Either way, the Web service is declared in the .asmx file by adding the @ *WebService* directive to the file. The syntax for declaring a Web service in which the class will be defined within the .asmx files is

```
<%@ WebService Language="VB" Class="ClassName" %>
```

ClassName is the name of the class that contains the Web service methods. The syntax for declaring a Web service in which the code that defines the class and methods resides in a compiled class is

```
<%@ WebService Class="NamespaceName.ClassName,AssemblyName" %>
```

NamespaceName is the name of the namespace in which the class for the Web service resides, *ClassName* is the name of the class that contains the Web service methods, and *AssemblyName* is the name of the assembly that contains the compiled code for the Web service. This assembly should reside in the bin directory of the Web application in which the .asmx file resides. The *NamespaceName* portion of the *Class* attribute is optional if you have not specified a namespace for your class, but it is good practice to always specify a namespace for your classes. The *AssemblyName* portion of the *Class* attribute is also optional because ASP.NET will search the bin directory for the assembly if no assembly name is provided. However, you should always provide an assembly name to avoid the performance impact of doing a search the first time the Web service is accessed.

note

Unlike using code-behind with ASP.NET Web Forms, you cannot use the *src* attribute with a Web service. This means that you must precompile the code-behind class that is to be used as the basis for the Web service, either manually using the command-line compiler, or by building a Visual Studio .NET Web Service application.

> **important**
>
> Visual Studio .NET provides a default framework for any Web service you create inside its IDE. The following section describes the specifics of creating a Web service class. In the following section, examples will be created using Visual Studio .NET, so many of the tasks required to get a basic Web service class will be in place with the default class created in the IDE. Nonetheless, it is important to understand the base classes and attributes used to create a Web service.

Creating the *WebService* Class

Each .asmx file is associated with a single class, either inline in the .asmx file or in a code-behind class. Either way, the syntax of a Web service class is as follows:

```
using System.Web.Services;

namespace NamespaceName
{
  public class ClassName : System.Web.Services.WebService;
  {
  // Methods exposed by the Web service
  }}
```

NamespaceName is the name of the namespace containing the *WebService* class. *ClassName* is the name of the *WebService* class.

Inheriting from *WebService*

In this syntax example, there is a *Using* statement specifying the *System.Web.Services* namespace. This namespace contains the classes and attributes that provide ASP.NET's built-in support for XML-based Web services. In this case, the class we care about is *WebService*, which is inherited in this example using the C# syntax that indicates the ancestor class. Note that the class name in the declaration is followed by a colon and the name of the WebServices class. Inheriting from the *WebService* class is not required for a class to function as a Web service, but the *WebService* class provides useful plumbing for Web services. This includes access to *Application*, *Session*, and other ASP.NET objects, including the *Context* object, which provides access to information about the HTTP request that invokes the Web service. Any Web service you create using Visual Studio .NET will use the WebService class as the base class.

Metadata Attributes

Prior to this chapter, the term *attributes* has referred to the key/value pairs added to HTML or ASP.NET server control tags to define specific properties of those entities or controls. This chapter introduces the concept of *Metadata* attributes.

ASP.NET and the Microsoft .NET Framework make extensive use of attributes to provide programmatic plumbing for classes, and add descriptive information to managed assemblies. You can also use your own attributes (by creating classes derived from *System.Attribute*) to add your own descriptive information to your classes.

Attributes in ASP.NET Web services, in addition to providing access to the XML namespace used for the Web service, are used to tell ASP.NET that a given method is to be exposed as a *WebMethod*. ASP.NET then provides all the runtime functionality necessary for clients of the Web service to access the *WebMethod* without requiring the programmer to write additional code.

Using the *WebService* Attribute to Specify XML Namespace

XML-based Web services use XML namespaces to uniquely identify the endpoint or listener to which a client sends requests. By default, ASP.NET sets the XML namespace for a Web service to *<http://tempuri.org/>*. If you plan to make your Web service available publicly over the Internet, change the default namespace to avoid potential conflicts with other XML-based Web services using the same name as your Web service, and that also might use the default namespace.

You can modify the default namespace for a Web service class by adding the *WebService* metadata attribute to the class definition and setting its *Namespace* property to the desired value for the new namespace. This value can be any unique URI that you control, such as your organization's domain name. The namespace is used only for identification; the URI specified is not used in any other way and need not be a valid, accessible Web site.

In C#, metadata attributes use the syntax *[AttributeName(PropertyName=value)]* and are placed just preceding the declaration for the entity (class, method, and so on) that they modify. For instance:

```
[WebService(Namespace="http://www.aspnetsbs.com/webservices/")] _
public class ClassName
```

Multiple properties can be set in an attribute declaration and are separated by commas.

Using the *WebMethod* Attribute to Expose Methods

After you've declared the class that implements the Web service, you will need to add one or more methods that provide functionality for the Web service. Each method will use the *WebMethod Metadata* attribute to declare the method as one for which ASP.NET should provide the necessary plumbing to expose it to clients.

To add the *WebMethod* attribute to a C# method, use the following syntax:

```
[WebMethod()]
public <ReturnType> MethodName()
{
    // method code
}
```

MethodName is the name of the method to be exposed by the Web service, and *ReturnType* is the type of the value (if any) to be returned by the method. Even if your method does not return a value that is a result of a calculation or other action, it is usually a good idea to at least return a value that indicates the success or failure of the method rather than declaring a void method.

WebMethod Attribute Properties

Like the *WebService* attribute, the *WebMethod* attribute has properties that you can use to alter the behavior of the Web method. These properties are described in the following table.

Table 11-1. *WebMethod* Properties	
Property	**Description**
BufferResponse	Determines whether output from the method is buffered in memory before being sent to the client. The default is *True*.
CacheDuration	Allows the output of a Web service method to be cached on the server for the specified duration, in seconds. The default is *0*, which turns off caching for the method.
Description	Sets a text description of the Web service method. This description is shown in the documentation pages auto-generated by ASP.NET, and it's included in the Web Service Description Language (WSDL) contract for the Web service.

Property	Description
EnableSession	Determines whether session support is enabled for the Web service method. Default is *False*. Enabling session state requires the Web service class to inherit from *WebService*. Note that enabling session state for a Web service might have a negative impact on performance.
MessageName	Allows methods to be given alias names. This can be useful when you have an overloaded method in which the same method name has multiple implementations that accept different input parameters. In this case, you can supply a different *MessageName* for each overloaded method version, allowing you to uniquely identify each one. The default is the method name.
TransactionOption	Allows adding support for COM+ transactions in a Web service method. Allowable values are *Disabled*, *NotSupported*, *Supported*, *Required*, and *RequiresNew*. The default is *Disabled*. Note that this property requires the use of an @ *Assembly* directive to load the *System.EnterpriseServices* assembly into the Web service application.

Create a HelloWorld Web service

1 Create a new project in Visual Studio .NET. Unlike previous projects, this project should be an ASP.NET Web Service rather than an ASP.NET Web Application. Name the project Chapter_11, and click OK. The resulting screen should show the default page, Service1.asmx.cs in design view, as in the following illustration:

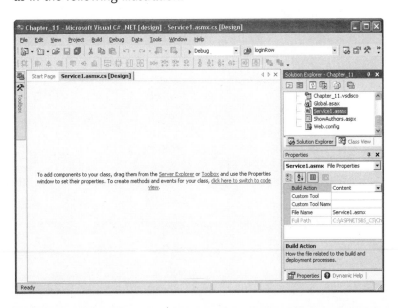

2   Unlike Web Applications, where a great deal of the work of building the page is done in Design view, Web services are generally modified using code directly. You can click the link provided in Design view to switch to Code view, or use the standard Visual Studio .NET key, F7. However you switch to Code view, the screen should look something like the following illustration:

3   Scroll to the bottom of the file, and locate a comment titled WEB SERVICE EXAMPLE. The code will look like the following:

```
// WEB SERVICE EXAMPLE
// The HelloWorld() example service returns the string Hello
World
// To build, uncomment the following lines then save and
build the project
// To test this web service, press F5

//    [WebMethod]
//    public string HelloWorld()
//    {
//        return "Hello World";
//    }
```

4   Remove the comments from the beginning of each line from *[WebMethod]* to the closing bracket of the *HelloWorld* method. Rather than leave this example exactly as it is created by Visual Studio .NET, add a parameter to *HelloWorld*, and append the parameter to the value returned. The finished method should look like the following code:

```
[WebMethod]
public string HelloWorld(string name)
{
    return "Hello World, from " + name;
}
```

5   To save the file, on the File menu, click Save Service1.asmx.cs. To build the application, on the Build menu, click Build Chapter_11.

6   Right-click Service1.asmx in Solution Explorer. On the shortcut menu, click Browse With, and then click Microsoft Internet Explorer in the browser list, and click the Browse button. The resulting screen should look like the following illustration:

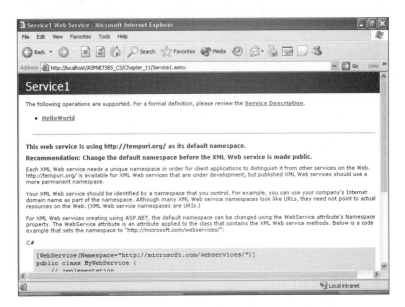

7   One thing that stands out on the illustration is the warning that the Web service is using the *http://tempuri.org/* namespace. There is a recommendation to change the namespace before the XML Web service is made public. Although it is unlikely this Web service will ever be made public, let's fix this now. Close the browser and return to the source code.

8 Add a line directly below the closing summary tag just above the top of the class declaration. Note that if you press Enter at the end of the line with the closing summary tag, you should see that Visual Studio .NET will insert three slashes (as a convenience, presuming you are adding more comments). Delete the three slashes if they appear. On the line just below the closing summary tag, add the following:

```
[WebService(Namespace="http://www.aspnetsbs.com/webservices/")]
```

9 To save the file, on the File menu, click Save Service1.asmx.cs. To build the application, on the Build menu, click Build Chapter_11.

10 Right-click Service1.asmx in Solution Explorer. On the shortcut menu, click Browse With, click Microsoft Internet Explorer in the browser list, and click the Browse button. The resulting screen should look like the following illustration:

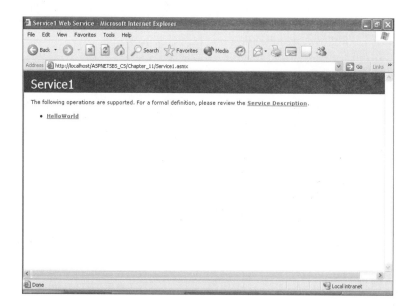

11 This screen is much cleaner. There are two links on this page. Click the first link, *Service Description*, and a screen like the following illustration will appear:

12 You can scroll through the entire document and see the complete WSLD contract for the Web service method. Click the Back button on the browser and select the other link on the page, *HelloWorld*. The screen should look like the following illustration:

13   In the text box provided for the name, enter your name, and click the Invoke button. The resulting screen should look something like this illustration:

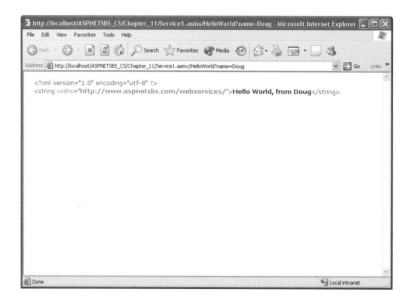

The complete source for the .asmx file and the code-behind file is shown here:

Service1.asmx

```
<%@ WebService Language="c#" Codebehind="Service1.asmx.cs"
Class="Chapter_11.Service1" %>
```

Service1.asmx.cs

```
using System;
using System.Collections;
using System.ComponentModel;
using System.Data;
using System.Diagnostics;
using System.Web;
using System.Web.Services;

namespace Chapter_11
{
  /// <summary>
  /// Summary description for Service1.
  /// </summary>
  [WebService(Namespace="http://www.aspnetsbs.com/webservices/")]
```

```csharp
public class Service1 : System.Web.Services.WebService
{
  public Service1()
  {
    //CODEGEN: This call is required by the ASP.NET Web Services
Designer
    InitializeComponent();
  }

  #region Component Designer generated code

  //Required by the Web Services Designer
  private IContainer components = null;

  /// <summary>
  /// Required method for Designer support - do not modify
  /// the contents of this method with the code editor.
  /// </summary>
  private void InitializeComponent()
  {
  }

  /// <summary>
  /// Clean up any resources being used.
  /// </summary>
  protected override void Dispose( bool disposing )
  {
    if(disposing && components != null)
    {
      components.Dispose();
    }
    base.Dispose(disposing);
  }

  #endregion

  // WEB SERVICE EXAMPLE
  // The HelloWorld() example service returns the string Hello
World
  // To build, uncomment the following lines then save and
  // build the project
  // To test this web service, press F5
```

```
    [WebMethod]
    public string HelloWorld(string name)
    {
      return "Hello World, from " + name;
    }
  }
}
```

important

The example Web services in this chapter all use the XML namespace *http://www.aspnetsbs.com/webservices/*. As with the default *http://tempuri.org* namespace, if you intend to make your XML-based Web services publicly available over the Internet, you should not use *http://www.aspnetsbs.com/webservices/* as the namespace for your Web service. Instead, use a URI that you control, and one that will allow you to be sure that your Web service can be uniquely identified.

Using Primitive Data Types

The *HelloWorld* example takes a single string as an input parameter, and it returns a value of type *String*. But XML-based Web services are not limited to strings and can accept input parameters of most types as well as returning values.

XML-based Web services in ASP.NET use the XML Schema Definition (XSD) draft specification to specify the datatypes that are supported by ASP.NET Web services. This includes primitive datatypes such as string, int, boolean, long, and so on, as well as more complex types such as classes or structs.

The definition for a Web service method that adds two numbers and returns the result would look like the following:

```
[WebMethod()]
public int Add(int Num1, int Num2)
{
    return (Num1 + Num2);
}
```

Accessing Data in a Web Service

In addition to primitive types, classes, and structs, ASP.NET Web services can also return or accept ADO.NET datasets as input parameters. This is possible because the *DataSet* class has built-in support for being serialized as XML, which can be easily sent over an HTTP connection.

Return data from a Web service

1   In Visual Studio .NET, open the Chapter_11 project, if it is not already open.

2   Create a new Web service. Right-click the root of the project, click Add on the shortcut menu, and then click Add Web Service. In the resulting dialog box, name the file AuthorsService.asmx, and click Open. When the Design view of the new Web service appears, click the link provided on the design surface to switch to Code view.

3   At the top of AuthorsService.asmx.cs, add the following line to the series of uses clauses at the top of the file:

```
using System.Data.SqlClient;
```

4   Just above the class declaration for the *AuthorsService* class, add the following line. If you press Enter at the end of the line with the closing Summary tag, Visual Studio .NET will add a new line with three slashes. Delete these before adding the line.

```
[WebService(Namespace="http://www.aspnetsbs.com/webservices/
")] _
```

5   Scroll to the bottom of the code file, and uncomment the commented *HelloWorld* method. Change the *HelloWorld* method to *GetAuthors*, and change the return type of the *GetAuthors* method from *string* to *DataSet*. Add a description to the following *WebMethod* attribute (just before the *GetAuthors* method), so that it looks like the following line:

```
[WebMethod(Description="Returns the Pubs Authors table.")]
```

6   Modify the *GetAuthors* method so that it looks like the following code, including removing the original return statement and replacing it in the code segment below. Much of the database access code should look very familiar from previous examples. Note that the connection is neither opened nor closed in this example. When the connection passed into the SqlAdapter constructor is closed, the SqlAdapter opens and closes the connection as needed.

```
public DataSet GetAuthors()
{
   DataSet dsAuthors = new DataSet();
   SqlConnection cn = new SqlConnection();
   SqlDataAdapter da;
   string strCn;

   strCn=@"server=(local)\vsDotNet;database=pubs;" +
     "Trusted_Connection=yes";
   cn.ConnectionString=strCn;
```

```
da=new SqlDataAdapter(
  "SELECT * FROM Authors ORDER BY au_LName,au_FName",cn);
da.Fill(dsAuthors,"Authors");
return dsAuthors;
}
```

7   On the File menu, click Save AuthorsService.asmx.cs. On the Build menu, click Build Chapter_11. Right-click AuthorsService.asmx in Solution Explorer. On the shortcut menu, click Browse With, and click Microsoft Internet Explorer, and click the Browse button. The screen should look like the following illustration:

8   Note that the description is specified as the WebMethod description. Click the *GetAuthors* link. This page looks similar to the last example page, which enabled you to invoke the Web service, except in this case, there will be the Invoke button, but no text box (because there are no parameters). Click the Invoke button, and you will be brought to a screen like the following illustration:

9   The schema for the resulting data is at the top of the result you saw when you invoked the Web service. Scroll down the screen a little way, and you will see actual data, as in the following illustration:

> **note**
>
> The descriptions of the data types supported by XML-based Web services in ASP.NET are specific to Web services that use SOAP for requests and responses. When using *HTTP GET* or *HTTP POST* for Web service requests (as in these examples), a more limited set of data types are supported, all of which are represented to the client as strings. Additionally, input parameters can only be passed by value, whereas parameters for SOAP requests can be passed either by value or by reference.

Advertising a Web Service

After you've created a Web service using the techniques in either of the previous examples, the Web service is ready to be accessed by clients. The challenge at this point is how to give clients the information necessary to enable them to access your Web service.

In an intranet-based scenario, this is relatively simple. You can provide potential internal clients with the URL to your Web service directly, either by e-mailing it to those who need it or by creating a centrally located Web page that users within your organization can browse to find the appropriate URL. In an Internet-based scenario, however, you might not know who your potential clients are. This makes it much more difficult to ensure that they can find and use your Web services.

There are two solutions to this dilemma: Web services discovery and Web services directories using Universal Description, Discovery, and Integration (UDDI).

Advertising Web Services Through a Discovery Document

A discovery document is an XML-based document containing references to Web services and/or other discovery documents. Through the use of discovery documents, you can easily catalog all the available Web services on a Web server at a single location.

By publishing a discovery document to a publicly available URL, you can make it possible for clients to easily locate and consume Web services you have made available. Clients can access the discovery document using tools such as the wsdl.exe command-line utility supplied with the .NET Framework, or Visual Studio .NET's Add Web Reference dialog box. We'll discuss this process in greater detail in "Using a Web Service" on page 439.

A discovery file uses the extension .disco and contains two types of nodes: *contractRef* nodes and/or *discoveryRef* nodes. The *contractRef* nodes refer to WSDL files that can be used to create clients for a Web service, while *discoveryRef* nodes refer to additional discovery documents. The discovery document for the two Web services examples created in this chapter is shown in the following listing, Chapter11.disco. The *ref* attribute of the *contractRef* node contains the URL to the WSDL contract for the Web service, in this case generated by ASP.NET, by appending the *?WSDL* argument to the URL for the .asmx file that implements the Web service. The *docRef* attribute contains the URL to the documentation for the Web service, in this case simply the URL, to the .asmx file because ASP.NET automatically generates documentation for Web services implemented in an .asmx file. The *xmlns* attributes in the *discoveryRef* and *contractRef* nodes establish the XML namespaces in which these nodes reside.

Chapter_11.disco

```
<?xml version="1.0" encoding="utf-8" ?>
<discovery xmlns="http://schemas.xmlsoap.org/disco/">
  <contractRef ref="AuthorsService.asmx?wsdl"
    docRef="AuthorsService.asmx"
    xmlns="http://schemas.xmlsoap.org/disco/scl/" />
  <contractRef ref="Service1.asmx?wsdl"
    docRef="Service1.asmx"
    xmlns="http://schemas.xmlsoap.org/disco/scl/" />
</discovery>
```

Note that for the sake of readability, relative URLs were used in this listing. Discovery documents can contain either relative or absolute URLs. When relative URLs are used, they are assumed to be relative to the location of the URL of the discovery document. If you browse to the disco file, it will be displayed just as any other XML file, as shown in the following illustration:

Visual Studio .NET creates a different kind document for discovery. ASP.NET supports dynamic discovery, using an XML-based file with a .vsdisco extension. For instance, in the example project for this chapter, the name of the .vsdisco file is Chapter_11.vsdisco. The file contains a set of paths that should be excluded from dynamic discovery. To maintain control over which services are exposed, dynamic discovery is appropriate only for development environments, so the .vsdisco file should not be copied to a development server.

Advertising Web Services Through UDDI

Another option for advertising Web services to potential clients is UDDI. This is a multivendor initiative, spearheaded by Ariba, IBM, and Microsoft, and is designed to provide an Internet-based business registry (or registries) in which creators of Web services can register their publicly available Web services. The UDDI specification describes how Web services can be registered in such a way as to allow clients to easily search for the type of Web service desired, or to discover all the Web services offered by a particular partner or company.

> **note**
>
> Although the UDDI initiative is based on Web standards and proposed standards such as DNS, HTTP, XML, and SOAP, UDDI itself is not a proposed standard. Rather, it's a multivendor specification, created and maintained by Ariba, IBM, and Microsoft, with input from other companies. It is the stated intent of the UDDI specification to be transitioned to a standards body eventually.

The model for UDDI is multiple identical versions of the UDDI business registry hosted by multiple participants, providing redundancy and load balancing for the registry. Web service providers can register their Web services at any node, and the information will be replicated to all registries daily, allowing potential clients to find these services from any registry.

Currently, both Microsoft and IBM provide online UDDI registries, and both can be reached from *http://www.uddi.org/*. You can also find a number of helpful white papers on UDDI there.

Securing a Web Service

One challenge of implementing a Web service comes when you need to limit who can access it. You might want to limit access to only those clients who have paid a subscription fee, for example. Or if your Web service stores and uses data that's specific to individual users, you might want to implement some sort of login process to allow clients to view and modify only data that is specific to them.

One potential issue with this is that the SOAP protocol, on which Web services are based, does not provide any specifications for securing Web services. Actually, the problem is not a total lack of standards, just the lack of a single standard that all sides agree on. This means that it's up to you to choose a means of securing your Web service that provides the level of security you need but that's also relatively easy to implement, for both you and your clients. The last thing you want is to make your Web service so difficult to use that potential clients go elsewhere.

Exploring Authentication Options

The first choice you must make is how to authenticate users of your Web service. There are a number of options, each with its own advantages and disadvantages.

Although ASP.NET does not define any specific authentication and authorization method for Web services, you can take advantage of the authentication mechanisms that IIS offers. These mechanisms are described in detail in Chapter 6, in the section titled "Using Windows-Based Authentication."

The advantage of using one of the IIS authentication mechanisms is that the infrastructure for them already exists. You do not need to create your own credential store for user account information. One disadvantage is that each of the authentication methods offered by IIS requires the creation of NT accounts for each client of your application. This can be difficult to administer, depending on how your Web server is set up (whether it is part of an NT domain, whether it uses Active Directory, and so on). Another disadvantage is that the Integrated Windows authentication method, although secure, requires the client to belong to the same domain (or a trusted domain) as the server, making it impractical for Internet use. Basic authentication is suitable for Internet use, but it sends user name and password as clear text, making it easy for them to be compromised. It can use SSL encryption to prevent this problem, but this might add an unacceptable performance overhead if user credentials must be passed with each Web service request.

Another option for authenticating users is a third-party authentication mechanism such as Microsoft Passport. Unfortunately, the developer tool support for Passport is still poor at present, and most available tools focus on allowing the use of Passport to authenticate users from Web sites, rather than Web services. Although it is likely that Passport and other third-party authentication mechanisms will add support for simple implementation in Web services eventually, today these mechanisms will probably require too much effort on the part of your clients.

Finally, you can "roll your own" Web services authentication by implementing a login function in one or all of your Web services, with the login method returning a unique key (which should be hashed or encrypted) identifying the logged-in user. This key is then passed as a parameter of each Web service request, indicating that the user is an authenticated user. To protect the user name and password, the login Web service method should be requested over an SSL connection. Subsequent requests can be made over a standard HTTP connection, however, so as to avoid the performance overhead of SSL encryption. To reduce the risk of a user being impersonated by someone who has intercepted the login key, these keys should be stored in such a way that they can be easily expired after a predetermined timeout value (in a back-end database, for example).

Although this authentication method is more difficult to implement and maintain than some of the others, it's the simplest for your clients to use. After you have given a client his or her account information (user name and password), all the client needs to do is make the request to the login Web service (over an SSL connection) and store the login key. With each subsequent request, the client passes the key as one of the parameters of the Web service method he or she is calling. If the timeout value expires between one request and the next, the client must call the login method again to receive a new key. Therefore, the value should be set to provide a balance between security and convenience. In addition to the login method, you could also implement a logout method in your Web service to explicitly expire the login key.

important

In addition to controlling access to a Web service with authentication, you should also consider using SSL to encrypt communications if you are passing sensitive data to or from the Web service. This includes user names and passwords sent when authenticating users. This also would include information such as patient information in the healthcare setting, where the requirement to protect personal data is not only common sense, it is the law!

Using a Web Service

Now that you've got a couple of nifty Web services, you'll probably want to know how to use them, beyond testing them by invoking them from a browser. Although the formatting of SOAP requests and responses necessary to call a Web service can be somewhat complicated, the .NET Framework abstracts away much of this complexity.

Nonetheless, you still need to know how to locate and use a Web service, including the following:

- Locating a Web service, using either a discovery document or UDDI
- Using the WSDL.EXE utility to create a proxy class for the Web service
- Using the proxy class from an ASP.NET page or console application to access the Web service

Locating a Web Service

The first step in using an XML-based Web service is to locate it. If you're dealing with a Web service that you or someone in your organization created, you might already know the location of the Web service. If so, you can skip this step.

Locating a Web service is essentially the mirror image of advertising a Web service, so the same techniques apply here. There are two techniques for locating a Web service in ASP.NET: discovery documents and UDDI.

Locating a Web Service with a Discovery Document

To use a discovery document to locate Web services, you need the URL for the discovery document that describes the services in which you're interested. You might get the URL for the document from a listing on an organization's public Web site, from an e-mail promotion, or from a catalog.

After you have the URL for a discovery document, you can use the disco.exe command-line utility to generate WSDL contracts for using the Web services described in the discovery document. The syntax for the disco.exe utility is

```
disco [options] URL
```

Here, *options* represents one or more command-line options for the utility, and *URL* represents the URL to the discovery document. The options for the disco.exe utility are shown in the following table.

Table 11-2. disco.exe Options	
Option	Description
/d:*domain* or /domain:*domain*	Sets the domain to use when connecting to a site that requires authentication.
/nosave	Prevents disco.exe from saving files for the discovered WSDL and discovery documents.
/nologo	Prevents the start-up banner from being displayed.
/o:*directory* or /out:*directory*	Provides the directory name where output should be saved.
/p:*password* or /password:*password*	Sets the password to use when connecting to a site that requires authentication.
/proxy:*url*	Sets the proxy to use for HTTP requests.
/pd:*domain* or /proxydomain:*domain*	Sets the domain to use when connecting to a proxy server that requires authentication.
/pp:*password* or /proxypassword:*password*	Sets the password to use when connecting to a proxy server that requires authentication.
/pu:*username* or /proxyusername:*username*	Sets the user name to use when connecting to a proxy server that requires authentication.
/u:*username* or /username:*username*	Sets the user name to use when connecting to a site that requires authentication.
/?	Provides help for command-line options.

Locating a Web Service with UDDI

Unlike using a discovery document to locate a Web service, UDDI does not require you to know in advance the URL of a document describing the desired Web service. Any provider of a UDDI business registry usually will provide a tool for searching their instance of the registry for businesses or Web services that meet your needs. The criteria you can search on will depend on the organization hosting that instance. For example, Microsoft's UDDI registry at *http://uddi.microsoft.com* supports searching by business name, business location, discovery URL, keyword, and a variety of other criteria. The following illustration shows the list of available criteria for searching the Microsoft UDDI registry.

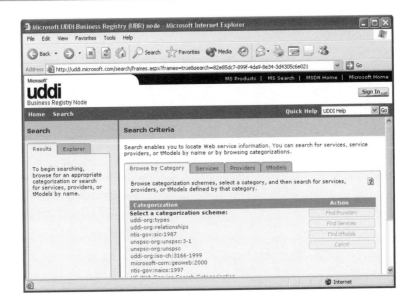

One effective technique for searching for Web services on the *http:
//uddi.microsoft.com* registry is to search by discovery URL and search
for URLs that contain "wsdl." These URLs are the most likely to point
to live WSDL contracts that you can use to access available Web services.

Understanding WSDL Files

WSDL is an XML-based standard for documents that describe the services
exposed by a Web service. You can view the WSDL contract for any of the Web
services you create with ASP.NET by calling up the URL for a Web service in a
browser and appending *?WSDL* to it.

WSDL contracts are similar to COM type libraries or .NET assembly metadata
in that they are used to describe the public members of the Web service, including
all publicly available methods, the parameters (and datatypes) those methods
expect when called, and the return type of any return value. Because this information is encoded in a standard XML-based format, any client that can read
XML and understand WDSL and SOAP should be able to effectively consume
the Web application that the WSDL contract describes.

Creating Web Services

11

> **important**
>
> The SOAP and WSDL specifications are still in the process of being standardized. In the short term, this means that there might be inconsistencies between different implementations of WSDL on different platforms because these implementations might be based on different drafts of the proposed standard. Until SOAP and WSDL become settled standards (W3C recommendations), you might need to tweak your WSDL contracts to achieve interoperability between different Web services implementations. This should become a nonissue after these specifications have received approval as W3C recommendations. In the meantime, there is an interesting article on interoperability between various Web services implementations on the MSDN Library Web site at *http://msdn.microsoft.com/library/en-us/dn_voices_webservice/html/service08152001.asp.*

Creating a Proxy Class

Consuming a Web service through SOAP is a fairly complex affair. It involves creating and formatting a SOAP envelope, a set of SOAP headers, and a SOAP body, all with the correct elements and attributes for the Web service you're targeting. Fortunately, thanks to the built-in support for Web services in the .NET Framework, all the plumbing necessary for accessing a Web service is provided for you. The .NET Framework provides another command-line utility, wsdl.exe, to help you by creating a .NET proxy class for a Web service described by a WSDL contract.

Using the wsdl.exe Utility

The wsdl.exe utility generates a proxy class in C#, Visual Basic .NET, or JScript .NET for a WSDL contract specified by URL or path. This proxy class can be instantiated and its methods called by any client, just like any other .NET class. Visual Studio .NET provides an easier way to generate a proxy class, which will be covered in the next example. However, there might be times (especially if you have special requirements not met by the standard proxy classes) when manually creating the proxy class might be handy.

The syntax for the wsdl.exe utility is as follows:

```
wsdl [options] {URL | path}
```

Here, *options* represents one or more command-line options for the utility, and *URL* represents the URL to the WSDL contract. Alternately, a file path to the WSDL contract can be passed as the *path* argument. The options for the wsdl.exe utility are shown in the following table.

Table 11-3. wsdl.exe Options	
Option	**Description**
/appsettingurlkey:*key* or /urlkey:*key*	Sets the key of the configuration setting from which to read the default URL for generating code.
/appsettingbaseurl:*baseurl* or /baseurl:*baseurl*	Sets the base URL to use for calculating relative URLs when a URL fragment is specified for the *URL* argument.
/d:*domain* or /domain:*domain*	Sets the domain to use when connecting to a site that requires authentication.
/l:*language* or /language:*language*	Sets the language to use when generating the proxy class. Valid values include CS, VB, JS, or the fully qualified name of any class that implements the *System.CodeDom.Compiler. CodeDomProvider* class. Default is CS (C#).
/n:*namespace* or /namespace:*namespace*	Sets the namespace to be used when generating the proxy class.
/nologo	Prevents the start-up banner from being displayed.
/o:*filename* or /out:*filename*	Provides the file name (and path) to use for saved output.
/p:*password* or /password:*password*	Sets the password to use when connecting to a site that requires authentication.
/protocol:*protocol*	Sets the protocol (SOAP, HTTP-GET, or HTTP-POST) to use for requests. Default is SOAP.
/proxy:*url*	Sets the proxy to use for HTTP requests.
/pd:*domain* or /proxydomain:*domain*	Sets the domain to use when connecting to a proxy server that requires authentication.
/pp:*password* or /proxypassword:*password*	Sets the password to use when connecting to a proxy server that requires authentication.
/pu:*username* or /proxyusername:*username*	Sets the user name to use when connecting to a proxy server that requires authentication.
/server	Creates an abstract base class with the same interfaces as specified in the WSDL contract.
/u:*username* or /username:*username*	Sets the user name to use when connecting to a site that requires authentication.
/?	Provides help for command-line options.

11

Creating Web Services

Create proxy classes in C#

1   Open a command line and navigate to the directory where you would like the proxy classes to be generated. (Or use the /o option to specify a path and file name for saving the proxy class.)

2   Execute the wsdl.exe utility, using the /l option to specify C# as the language and passing the URL to the HelloService.asmx file, including the *?WSDL* parameter, which tells ASP.NET to return the WSDL contract for the .asmx file. If you do not have wsdl.exe on your path, you can either add the folder with wsdl.exe to your path, or copy wsdl.exe to the folder you are working in. (Both lines below should form a single command.) The URL you specify should match the location of the .asmx file on your Web server, and it might differ from the following URL.

```
wsdl /l:cs /n:ASPNETSBS_CS
http://localhost/aspnetsbs_cs/Chapter11/Service1.asmx?WSDL
```

3   Execute the wsdl.exe utility again for AuthorsService.asmx, using the same syntax as shown in step 2 but modifying the URL to point to AuthorsService.asmx.

4   Optionally, you can create a batch file (with the .bat extension) containing both of the preceding commands. If you want to see the results of the batch execution before the command window closes, add a *pause* command at the end of the batch file.

After you've created your proxy class(es), you'll need to compile the class(es) using the command-line compiler for the language you chose to generate (in this example, C#). You should add the folder with the C# compiler (csc.exe) to your path. The following listing, MakeServices.bat, shows the command-line compiler syntax to compile these classes and output the resulting assembly to the bin subdirectory of the directory from which the command is run. Note that this listing represents a single command and has been wrapped to multiple lines for readability.

MakeServices.bat

```
csc /t:library /r:System.Web.dll /r:System.dll
/r:System.Web.Services.dll /r:System.Xml.dll /r:System.Data.dll
/out:bin\Services.dll Authors.cs Service1.cs
```

Consume a Web service from Visual Studio .NET

1 Open the project for this chapter, Chapter_11, in Visual Studio .NET, if it is not already open.

2 Right-click the root of the project in Solution Explorer, and on the shortcut menu, click Add Web Reference. In the Add Web Reference dialog box, fill in the URL to the AuthorsService.asmx file, and press Enter. The resulting screen should look something like the following illustration:

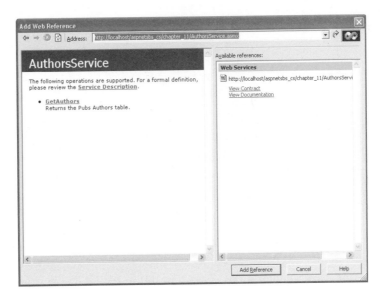

3   Click the Add Reference button in the bottom right corner of the Add Web Reference dialog box. When the Add Web Reference dialog box closes, look in Solution Explorer. Under Web References, there will be a node added called localhost (presuming the URL entered in step 2 was on the localhost domain. Expand that element, and Solution Explorer should look something like the following illustration:

4   Right-click localhost, and click Rename on the shortcut menu. Rename localhost as **Authors**. When you add a Web Reference, Visual Studio .NET creates a folder with the same name as the Web reference under the Web References folder that is under the main project folder. There are several files created by Visual Studio .NET in this folder. Most interesting is Reference.cs. This file will be discussed a little further after this example.

5   Right-click the root of the project in Solution Explorer, point to Add and then click Add Web Form on the shortcut menu. Change the name of the new form to ShowAuthors.aspx, and click Open. Right-click ShowAuthors.aspx in Solution Explorer and click Set As Start Page on the shortcut menu.

6   Drag a DataGrid component from the toolbox to the surface of the page of ShowAuthors.aspx.

7   Press F7 to change to Code view. Scroll down to the *Page_Load* method, and modify it so that it looks like the following code:

```
private void Page_Load(object sender, System.EventArgs e)
{
  DataSet ds;
  Authors.AuthorsService svc=new Authors.AuthorsService();
  ds=svc.GetAuthors();
  DataGrid1.DataSource=ds.Tables["Authors"];
  DataBind();
}
```

8   To save the page, click Save ShowAuthors.aspx.cson the File menu. To build the project, on the Build menu, click Build Chapter_11. To run the application click Start on the Debug menu, or press F5. The resulting screen should look like the following illustration:

The important thing to notice about this example is that although the table we are displaying is a SQL Server table, we do not reference System.Data.SqlClient. We do not have to because this application is not directly connecting to a SQL Server database. Rather, the application connects to the Web Service created earlier, and from there the Web service itself connects to SQL Server. Of course, in a real application, we would have used the tools that Visual Studio .NET provides to customize the appearance of the grid.

Looking at the Proxy Code

Web services use a proxy class on the client to allow access to the methods of the Web service. The proxy class contains all the methods and properties of the real class that you want to call using the Web service. Rather than actual functionality (in our case, the code that connects to the SQL Server database), the proxy code descends from *SoapHttpClientProtocol* and calls out to the required method indirectly using its own *Invoke* method. The proxy for the *AuthorsService* is shown here (reformatted somewhat for ease of viewing).

Reference.cs

```
//------------------------------------------------------------------
// <autogenerated>
//   This code was generated by a tool.
//   Runtime Version: 1.0.3705.209
//
//   Changes to this file may cause incorrect behavior and will be
//   lost if the code is regenerated.
// </autogenerated>
//------------------------------------------------------------------


//
// This source code was auto-generated by Microsoft.VSDesigner,
// Version 1.0.3705.209.
//
namespace Chapter_11.Authors {
  using System.Diagnostics;
  using System.Xml.Serialization;
  using System;
  using System.Web.Services.Protocols;
  using System.ComponentModel;
  using System.Web.Services;


  /// <remarks/>
  [System.Diagnostics.DebuggerStepThroughAttribute()]
  [System.ComponentModel.DesignerCategoryAttribute("code")]
  [System.Web.Services.WebServiceBindingAttribute(Name="AuthorsServiceSoap",
Namespace="http://www.aspnetsbs.com/webservices/")]
```

```csharp
public class AuthorsService :
System.Web.Services.Protocols.SoapHttpClientProtocol {

    /// <remarks/>
    public AuthorsService() {
        this.Url = "http://localhost/aspnetsbs_cs/chapter_11/
AuthorsService.asmx";
    }

    /// <remarks/>
    [System.Web.Services.Protocols.SoapDocumentMethodAttribute(
    "http://www.aspnetsbs.com/webservices/GetAuthors",
    RequestNamespace="http://www.aspnetsbs.com/webservices/",
    ResponseNamespace="http://www.aspnetsbs.com/webservices/",
Use=System.Web.Services.Description.SoapBindingUse.Literal,
ParameterStyle=System.Web.Services.Protocols.SoapParameterStyle.Wrapped)]
    public System.Data.DataSet GetAuthors() {
        object[] results = this.Invoke("GetAuthors", new object[0]);
        return ((System.Data.DataSet)(results[0]));
    }

    /// <remarks/>
    public System.IAsyncResult BeginGetAuthors(
    System.AsyncCallback callback, object asyncState) {
    return this.BeginInvoke("GetAuthors",
    new object[0], callback, asyncState);
    }

    /// <remarks/>
    public System.Data.DataSet EndGetAuthors(
    System.IAsyncResult asyncResult) {
        object[] results = this.EndInvoke(asyncResult);
        return ((System.Data.DataSet)(results[0]));
    }
  }
}
```

The *GetAuthors* method is quite simple, merely calling Invoke and returning the result. In addition to the *GetAuthors* method, there are two other methods that allow asynchronous invocation of *GetAuthors*.

tip

It's important to note that Web services clients are not limited to ASP.NET Web Forms. You can just as easily consume Web services from Windows Forms applications, Console applications, Windows Services, or even other Web services.

Chapter 11 Quick Reference

To	Do this
Create an XML-based Web service using ASP.NET	In Visual Studio .NET, create a new ASP.NET Web Service project. Visual Studio .NET will create the application in IIS and create a default Web service file with an .asmx extension.
Test a Web service	Browse the .asmx file containing the Web service from a Web browser. ASP.NET will generate documentation pages for the Web service, as well as allowing you to invoke the Web service.
Change the default name-space of a Web Service	Add or modify the *WebService* attribute, adding a Namespace="<new URL>" parameter.
Advertise a Web service	Either create a discovery document for your Web services and publish the document to a public location, such as your organization's Web site, or register your Web services in one of the publicly available UDDI business registries, making sure to provide the URL to the WSDL contract for each Web service you register.
Consume a Web service from ASP.NET	Use the wsdl.exe utility to create a proxy class-based on the WSDL contract for the Web service, compile the proxy class, and instantiate the proxy class from your client application as you would any other .NET class. Alternatively, simply right-click the project root in Visual Studio .NET, click Add Web Reference on the shortcut menu, and then enter a URL. If the URL is recognized and the methods available are displayed, click Add Reference.

12

Using Caching to Improve Performance

In this chapter, you will learn how to

✔ *Use output caching for Web Forms pages and user controls.*

✔ *Use caching for data retrieved with ADO.NET.*

✔ *Use the Cache APIs to get fine-grained control over expiration, dependencies, and other properties of cached items.*

The improvements in ASP.NET, from the use of compiled languages rather than interpreted languages to the complete rewrite of the ASP.NET execution engine, make it easy to get the performance that many applications need. Well-designed applications written in ASP.NET will almost always be faster than the equivalent applications written in classic ASP. But there is a class of applications for which these performance improvements alone will not be sufficient. This can include applications whose pages are computationally intensive (such as pages that use recursive procedures), applications that access large amounts of data, or applications that need to scale to large numbers of concurrent users. ASP.NET offers new features for this class of applications, including a simple API for output caching and a rich and robust caching engine and API.

Understanding Caching

Caching is the process of temporarily storing expensive resources in memory. These resources are called *expensive* because of the amount of processor time necessary to render them, because they reside on disk, or because they reside in a back-end database on another machine.

Pages that are expensive to render can consume so much processor time that the Web server becomes unable to fulfill additional requests in a timely fashion. Retrieving pages and other content from disk is much slower than serving them from memory, and this performance difference is magnified when the server needs to fulfill many requests simultaneously. Requests for large amounts of data from a back-end database often encounter both disk-based and network-based performance delays. (This makes calls from one server to another substantially more expensive than fulfilling a request on the same machine.)

For these reasons, Web applications that need high performance have long used caching to mitigate the performance costs of expensive operations. The output from recent requests, or requested data, is cached in memory. Subsequent requests are served from this in-memory cache, rather than rendering a page or querying a database again. This can substantially improve the performance and scalability of an application. Unfortunately, in the past this has come with a cost. Developers using classic ASP were limited to using the *Session* and *Application* intrinsic objects for caching, or rolling their own caching engine.

ASP.NET now offers a rich, robust framework for caching both page output and arbitrary data that developers can access easily using declarative and programmatic means. ASP.NET output caching enables developers to declaratively cache page and user control output to avoid wasting resources by repeatedly rendering content that does not need to change from request to request. The cache API provides a number of methods that enable developers to add and remove items from the cache and set properties that determine the lifespan of items stored in the cache.

Using Output Caching

Output caching enables you to cache the rendered output of any ASP.NET Web Forms page or user control and serve subsequent requests from the cache. This can substantially reduce the processor load on the Web server because the processor isn't busy rendering pages whose content hasn't changed. There are two basic techniques for enabling output caching: declarative and programmatic. The declarative technique uses the @ *OutputCache* directive and its associated attributes to enable output caching, whereas the programmatic technique uses the *Response.Cache* property to programmatically set caching parameters.

Using the *@ OutputCache* Directive

The simplest method to quickly set up output caching for a given page or user control is to add the *@ OutputCache* directive. This directive and its attributes enable you to set the length of time the content should be cached, the location where it should be cached, and any parameters to be used to cache multiple versions of a page. The following table describes the available attributes for the *@ OutputCache* directive.

Table 12-1. *@ OutputCache* Attributes		
Attribute	**Description**	**Value**
Duration	Sets the number of seconds to cache the content. This attribute is required.	
Location	Sets the location to be used to cache content.	*Any* Content can be any cache-aware application (such as a proxy server) in the request stream, by the Web server, or by the client browser. This is the default. *Client* Content is cached by the requesting client's browser. *Downstream* Content can be cached by any cache-aware application downstream of the Web server fulfilling the request. *Server* Content is cached on the Web server. *None* No caching.
VaryByControl	Sets the names of properties of a user control by which to vary the caching of the user control output. Multiple properties are separated by semicolons. This attribute can be used with user controls *only*.	
VaryByCustom	Allows varying of cached content by browser user agent, browser capabilities, or custom logic. When set to any value other than *browser*, this attribute requires that the *HttpApplication.GetVaryByCustomString* be overridden in Global.asax in order to implement the custom logic.	

(continued)

12

Using Caching

Table 12-1. @ *OutputCache* Attributes (continued)		
Attribute	**Description**	**Value**
VaryByHeader	Allows varying of cached content based on the value of one or more HTTP request headers. Multiple properties are separated by semicolons. This attribute can be used with Web Forms pages *only*.	
VaryByParam	Allows varying of cached content based on the value of one or more querystring values sent with a *GET* request or form fields sent with a *POST* request. Multiple key or field names are separated by semi-colons. You can also set the value of this attribute to * to vary by all parameters, or to *None* to use the same cached page regardless of *GET/POST* parameters. This attribute is required.	

Among the most important features of the @ *OutputCache* directive are the *VaryBy*X attributes, where X is Controls, Headers, Param or Custom, among other things. These attributes make it possible to cache pages and user controls even when those pages are dynamically generated based on querystring values, form field values, HTTP header values, or even browser capabilities.

You can use the *Duration* attribute to limit the length of time that output is cached. For pages that are updated periodically but not at every request, the *Duration* attribute enables you to fine-tune the output caching so that you can maximize the benefit gained by caching while being reasonably sure that users will not get stale content. For example, if you had a page that was updated every two hours on average, you could set the *Duration* attribute of the @ *OutputCache* directive to *15*. This would cache the output of the page for 15 minutes from the last time the page was requested (subject to the *VaryBy* attributes). This would ensure that the page would only need to be rendered once every 15 minutes regardless of how many requests were received for the page, and that there would only be a 15-minute window in which users would get a cached page rather than updated data.

Finally, the *Location* attribute determines where the output cache is located. Setting certain values for the *Location* attribute causes ASP.NET to set the *If-Modified-Since* HTTP header to allow caching of page or control output.

Cache Web Forms output

1 Open Microsoft Visual C# .NET. On the File menu, point to New, and then click Project. In the New Project dialog box, click ASP.NET Web Application. Name the new project *Chapter_12*.

2 To rename the initial default page to *OutputCache.aspx,* on the File menu, click Save WebForm1.aspx As. In the Save File As dialog box, enter **OutputCache.aspx** as the new file name, and click the Save button.

3 Right-click OutputCache.aspx in Solution Explorer, and click Set As Start Page on the shortcut menu.

4 Add two labels to the form. In the Properties pane, change the *ID* of the first label to **Message**. Change the text in the second label to **The text above was rendered with an ASP.NET Label Server Control, and then the output was cached for 10 seconds.** Expand the label as needed so that the resulting screen looks like the one shown here:

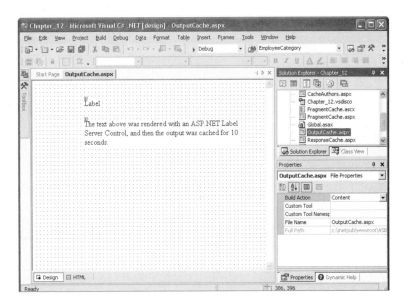

5 On the View menu, click Code, or press F7 to move to the code window.

6 Scroll down to the *Page_Load* event handler, and add the following code:

```
Message.Text=DateTime.Now.ToString();
```

7 To save the project, on the File menu, click Save All. To compile the project, on the Build menu, click Build Solution or press Ctrl+Shift+B.

8   Run the project. When you browse the page, refresh the browser several times. Each time you refresh the browser (as long as you wait at least one second before refreshing again) the time displayed in the Message label will change.

9   Go back to OutputCache.aspx and switch to HTML view. Add an *@ OutputCache* directive to the page, set the *Duration* attribute to **10** and set the *VaryByParam* attribute to **None**. This directive should appear on the line directly below the *@ Page* directive. The complete directive should look like this:

```
<%@ OutputCache Duration="10" VaryByParam="None" %>
```

10 To save the project, on the File menu, click Save All. To compile the project, on the Build menu, click Build Solution or press Ctrl+Shift+B.

11 Run the project. When you browse the page, refresh the browser several times. You should see the time displayed change only about once every ten seconds. The screen should look like the one shown here:

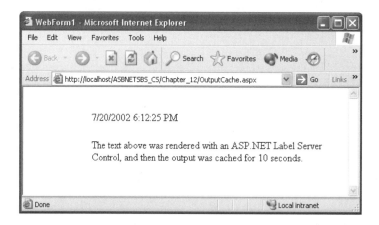

> **note**
> In the previous illustration, notice that even though we renamed the form toOutputCache.aspx, the title (displayed in the title bar) remains WebForm1. Microsoft Visual Studio .NET uses the default title as the file name when the form is created and does not update that when the file is renamed.

Caching User Controls

Caching the output of Web Forms pages can be very useful, but sometimes you might not be able to cache an entire page because of how frequently its content is updated. Don't fret—you can still take advantage of output caching by moving less frequently updated portions of a page into one or more ASP.NET user controls and then caching the output of the user controls.

Caching the output of user controls is nearly identical to caching page output. Instead of adding the @ *OutputCache* directive to the page containing the user controls, add the directive to the user controls themselves. As noted in the table on page 453, certain @ *OutputCache* attributes, such as *Location* and *VaryByHeader*, can only be used with Web Forms pages and will cause an error if included in a user control.

Cache user control output

1   In the same project as the last exercise, add a user control named **FragmentCache.ascx**. Right-click the root of the project in Solution Explorer, and click Add/Add Web User Control on the shortcut menu. Name the user control **FragmentCache.ascx**,and click the Open button.

2   The default layout in User Controls in Visual Studio .NET is Flow Layout. To add two labels (as we did in the last example, Outputcache.aspx), drag one label from the Toolbox to the form, click just after the label, press Enter, and then add the second label. In the Properties pane, change the ID of the first label to **Message**. In the Properties pane, change the text in label2 to **The text above was rendered from the User Control**.

3   On the View menu, click Code, or press F7 to move into the code window.

4   Scroll down to the *Page_Load* event handler, and add the following code:

```
Message.Text=DateTime.Now.ToString();
```

5   To save the project, on the File menu, click Save All. To compile the project, on the Build menu, click Build Solution, or press Ctrl+Shift+B.

6   In the same project, add a Web Form named **FragmentCache.aspx**. Right-click the root of the project in Solution Explorer, and click Add/Add Web From on the shortcut menu. Name the Web Form **FragmentCache.aspx**, and then click the open button.

7   Leaving room at the top of the page, add two labels to the form. In the Properties pane, change the ID of the first label to **Message**. Change the text in the second label to **The text above was rendered from the Web Forms page**.

8   Switch to HTML mode by clicking the tab control at the bottom of the Design window. Add the following @ **OutputCache** directive to the top of the HTML, just below the @ *Control* directive:

```
<%@ OutputCache Duration="10" VaryByParam="None" %>
```

9   On the View menu, click Code, or press F7 to move to the code window. Scroll down to the *Page_Load* event handler and add the following code:

```
Message.Text=DateTime.Now.ToString();
```

10   Switch to FragmentCache.aspx by double clicking on FragmentCache.aspx in Solution Explorer. You should be in Design mode. If not, switch to Design mode by clicking the tab control at the bottom of the Design window.

11   Drag FragmentCache.ascx from Solution Explorer onto the form. No matter where you place it, it will end up in the upper left hand corner of the Design window.

12   To set FragmentCache.aspx as the start page, right-click it in Solution Explorer, and click Set As Start Page on the shortcut menu.

13   To save the project, on the File menu, click Save All. To compile the project, on the Build menu, click Build Solution, or press Ctrl+Shift+B.

14   Run the project. When you browse the page, refresh the browser. The screen will look like this:

When you first run the page, both timestamps will be the same. If you click the browser's Refresh button several times, you'll notice that the time displayed by the page is updated with each page request, as shown in the illustration, whereas the time displayed by the user control is updated only once every ten seconds.

Caching Multiple Versions of Output

If your page uses either querystring values (*GET* requests) or form fields (*POST* requests) to dynamically generate content, you can use output caching. Add the *VaryByParam* attribute to the @ *OutputCache* directive with the values set to the names of the parameters by which to vary the cache. ASP.NET will cache a copy of the output from the page for each unique combination of parameters so any user who requests the page within the period specified by the *Duration* attribute with the same set of parameters as a previous request will have his or her request fulfilled from the cache.

caution

Because ASP.NET will cache a copy of the output for each unique combination of parameters, you should avoid using an excessive number of parameters to vary the cache. This can result in a great deal of memory use. This caution also applies to the *VaryByHeader* and *VaryByControl* attributes as well.

Use *VaryByParam* to cache multiple versions of a Web Form

1   In the same project as the last exercise, add another Web Form named **VaryByParam.aspx**. Right-click the root of the project in Solution Explorer, and click Add/Add Web Form on the shortcut menu. Click Web Form, and name the Web Form **VaryByParam.aspx** and click Open.

2   Add two labels to the form, one above the other. Add a text box on the right of the top label. In the Properties pane, change the text of the first label to **Enter Your Name**. Change the ID of the Text Box to **Name**. Set the text of the second label to **The text above was rendered with an ASP.NET Label Server Control,and then the output was cached for 30 seconds.** Set the *Visible* property of this second label to *false*. The result should look like this:

3 Add an @ *OutputCache* directive to the page, specifying the duration as 30 seconds and the parameter to vary by as the name of the *TextBox* control. To do this, switch to HTML view by clicking the tab control at the bottom of the Design window. The output directive must go just below the @ *Page* directive, and looks like this:

```
<%@ OutputCache Duration="30" VaryByParam="Name" %>
```

4 On the View menu, click Code, or press F7 to move to the code window.

5 Scroll down to the *Page_Load* event handler and add the following code:

```
if ( IsPostBack )

{
    Name.Visible=false;
    Label2.Visible=true;
    Label1.Text="Hello " + Name.Text;
    Label1.Text+=". The current date and time is ";
    Label1.Text+=DateTime.Now.ToString();
}
```

6 To make *VaryByParam.aspx* the start page, right-click it in Solution Explorer, and click Set As Start Page on the shortcut menu.

7 To save the project, on the File menu, click Save All. To compile the project, on the Build menu, click Build Solution, or press Ctrl+Shift+B.

8 Run the project. When you first browse the page, the screen will look like this:

9 Type your name and press Enter. The screen will look like this:

If you click the browser's Refresh button (and click Retry or OK to repost the form), the page will refresh from the cache. If you click Back and enter a different name, you will get a fresh version of the page. Try entering different names, refreshing, and then going back and entering the same names as earlier requests. You should see that all requests with the same name are cached for 30 seconds.

Using Response.Cache

In addition to using the @ *OutputCache* directive, you can also enable output caching for a page using the methods of the *HttpCachePolicy* class, which is exposed by the *Response.Cache* property.

The code required to perform the same output caching as shown in the OutputCache.aspx example is shown in the following listing. This code should be placed in the *Page_Load* event handler.

```
Message.Text=DateTime.Now.ToString();
Response.Cache.SetExpires(
DateTime.Now.AddSeconds(10));Response.Cache.Setcacheability(
HttpCacheability.Public);
```

This code is equivalent to an @ *OutputCache* directive with a duration of *10* and a location of *Any* (or no location attribute). To set the cache location to client, use the *HttpCacheability.Private* enumeration member instead of *HttpCacheability.Public*. To turn off caching entirely, use *HttpCacheability.NoCache*.

12
Using Caching

In addition to the *SetExpires* and *SetCacheability* methods you can also use the *SetNoServerCaching* method in combination with the code from ResponseCache.aspx to provide the equivalent of an @ *OutputCache* directive with a duration of *10* and a location of *Downstream*.

Caching Arbitrary Data

Like the *Application* and *Session* ASP intrinsic objects, the ASP.NET Cache engine offers a simple, straightforward means of saving arbitrary data to the cache and accessing that data through key/value pairs. The following code shows how to add a simple text value to the cache and retrieve it:

```
Cache["myFoo"] = "foo";
Response.Write(Cache["myFoo"]);
```

An important difference from the *Application* and *Session* collections, which can be accessed by either key or numeric index, is that cache items can only be accessed by their keys.

You can use this technique to store more than just strings, too. For example, the code in the following example, CacheAuthors.aspx, checks the cache to see if a dataset already exists. If not, it calls a method that creates a dataset containing data from the Authors table of the Pubs sample SQL Server database, and then it saves that dataset to the cache before setting the *DataSource* property of an ASP.NET *DataGrid* control to the default view of the first table in the dataset (0). In this example, rather than adding controls through the Design window, you will add controls in HTML view and then see the results in the Design window. Visual Studio .NET is a true two-way design tool.

> **note**
>
> To use a trusted connection to connect to SQL Server as shown in the preceding listing, you will need to either enable Windows authentication and impersonation or set up the ASPNET worker process account as a SQL Server login, as described in Chapter 9.

Cache DataSets

1   In the same project as the last exercise, add another Web Form named **CacheAuthors.aspx**. Right-click the root of the project in Solution Explorer, and click Add/Add Web Form on the shortcut menu. Name the Web Form **CacheAuthors.aspx** and click Open.

2 Switch to HTML view by clicking the tab control at the bottom of the Design window. Between the beginning and ending *<form>* tags, add the following code:

```
<asp:label id="title" text="DataSet Caching Example"
    font-name="Verdana" font-size="18" runat="server"/><br>
<asp:datagrid id="MyGrid" bordercolor="black"
    borderwidth="2" cellpadding="3" runat="server">
<headerstyle backcolor="silver" font-bold="true"/>
    <itemstyle backcolor="black" forecolor="white"/>
    <alternatingitemstyle backcolor="white" forecolor="black"/>
</asp:datagrid><br>
<asp:label id="Message" font-style="italic" runat="server"/>
```

3 Switch to Design mode by clicking on the tab control at the bottom of the Design window. The resulting screen should look something like this:

4 On the View menu, click Code, or press F7 to move to the code window.

5 Add the following line toward the top of the file just under the line *using System.Data*:

```
using System.Data.SqlClient;
```

6   Scroll down to the *Page_Load* event handler and add the following code:

```
DataSet DS = (DataSet)Cache["myDS"];
if ( DS!=null )
{
    Message.Text = "Dataset retrieved from cache";
}
else
{
    DS = GetData();
    Cache["myDS"] = DS;
    Message.Text = "Dataset retrieved from database";
}
MyGrid.DataSource = DS.Tables[0].DefaultView;
MyGrid.DataBind();
```

7   Below the *Page_Load* event handler, add the following method:

```
private DataSet GetData()
{
    DataSet myDS = new DataSet();
    string ConnStr;

    // Use @ so we do not need to escape
    //     backslash character.
    ConnStr = @"server=(local)\VsDotNet;";
    ConnStr += "database=pubs;Trusted_Connection=yes";
    string SQLSelect;
    SQLSelect = "SELECT au_id, au_lname, au_fname, ";
    SQLSelect += "zip FROM Authors WHERE zip = '94609'";
    SqlConnection mySqlConn = new SqlConnection(ConnStr);
    SqlDataAdapter mySqlDA = new SqlDataAdapter(SQLSelect,
ConnStr);
    mySqlDA.Fill(myDS);
    return myDS;
}
```

8   To make *CacheAuthors.aspx* the start page, right-click it in Solution Explorer, and click Set As Start Page on the shortcut menu.

9 To save the project, on the File menu, click Save All. To compile the project, on the Build menu, click Build Solution, or press Ctrl+Shift+B.

10 Run the project. When you first browse the page, the screen will look like the following illustration. Note that the data was retrieved from the database.

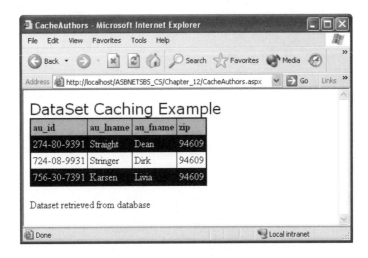

11 Refresh the browser. The screen will look like the following illustration. Note that now the data was retrieved from the cache.

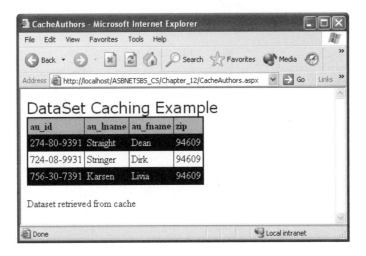

Using the Cache APIs

The question that comes to mind is, "How do I remove the dataset from the cache?" There are a couple of answers to this question, one simple and one more complex. Let's leave the more complex answer for the next section. The simple answer is that you can remove an item from the cache programmatically by calling the *Remove* method of the *Cache* class and passing it the key of the item to be removed. For example, you could add an ASP.NET button to the preceding example, and add the following line to the *Click* event handler for the button:

```
Cache.Remove("myDS");
```

This would clear the dataset from the cache and force the page to be rendered again using fresh data. (Note that because the *Page_Load* event fires before the *Click* event for the button, you might need to click the button twice before the datagrid and the label are updated.)

Understanding Expiration and Scavenging

The more complex answer to the question of how to remove items from the cache is that ASP.NET will actually do it for you. The complex part is that if you want to control *how* ASP.NET decides which items to remove from the cache, and when it does so, you need to provide ASP.NET with that information when you add an item to the cache.

You can do that by using the *Add* or *Insert* methods of the *Cache* class. Both let you pass parameters that tell ASP.NET when and/or on what basis to expire your cached content, as well as the priority your cached content should have when ASP.NET scavenges the cache for items that can be removed to free memory.

ASP.NET determines the order in which items are scavenged from the cache based on their priority. Over time, if an item is not accessed, ASP.NET will reduce its priority periodically. When its priority reaches a predetermined point, it might be scavenged. You can set the priority of an item by passing one of the values of the *CacheItemPriority* enumeration when calling the *Add* or *Insert* method. The following code is an example of the *Insert* method:

```
Cache.Insert("myDS", myDS, null, DateTime.Now.AddMinutes(2),
    TimeSpan.Zero, CacheItemPriority.High, null);
```

This inserts a dataset into the cache with the key *"myDS"*, passes *null* as the *CacheDependency* parameter, sets the expiration for two minutes from the time when the item is added to the cache, sets the *SlidingExpiration* parameter to *TimeSpan.Zero* (no sliding expiration), sets the cache priority for the item to *High*, and sets the callback function for the item to *null* (no callback function).

note

The *Add* and *Insert* methods of the *Cache* class provide essentially the same functionality, with two differences. The first difference is that all parameters of the *Add* method are required, so even if you are not using a particular parameter, you must still pass a placeholder parameter. The *Insert* method is overloaded, which makes this method easier to use when you want to pass only some of the possible parameters.

The second difference is that the *Add* method returns an object that represents the item just added to the cache, whereas the *Insert* method doesn't return a value.

You can also call the *Insert* method passing just the *Key (String)* and *Item (Object)* parameters, passing the *Key*, *Item*, and *CacheDependency* parameters, or passing the *Key*, *Item*, *CacheDependency*, *AbsoluteExpiration (DateTime)*, *SlidingExpiration*, and *(TimeSpan)* parameters.

Understanding File and Key Dependencies

Another important parameter that can be passed to either the *Add* or *Insert* method is the *CacheDependency* parameter, which takes an instance of the *CacheDependency* class as its value. The *CacheDependency* class enables you to create a dependency for a cached item on one or more files or directories (file dependency), or on one or more other cache items (key dependency). The constructor for the *CacheDependency* class has the following three forms:

```
// Monitor a file or directory for changes
CacheDependency myDependency;
myDependency = New CacheDependency("myFileorDirName");
// Monitor an array of file names and/or paths for changes
CacheDependency myDependency;
string[] myFileorDirArray;
myDependency = New CacheDependency(myFileorDirArray);
// Monitor an array of file names and/or paths, and an
// array of keys for changes
CacheDependency myDependency;
myDependency = New CacheDependency(myFileorDirArray, myKeyArray);
```

Note that to set up a key dependency without any file dependencies, you must create an array of keys (even if there is only one key) and pass *Nothing* (or *null* in C#) as the first argument to the constructor, passing the array of keys as the second.

```
string[] Keys = new string[1];
Keys[0]="myKeyName";
CacheDependency myDependency = new CacheDependency(null,Keys);
```

After the instance of *CacheDependency* has been created, it can be passed as a parameter to the *Add* or *Insert* method of the *Cache* class.

```
Cache.Insert("myDS", myDS, myDependency);
```

Invalidating the Cache Automatically on Data Change

One of the biggest challenges in using caching in your application is how to get the most out of it, even when you're dealing with data that is either frequently updated or must always be fresh. Although setting absolute and/or sliding expiration times for a cached item might reduce the likelihood of a user getting stale data, it's still possible.

What you need is a way to notify the ASP.NET cache to remove an item from the cache when a table has been updated. Fortunately, the *CacheDependency* class and the SQL Server Web Assistant make this easy.

To force a cached copy of the *Authors* query seen in the CacheAuthors.apsx example to be expired whenever the data in the Authors table is modified, follow these steps. Because this example uses the SQL Server Web Assistant, which does not ship with MSDE, it requires a full SQL Server installation.

Use a trigger to invalidate the cache

1   Create a trigger on the Authors table that uses the SQL Server Web Assistant to write a new HTML file when the data in the table changes.

2   Open SQL Server Enterprise Manager and select the *Tables* node of the Pubs database. This should be the Pubs database in your SQL Server instance, rather than the VSdotNET MSDE instance you've used for other examples.

3   Right-click the authors table in the table list, point to All Tasks, and click Manage Triggers.

4 Make sure that the *<new>* item is showing in the Name drop-down list. Add the following text to the trigger, replacing *filepath* with the path to the directory where you have saved the examples for this chapter and the file name *authors.htm*, and click OK.

```
CREATE TRIGGER WriteFile ON [dbo].[authors]
FOR INSERT, UPDATE, DELETE
AS
EXEC sp_makewebtask filepath, 'SELECT * FROM authors'
```

Follow these steps to create the page that will use the cache:

1 In the same project as the last exercise, add a copy of CacheAuthors.aspx, and name it **AuthorsTrigger.aspx**. Right-click CacheAuthors.aspx and click Copy on the shortcut menu. Right-click the root of the project, and click *Paste*. Double click *Copy of CacheAuthors.aspx* and then on the File menu, click Save Copy of CacheAuthors.aspx As to save the file as AuthorsTrigger.aspx.

2 Click the title, and change the *Text* property of the title to **Cache invalidate with trigger Example**.

3 On the View menu, click Code, or press F7 to move to the code window. Add the following line to the using clauses at the top of the code file:

```
using System.Web.Caching;
```

4 Change the name of the class in *CacheAuthors* to **AuthorsTrigger.aspx**.

5 Replace the line that reads *Cache["myDS"]=DS;* with the following code, which adds a file dependency on the file created by the SQL Web Assistant:

```
Cache.Insert("myDS", DS, New
    CacheDependency(Server.MapPath("authors.htm")));
```

6 Modify the connection string in the file to point to the SQL Server instance in which you created the trigger.

7 To make *AuthorsTrigger.aspx* the start page, right-click it in Solution Explorer, and click Set As Start Page on the shortcut menu.

8 To save the project, on the File menu, click Save All. To compile the project, on the Build menu, click Build Solution, or press Ctrl+Shift+B.

Using Caching

12

9   Run the project. When you first browse the page, the screen will look like the following illustration. Note that the data was retrieved from the database.

10   If you click the Refresh button on the browser, the data will be served from the cache and the output will look like this:

11   To make sure this works, open the Authors table in SQL Enterprise Manager (right-click the Authors table, point to Open Table, and click Return All Rows) and change one of the values in a row in the table that matches the query criteria for AuthorsTrigger.aspx (zip=94609). (Move the mouse pointer off the row being updated to make sure the update occurs.) Refresh the browser. The output should look like the illustration just shown.

Chapter 12 Quick Reference

To	Do this
Cache page or user control output	Add the @ *OutputCache* directive to the page or user control, or use the methods exposed by *Response.Cache*.
Vary the cache based on user input	Add the *VaryByParam*, *VaryByHeader*, or *VaryByControl* attributes to the @ *OutputCache* directive.
Cache arbitrary data	Insert items into the cache using either the simple syntax *Cache["myKey"] = myItem;* or by calling the *Add* or *Insert* methods of the *Cache* class.
Expire a cache item when another item changes	Insert the item to be expired with a key dependency on the other cache item.

13

Deploying an ASP.NET Application

In this chapter, you will learn how to

✔ *Store application-specific configuration settings for easy deployment.*

✔ *Set up a target IIS application.*

✔ *Copy content, Web Forms pages, Web services, and assemblies.*

✔ *Deploy using Microsoft Visual Studio .NET.*

Deploying applications has been a long-standing bane of many a classic ASP developer's existence, and for good reason. Although it was easy enough to deploy or replace static content and the ASP files themselves, other portions of the applications, such as components and application-specific configuration settings, required greater effort to deploy and often necessitated a shutdown of the application to replace.

Deployment is another one of the areas in which the improvements in ASP.NET truly shine. ASP.NET eliminates many of the deployment shortcomings in classic ASP, making it possible for the first time to deploy an ASP.NET application simply by copying all the necessary files to the IIS application directory where the application will be deployed.

This chapter will discuss the steps for deploying ASP.NET Web applications, both manually and through Visual Studio .NET.

Understanding the Structure of ASP.NET Applications

Although you learned about the structure of ASP.NET Web applications in Chapter 5, it is worthwhile to review this information. Understanding the structure of an ASP.NET application will make the deployment process smoother, and can help prevent unexpected errors and problems in your deployed applications.

Each ASP.NET application needs to have a corresponding IIS application root to function properly. Each time you create a new ASP.NET project in Visual Studio .NET, an IIS application root is created automatically. The application root provides the boundary for the application. The physical file system directory that maps to the application root is the location where the root Web.config file for the application, as well as the application's bin directory (which contains all managed assemblies related to the application) and the Global.asax file (if you choose to use one), are deployed. If the IIS directory that is the root of the application is not configured as an application root, certain configuration settings might fail and the assemblies located in the bin directory (if present) will not be loaded.

important

Windows XP offers multiple views of the Control Panel. The default view is called *Category* view and the optional view is called the *Classic* view. For this chapter, all instructions will be for the Classic view. To switch to Classic view click on the Switch To Classic View link on the left side of Control Panel.

Determine if a directory in IIS has been configured as an application

1   Open the Internet Services Manager plug in (called Internet Information Services in Windows 2000) by clicking Start, Control Panel, Administrative tools and then clicking Internet Information Services. (In Windows 2000, click Start, Programs, Administrative Tools, Internet Services Manager.)

2   Navigate to the directory whose configuration you want to check by expanding the Web site containing it and expanding other nodes as necessary. If the directory is configured as an application root, it will show an icon of a black globe in a gray box. If the directory is not configured as

an application, it will either show a folder icon (for content that resides directly within the path of the parent application root) or a folder icon with a small globe (for content that resides elsewhere in the file system). The following illustration shows examples of these icons:

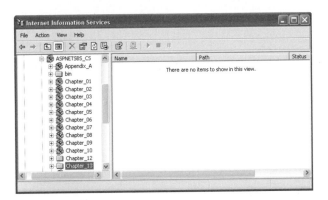

3 If the directory is not configured as an application, you can create an application root at this level. Right-click the directory, click Properties, and then click the Create button on the Directory tab (or Virtual Directory tab) of the Properties dialog box. The Properties dialog box for the Chapter_13 directory is shown in the following illustration:

4   Click OK to update the directory with the new setting. The directory should now show the icon for an application root, as shown in the following illustration:

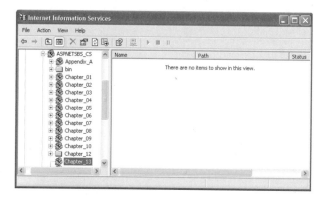

As you can see in these illustrations, IIS application roots can be nested one beneath the other. However, each application root defines its own application boundary. One advantage of this is that it enables you to partition your application as necessary. For example, you can provide customized configuration settings or use different versions of a private assembly with different parts of your application. The most important thing to remember, however, is that the application root is where the bin directory and Global.asax and Web.config files should be located.

Distinguishing Between Physical Path and URL

An important distinction to make when discussing deployment is between the physical path of an application (that is, the application's location within the file system of its server) and the URL of the application. This distinction becomes important when discussing the array of different tools available for deployment, some of which (like the DOS XCOPY command) use file or network paths, and some of which (like FTP and WebDAV) use URLs.

There is only a single file path for a given application root in IIS. However, there can be more than one directory in IIS that maps to a single physical directory in the file system. This enables you to set up URLs for both public and private access to a given application, with different IIS settings for each. If more than one IIS application root points to the same physical directory in the file system, each IIS application root will have its own IIS-specific settings. It is important to note, however, that if the physical directory contains ASP.NET-specific configuration and start-up files (Web.config and Global.asax), the settings in these files will be shared by both IIS applications.

One important caveat to this sharing is that when a subfolder containing a Web.config file and/or Global.asax file is defined as an application root in one of the IIS applications, it's not configured as an application root in the second IIS application. In the first case, which is illustrated by the following graphic, requests to this subfolder will use the Global.asax file for start-up code.

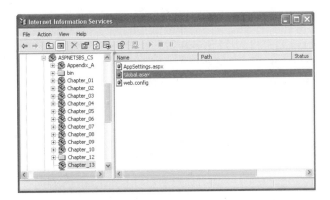

In the second case, illustrated by the following graphic, the Global.asax file contained within this subfolder will be ignored because the folder is not configured as an application in IIS.

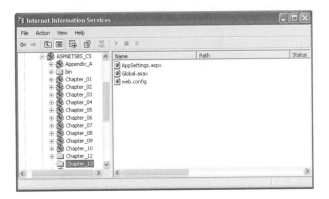

You should also note that there are certain settings in the Web.config file that are only applicable at the application root level. For example, if the Web.config file contained in the Chapter13 folder illustrated in the preceding graphic contains an *<authentication>* section, a configuration error will result because this section can only be defined at the machine (Machine.config) or application root level.

The URL for a specific application root in IIS is a product of the domain name (if any) associated with the IP address that is assigned to the IIS Web site, plus the folder hierarchy between the IIS Web site and the application root. Thus, in the previous graphic, where the aspnetsbs_CS application root resides under the default Web site, the URL to reach the Chapter13 directory would be either *http://localhost/aspnetsbs_CS/Chapter13/* or *http://*servername*/aspnetsbs_CS/Chapter13/*.

This works if you request the URL from the server containing the application because requests for *localhost* or *servername* (where *servername* represents the name of the Web server containing the application) are automatically directed to the default Web site. If you wanted to make the content of the Chapter13 application root available on the Internet, you'd need to create a new IIS Web site, assign a publicly available IP address on the machine to the Web site, and then create (or have a DNS provider create) a DNS entry that maps your chosen domain name (say, *www.aspnetsbs.com*) to that IP address. Then you would create a new application root under the new Web site that maps to the Chapter_13 directory in the file system. Then you could access this application from the Internet using the URL *http://www.aspnetsbs.com/Chapter_13/*.

Note that if you have directory browsing disabled (the default), you will need to set a default document on the Documents tab of the Properties dialog box for the directory, in case the user does not enter a document name. The name of the default document should match the name of a page that exists in the directory. This will allow access to content using a URL that does not contain a document name, such as the preceding URLs. If the name of the desired file is not appended, an error will occur.

Storing Application-Specific Configuration Settings

One of the challenges of deploying most non-trivial Web applications in classic ASP is figuring out where to store application-specific configuration information. In classic ASP, there were a number of approaches, including using custom keys in the system registry, storing configuration information in a back-end database, reading configuration settings from a custom configuration file, and building settings into components. Each approach has its own set of drawbacks that make it less than ideal.

For example, storing configuration information in the system registry makes that information relatively secure (particularly if proper registry security procedures are followed). However, adding that information to the registry or modifying it from a remote machine can be difficult, if not impossible, due to permission settings designed to protect the registry from remote tampering. Additionally, accessing settings within the registry can be expensive from a performance standpoint.

Storing configuration information in a back-end database or in custom configuration files won't provide easily repeatable procedures for multiple applications. The database solution requires that changes to the Web application and the configuration database be synchronized so that users always get the correct information. The custom configuration file solution requires building logic into pages or components to parse and cache the application settings, while periodically checking to see if settings have been modified and loading the new settings if they have.

To simplify this situation, ASP.NET provides a special section of the Web.config and Machine.config files called appSettings, which enables you to store application-specific configuration settings as a set of key/value pairs.

```
<appSettings>
    <add key="myConfigKey" value="myConfigValue" />
</appSettings>
```

When your application starts up, ASP.NET caches the values of the appSettings section in a string collection called *ConfigurationSettings.AppSettings*. These settings can be accessed by passing the desired key to this collection, as shown here:

```
Label1.Text = ConfigurationSettings.AppSettings["myConfigKey"];
```

In addition to automatically loading and caching these values for you at application start-up, ASP.NET monitors the Web.config file(s) for changes and dynamically reloads the appSettings if changes are detected.

important

Although appSettings provides a storage location for application-specific configuration settings that is almost ideal in its ease of use and performance, it should be noted that because the values are stored as plain text in a file in the Web space, there is some security risk associated with this approach.

note

If a vulnerability in the Web server allows access to the Web.config file, any sensitive information stored in appSettings could be compromised. For this reason, it is important to avoid storing sensitive information, such as user names, passwords, or credit card or account numbers, in the appSettings section of Web.config. For items of medium sensitivity, one solution would be to add the items to the appSettings of the Machine.config file, which is not located within the Web space, making it harder to compromise. Keep in mind, however, that the appSettings stored in Machine.config are available to every application on the server unless they are locked down using the *<location>* tag. (See Chapter 5 for more information about locking down configuration settings.)

Deploying a Web Application Manually

If you're developing ASP.NET applications against the Microsoft .NET Framework without the benefit of Visual Studio .NET, most (if not all) of your deployment work will be manual. The great news is that ASP.NET applications are simple to deploy. Even if you are using Visual Studio .NET, you might need to or want to deploy your Visual Studio .NET ASP.NET application manually.

Setting Up the Target Deployment Directory

To successfully deploy an ASP.NET application, the first thing you need is a target directory on the server that will host the application. This directory must be set up in IIS as an application root if you want to use the automatic loading of assemblies in the bin subdirectory or use a Global.asax file, and if you want to have a root Web.config file for the application. (Certain configuration sections cannot be set below the application level and they will cause errors if used in a Web.config file that resides in a subdirectory.)

Copying Files to the Target Directory

After you've set up the target directory in IIS (mapped to a physical folder on the host machine), you're ready to copy all the necessary files to the target directory. This can be done using any number of commonly available tools, from the XCOPY command to WebDAV. You can even drag and drop files to and from a network share using Windows Explorer.

If you're using code-behind in your Web Forms pages and/or user controls, you'll need to decide whether or not to deploy the code-behind class files containing your source code to the target server. If you're using the *Src* attribute of the *@ Page* or *@ Control* directive to have ASP.NET dynamically compile your code-behind classes, you will have to deploy the class files or the application will not function. If you want to avoid deploying the code-behind class files, you can use the *Inherits* attribute of the *@ Page* or *@ Control* directive instead of the *Src* attribute. Recall from Chapter 7 that using the *Inherits* attribute requires you to manually compile your code-behind classes and put the resulting assemblies in the application's bin subdirectory. Projects created with Visual Studio .NET will be created using the *Inherits* attribute of the *@ Page* or *@ Control* directive.

Deploying Content

Deploying static content (such as HTML pages and images), Web Forms pages, user controls, and code-behind classes is as simple as copying them from the development application directory to the deployment target directory. For example, you would use the following command to deploy content from a local directory, *C:\inetpub\wwwroot\myDevApp*, to a remote directory for which a mapped drive, *X:*, has been created:

```
xcopy c:\inetpub\wwwroot\ASPNetApp1 x:\ /E /K /O
```

XCOPY is a command line program that is a standard part of Windows, and should be on the system path. The parameters passed to XCOPY are as follows:

- */E* specifies that all subdirectories are to be copied, whether empty or not.
- */K* specifies that file and directory attributes on the destination should be set to match the source.
- */O* specifies that ownership and ACL information should be copied to the destination. This is useful when using domain accounts to set ACLs.

You can find out about all of the command-line parameters available with XCOPY by executing XCOPY /?.

Deploying Assemblies

One of the areas of great improvement in deployment is Microsoft .NET-managed assemblies over COM components. With classic ASP applications that used custom COM components, not only did you need to copy the component file to the machine on which the application was being deployed, you also needed to register that component in the system registry, which was difficult to do remotely. Additionally, registering a component made it available to any application on the server, which is not allowed in a shared server environment.

Because .NET assemblies are self-describing and assemblies are private to an application by default, you can simply copy an assembly to the bin subdirectory of an application and it will be available for use by the application automatically. Private assemblies do not need to be registered to be used, and they are available only to the application in whose bin directory they reside.

Global Assemblies

The exception to the rule of XCOPY deployment applies to assemblies that you want to make available to more than one application on the server without having multiple copies of the assembly (one for each application). These assemblies need to be installed in the Global Assembly Cache or GAC. Remember that assemblies installed in the GAC must be strongly named. This can be done by using the al.exe command-line tool. After you have a strongly named assembly, there are several ways to install it into the GAC.

- **Windows Installer 2.0**   This is the preferred method for installing assemblies into the GAC because Windows Installer performs reference counting and provides transactional installation, neither of which are available with the other options. See the Windows Installer documentation included in the Visual Studio .NET for more information on packaging and installing applications with Windows Installer 2.0.

- **gacutil.exe**   This command-line utility lets you add assemblies to the GAC, remove assemblies from the GAC, and list the contents of the GAC.

- **Windows Explorer**   The .NET Framework installs a shell extension that lets you simply drag and drop strongly named assemblies into the GAC from any Windows folder. The GAC is located at %WinDir%\assembly.

Deployment and Assembly Versioning

One nifty thing about global assemblies that compensates for the additional overhead of installing and removing them from the GAC is that they can contain versioning information. This allows two or more versions of the same assembly to be executed side-by-side, and client applications can request the version of an assembly they want to use, or accept the latest revision of an assembly.

Updating Assemblies

In addition to the problems of registering COM components, IIS locked any COM component as soon as it was called. Because of this, replacing or updating a COM component often required stopping the IIS Web service, unregistering the old component, copying over the new component, registering the new component, and restarting the Web service. For many applications, this meant an unacceptable amount of downtime.

With private assemblies, this is no longer a problem because of the way ASP.NET loads assemblies. Unlike IIS under classic ASP, which loaded a component into memory and locked it on disk until the Web application (or IIS) was shut down, ASP.NET first makes a shadow copy of each assembly file and then loads and locks the shadow file instead of the original. ASP.NET then monitors the original files for changes. If changes are detected, ASP.NET fulfills any existing requests with the current copy of the assembly, and then it loads the new assembly and fulfills new requests using the updated assembly, discarding the old assembly. This enables you to easily update any private assembly used by your application without needing to shut down the Web server, even temporarily.

Setting IIS Permissions for Subdirectories

After you've copied your content and assemblies to the target directory, it's a good idea to double-check the IIS permissions on any subdirectories in the application.

Fortunately, ASP.NET actually takes care of one of the most important checks for you. It automatically removes all permissions on the bin subdirectory of the application, effectively preventing the contents of the directory from being listed, read, downloaded, or executed.

Preventing IIS from executing the assemblies on behalf of clients might sound like a *bad* thing, but it's not. In fact, when a request comes in for a resource that ASP.NET handles, such as an .aspx, .ascx, or .asmx file, IIS simply hands the request over to ASP.NET, which processes the request from there. Because ASP.NET alone is responsible for loading assemblies, preventing IIS from attempting to execute assemblies is a *good* thing.

If you have subdirectories that contain static content, such as images, you should ensure that the only permission allowed on these subdirectories is *Read*.

Most importantly, if you need to allow users to upload content to your Web application, it is absolutely essential that you set up a separate subdirectory for this purpose, and set only the *Write* permission. *Read* must not be allowed on this subdirectory, nor should the *Execute* permissions be set to anything other than *None*. Failure to follow these guidelines could allow an attacker to upload and execute hostile code in your application.

You can view and modify the IIS permissions for any directory by right-clicking the directory name in Internet Services Manager and clicking Properties. The permissions are set on the Directory (or Virtual Directory) tab, which is shown in the following illustration:

Deployment Options in Visual Studio .NET

If you are developing Web applications with Visual Studio .NET, it is still possible to manually deploy your applications using XCOPY, WebDAV, and the like. However, you will probably find that it is more efficient to take advantage of one of the built-in deployment features available in the Visual Studio .NET IDE. These include the *Copy Project* command, which provides a fast and simple method for copying a project from one machine to another or from one directory to another on the same machine, and the Setup And Deployment Projects type, which provides much more fine-grained control over how your application is deployed.

Using Copy Project to Deploy a Web Application

The Copy Project command, which is accessed by clicking Project, Copy Project, enables you to copy just the files needed to run an application (only the .aspx files and related assemblies, plus any static content; code-behind class files are not copied), all the files in the project, or all the files in the source project folder, whether they are a part of the project or not.

You can copy files to either a URL using the FrontPage server extensions or to a file share. The Copy Project dialog box is shown in the following illustration:

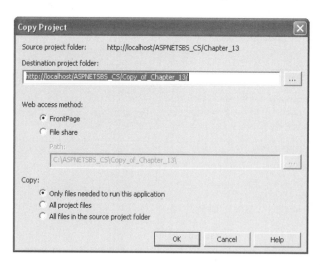

Using Copy Project is simple and straightforward, but it offers only limited control over which project files are copied and how they're copied.

important

The following section describes a feature available only on Visual Studio .NET Professional, Enterprise Developer, or Enterprise Architect editions. This will not work with the Deluxe Learning edition.

Using a Web Setup Project to Deploy a Web Application

Another method that Visual Studio .NET offers for deploying Web applications is the Web Setup Project, which is one of the templates available in the Setup And Deployment Projects project type. The following illustration shows the Web Setup project selected in the New Project dialog box:

A Web Setup project enables you to specify a variety of options about how the application will be deployed, including which files to include, the name of the deployed application, and the location of the deployed files. When built, the Web Setup project creates a Windows Installer .msi file that can be copied to the target machine and executed to deploy the application.

Create a Web Setup Project in Visual Studio .NET

1 Open an existing Web application solution in Visual Studio .NET Professional, Enterprise Developer, or Enterprise Architect editions.

2   Right-click the solution name in Solution Explorer, point to Add, and click New Project. The New Project dialog box will appear. Click the Setup And Deployment Projects type. (See the illustration on page 485.)

Click the Web Setup Project icon, and then click OK to accept the default project name. Make sure that the Add To Solution option (above the More button at the bottom left of the dialog box) is selected. The File System editor for the Web Setup project will appear.

3   With WebSetup1 selected in Solution Explorer, in the Properties pane, modify the *ProductName* property to match the name of the Web application project you opened in step 1.

4   Right-click the Web Application Folder node in the left pane of the File System editor, and click Add, Project Output. The Add Project Output Group dialog box will appear, as shown in the following illustration:

5   Click both Primary Output and Content Files in the list. Use the Ctrl key to select multiple items. Then click OK.

6   Click the Web Application Folder node in the File System editor. Then locate the VirtualDirectory entry in the Properties pane and change it to the name of a target directory on the deployment target. This directory does not need to exist; it will be created.

7   Also in the Properties pane, set the *DefaultDocument* property to the name of the default document for the Web application opened in step 1.

8   To build the solution, click Build Solution on the Build menu.

9   Locate the set-up package created by the Web Setup project. It should be located in the Debug or Release subdirectory of the directory containing the

Web Setup project, and will be called WebSetup1.msi if you used the default project name of WebSetup1. Copy the file to the target server and execute it. The initial screen of the installation program is shown in the following illustration:

10 Browse the newly deployed application using the URL *http://machinename /vdirname/*, where *machinename* is the name of the machine where you installed the set-up package and *vdirname* is the name that you specified for the VirtualDirectory property in step 7. If the deployment worked correctly, you should see the default page for the Web application.

warning

The installation created by Visual Studio .NET does not install the .NET framework. You can run the program dotnetfx.exe on the Windows Components Update CD before the executing the installation package to allow the project to install if the target machine does not already have the framework installed.

In addition to providing fine-grained control over the files and outputs included in the installation package, this method also enables you to automatically install shared assemblies in the GAC. It also enables you to uninstall a Web application with a single command, either by right-clicking the installation package and clicking Uninstall or by locating the application's entry in the Windows Add/ Remove Programs applet, which can be accessed from the Control Panel.

Chapter 13 Quick Reference

To	Do this
Verify that a directory in IIS is an application root	Navigate to the directory in Internet Services Manager and look at the icon for the directory. If the directory is not an application root, you can make it one by right-clicking the directory, clicking Properties, and clicking Create on the Directory tab.
Store application-specific configuration settings	Add an appSettings section to your Web.config or Machine.config file, with an *<add>* tag for each item to be added to the appSettings.
Deploy content and private assemblies	Set up the target directory in IIS on the machine where the content will be deployed. Then use XCOPY, WebDAV, Windows Explorer, or another means to copy the files and folders of the application to the target directory.
Create an installation package with fine-grained control of installation items and uninstall ability	Add a Web Setup project to the solution for the Web application to be packaged and set its properties and outputs as desired.

14

Tracing and Debugging ASP.NET Applications

In this chapter, you will learn how to

✔ *Use tracing to learn how your application is running.*

✔ *Debug ASP.NET applications.*

✔ *Use the Microsoft .NET Framework SDK debugger.*

This book covers a wide variety of topics related to ASP.NET development. Hopefully, you'll be able to avoid most problems while developing your ASP.NET Web applications. Inevitably, however, there will be times when your code doesn't do what you expect, or you'll run into errors or problems that prevent your application from working. This chapter will look at what to do when that happens. It's not intended to make you an expert debugger but rather give you an overview of the tools available for debugging in ASP.NET.

To say that classic ASP did not offer developers much support for debugging their applications would be a colossal understatement. Despite being a very simple and productive development environment, classic ASP left a lot to be desired in terms of debugging and error messages.

For example, in classic ASP there was no convenient way to access the state of the current HTTP request (apart from writing code in each application to access and log or write to the page the contents of the *Request.Headers* collection) or of the other collections, such as *QueryString* or *Forms*. ASP.NET addresses this through a new feature called *tracing*, which is discussed in the first part of this chapter.

Additionally, classic ASP error messages were often cryptic at best. If you were lucky, they told you the line of the ASP page on which the error occurred. Unfortunately, this information could be misleading. The error might have occurred in a function called by that page, but you wouldn't know that from the error message. ASP.NET provides much richer error reporting than classic ASP, including a stack trace of the functions that led up to an error condition, making it much easier to locate the root cause of the error.

The .NET Framework SDK ships with its own debugger, so developers who are not using Microsoft Visual Studio .NET can attach it to the process of their ASP.NET application and step through their code to find and fix problems. Most often, using Visual Studio .NET's debugger is the most efficient way to debug your application. This improved error reporting and the SDK debugger are discussed in the second half of this chapter.

Tracing

As mentioned, one weakness of classic ASP was the lack of an easy way to get information about the current request. Apart from creating reusable include files to write out the contents of the various collections of the request object, there was no simple method of making this information available. ASP.NET provides a solution. Tracing provides a substantial amount of information about requests that have been executed, either at the page level or the application level, as well as a way to get your own custom debug information without exposing it to the users of your application.

Enabling Page-Level Trace Output

The simplest way to access trace information is through the *Trace* attribute of the @ *Page* directive. By adding the *Trace* attribute to any .aspx page, you can instruct ASP.NET to append the trace output for that page to the rendered content of the page. The following example shows how to enable tracing on a simple ASP.NET page.

Display tracing information

1   Open Visual Studio, and create a new project called Chapter_14. Click Save WebForm1.aspx As on the File menu and rename the default Web Page created by Visual Studio **SimpleTrace.aspx**.

2   To make SimpleTrace.aspx the start page, right-click it in Solution Explorer, and click Set As Start Page on the shortcut menu.

3   Right-click anywhere on the page, and click Properties on the shortcut menu. In the Property Pages dialog box, change the page title to **Simple**

⌐ **Trace**. Change the Page Layout from GridLayout to FlowLayout. Tracing does not work quite right using GridLayout. Click the Apply button, and then click OK.

4 Add a label to the page by dragging a label from the Toolbox onto the form. Because this is FlowLayout, the label will move to the upper left corner of the form no matter where you place it on the form. Change the *Text* property to **Trace is enabled for this page**.

5 Click the HTML tab at the bottom of the design window.

6 Add **Trace="true"** to the @ *Page* directive at the top of the HTML in the HTML Window.

7 To save the solution, click Save All on the File menu.

8 To build the application, click Build Chapter_14 on the Build menu.

9 To run the application, press F5 or click Start on the Debug menu. The resulting screen should look similar to the following illustration (some details might be different):

The trace output includes such information as the contents of the cookies, forms, and querystring collections. Therefore, page-level tracing using the *Trace* attribute of the @ *Page* directive should be restricted to nonproduction systems because the output is visible to any client requesting that page. Although it is possible to use one of the configuration options detailed in the next section to configure ASP.NET to provide page-level trace output only for requests from the local system, it is probably best to stick to application-level tracing on publicly available applications.

Enabling Application-Level Trace Output

In addition to providing trace output at the page level, ASP.NET can be configured to log trace output for a specified number of requests for later review. The primary advantages of this approach are that it hides trace output from users of the page, allowing its use on production or customer-facing systems, and it allows tracing to be enabled for an entire site at once.

Application-level tracing is enabled by adding the *<trace>* section to the Web.config file for the application and setting its attributes to the desired values. The following listing shows a *<trace>* section that enables application-level tracing and tells ASP.NET to log the last 40 requests. (Logged requests must be cleared manually when the request limit has been reached.) The attributes for the *<trace>* section are detailed in Chapter 7.

Enable application-level tracing in Web.config

1   In Visual Studio, open the project created in the previous example, Chapter_14.

2   To edit the Web.Config file, double-click it in Solution Explorer. Search for **<trace** in Web.Config by clicking Edit on the main menu. Point to Find And Replace, type **<trace**, and then click Find. This will move your cursor to the beginning of the <trace> section. Change enabled to *true*, change requestLimit to 40, and change traceMode to SortByCategory. Change the trace options so that it looks like the following example:

```
<trace
    enabled="true"
    requestLimit="40"
    pageOutput="false"
    traceMode="SortByCategory"
    localOnly="true"
/>
```

3   To save the changes, click File on the main menu, and then click Save Web.Config.

To allow access to the logged trace output, ASP.NET provides an *HttpHandler* that is mapped to a special URL called *trace.axd*. Appending *trace.axd* to the base URL for the application will display the list of currently available traces, as shown in the following illustration. Clicking the View Details link for a particular trace displays its output. Clicking the clear current trace link clears all current entries from the trace log and allows more requests to be logged.

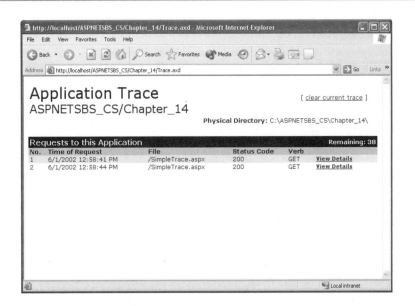

Writing to the Trace Output

Most developers who have ever tried debugging a classic ASP application have resorted at one time or another to using *Response.Write* to output the value of variables to the page. Another trick is placing flags within their code to determine where the code breaks by seeing how much of the page is executed before execution is halted. Although these are very useful techniques for debugging, they should only be used for development machines that are not accessible by users. And many of those aforementioned developers have received calls from their supervisors because they forgot to take the *Response.Write* statements out before migrating a page to a production server.

---

important

The page-level setting for trace functionality will override the setting in Web.config. So even if you have tracing enabled in Web.config, setting the *Trace* attribute of the @ *Page* directive to *false* will still disable tracing for that page. Likewise, even if tracing is disabled at the application level in Web.config, setting the page-level *Trace* attribute to *true* will still enable tracing for that page. For this reason, if you use page-level tracing, you should always double-check your pages before publishing them to a public server to ensure that the *Trace* attribute for each page has been removed or set to *false*.

ASP.NET's trace functionality solves this problem by enabling developers to write to the trace output instead of writing to the page output. Assuming that page-level trace output has not been enabled, this prevents users from seeing the trace statements written by the developer.

important

Enabling tracing for a page or an application carries some performance overhead. Even though the ASP.NET trace functionality makes it possible to leave tracing enabled without trace output being viewed by end users, when performance is important, it is a good idea to disable tracing for an application at both the page and application level.

The trace output is exposed to developers through the *TraceContext* class, which is available from the *Page.Trace* property (which can be accessed within a page simply by *Trace* because the *Page* is assumed). There are two methods for writing to the trace output: *Trace.Write* and *Trace.Warn*.

Determining If Tracing Is Enabled

To keep developers from wasting time attempting to write to the trace output when tracing is not enabled, the *TraceContext* class exposes a boolean property called *IsEnabled*, which contains the current status of tracing for the page. This is especially helpful if you are performing expensive processing or database lookups as a part of your trace logging.

Using *Trace.Write*

The *Trace.Write* method of the *TraceContext* class is overloaded, and it can be called in one of the following three ways:

```
Trace.Write(message);
Trace.Write(category, message);
Trace.Write(category, message, errorInfo);
```

The string *message* contains the message to be written to the trace output. The string *category* contains a description of the message (variable, statement, or whatever the developer desires as a category). And *errorInfo* is an exception object that allows exceptions to be logged to the trace output. The *category* and *errorInfo* parameters enable developers to set up sophisticated application-wide tracing by defining specific categories of logged information and using them consistently across an application.

The following example shows how to create a page that tests if tracing is enabled for the page and then writes a simple message to the trace output.

Write trace messages

1   In Visual Studio, open the project created in the previous example, Chapter_14. To add a new page, right-click the root of the project in Solution Explorer, point to Add, and then click Add Web Form. Name the form **TraceWrite.aspx**. Right click TraceWrite.aspx in Solution Explorer, and click Set As Start Page.

2   Right-click anywhere on the page, and click Properties on the shortcut menu. In the Properties dialog box, change the Page Layout from GridLayout to FlowLayout. Click the apply button, and then click OK.

3   Add a label to the page by dragging a label from the Toolbox onto the page.

4   Change to HTML mode by clicking the HTML tab on the bottom of the design window. *Add Trace="true"* to the @ *Page* directive.

5   Change to the code page by pressing F7. Scroll down to the *Page_Load* event handler, and add the following code:

```
if ( Trace.IsEnabled )
{
    Label1.Text="Writing 'Hello from Page!' to Trace Log...";
}
Trace.Write("Hello from Page!");
```

6   To save the solution, on the File menu, click Save All.

7   To build the application, on the Build menu, click Build Chapter_14.

8   To run the application, press F5 or click Start on the Debug menu. The resulting screen should look like the following illustration:

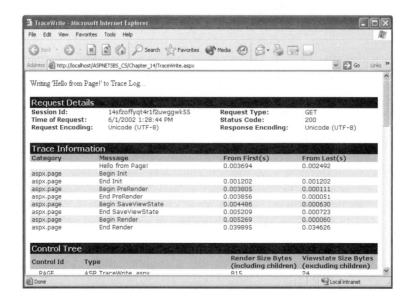

Using *Trace.Warn*

Another method offered by the *TraceContext* class for writing to the trace output is *Trace.Warn*. The primary difference between the two methods is that output written with *Trace.Warn* appears in the trace output as red text, making it ideal for highlighting important entries such as exceptions.

Understanding the Trace Output

The trace output for a page contains a great deal of information. The following table lists the sections of the trace output and describes the information contained in each.

Table 14-1. Trace Output Sections	
Section	**Description**
Request Details	Displays request-specific information such as session ID, request type, request status code, and encoding.
Trace Information	Displays messages relating to stages of page processing as well as execution times for these stages.

Section	Description
Control Tree	Displays a tree representation of all controls on the page, including *LiteralControls* for static HTML text within the source file. Also displays the render size and *ViewState* size of each control.
Cookies Collection	Displays the name, content, and size of all cookies sent as part of the request.
Headers Collection	Displays a list of all HTTP headers sent as a part of the request.
Form Collection	Displays a list of the names and values of all form fields sent as part of a *POST* request.
Querystring Collection	Displays a list of the names and values of all querystring values sent as part of a *GET* request.
Server Variables	Displays a list of the server variables for the request.

Debugging

In an ideal world, all programmers would be sufficiently skilled and attentive to detail as to write bug-free code. Unfortunately, we do not live in an ideal world. As such, debugging, or tracking down the source of errors and erroneous results in your programs, is an important task that all developers need to perform before they allow end-users to use their applications. This section will discuss some techniques for reducing the number of bugs in your code up-front, as well as the tools and techniques in ASP.NET and the .NET platform for debugging applications.

Understanding Bug Categories

There are three broad categories of bugs: each has different characteristics and levels of difficulty.

- **Syntax errors**   These errors occur when code breaks the rules of the language you're using, such as forgetting a closing curly brace in C#. These errors are the easiest to locate. The language compiler or IDE will alert you to them and will not allow you to compile your program until they are corrected.

- **Semantic errors**   These errors occur in code that is correct according to the rules of the compiler but that causes unexpected problems such as crashes or hanging on execution. A good example is code that executes in a loop but never exits the loop, either because the loop depends on a variable whose value was expected to be something different than it actually was or because the programmer forgot to increment the loop counter. Another type of error in this area occurs when trying to retrieve a field from a dataset. Unless you are using a typed dataset, there is no way to tell if the field actually exists at compile time. These bugs are harder to detect and are one type of run-time error.

■ **Logic errors**   These errors are similar to semantic errors in that they are run-time errors. That is, they occur while the program is running. But unlike semantic errors, they do not cause the application to crash or hang. Instead, logic errors result in unexpected values or output. This can be due to something as simple as a mistyped variable name that happens to match another declared variable in the program (an argument for descriptive variable names rather than simple ones, for example). This type of error can be extremely difficult to track down and eliminate, particularly because in complex programs it can be difficult (if not impossible) to reproduce a logic error reported by a user.

Preventing Bugs

Before we get into the discussion of how to debug the various errors you're apt to run into in your applications, let's take some time to look at strategies for preventing bugs in the first place. Preventing bugs is a much more efficient and less expensive way to produce bug-free software.

The following list contains a few strategies that will help. This is not a comprehensive list by any means, but applying these strategies consistently will help you spend less time debugging code and more time enjoying the rewards of having written it.

■ **Write readable code**   Use consistent naming and coding standards. It's not that important which standard you use as long as you use one. You should also strive for consistency in comments and encourage liberal commenting of code. Anything that makes code more readable and easier to understand will help eliminate bugs from the get-go.

■ **Create effective test plans**   The only effective way to eliminate logic errors is to test every path of your application with every possible data value (or representative range of data) that could be entered by a user. This is difficult to manage without effective planning. Test plans should be created at the same time that the application is being designed, and they should be updated as the application design is modified. To be effective, the test plans need to describe how to test each area of functionality in the application. Test plans and other design documents can also help highlight design problems before they are implemented, preventing a wide array of bugs.

■   **Use a rich IDE**   You don't necessarily need to use Visual Studio .NET to develop your Web applications because ASP.NET does not require it, but you should consider developing in an IDE that provides syntax checking as you type. If you develop with Notepad, it is too easy to amass a number of syntax errors that go unnoticed until you try to run the page. Then you get to spend the next half-hour or more eliminating the errors, one at a time, until you finally get the code to run. This is not an efficient way to write code.

■   **Get another pair of eyes**   Whether you're working on a team or building an application on your own, it is important to have someone else review your code (and test it, if possible). Developers are simply too close to their own code to catch every bug before testing, and sometimes even after. A review by a different pair of eyes can help a lot.

Compiling Web Forms Pages in Debug Mode

As mentioned in the introduction to this chapter, ASP.NET provides a great deal of information to developers when a bug or error halts execution of an application by throwing an exception. Some of this information, such as the stack trace, is available regardless of the mode in which the code was compiled. The following example shows what happens by default when a project created in Visual Studio .NET divides by zero in code to force an exception to be thrown.

Show the result of a divide by zero exception

1   In Visual Studio, open the project created previously for this chapter, Chapter_14. To add a new page, right-click the root of the project in Solution Explorer, point to Add, and then click Add Web Form. Name the form **DivByZero.aspx**. Right click DivByZero.aspx in Solution Explorer, and click Set As Start Page.

2   Add a label to the page by dragging a label from the Toolbox onto the page.

3   Change to the code page by pressing F7. Add the following line to the top of the file, with the other using clauses:

```
using System.Diagnostics;
```

Scroll down to the *Page_Load* event handler and add the following code:

```csharp
int One=1;
int Zero=0;
int Result;
Debug.Assert(Zero!=0,"Value of Zero will result in excep-
tion.");
Result=One/Zero;
Label1.Text="Got past the error.";
```

4 To save the solution, on the File menu, click Save All.

5 To build the application, on the Build menu, click Build Chapter_14.

6 To run the application, press F5 or click Start on the Debug menu.
The resulting screen should look like the following illustration:

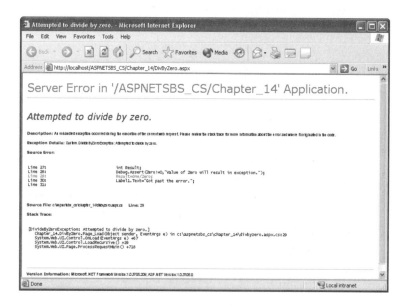

The previous illustration shows the information available when the application is compiled in Debug mode, the default when an application is created using Visual Studio .NET. Information such as the code with the error shown in context, as well as a stack trace is available only in Debug mode. The following example shows the output when an error occurs and debugging is not enabled.

Divide by zero exception without debugging enabled

1   In Visual Studio, open the project created previously for this chapter, Chapter_14. Open Web.Config by double-clicking it in Solution Explorer.

2   To search for <compilation in Web.Config, click Edit on the main menu. Point to Find And Replace, and then click Find. Enter **<compilation** in the Find What text box, and then click the Find Next button. This will move your cursor to the beginning of the <compilation> section. Change the *debug* attribute to *false*.

3   To save changes to Web.Config, on the File menu, click Save Web.Config.

4   Select Build from the main menu, and then click Configuration Management. In the Configuration Manager dialog box, change the configuration for Chapter_14 from Debug to Release. Alternately, you can click Release in the Active Solution Configuration drop down list. You should rebuild the application whenever you change configuration settings.

5   To save the solution, on the File menu, click Save All.

6   To build the application, on the Build menu, click Build Chapter_14.

7   To run the application, press Ctrl+F5 or click Start Without Debugging on the Debug menu. Because debugging is disabled, we cannot run the application cleanly by just pressing F5 or by clicking Start. The resulting screen should look like the following illustration:

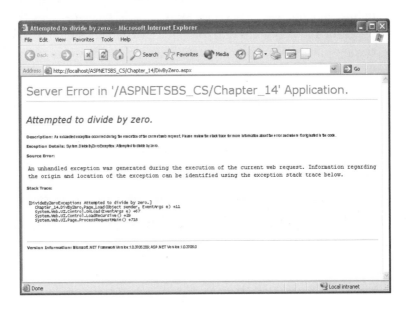

There is considerably less information that could be dangerous if exposed in this error message. For instance, none of the actual code is reproduced. Although it is not a good idea to embed passwords and other security related information in code, exposing only the limited information shown in the illustration is a better idea for a production system than the more complete error message shown previously. In any event, it is better still to provide custom error handling pages wherever possible, as explained in Chapter 5.

Understanding ASP.NET Error Messages

Anyone who's seen the infamous ASP 015 error probably realizes just what a dramatic improvement the information in the previous illustration represents. ASP.NET will provide descriptive information for both semantic and syntax errors, including the type of exception thrown (which enables you to provide effective and specific exception handling when you cannot completely prevent the exception) and the stack trace for the current request. As mentioned previously, you can also write to the trace output, and any trace statements that occur before execution is halted by an exception will be shown in the trace output.

Using the Visual Studio .NET Debugger

Although the error information provided by ASP.NET at runtime can be useful in locating and eliminating syntax errors, most errors in semantics and logic require a *debugger*. The Visual Studio .NET debugger uses the source code for a program and an executable compiled with debug symbols to let a developer step through his code line by line, set breakpoints, and examine the state or values of variables during program execution. You can also use the *Assert* method of the *Debug* class (part of the *System.Diagnostics* namespace) to test for certain conditions in your code and write messages to the output window of the debugger when the assertions fail.

The .NET Framework SDK comes with its own debugger, which provides rich debugging functionality for ASP.NET applications. The debugger is installed in the \Program Files\Microsoft Visual Studio .NET\FrameworkSDK\GuiDebug folder and is named DbgCLR.exe. You can execute the runtime debugger by double-clicking this file in Windows Explorer or by entering the path and file name in the Run dialog (Start, Run).

Generally, however, you will find the integrated debugger included with Visual Studio .NET to be superior to the SDK debugger. To show some of the features of Visual Studio .NET's debugger, lets take the DivByZero.aspx page as an example.

Debug a divide by zero exception

1   In Visual Studio, open the project created previously for this chapter, Chapter_14. Double click Web.Config in Solution Explorer, and set the *debug* attribute in the *compilation* tag to *true*. On the Build menu, click Configuration Manager and in the Configuration Manager dialog box, click Debug in the Configuration drop-down list. Close the Configuration Manager dialog box.

2   Open DivByZero.aspx.cs, if it is not already open.

3   Although our variable names give it away in this example, suppose you needed to determine exactly why the divide by zero exception was happening. Scroll down to the *Page_Load* event handler. Along the left side of the code window is a gray bar. Click the gray bar next to the line that begins Debug.Assert. A red dot will appear on the gray bar, and the line will be highlighted. The following illustration shows the breakpoint set in Visual Studio .NET:

The dot and the highlighting indicate that a breakpoint has been set. This means that while debugging the application, when this line of code is reached, the debugger will appear before the line is executed. If you are used to Visual Basic, this will be no big deal, but being able to set a breakpoint by simply clicking the line is a huge improvement for Microsoft Visual C++ programmers. In Visual C++, you needed to right click the line and then click Insert Breakpoint on the shortcut menu.

4 Run the application. Because the breakpoint you just set is in the *Page_Load* event handler, it will be reached immediately. The screen will look something like the following illustration:

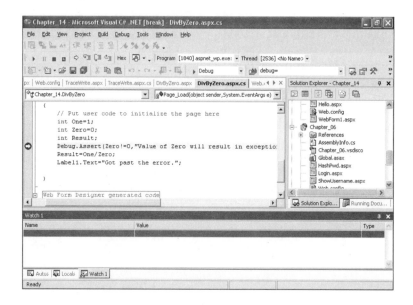

5 There are several ways to determine the values of variables while in the debugger. The first is to simply move your mouse pointer over a variable and leave it there. A ScreenTip appears telling you the scope, type, name, and value of the variable. Also, note that there is a Watch pane at the bottom of the screen just shown. Click the first line in the Watch pane and you will be able to enter a variable name in the Name column. Zero is the default value, and that is the desired value. Press Enter, and the Watch pane will look like the following illustration:

6 An easier way to see the value of a local variable is to click the Locals tab. The Locals pane is one of several different panes that might appear at the bottom of the Visual Studio .NET debugging screen. The Watch pane enables you to set a variable to be watched and observe its value. The Auto pane will automatically change to show variables involved with whatever the current line of code will evaluate or modify. The Locals pane shows all local variables, as shown in the following illustration:

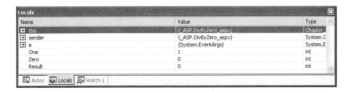

7 Press F10 to single step through the code. In this case, you should move to the line with the actual division, and the screen should look like the following illustration:

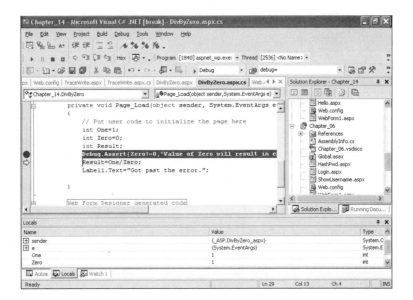

8 To make the Output pane visible, on the View menu, point to Other Windows, and then click Output. The Output pane will display the assert failure, as shown in the following illustration:

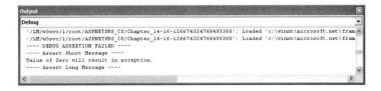

9   Because zero is indeed equal to 0, we could just stop debugging. We could also change the value of zero. Highlight the line with zero on it in the Locals pane, and then click the Value column. Change the value to 1, and press Enter. The value changes to 1, and the value appears in red by default (or in a color defined as meaning the value has changed).

10 Press F10 again to single step to the next statement. If a line calls a method that is compiled for debugging and you have access to the source, press F11 to step into the code. Press F5 to continue. The browser screen should appear with the message Got Past The Error displayed.

11 Close the browser. Now lets add some exception handling code. To create a safer version, make sure that DivByZero.aspx is the current file in the editor. On the File menu, click Save DivByZero.aspx As, and save the file as SafeDivByZero.aspx.

12 Change the code in the *Page_Load* event handler to the following:

```
int One=1;
int Zero=0;
int Result;
Debug.Assert(Zero!=0,"Value of Zero will result in excep-
tion.");
try
{
    Result=One/Zero;
}
    catch ( System.Exception ex )
{
    Label1.Text+="Exception! " + ex.ToString() + "<br/>";
}
Label1.Text+="Got past the error.";
```

13 Set a breakpoint on the assert line if not already present. This time, after the breakpoint is set, right-click the line and click Breakpoint Properties on the shortcut menu. The following form will appear:

Breakpoint Properties

Function | File | Address

Break execution when the program reaches this location in a file.

File: C:\ASPNETSBS_CS\Chapter_14\SafeDivByZero.aspx.cs

Line: 28

Character: 4

Condition...   (no condition)

Hit Count...   break always

OK   Cancel   Help

14   Click the Condition button. In the Breakpoint Condition dialog box that appears, enter Zero!=0 in the text box. Before you click OK, the dialog box should look something like the following illustration. When it does, click OK.

Breakpoint Condition

When the breakpoint location is reached, the expression is evaluated and the breakpoint is hit only if the expression is either true or has changed.

☑ Condition

Zero!=0

⦿ is true
◯ has changed

OK   Cancel   Help

15   Click the Hit Count button. Change the value of the When The Breakpoint Is Hit drop-down list to Break When The Hit Count Is Equal To. A text box should appear; leave it set to 1. When the dialog box looks like the following illustration, click OK.

Breakpoint Hit Count

A breakpoint is hit when the breakpoint location is reached and the condition is satisfied. The hit count is the number of times the breakpoint has been hit.

When the breakpoint is hit:

break when the hit count is equal to   ▼   1

Reset Hit Count   Current hit count: 0

OK   Cancel   Help

Tracing and Debugging   14

16 Run the application. It will run without breaking for the exception and display a screen similar to the following illustration:

17 Change the properties of the break point as shown earlier, setting the condition to Zero==0. Run the application. This time, the breakpoint will be reached with a condition that is true, and you will be brought to the debugger. Use F10 to single step through the code. You will see exactly how the exception is thrown, and you can confirm that the catch clause is reached. Often just seeing how the code runs by single stepping through it can be a huge help.

tip

There is a bug in Visual Studio .NET that under some circumstances (apparently related to quickly changing a page from design to HTML view) can cause lines of code to disappear in the *InitializeComponent* method that set event handlers. If you have a section of code that does not seem to be working, check that the *InitializeComponent* method that Visual Studio .NET places in Web Form Designer generated code has at least a single line of code setting the event handler for *this.Load*, as follows:

```
this.Load += new System.EventHandler(this.Page_Load);
```

If you have other event handlers, such as button click handlers, there will be additional code as well. If you have any doubt about a bit of code being executed, set a breakpoint. If the breakpoint is never reached, something is causing the code to be bypassed.

Using Debug.Assert

As mentioned, you can add *Debug.Assert* messages to your code to test certain conditions. The *Assert* method is overloaded and takes the following forms:

```
Debug.Assert(condition);
Debug.Assert(condition, shortmessage);
Debug.Assert(condition, shortmessage, longmessage);
```

The *condition* expression evaluates to *true* or *false*, the *shortmessage* string contains a brief message to display when *condition* returns *false*, and the *longmessage* string contains a detailed message to display when *condition* returns *false*. The following illustration shows the runtime debugger after stepping past an *Assert* statement.

Chapter 14 Quick Reference

To	Do this
Enable page-level tracing	Add the *Trace* attribute to the @ *Page* directive and set its value to *true*.
Enable application-level tracing	Add the *<trace>* configuration section to Web.config with the desired attributes. At a minimum, the *enabled* attribute is required and should be set to *true*.
Write to the trace output	Call either the *Trace.Write* or *Trace.Warn* method, passing the appropriate arguments.
View detailed error information or prepare for using the runtime debugger	Compile your page or pages in debug mode by either adding the *Debug* attribute to the @ *Page* directive with a value of *true* or adding the *<compilation>* section to the Web.config file and setting its *debug* attribute to *true*.
Invoke the runtime debugger	Locate the file DbgCLR.exe and execute it.
Debug a page using the Visual Studio .NET debugger	Ensure that the page is set to compile in debug mode, which is the default in Visual Studio .NET. Set breakpoints by clicking on the gray bar on the left side of the code window.
Make a breakpoint conditional	Set a breakpoint by clicking on the gray bar on the left side of the code window. Right-click the line, and click Breakpoint Properties on the shortcut menu. Set a condition (to break only when a condition is met) or a hit count (to break only after some number of passes through the line where the breakpoint is located).
Disable debugging when moving an application to production	In Web.Config, in the <compilation> tag, set *debug* to *false*. On the Build menu, click Configuration, change the configuration for the project involved to *Release*, and rebuild the application.

PART 5

Appendices

Migrating from ASP to ASP.NET

In this appendix, you will learn how to

✔ *Recognize issues common to the migration process.*

✔ *Migrate a page that accesses data using ADO.*

✔ *Use programming practices with classic ASP that will make migration easier.*

The one disadvantage of moving from ASP to ASP.NET using C# is that there is not a convenient way to migrate applications bit by bit or to modify the VBScript used by ASP so that it will compile as Visual Basic C# .NET in ASP.NET. Of course, migrating VBScript ASP pages to C# is a lot harder than converting VBScript to Visual Basic .NET, but if your experience is with C++, the C# transition will be worth the effort.

Migration Overview

Almost all the issues you encounter when migrating your classic ASP applications to ASP.NET fall into two categories: page structure changes and language changes. The next two sections discuss the types of changes in each category and the ways you need to update your code to work with them.

Page Structure Changes

The page structure changes from classic ASP to ASP.NET can be broken down into two areas: changes in the structure of code blocks and changes to the syntax of page directives.

Code Blocks

As discussed in Chapter 7, there are significant changes between how code was structured in classic ASP and how it is structured in ASP.NET. These changes, which are designed to make your code more readable and maintainable, are likely to be the most common issue in migration.

In classic ASP, server-side code is written in either code render blocks, indicated by the syntax <% %>, or code declaration blocks, indicated by the <script runat="server"></script> syntax. Either syntax can be used anywhere in the page and can contain either statements or procedures.

One problem with classic ASP was that it can be difficult to tell the order in which its code will execute, which can cause bugs. It's also all too easy to write spaghetti code, wind up with a page covered in render blocks, and mix procedures and raw statements. This can make the code difficult to read and maintain, and mixing HTML and render blocks often negatively affects page performance.

In ASP.NET, the purpose of render blocks and code declaration blocks has been narrowed considerably. Render blocks in ASP.NET can contain only executable statements, not procedures, whereas code declaration blocks can contain only global variable declarations and procedures.

important

In addition to the performance and reliability implications of mixing code within render blocks and HTML, using render blocks also makes for an unclear separation of presentation and program logic. ASP.NET enables one team to work on the presentation logic (in the *.aspx* files) while another group works on the guts of the application logic (in the *.cs* files).

Another significant difference between classic ASP and ASP.NET is that in classic ASP, multiple <script runat="server"> code declaration blocks can be used on a page. Each code declaration block could use a different language through the *language* attribute, which could be set to VBScript or JScript. ASP.NET only supports a single language per page, which is Visual Basic .NET by default.

Top-to-Bottom vs. Event-Driven Programming

Classic ASP pages using render blocks always executed from top to bottom. Code in <% %> render blocks was executed and output to the response stream as the ASP interpreter encountered it.

ASP.NET code is compiled into an instance of the *Page* class, and execution is event-based. Rather than placing start-up code in the first render block in a page, start-up code in ASP.NET is placed in the *Page_Load* event handler, which is fired when the instance of the *Page* class that represents the page is loaded into memory. Likewise, a *Page_UnLoad* event is fired just before the page is removed from memory and can be used to run any clean-up code that is necessary.

Page Directives

In classic ASP, the primary directive used in pages was the @ *Language* directive, which specified the language to be used for render blocks. Other less commonly used directives included @ *Codepage*, @ *EnableSessionState*, @ *LCID*, and @ *Transaction*.

In ASP.NET, these directives are attributes of the @ *Page* directive, which should appear at the top of each ASP.NET Web Form page. See Chapter 7 for a full discussion of the @ *Page* directive and its attributes.

One new attribute of the @ *Page* directive that is important to discuss in relation to classic ASP is the *AspCompat* attribute. By default, ASP.NET runs as a multi-threaded apartment (MTA) process. This means that single-threaded apartment (STA) components, such as those written in Visual Basic 6, are not compatible with ASP.NET. This includes the ADO components, which are installed to run as STA components by default. (You can modify this by running a batch file that changes the registry settings for ADO, but that is beyond the scope of this discussion.) Setting the *AspCompat* attribute to *true* forces ASP.NET to run in STA mode, making it possible to use STA components in ASP.NET pages.

important

Setting AspCompat to *true* should be considered a short-term solution when migrating from ASP to ASP.NET, because this setting can have a significant negative impact on the performance of your application. For best performance, you should rewrite components written in earlier versions of Visual Basic using Visual Basic .NET, and migrate existing ADO code to use ADO.NET.

Language Changes

In addition to changes to the structure of pages in ASP.NET, there are some significant changes when moving code from VBScript to C# that will require modifications to your code. These include the following:

- *Set* and *Let* are not needed or supported. Object references can be set by simple assignment:

```
Object1 = Object2
```

- Parentheses are required for calling all methods in C#, including methods that do not have parameters:

```
Response.Write("Hello, World!");
```

- All statements are terminated with semicolons.

- Blocks that are associated with control structures like *if* and *while* statements are delimited by curly braces ({ *and* }) rather than words, such as *Endif* or *End While*.

- The *Variant* data type does not exist in C# .NET. The replacement is *Object*.

- Default properties are not supported. All properties must be called explicitly:

```
MyString = TextBox1.Text;
```

- Property declaration syntax is different in C#. Instead of *Property Set*, *Property Get*, and *Property Let*, C# .NET uses the following syntax (keep in mind that *value* is a special keyword that contains the value submitted to the *set* portion of the *public variable* statement):

```
public string MyProperty
{
    get
    {
        return MyInternalVariable;
    }
    set
    {
        if ( value!=MyInternalVariable )
        {
            MyInternalVariable=value;
        }
    }
```

important

The property just shown acts as a simple shell for *MyInternalVariable*. You can use any code while setting or getting the property. In this example, I only set *MyInternalVariable* in the setter if it is different from the current value. Properties can be used to expose values that don't really exist as explicit fields in the class. For instance, you might create an Invoice class that exposes an *InvoiceTotal* property that cannot be set, and when read actually totals the amounts in each invoice line. You can also use properties to expose objects that might take some time to create. By doing so, you can postpone the expensive creation until the object is first requested, allowing Just-In-Time initialization.

■ By default, parameters are passed to procedures in C# by value. Parameters can be passed by reference using the *ref* keyword. You can change the value of Reference parameters in the procedure to which they're passed and then retrieve their value outside the procedure:

```
public void MySub(ref string MyValue)
{
    MyValue="Hello!";
}
```

Migrating a Data Access Page to ASP.NET

To demonstrate some of these changes and show you how to deal with them, let's walk through the process of migrating a classic ASP page that accesses data in a SQL Server database through ADO and writes it to the page as an HTML table. You will migrate the ADO to ADO.NET and change the language from VBScript to C#. Rather than rendering a table directly, the ASP.NET version uses a DataGrid component. The following listing shows the classic ASP page you'll use to start. You will need to set the *pwd* attribute in the connection string to the appropriate password for your VSdotNET MSDE instance. You might also want to change the *uid* attribute to the name of an account with fewer privileges than the *sa* account. You can get the values of both of these attributes from your SQL Server administrator.

GetAuthors.asp

```
<%@ Language=VBScript %>
<html>
<head>
<%
Dim objConn
Dim objCmd
Dim objRS
Dim strConn

strConn = "PROVIDER=SQLOLEDB;INITIAL CATALOG=PUBS;" _
    &"SERVER=(local)\VSdotNET;uid=sa;pwd=;"
Set objConn = Server.CreateObject("ADODB.Connection")
Set objCmd = Server.CreateObject("ADODB.Command")
Set objRS = Server.CreateObject("ADODB.Recordset")

objCmd.CommandText = "SELECT * FROM Authors"
objConn.Open strConn
Set objCmd.ActiveConnection = objConn
Set objRS = objCmd.Execute

Sub FormatTable

    Dim objField

    If Not objRS.EOF Then
        Response.Write "<table border=2 cellspacing=0>"
        Do While Not objRS.EOF
            Response.Write "<tr>"
            For Each objField In objRS.Fields
                Response.Write "<td>" & objField & "</td>"
            Next
            Response.Write "</tr>"
            objRS.MoveNext
        Loop
        Response.Write "</table>"
    Else
        Response.Write "No Records!"
    End If
```

```
End Sub
Sub CleanUp()
    objConn.Close
    Set objConn = Nothing
    Set objCmd = Nothing
    Set objRS = Nothing
End Sub
%>
</head>
<body>

<%
FormatTable()
CleanUp()
%>

</body>
</html>
```

The output of this page is shown here:

The page in the previous listing accesses the Authors table of the Pubs SQL Server sample database (in this case in the NetSDK MSDE instance installed with the .NET Framework SDK samples), calls a render function to write the data to the page as an HTML table, and then calls a clean-up function to close the connection to the database and set the object references to *Nothing* to ensure that the COM subsystem knows these objects can be destroyed.

warning

One thing this sample code has in common with much of the sample code you will encounter (and unfortunately, some production code as well) is its use of the *sa* SQL Server login account with a blank password. (This is the default for SQL Server 6.5 and 7.0 installs. You must explicitly choose a blank password to use a blank *sa* password in SQL Server 2000.) In practice, the *sa* account should always be given a strong password because this account has full administrative rights on the SQL Server machine. This includes the ability to run operating system commands through an extended stored procedure. In a production application, never use the *sa* account for accessing data from a page.

If you cannot use a trusted connection to SQL Server, you should set up one or more special user accounts for each Web application with the absolute minimum rights necessary to allow access to that application's data. This will reduce the risk of overbroad rights, which can cause data to be compromised.

Another security issue in the sample is the placing of user ID and password information directly in the page. In practice, connection string information should be stored somewhere more secure. In order of increasing security, options include storing it as an *appSetting* in Web.config, storing it as an *appSetting* in Machine.config (not appropriate in a shared server environment), and hard-coding it as a private member of a compiled component.

Short-Term Migration

In the short term, your goal might be to simply move your pages over to ASP.NET while still using most of the existing logic in the page. Although this choice has performance implications, it might make your migration easier by letting you do it in stages. Making the code in the previous listing work as an ASP.NET page is largely a matter of modifying it to comply with the rules for ASP.NET code using Visual Basic .NET. The conversion from VBScript to Visual Basic .NET is beyond the scope of this book.

Long-Term Migration

Doing a quick-and-dirty conversion to allow your VBScript ASP pages to run as ASP.NET pages using Visual Basic .NET is a stopgap measure that will enable you to get the page up and running quickly. Among other compromises, you will need to modify the ASP.NET default to allow STA components to work correctly with ASP.NET. In the long run, it's best to fully migrate your code to take advantage of the features offered by ASP.NET and ADO.NET. The following steps show how to migrate the ASP page to run under ASP.NET in C#.

Migrate a page to ASP.NET

1   Open Visual C# .NET. Create a new project called Appendix_A.

2   To rename the initial default page, on the File menu, click Save WebForm1.aspx As. In the resulting dialog box, enter **GetAuthors.aspx** as the new file name, and click the Save button.

3   Move the mouse pointer to the Toolbox, and drag a DataGrid onto the Web form. Change the ID of the DataGrid to **MyGrid**.

4   On the View menu, click Code, or press F7 to move to the code window.

5   Add the following line to the using clauses:

```
using System.Data.SqlClient;
```

6   Scroll down to the *Page_Load* event handler and replace the following lines:

```
Dim objConn
Dim objCmd
Dim objRS
Dim strConn
```

with these lines:

```
DataSet MyDS = new DataSet();
SqlConnection MySqlConn;
SqlDataAdapter MySqlDa;
string ConnStr;
string SQLSelect;
```

7   Next change the SQL Connection string to the new format required by SqlClient, and add the following line setting the *ConnStr* variable just below the previously inserted lines inside the Page_Load event handler. Note that I am using the @ at the beginning of the string so the backslash is treated as a normal string (see the note after Step 13 for information regarding trusted connections).

```
ConnStr=@"server=(local)\VsDotNet;database=pubs;" +
    "Trusted_Connection=yes";
```

8   The SQL select statement line is almost identical to the VBScript version (there is a semicolon appended). Add this line just below the code setting the connection string:

```
SQLSelect="SELECT * FROM Authors";
```

9   Create the connection and the data adapter. The connection is similar to the ADO connection object. The data adapter is used to fill a DataSet that will be bound to the DataGrid. Add these lines to the bottom of the Page_Load handler:

```
MySqlConn=new SqlConnection(ConnStr);
MySqlDa=new SqlDataAdapter(SQLSelect,MySqlConn);
```

10   Use the *Fill* method to fill the DataSet, and then assign the DataSource property to the DataSet to set it as the data source of the DataGrid. Add these lines to the end of the Page_Load handler:

```
MySqlDa.Fill(MyDS);
MyGrid.DataSource=MyDS.Tables[0].DefaultView;
```

11   The final statement to add is the call to DataBind. This is the call that will actually fill the DataGrid as the page loads, causing the DataGrid to render an HTML table. Calling DataBind without qualifying the name binds all bindable controls on the page. You could also call DataBind on the DataGrid directly. Add the following line just below the previously added code.

```
DataBind();
```

12 The page will work as written, but there is one last step to take. Just below the area where the connection object is created, you should begin a try/finally block, with the connection being closed in the finally block. The final *Page_Load* should look like this:

```
private void Page_Load(object sender, System.EventArgs e)
{
    // Put user code to initialize the page here
    DataSet MyDS = new DataSet();
    SqlConnection MySqlConn;
    SqlDataAdapter MySqlDa;
    string ConnStr;
    string SQLSelect;
    ConnStr=@"server=(local)\VsDotNet;database=pubs;" +
        "Trusted_Connection=yes";
    SQLSelect="SELECT * FROM Authors";
    MySqlConn=new SqlConnection(ConnStr);

    try
    {
        MySqlDa=new SqlDataAdapter(SQLSelect,MySqlConn);
        MySqlDa.Fill(MyDS);
        MyGrid.DataSource=MyDS.Tables[0].DefaultView;
        DataBind();
    }
    finally
    {
        MySqlConn.Close();
    }
}
```

13 To save the project, on the File menu, click Save All. Right click GetAuthors.aspx and select *Set as Start Page* from the shortcut menu. To compile the project, on the Build menu, click Build Solution, or press Ctrl+Shift+B.

note

To use a trusted connection to connect to SQL Server as shown in the preceding listing, you will need to either enable Windows authentication and impersonation or set up the ASPNET worker process account as a SQL Server login, as described in Chapter 9.

14   Run the project. As you browse the page, refresh the browser. The screen will look like this:

15   Switch to GetAuthors.aspx by clicking the appropriate tab near the top of the Visual Studio .NET editing window. Ensure that you are in Design mode by clicking Design on the tab control at the bottom of the Design window.

16   Right-click the DataGrid and click Auto Format on the shortcut menu. The screen that appears will look like this:

17   In the AutoFormat dialog box, click Professional 1 in the Select A Scheme box, and save and run the application. The screen that appears will look like this:

note

The code in the preceding listing offers better performance than a quick-and-dirty conversion of the VBScript code to Visual C# .NET because it does not rely on *AspCompat* to run. It takes advantage of ADO.NET instead of using ADO through COM Interop, which carries some performance overhead. The code could be made even more efficient by using an ADO.NET DataReader to access the data. The code in the preceding listing also provides greater flexibility for modifying the look of the rendered table. You can modify this by adding attributes to the *DataGrid* tag. Using an ASP.NET *DataGrid* also provides built-in support for paging, editing, and filtering. Fancy formatting (including alternating item formatting) is also easy to add, as shown in Step 17 of the previous procedure, using Visual Studio .NET's Auto Format. See Chapter 9 for more information on these features.

Best Practices for Preparing for ASP.NET

As you can see from this appendix, migrating from classic ASP to ASP.NET does not need to be terribly painful. However, a lot depends on how your classic ASP code is written in the first place. Code that is written with a great deal of intermingled HTML and render blocks will be more difficult to migrate, as will code that does not follow good coding practices. The following are several coding practices you can put in place in your ongoing classic ASP development to make migrating it to ASP.NET easier:

- Use *ByVal* or *ByRef* to explicitly state which type of parameter is desired in procedures that take parameters. This will remind you what types of parameters are expected when moving to ASP.NET and C#.

- Write all procedures in *<script>* code declaration blocks, rather than in render blocks.

- Use render blocks sparingly, particularly when intermingled with HTML tags.

- Do not rely on default properties. Instead, explicitly name properties such as *objRS.Value*.

- Do not use multiple languages in server-side *<script>* blocks. Choose the language you're most comfortable with and use it exclusively on a per-page basis.

APPENDIX

B

ASP.NET
Configuration Elements

Elements

In this appendix, you will learn how to

✔ *Use the syntax for each configuration element.*

This appendix lists the syntax for each configuration element and describes the attributes and child elements available for that element (where applicable). The names of configuration elements and their attributes are case sensitive and are in what is referred to as *camel case*. In *camel case*, the entire first word of a name is lowercase, and the first letter of each additional word is capitalized. For example, the *sessionstate* configuration element becomes *sessionState*. If you don't use camel case with both configuration element names and attribute names, you'll get an error when you try to access a page in the application.

<trace>

The *<trace>* element allows you to enable or disable application-wide tracing (see Chapter 14 for more on this useful feature), as well as set the parameters for the tracing functionality. When tracing is enabled, you can review information about requests received by the Web server with the special URL *http://<servername>/<appname>/trace.axd*. The *<trace>* element has the following syntax:

```
<trace
    enabled="true|false"
    localOnly="true|false"
    pageOutput="true|false"
    requestLimit="integer"
    traceMode="SortByTime|SortByCategory" />
```

For information on *<trace>* element attributes, consult the following table.

Table B-1.   *<trace>* Element Attributes

Attribute	Description	Options
enabled	Determines whether application-level tracing is enabled for the application.	When set to *true*, application-level tracing is enabled. When set to *false*, application-level tracing is disabled. The default is *false*.
localOnly	Determines whether trace information is viewable by computers other than the local Web server.	When set to *true*, trace output can be viewed only from the local Web server. When set to *false* the trace output can be viewed from any machine. The default is *true*.
pageOutput	Determines whether trace output is appended to each ASP.NET page in the application or is available only through trace.axd.	When set to *true*, Trace output is appended to each page within the scope of the configuration file. When set to *false*, trace output is available only by browsing the special trace.axd URL. The default is *false*.
requestLimit	Determines the number of requests that are stored for review through the trace.axd URL. After this limit has been reached, the current trace must be cleared by browsing trace.axd to collect information on additional requests.	The default is 10. The higher this number, the more overhead is involved in tracing. Set this number as low as is feasible.
traceMode	Determines the sort order of the requests stored.	The *SortByTime* option sorts trace information by the order in which events are processed. The *SortByCategory* option sorts trace information alphabetically by category. When used with the *Trace.Write* method, this can be useful for grouping *Trace.Write* statements using the same category argument. The default is *SortByTime*.

<globalization>

The *<globalization>* element controls globalization settings for ASP.NET applications. This includes the encoding used for requests, responses, and files, as well as settings for specifying the culture to be associated with Web requests and local searches. The *<globalization>* element has the following syntax:

```
<globalization
    culture="any valid culture string"
    fileEncoding="any valid encoding string"
    requestEncoding="any valid encoding string"
    responseEncoding="any valid encoding string"
    uiCulture="any valid culture string" />
```

For information on *<globalization>* element attributes, consult the following table.

Table B-2. *<globalization>* **Element Attributes**

Attribute	Description	Options
culture	Determines the culture (such as language defaults) used to process incoming Web requests.	This attribute must be set to a valid culture string. For a list of valid culture strings, see the Microsoft .NET Framework documentation entry for the *System.Globalization.CultureInfo* class.
fileEncoding	Determines the type of character encoding used for parsing ASP.NET application files (.aspx, .asmx, and .asax).	This attribute must be set to a valid encoding string. If this attribute is not included in either Machine.config or Web.config, encoding is based on the machine's Regional Options setting in Control Panel.
requestEncoding	Determines the type of character encoding used to process incoming Web requests.	This attribute must be set to a valid encoding string. If this attribute is not included in either Machine.config or Web.config, encoding is based on the machine's Regional Options setting in Control Panel. The default for *requestEncoding* is utf-8.
responseEncoding	Determines the type of character encoding used to encode outgoing responses.	This attribute must be set to a valid encoding string. If this attribute is not included in either Machine.config or Web.config, encoding is based on the machine's Regional Options setting in Control Panel. The default for *responseEncoding* is utf-8.
uiCulture	Determines the culture (such as language defaults) used to process searches that are culture-specific or locale-specific.	This attribute must be set to a valid culture string. For a list of valid culture strings, see the .NET Framework documentation entry for the *System.Globalization.CultureInfo* class.

Fully Qualified vs. Relative URLs

There are two basic types of URLs used for creating hyperlinks in Web pages: fully qualified URLs and relative URLs. Fully qualified URLs, also known as absolute URLs, contain all the information necessary for the browser (or other client program) to locate the resource named in the URL. This includes the protocol moniker being used (ftp://, http://, https://, and so on), the server's domain name or IP address (on local Windows networks, the machine name might also be used), and the path to the resource. A typical fully qualified URL would look like the following:

http://localhost/quickstart/aspplus/default.aspx

Relative URLs provide only the information necessary to locate a resource relative to the current document (known as document relative) or current server or domain (known as root relative). A document-relative URL used to link to the previously referenced page from another page in the same virtual directory would look like the following:

default.aspx

A root relative URL would look like the following:

/quickstart/aspplus/default.aspx

Because some controls or applications might not know how to use relative URLs, there might be times when you need to use a fully qualified URL.

<httpRuntime>

The *<httpRuntime>* element controls several aspects of the ASP.NET HTTP Runtime engine. The *<httpRuntime>* element has the following syntax:

```
<httpRuntime
    appRequestQueueLimit="number of requests"
    executionTimeout="seconds"
    maxRequestLength="kbytes"
    minLocalRequestFreeThreads="number of threads"
    minFreeThreads="number of threads"
    useFullyQualifiedRedirectUrl="true|false" />
```

For information on *<httpRuntime>* element attributes, consult the following table.

Table B-3.	*<httpRuntime>* Element Attributes	
Attribute	**Description**	**Options**
appRequestQueueLimit	Specifies the number of requests that ASP.NET will queue when no threads are available to process them, before returning a "503 - Server Too Busy" error message.	Increasing this value might result in unacceptably long wait times for users, so use caution and test carefully when making adjustments to this value. The default is 100.
executionTimeout	Determines amount of time, in seconds, that an ASP.NET request can continue executing before being shut down.	This attribute, which is similar to classic ASP's *Server.ScriptTimeout* property, can be used to prevent hung or long-running requests from consuming more resources than necessary. This attribute should be set higher than the average time it takes to process requests, but not so high as to allow processor overutilization by errant or inefficient pages. The default is 90 seconds.
maxRequestLength	Determines maximum size of incoming file uploads, in kilobytes.	This attribute is designed to help prevent denial of service attacks mounted by uploading large files to a server. Set it to the smallest size feasible for files you expect your users to upload. The default is 4,096 Kb.
minFreeThreads	Configures the minimum number of threads ASP.NET will keep free for processing new requests.	The default is 8.

(continued)

Table B-3. *<httpRuntime>* Element Attributes *(continued)*		
Attribute	**Description**	**Options**
minLocalRequestFreeThreads	Configures the minimum number of threads ASP.NET will keep free for processing requests coming from the local machine. Maintaining these free threads can help prevent deadlocks in multi-threaded processing. Note this is incorrectly identified in the current .NET Framework documentation as *minFreeLocalRequestFreeThreads*.	The default is 4.
useFullyQualifiedRedirectUrl	Determines whether relative or fully qualified URLs are used for client-side redirects. This attribute enables developers to support certain mobile controls that require fully qualified URLs for client-side redirects.	When set to *true*, client-side redirects are fully qualified. When set to *false*, client-side redirects are relative. The default is *true*.

<compilation>

With ten attributes and two child elements, the *<compilation>* element is one of the more extensive ASP.NET configuration elements, and it contains settings that determine how ASP.NET compiles code in your Web applications and Web Services. The settings you'll see most frequently are the *debug* and *defaultLanguage* attributes, which are placed in your application's Web.config file by default when you're using Microsoft Visual Studio .NET. Other settings, such as the *<assemblies>* and *<namespaces>* child elements, are equally important but usually are inherited from the settings in Machine.config, unless overridden by a developer.

The *<compilation>* element has the following syntax:

```
<compilation
    batch="true|false"
    batchTimeout="seconds"
    debug="true|false"
    defaultLanguage="language"
    explicit="true|false"
    maxBatchSize="number of pages"
    maxBatchGeneratedFileSize="kbytes"
```

```
numRecompilesBeforeAppRestart="number"
strict="true|false"
tempdirectory="directory" >
<compilers>
    <compiler
        extension="file extension"
        language="language"
        compilerOptions="compiler options"
        type=".NET type"
        warningLevel="number" />
</compilers>
<assemblies>
    <add assembly="assembly name" />
    <remove assembly="assembly name" />
    <clear />
</assemblies>
</compilation>
```

For information on *<compilation>* element attributes, consult the following table.

Table B-4. *<compilation>* Element Attributes			
Element	**Attribute**	**Description**	**Options**
<compilation>		Determines compiler options for the application. Supports the *<compilers>* and *<assemblies>* child elements.	
	batch	Determines whether the application supports batch compilation of ASP.NET pages. When batch compilation is enabled, ASP.NET will attempt to compile all ASP.NET pages within the application directory on the first request. This prevents later page requests from having to be compiled on request.	When set to *true*, batch compilation is supported. When set to *false*, pages will be compiled one by one as they are requested. The default is *true*.

(continued)

Table B-4. *<compilation>* Element Attributes *(continued)*			
Element	**Attribute**	**Description**	**Options**
	batchTimeout	Determines the amount of time, in seconds, before timeout of batch compilation. If the timeout is exceeded, the compiler will switch to per-request compilation mode.	This setting will vary depending on the size of an application and the amount of time you are willing to allow for batch compilation. The default is 15 seconds.
	debug	Determines whether debug information is included in compiled assemblies for ASP.NET pages and Web Services. This attribute should always be set to false in a production application because debug assemblies are larger and don't perform as well as release-type assemblies.	When set to *true*, assemblies are compiled with debug info. When set to *false*, assemblies are compiled without debug information. The default is *false*.
	defaultLanguage	Determines the language(s) to be used during dynamic compilation.	This attribute is the name of a language, as specified by one of the *<compiler>* child elements. The default is vb. For C#, use C#.
	explicit	Determines whether ASP.NET compiles pages written in Visual Basic .NET using the Visual Basic Option Explicit compiler option (which forces explicit declaration of variables). Enabling this setting makes it easier to locate and fix common problems, such as misspelled variable names, that otherwise wouldn't be discovered until runtime.	When set to *true*, the option is enabled. When set to *false*, the option is disabled. The default is *true*. Not meaningful for C# applications.

Element	Attribute	Description	Options
	numRecompiles BeforeApp Restart	Determines how many times application resources can be dynamically recompiled before the application is automatically restarted. This setting can be configured at the application level and at the global level through Machine.config The default is 15.	
	strict	Determines whether ASP.NET compiles pages written in Visual Basic .NET using the Visual Basic Option Strict compiler option (which prevents type conversions that would result in data loss, late binding, and other error-prone coding habits) to your .aspx files before compilation.	When set to *true*, the option is enabled. When set to *false*, the option is disabled. It's a good practice to enable this through either Machine.config or Web.config, the Visual Studio .NET properties dialog box for the project (the Build choice under Common Properties), or by adding Option Strict to the page or module you're working on. This makes it easier to fix common problems, such as overflows or rounding errors, that otherwise wouldn't be discovered until runtime. Not meaningful for C# applications. The default is *false*.
	tempDirectory	Determines the directory in which the temporary ASP.NET files resulting from dynamic compilation will reside.	Any valid directory.
<compilers>		Child element containing individual *<compiler>* child elements.	

(continued)

Table B-4. *<compilation>* Element Attributes *(continued)*			
Element	**Attribute**	**Description**	**Options**
<compiler>		Determines options for specific language compilers. One or more of these child elements can be contained within the *<compilers>* element.	
	extension	Determines the file extension used by dynamically compiled code-behind modules for a specifc compiler. The extensions for the three most commonly used ASP.NET languages (Visual Basic .NET, C#, and JScript .NET) are included in Machine.config, so you don't need to set them yourself unless you want to add additional extensions for one of these languages.	String representing the file extension (.vb, .cs, and so on). Multiple extensions should be delimited by semicolons. This setting should match the language specified in the language attribute. This attribute is required.
	language	Determines the list of language names to be handled by a specific compiler. The names for the three most commonly used ASP.NET languages (Visual Basic.NET, C#, and JScript .NET) are included in Machine.config, so you don't need to set them yourself unless you want to add additional names for one of these languages.	String representing the language name (vb;visualbasic; vbscript). Multiple names should be delimited by semicolons. This setting should match the language specified in the extension attribute. This attribute is required.
	compilerOptions	Determines any compiler-specific options to bepassed along during compilation.	Consult the .NET Framework SDK documentation to determine available options.

Element	Attribute	Description	Options
	type	Determines which .NET class and/or assembly is used to compile resources using the language specified in the language attribute, or the extension in the extension attribute. The types for the three most commonly used ASP.NET languages (Visual Basic .NET, C#, and JScript .NET) are included in Machine.config, so you don't need to set them yourself unless you want to modify the type for one of these languages (not recommended).	This attribute is a comma-delimited list that can include the class name, assembly name, and version information. The Machine.config file contains good examples of the syntax for this attribute. This attribute is required.
	warningLevel	Determines the compiler warning levels, which determine the types of warning messages (and the severity) that are emitted by the compiler.	The value for this attribute depends on the language compiler being configured. The default for C# is 1.
<assemblies>		Contains child elements containing one or more of the *<add/>*, *<remove/>*, or *<clear/>* child elements.	The child elements of the *<assemblies>* element are used to add references to assemblies to be used during compilation. ASP.NET automatically links in the assemblies specified here during dynamic compilation.
<clear>		Specifies that all current or inherited assembly references should be removed.	

(continued)

Table B-4.	*<compilation>* Element Attributes	*(continued)*	
Element	**Attribute**	**Description**	**Options**
<add>	*assembly*	Specifies an assembly, by its assembly name, to be referenced during dynamic compilation.	This setting should be the assembly name, not the DLL name, of the desired assembly. You can also use the wildcard (*) to add all assemblies from the application's private assembly cache (by default, in the bin subdirectory).
<remove>	*assembly*	Specifies an assembly, by its assembly name, to be removed from use during dynamic compilation.	The assembly name used must match exactly the name of an assembly added by a previous add directive (for example, from a parent Web.config). You cannot use wildcards for this attribute.

<pages>

The *<pages>* element enables you to set the defaults for the page-level attributes that are more commonly associated with the attributes of the @ *Page* ASP.NET directive. The settings in this element apply to all pages for which specific attributes of the @ *Page* directive do not appear. If these attributes appear in an ASP.NET page, their settings will override those in either the Machine.config or Web.config configuration files. As such, the *<pages>* element provides a great way of configuring the *SessionState*, *ViewState*, and other settings at an application or subfolder level, giving you a great deal of control over your application.

The *<pages>* element has the following syntax:

```
<pages
    autoEventWireup="true|false"
    buffer="true|false"
    enableSessionState="true|false|ReadOnly"
    enableViewState="true|false"
    enableViewStateMac="true|false"
    pageBaseType="typename, assembly"
    smartNavigation="true|false"
    userControlBaseType="typename" />
```

For information on *<pages>* element attributes, consult the following table.

Table B-5. *<pages>* Element Attributes		
Attribute	**Description**	**Options**
AutoEventWireup	Determines whether support for page events (Page_Load, and so on) is automatically provided in an application's ASP.NET pages.	When set to *true*, event support is provided automatically. When set to *false*, event support is not provided. Event handlers must be manually wired by developers. The default is *true*. Pages created in Visual Studio .NET will have *autoEventWireup* set to *false* by default.
Buffer	Determines whether responses are buffered before being sent to the client. This setting is analogous to the classic ASP *Response.Buffer* property.	When set to *true*, buffering is enabled. Page output will be buffered until the page is completely processed, or until either the *End* or *Flush* method of the *HTTPResponse* class is called. When set to *false*, buffering is not enabled. Page output is sent to the client as it is rendered. The default is *true*.
pageBaseType	Provides the type or assembly name of a class from which ASP.NET pages should inherit. In the absence of this attribute, the default is to inherit from the Page class of the *System.Web.UI* namespace.	Set this attribute to the name of a class derived from the *Page* class if you want to provide additional functionality not included in the base *Page* class. This is a simple yet powerful way to extend ASP.NET applications.
userControlBaseType	Provides the type or assembly name of a class from which ASP.NET UserControls (.ascx files) should inherit. In the absence of this attribute, the default is to inherit from the *UserControl* class of the *System.Web.UI* namespace.	Set this attribute to the name of a class derived from the *UserControl* class if you want to provide additional functionality not included in the base *UserControl* class. This is a simple yet powerful way to extend ASP.NET applications.

(continued)

Table B-5. <pages> Element Attributes (continued)		
Attribute	**Description**	**Options**
enableSessionState	Determines whether a new session is created by default for the current user by an ASP.NET page. Note that if the user already has a session from a prior page in which this attribute is set to false, this attribute will not affect that session. However, if it's set to ReadOnly, it will prevent the page from modifying values set in previous pages.	When set to *true*, if the user does not have a current session when he or she requests a page, a new session will be created. When set to *false*, if the user does not have a current session, one will not be created. If the user does have a session, it will not be affected, but its values cannot be accessed from pages. When set to ReadOnly, if the user does not have a current session, one will not be created. If the user does have a session, its values can be read from within a page where this attribute has been set to ReadOnly, but they cannot be modified. The default is *true*.
enableViewState	Determines whether *ViewState* (the method by which ASP.NET Server Controls store their state between page requests) is enabled.	When set to *true*, *ViewState* is enabled. Server Controls will maintain their values from one request to the next. When set to *false*, ViewState is not enabled. Server control state will be reset with each request. The default is *true*.
enableViewStateMac	Determines whether a Machine Authentication Check (MAC) is performed on *ViewState* data when a Web Form is posted back to the server. The MAC can help identify client-side tampering with the *ViewState* hidden field.	When set to *true*, MAC is enabled for *ViewState*. When set to *false*, MAC is not enabled for *ViewState*. The default is *true*.

<customErrors>

The *<customErrors>* element enables you to customize how your ASP.NET application responds to error conditions. In this element, you can specify whether the raw error messages generated by ASP.NET should be visible to local or remote clients, or whether to redirect the client to either a custom error page or a page specific to the error that occurred (based on the status code of the error). The *<customErrors>* element supports one child element, *<error>*, and has the following syntax:

```
<customErrors
    defaultRedirect="url"
    mode="on|off|RemoteOnly">
```

```
<error
    redirect="url"
    statusCode="status code"/>
</customErrors>
```

For information on *<customErrors>* element attributes, consult the following table.

Table B-6. *<customErrors>* Element Attributes

Element	Attribute	Description	Options
<customErrors>		Determines how ASP.NET errors are handled.	
	defaultRedirect	Determines the page to which a user is redirected if an error occurs.	The page to which this URL points can be either an .aspx page, in which you attempt to clean up or recover from the error, or a static HTML page, to inform the user of the error and offer guidance on what to do.
	mode	Determines whether raw ASP.NET error messages are sent to the client.	When set to On, custom errors are enabled. When an error occurs, the client, whether on a local or a remote Web server, will be redirected to the custom error page specified by the *defaultRedirect* attribute (or to a page specified in an *<error>* child element). When set to Off, custom errors are not enabled. When an error occurs, the client will see the error page generated by ASP.NET. Note that depending on how your application is designed, this can expose proprietary information to clients, so you should rarely use this setting. When set to RemoteOnly, custom errors are enabled for remote clients. When an error occurs, remote clients will be redirected to a custom error page, whereas clients on the local Web server will see the

(continued)

Table B-6.	*<customErrors>* Element Attributes		*(continued)*
Element	**Attribute**	**Description**	**Options**
			error page generated by ASP.NET. This enables developers to track down errors without having clients see raw error pages. RemoteOnly is the default.
<error>		Determines redirect page for a specific error type, based on the HTTP status code for the error.	Adding *<error>* tags provides finer-grained control over how errors are handled.
	redirect	Determines the page to which a user is redirected if an error of the type specified in the *statusCode* attribute occurs.	
	statusCode	Determines the HTTP status code (404-Not Found, and so on) that is handled by this *<error>* child element.	

<authentication>

The *<authentication>* element controls configuration of authentication in ASP.NET. You can choose from one of three authentication methods, set appropriate parameters for the method you choose, or choose no authentication at all. The *<authentication>* element supports two child elements, *<forms>* and *<passport>*. Additionally, the *<forms>* element supports one child element, *<credentials>*, which in turn supports one child element, *<user>*, as shown in the following example:

```
<authentication mode="Windows|Forms|Passport|None">
    <forms
        loginUrl="url"
        name="name"
        path="/"
        protection="All|None|Encryption|Validation"
        timeout="number">
        <credentials passwordFormat="Clear|MD5|SHA1">
            <user name="username" password="password" />
```

```
    </credentials>
  </forms>
  <passport redirectUrl="url" />
</authentication>
```

For information on *<authentication>* element attributes, consult the following table.

Table B-7.	*<authentication>* Element Attributes		
Element	**Attribute**	**Description**	**Options**
<authentication>		Determines how ASP.NET authentication is handled.	
	mode	Determines the authentication mode to be used. This is discussed in greater detail in Chapter 6.	When set to the Windows option, ASP.NET will use Windows authentication by default. Works with IIS' Basic, Digest, NTLM, or Certificate-based authentication methods. When set to the Forms option, ASP.NET will use Forms-based authentication, which provides basic support for "roll-your-own" security scenarios, by default. When set to the Passport option, ASP.NET will use Microsoft Passport as the default authentication method. When set to the None option, no authentication will be performed by ASP.NET.
<forms>		Determines the parameters associated with Forms-based authentication.	
	loginUrl	Determines the URL where a user is redirected if he doesn't have a valid authentication cookie.	This can be any page in your ASP.NET application that allows a user to log in. The default is login.aspx.
	name	Determines the name of the cookie used for authenticating a user.	The default is .ASPXAUTH.

(continued)

Table B-7. *<authentication>* Element Attributes *(continued)*			
Element	**Attribute**	**Description**	**Options**
	path	Determines the path to set for the authentication cookie.	The default is /. This is to prevent the possibility of missing cookies due to browser case sensitivity with respect to URL paths and cookies.
	protection	Determines the methods used to protect the authentication cookie from being compromised. Your choice of which method to use, or whether to use any at all, will depend on your security needs vs. the amount of resources you're willing to devote to security. Generally, the higher the level of security, the greater the performance overhead.	When set to the All option (the default), both encryption and data validation will be used to protect the cookie. This is the recommended setting. When set to the Encryption option, the authentication cookie will be encrypted, but it will not be validated. This leaves the cookie vulnerable to certain types of attacks. When set to the Validation option, the authentication cookie's contents will be validated to ensure that the cookie hasn't been changed between the browser and the server. When set to the None option, neither encryption nor validation are used (not recommended).
	timeout	Determines the amount of time, in minutes, until the authentication cookie expires.	Default is 30. You should set this value to the minimum amount that will enable users to use your site effectively. If you use persistent cookies with forms authentication, they will not time out.
<credentials>		In conjunction with the *<user>* child element, this element enables you to define credentials to authenticate against within a configuration file.	If you use this method to store credentials in a Web.config file within your application scope and your application is compromised, it might be possible for intruders to gain the passwords stored there, even if they're encrypted. Remember that no encryption method is perfect.

Element	Attribute	Description	Options
	passwordFormat	Determines the encryption used for stored passwords.	When set to the Clear option, no encryption is used (not recommended). When set to the MD5 option, passwords are encrypted using the MD5 hash algorithm. When set to the SHA1 option, passwords are encrypted using the SHA1 hash algorithm.
<user>		Determines the user name and password of a single user. Use one *<user>* child element for each set of credentials you want to store in the configuration file.	
	name	Specifies the user name of the user to authenticate against.	
	password	Specifies the password of the user to authenticate against.	This value should be an encrypted version of the password created with the hash algorithm specified by the passwordFormat attribute of the *<credentials>* tag.
<passport>		Child element used to set the parameters for Microsoft Passport-based authentication.	
	redirectUrl	Determines the URL where the user will be redirected if he has not been authenticated.	

<identity>

By default, requests made by ASP.NET applications for resources requiring authentication, such as files secured by NT Access Controls Lists (ACLs), are made in the context of either the IUSR_MACHINENAME or IWAM_MACHINENAME accounts, depending on whether the application is configured to run in-process or out-of-process relative to IIS. The *<identity>*

element allows ASP.NET applications to use impersonation, in which an application takes on the security context of the user making a request, or of a specified account. The *<identity>* element has the following syntax:

```
<identity
    impersonate="true|false"
    userName="username"
    password="password" />
```

For information on *<identity>* element attributes, consult the following table.

Table B-8.	*<identity>* Element Attributes	
Attribute	**Description**	**Options**
impersonate	Determines whether ASP.NET applications will use impersonation.	When set to true, impersonation of security accounts by ASP.NET applications is enabled. When set to false, impersonation of security accounts by ASP.NET applications is disabled.
userName	Specifies a user account that the affected ASP.NET application will impersonate.	Any valid user account. You should ensure that the account you choose has access to only the desired resources. For example, it is not a good idea to have an ASP.NET application impersonate an account in the Administrators group. If omitted, ASP.NET will impersonate the account of the logged on user (as provided by IIS).
password	Specifies the password for the account named in the *userName* attribute.	

<authorization>

The *<authorization>* element enables you to specify which accounts or roles (groups) are authorized to access resources within the scope of the configuration file. The *<authorization>* element supports two child elements, *<allow>* and *<deny>*, each of which has three attributes. The *<authorization>* element has the following syntax:

```
<authorization>
    <allow
        users="userlist"
        roles="rolelist"
        verbs="verblist" />
```

```
<deny
    users="userlist"
    roles="rolelist"
    verbs="verblist" />
</authorization>
```

For information on *<authorization>* element attributes, consult the following table.

Table B-9. *<authorization>* Element Attributes

Element	Attribute	Description	Options
<authorization>		Determines authorization settings for an application or directory. Contains one or more <allow> or <deny> child elements.	
<allow> or *<deny>*		Allows or denies access to resources based on user account, group membership, or HTTP request method.	
	users	Lists users (NT user accounts) granted or denied access to the resource(s).	This attribute takes a comma-delimited list. Access to anonymous users is allowed or denied using the Question mark (?) wildcard, and access to everyone is allowed or denied using the asterisk (*) wildcard.
	roles	Lists roles (NT groups) granted or denied access to the resource(s).	This attribute takes a comma-delimited list.
	verbs	Lists HTTP verbs (GET, POST, and so on) granted or denied access to the resource(s).	This attribute takes a comma-delimited list. Verbs available are GET, HEAD, POST, and DEBUG.

<machineKey>

The *<machineKey>* element enables you to specify the keys used for encryption and decryption of cookie data in Forms-based authentication. This element can be used at the machine level through Machine.config, as well as at the site and application levels through Web.config files, but it cannot be used at the subdirectory level. The *<machineKey>* element has the following syntax:

```
<machineKey
    decryptionKey="autogenerate|value"
```

```
validation="autogenerate|value"
validationKey="3DES|MD5|SHA1" />
```

For information on *<machineKey>* element attributes, consult the following table.

Table B-10. *<machineKey>* Element Attributes		
Attribute	**Description**	**Options**
decryptionKey	Determines whether the decryption key to be used is autogenerated, or specifies a key value to be used.	autogenerate (default) ASP.NET will generate a random key for decryption. The key value represents a string of characters (minimum 40, maximum 128) to be used as a decryption key. Note that 128 characters is the recommended length. For shorter-length keys, you should ensure that the key is randomly generated. This setting is necessary in Web farms to ensure that all servers are using the same keys, providing transparent user access while still taking advantage of encryption.
validation	Determines the type of encryption to be used by ASP.NET.	When set to the 3DES option, dData is encrypted using Triple-DES (3DES) encryption. When set to the MD5 option, data is encrypted using the MD5 hash algorithm. When set to the SHA1 option (the default), data is encrypted using the SHA1 hash algorithm.
validationKey	Determines whether the validation key to be used is autogenerated, or specifies a key value to be used.	autogenerate (default) ASP.NET will generate a random key for validation. The key value represents a string of characters (minimum 40, maximum 128) to be used as a validation key. Note that 128 characters is the recommended length. For shorter-length keys, it is recommended to ensure that the key is randomly generated. This setting is necessary in Web farms to ensure that all servers are using the same keys, providing transparent user access while still taking advantage of encryption.

<securityPolicy>

The *<securityPolicy>* element enables you to specify one of several named security policies, or a custom policy, for code-access security based on the name and *policyFile* attributes of its *<trustLevel>* child element. The *<trust>* element, described in the next section, specifies which of the named policies is implemented for a given site or application. The *<securityPolicy>* element supports one child element, *<trustLevel>*, with two attributes, and has the following syntax:

```
<securityPolicy>
   <trustLevel
      name="value"
      policyFile="value" />
</securityPolicy>
```

For information on *<securityPolicy>* element attributes, consult the following table.

Table B-11. *<securityPolicy>* Element Attributes			
Element	**Attribute**	**Description**	**Options**
<securityPolicy>		Determines the available named security policies for sites and/or applications.	
<trustLevel>		Each *<trustLevel>* child element sets up an available named policy based on its name and *policyFile* attributes.	
	name	Specifies the name to use for the policy.	The name specified by this attribute is also used by the *<trust>* element to implement the named policy.
	policyFile	Specifies the file name of the file that contains the code-access security settings to be used under the named policy.	The file name specified by this attribute is relative to the location of the Machine.config file.

<trust>

The *<trust>* element is used to implement one of the named security policies created by the *<securityPolicy>* element. This element can be used at the machine level through Machine.config, as well as at the site and application levels through Web.config files. However, it can't be used at the subdirectory level. The *<trust>* element has the following syntax:

```
<trust
    level="Full|High|Low|None|custom name"
    originUrl="url" />
```

For information on *<trust>* element attributes, consult the following table.

Table B-12.   *<trust>* Element Attributes

Attribute	Description	Options
level	Determines the applicable trust level, based on a named security policy.	When set to the Full option, code-access security is based on the Full named policy set up by default in Machine.config. When set to the High option, code-access security is based on the High named policy set up by default in Machine.config. When set to the Low option, code-access security is based on the Low named policy set up by default in Machine.config. When set to the None option, code-access security is based on the None named policy set up by default in Machine.config. When set to the Custom Name option, code-access security is based on a custom named policy set up in either Machine.config or a Web.config file at the site or application level.
originUrl	Specifies the origin URL for an application.	When set to the Optional option, this attribute can be used to support permissions for Socket and WebRequest requests that allow connectivity to the origin host.

<sessionState>

The *<sessionState>* element is used to configure the Session State HttpModule, including the type of state management to be used (in-process, out-of-process, or SQL Server), the default session timeout, and whether or not to use cookies for associating requests with user sessions. The *<sessionState>* element has the following syntax:

```
<sessionState
    stateConnectionString="IP address:port number"
    cookieless="true|false"
```

```
mode="Off|Inproc|StateServer|SQLServer"
sqlConnectionString="sql connection string"
timeout="number" />
```

For information on *<sessionState>* element attributes, consult the following table.

Table B-13. *<sessionState>* **Element Attributes**

Attribute	Description	Options
stateConnectionString	Specifies the server and port number to connect to when the mode attribute is set to StateServer.	This attribute is required when the mode is set to StateServer. The default is tcpip=127.0.0.1:42424.
cookieless	Determines whether user sessions are mapped to requests by using cookies or by adding a user's SessionID to the URL string for requests by that user.	When set to *true*, SessionIDs are added to request URLs, and cookies are not used. When set to *false*, cookies are used to map user requests to sessions. The default is *false*.
mode	Determines the type of session state management that applications will use.	When set to the Off option, Session state is disabled. When set to the Inproc option, Session state is stored in-process with the application, as in classic ASP. When set to the StateServer option, Session state is managed by an out-of-process NT Service, allowing multiple servers in a Web farm to share a single state store. When set to the SQLServer option, Session state is managed by SQL Server database, allowing multiple servers in a Web farm to share a single state store. This mode has the added advantage of providing persistent state storage in the event of a Web server crash. The default is InProc.
sqlConnectionString	Specifies the connection string used to connect to a SQL Server database where state information is stored.	This attribute is required when the mode is set to SQLServer.

(continued)

Table B-13.	*<sessionState>* Element Attributes	*(continued)*
Attribute	**Description**	**Options**
timeout	Specifies the amount of time, in minutes, before the user's session expires.	Like the classic ASP *Session.Timeout* property, this attribute uses sliding expiration. Each request by the user resets the amount of time before his session expires. The default is 20 minutes.

<httpHandlers>

The *<httpHandlers>* element enables you to assign requests of certain types or for certain resources to specific handler classes. For example, in Machine.config, the handling of ASP.NET pages (requests with the .aspx extension) is assigned to the *System.Web.UI.PageHandlerFactory* class. The *<httpHandlers>* element can also be used to prevent HTTP access to certain types of files by assigning them to the *System.Web.HttpForbiddenHandler* class, as is done by default for configuration files (*.config) and source files (*.cs and *.vb, for example).

The *<httpHandlers>* element supports three child elements, *<add>*, *<remove>*, and *<clear>*, and has the following syntax:

```
<httpHandlers>
   <add
      path="path"
      type="type, assembly name"
      validate="true|false"
      verb="verblist" />
   <remove
      path="path"
      verb="verblist" />
   <clear />
</httpHandlers>
```

For information on *<httpHandlers>* element attributes, consult the following table.

		Table B-14. *<httpHandlers>* Element Attribute	
Element	**Attribute**	**Description**	**Options**
<httpHandlers>		Determines the assignment of requests to *httpHandlers* for ASP.NET applications.	
<add>		Each *<add>* child element maps a specific type of request to a given *httpHandler*.	
	path	Specifies the URL path this *httpHandler* will handle.	This can be a single URL, as in the case of the default mapping of the trace.axd URL to *System.Web.Handlers.TraceHandler*, or can use a wildcard to specify that the *httpHandler* should handle all requests of a given type (such as *.aspx or *.asmx).
	type	Specifies the .NET class that should handle the requests specified by the path and verb attributes.	This is a string containing a comma-separated list with the class name and other information, such as version and public key that enables ASP.NET to locate the class in either the application's bin directory or the global assembly cache.
	verb	Specifies the HTTP verbs for which the *httpHandler* will handle requests.	Comma-separated list of verbs (GET, POST) or a wildcard (such as *, which specifies that all verbs should be handled).
<remove>		Removes an *httpHandler* mapping, based on the path and verb attributes specified.	
	path	Specifies path of the *httpHandler* to be removed.	This attribute must exactly match the path attribute of an *httpHandler* added by a previous *<add>* child element.
	verb	Specifies verb(s) of the *httpHandler* to be removed.	This attribute must exactly match the verb attribute of an *httpHandler* added by a previous *<add>* child element.

(continued)

Table B-14.	*<httpHandlers>*	Element Attribute	*(continued)*
Element	**Attribute**	**Description**	**Options**
<clear>		Removes all *httpHandler* mappings, both those configured by the current file and those inherited from parent configuration files.	

<httpModules>

HttpModules are classes that implement the *IHttpModule* interface and provide functionality to ASP.NET applications. For example, by default, the Machine.config file adds *HttpModules* for output caching, session-state management, authentication, and authorization. The *<httpModules>* element enables you to add *HttpModules* to ASP.NET applications.

The *<httpModules>* element supports three child elements, *<add>*, *<remove>*, and *<clear>*, and has the following syntax:

```
<httpModules>
    <add
        name="name"
        type="type\ assembly name" />
    <remove
        name="name"
    <clear />
</httpModules>
```

For information on *<httpModules>* element attributes, consult the following table.

Table B-15.	*<httpModules>*	Element Attributes	
Element	**Attribute**	**Description**	**Options**
<httpModules>		Determines the *httpModules* available for ASP.NET applications within the scope of the configuration file.	
<add>		Each *<add>* child element adds a specified *httpModule*.	

Element	Attribute	Description	Options
	Name	Specifies a name that can be used by ASP.NET applications to refer to the module identified by the type attribute.	
	Type	Specifies the .NET class that implements the desired *httpModule*.	This is a string containing a comma-separated list with the class name and other information, such as version and public key, which enables ASP.NET to locate the class in either the application's bin directory or the global assembly cache.
<remove>		Removes an *httpModule*, based on the name and type attributes specified.	
	name	Specifies the name of the *httpModule* to remove.	This attribute must exactly match the name attribute of an *httpModule* added by a previous *<add>* child element.
<clear>		Removes all *httpModules*, both those configured by the current file and those inherited from parent configuration files.	

<processModel>

The *<processModel>* element configures settings related to how ASP.NET applications run, and provides access to a number of features geared toward improving the availability of applications. These include automatic restart (which can be configured based on elapsed time or number of requests), allowed memory size, and Web garden, in which applications can be associated with specific processors in a multiprocessor machine. Note that when ASP.NET is running under IIS 6.0 in native mode, the settings in the *<processModel>* element are ignored in favor of the settings configured by the IIS administrative UI.

The *<processModel>* element has the following syntax:

```
<processModel
    clientConnectedCheck="time"
    comAuthenticationLevel="Default|None|Connect|Call|Pkt|
        PktIntegrity|PktPrivacy"
    comImpersonationLevel="Default|Anonymous|Identify|Impersonate|
```

```
        Delegate"
    cpuMask="number"
    enable="true|false"
    idleTimeout="time"
    logLevel="loglevel"
    maxIoThreads="number"
    maxWorkerThreads="number"
    memoryLimit="number"
    pingFrequency="hh:mm:ss"
    pingTimeout="hh:mm:ss"
    requestLimit="number"
    requestQueueLimit="number"
    responseDeadlockInterval="Infinite|hh:mm:ss"
    responseRestartDeadlockInterval="Infinite|hh:mm:ss"
    restartQueueLimit="number"
    serverErrorMessageFile="filename"
    shutdownTimeout="time"
    timeout="time"
    webGarden="true|false"
    username="user name"
    password="password" />
```

For information on *<processModel>* element attributes, consult the following table.

Table B-16.	*<processModel>* Element Attributes	
Attribute	**Description**	**Options**
clientConnectedCheck	Determines the frequency with which ASP.NET checks if the client is still connected while a request is queued.	This attribute takes a time value in the format hrs:min:sec. The default is 0:00:05. This attribute can be useful for preventing processor resources from being wasted on queued requests for which the client has disconnected.
comAuthenticationLevel	Specifies the DCOM authentication level.	When set to the Default option, DCOM will determine authentication level based on its normal security negotiation algorithm. When set to the None option, no authentication is used. When set to the Connect

Attribute	Description	Options
		option, DCOM authenticates the credentials of the client at the time the connection is established. When set to the Call option, DCOM authenticates the credentials of the client with each remote procedure call. When set to the Pkt option, DCOM authenticates that all received data is coming from the expected client. PktIntegrity Same as Pkt, but also verifies that data has not been modified in transport. When set to the PktPrivacy option, the same method used in PktIntegrity, is used, but encryption is added. The default value is Connect.
comImpersonationLevel	Specifies the COM authentication level.	When set to the Anonymous option, the client is anonymous. Not supported in the current release. When set to the Identify option, the server can obtain the client's identity and impersonate the client for ACL checking, but cannot access system objects using the client's identity. This allows the server to impersonate the client and access system resources using the client's security context, but this context can only be passed across a single machine boundary. When set to the Delegate option, the same method used in Impersonate is used, but the impersonation token can be passed across multiple machine boundaries.

(continued)

Configuration Elements

Table B-16.	*<processModel>* Element Attributes	*(continued)*
Attribute	**Description**	**Options**
cpuMask	Specifies the processors (on a multiprocessor server) that are allowed to run the ASP.NET application. This attribute works with the *webGarden* attribute. When *webGarden* is set to true, *cpuMask* determines the eligible processors for the application.	The default is 0xffffffff.
Enable	Enables or disables the *processModel* settings for ASP.NET applications.	When set to *true*, *processModel* settings are enabled. When set to *false*, *processModel* settings are disabled.
idleTimeout	Determines the amount of time, in minutes, before ASP.NET shuts down an inactive worker process.	The default is Infinite, in which case the process will not be shut down when idle.
logLevel	Specifies the types of process events that will be written to the event log.	When set to the All option, all process events are logged. When set to the Errors option, only unexpected shutdowns, memory limit shutdowns, and deadlock shutdowns are logged. When set to the None option, no events are logged. The default is Errors.
maxIoThreads	Specifies the maximum number of IO threads per CPU.	Any value from 5 to 100 is valid. The default is 25.
maxWorkerThreads	Specifies the maximum number of worker threads per CPU.	Any value from 5 to 100 is valid. The default is 25.
memoryLimit	Determines the maximum allowable memory size for an ASP.NET application.	This attribute takes a number representing the percentage of the total system memory that the application's worker processes can consume. If this value is exceeded, ASP.NET will launch a new process, reassign existing requests to it, and then shut down the old process.

Attribute	Description	Options
pingFrequency	Determines how often the ASP.NET ISAPI extension pings the worker process to see if it is running. If the process does not respond in the interval specified by pingTimeout, the worker process will be restarted.	The format of this value is hh:mm:ss. The default is 30 seconds.
pingTimeout	Determines the time interval after which an unresponsive worker process is restarted.	The format of this value is hh:mm:ss. The default is 5 seconds.
responseDeadlockInterval	Determines the time interval after which the process will be restarted when there are queued requests, and no responses have been generated for this interval.	The format of this value is hh:mm:ss. The default is 3 minutes.
responseRestartDeadlockInterval	Determines the time interval that must elapse before a second restart to cure a deadlock (as specified by *responseDeadlockInterval*) can occur.	The format of this value is hh:mm:ss. The default is 9 minutes.
requestLimit	Determines the number of requests an application can fulfill before ASP.NET launches a new worker process and shuts down the old one.	The default is Infinite, in which case the process will not be shut down, regardless of the number of requests. This setting can be used to restart the application after a given number of requests, and it can help deal with problems such as memory leaks in legacy COM components used by an application or blocked processes.
requestQueueLimit	Determines the number of requests that might be queued before ASP.NET returns the "503 - Server Too Busy" status error.	Default is 5000.
restartQueueLimit	Specifies the number of requests that are kept in the queue while the process is restarting.	Default is 10.

B

Configuration Elements

(continued)

Table B-16.	*<processModel>* Element Attributes	*(continued)*
Attribute	**Description**	**Options**
serverErrorMessageFile	Provides custom message for Server Unavailable error condition.	Path and file name to the desired file. If omitted, the default Server Unavailable message is used.
shutdownTimeout	Determines the amount of time that an ASP.NET worker process is given to shut itself down.	This attribute takes a time value in the format hrs:min:sec. If the time specified by this attribute is exceeded, ASP.NET will force the shutdown of the worker process. The default is 0:00:05.
timeout	Determines the amount of time, in minutes, before ASP.NET launches a new worker process and shuts down the old one.	This setting can be used to restart the application after a given period of time, and it can help deal with problems such as memory leaks in legacy COM components used by an application or blocked processes.
webGarden	Determines whether Web gardening is enabled.	When set to true, Web gardening is enabled. When set to false, Web gardening is disabled.
password	Specifies a password for the user account specified in the *username* attribute.	The default is autogenerate, which can be used with either the SYSTEM or MACHINE special accounts.
username	Determines the identity under which ASP.NET worker processes are run.	The default is MACHINE, which runs worker processes as an unprivileged ASP.NET service account called ASPNET. This provides a higher level of security than the beta releases of ASP.NET (which used the more privileged SYSTEM account), but might make certain techniques, such as using trusted connections with SQL Server, more difficult because the ASPNET account is not trusted. You can also use another special account,

Attribute	Description	Options
		SYSTEM, to run the ASP.NET worker processes, but for security reasons, this is not recommended.

<webControls>

The *<webControls>* element enables you to specify the location of script files used by client-side implementations of ASP.NET Server Controls, such as the validation controls. The *<webControls>* element has the following syntax:

```
<webControls
    clientScriptsLocation="path" />
```

For information on *<webControls>* element attributes, consult the following table.

Table B-17. *<webControls>* Element Attributes		
Attribute	**Description**	**Options**
ClientScriptsLocation	Determines where ASP.NET will look for client-side scripts for use with ASP.NET Server Controls.	This attribute is relative to the root Web of the Web server.

<clientTarget>

The *<clientTarget>* element enables you to set up aliases to be used by the *ClientTarget* property of the *Page* class. The *<clientTarget>* element supports one child element, *<add>*, and has the following syntax:

```
<clientTarget>
    <add
        alias="aliasname"
        userAgent="true|false" />
</clientTarget>
```

For information on *<clientTarget>* element attributes, consult the table on the following page.

Table B-18.	*<clientTarget>* Element Attributes	
Attribute	**Description**	**Options**
<clientTarget>		Creates aliases for specific browser user agents that can then be specified from the *Page.ClientTarget* property.
<add>		Maps a specific user agent string to an alias name.
	alias	Specifies the name of the alias.
	userAgent	Specifies the browser user agent that the alias looks for.

<browserCaps>

The *<browserCaps>* element contains settings used by ASP.NET to provide the functionality of the browser capabilities component (accessible through the *Request.Browser* property). It provides filtering processes that allow the browser capabilities component to populate its properties with information on the capabilities of a user's browser, based on the information contained in the user agent string passed by the browser. The *<browserCaps>* element supports three child elements, *<result>*, *<use>*, and *<filter>*. The *<filter>* element supports one child element, *<case>*. The *<browserCaps>* element has the following syntax:

```
<browserCaps>
    <result type="System.Web.HttpBrowserCapabilities" />
    <use var="HTTP_USER_AGENT" />
    list of default property values
    <filter>
        <case match="string1|string2|stringN">
            property=value
        </case>
    </filter>
</browserCaps>
```

For information on *<browserCaps>* element attributes, consult the following table.

Table B-19.	*<browserCaps>* Element Attributes		
Element	**Attribute**	**Description**	**Options**
<browserCaps>		Allows filtering and mapping of strings within the browser user agent string to properties of the browser capabilities component.	

Element	Attribute	Description	Options
<result>		Specifies the result type of the configuration element.	
	type	.NET class used as the result type.	The default is *System.Web.HttpBrowserCapabilities*.
<use>		Determines the server variables used while evaluating *<filter>* and *<case>* elements.	
	var	Server variable used in evaluating *<filter>* and *<case>* elements.	The default is *HTTP_USER_AGENT*.
<filter>		The *<filter>* contains one or more <case> child elements to search for specific strings within the user agent string.	
<case>		Each *<case>* child element searches for a specific string or strings within the user agent string.	
	match	Specifies the string or strings (separated by | characters) to look for in the code.	If a specified string is found, the property assignment enclosed by the *<case></case>* tags is executed. Setting and Retrieving Custom Application Settings
			The final configuration element is a special one because it allows you to configure your own custom application settings, which can then be easily retrieved from within your ASP.NET applications.

<appSettings>

The *<appSettings>* element enables you to create your own configuration settings as key/value pairs. You can use this configuration element to store configuration information such as DSNs for data access, and then retrieve them in your application using this syntax:

```
Dim DSN As String
DSN = ConfigurationSettings.AppSettings("dsn")
This is assuming that you've stored the DSN using "dsn" as the key.
The <appSettings> element has the following syntax:
<appSettings
    key="string"
    value="string" />
```

For information on *<appSettings>* element attributes, consult the following table.

Table B-20. *<appSettings>* Element Attributes	
Attribute	**Description**
key	Specifies the key by which the value in the appSettings hash table will be retrieved.
value	Specifies the value to be retrieved by the specified key.

C

Installing Microsoft Visual C# .NET Standard Edition

Installation

In this appendix, you will learn how to

✔ *Determine if your operating system supports building and running ASP.NET applications.*

✔ *Ensure that Internet Information Services is installed and running.*

✔ *Install the Microsoft .NET Framework and Visual C# .NET.*

To create ASP.NET applications using the Visual C# .NET development environment, you need to install both the .NET Framework and the Visual C# .NET software on a supported platform.

Before You Install

Although the Visual C# .NET development environment might be installed on Windows NT 4.0, Windows 2000, or Windows XP, support for running ASP.NET is limited to platforms that support Internet Information Services (IIS) 5.0 or above. This means that to run ASP.NET applications, you must be running Windows 2000 (any version), Windows XP Professional, or any later version that provides support for IIS 5.0 or above.

important

All the following instructions presume that you are using the Classic view of the Control Panel in Windows XP.

After you have determined that your operating system supports IIS, you should check that it is installed before installing the Visual C# .NET development environment. You can do this using the Add Or Remove Programs control panel applet. In the Add Or Remove Programs control panel applet, click Add/Remove Windows Components. Note that you must be logged in as an administrator to verify/install IIS.

note

In addition to IIS, you must also install and configure the FrontPage Server Extensions (FPSE) 2002 if you want to access projects through the server extensions. (The default access mode is File Share, but you can change this in the Visual Studio .NET Options dialog box.) For more information about the steps necessary for installing and configuring FPSE, refer to the document \setup\WebServer.htm on Disc 1 of the Visual C# .NET Standard software. If your CD-ROM drive uses D: as the drive letter, you would access the file by navigating to D:\setup\WebServer.htm.

Check for IIS

1   Open the Control Panel folder by clicking the Start button and clicking Control Panel. In windows 2000, click Start, then Settings, and then Control Panel.

2   Double-click the Add/Remove Programs link.

The Add/Remove Programs applet will be displayed, listing the currently installed programs, as in the following illustration:

3   Click the Add/Remove Windows Components button in the left column.

The Windows Component Wizard appears. If the Internet Information Services (IIS) check box is not selected, IIS is not installed.

4   To install IIS, select the check box next to Internet Information Services (IIS), and then click Next.

Installing Visual C# .NET

The Windows Component Wizard begins installing the files for IIS, as in the following illustration:

5   If you see the prompt shown in the following illustration, insert your Windows XP (or Windows 2000) CD, then click OK.

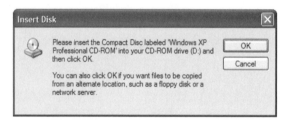

6   When the Windows Component Wizard has finished copying files, click the Finish button to complete the installation process on the screen that appears:

7   Click the Close button to close the Add Or Remove Programs applet.

note

The default installation of IIS includes sample files that might present a security risk if installed on production systems. When installing IIS, you can choose not to install these samples by clicking the Details button in the Windows Component Wizard shown in step 3, and clearing the Documentation check box, which will remove the samples. You might also want to clear the check box for services you don't plan to use, such as the FTP, SMTP, and NNTP services because unused services might also present a security risk. By removing these samples and services, you can eliminate a whole range of potential vulnerabilities. For more information about samples and services, and how they impact server security, see Chapter 8, "Security in ASP.NET"

Installing Visual C# .NET Standard Edition

Installing the Visual C# .NET development environment requires two steps, both of which can be accomplished using the CDs included with the Deluxe Learning Edition package. First you must install the components from the Windows Component Updates CD, which includes the .NET Framework and other software required to support the Visual C# .NET development environment. After these updates have been completed, install the Visual C# .NET development environment.

To install the Windows Component Updates or Visual C# .NET, you must be logged in as an administrator or have access to an administrative account valid for the machine on which you want to install the software. If you are not an administrator, you will see a dialog box similar to the one shown here:

Installing Visual C# .NET

If this dialog box appears, you can either log out and log back in using an administrator account, or specify the user name and password of an administrative account from which to run the installation program.

Install the Windows Component Updates

1   Insert Disc 1 of Visual C# .NET Standard into your CD-ROM drive. If autorun is enabled, setup will begin automatically, and the dialog box shown in the following illustration will appear. (If autorun is not enabled, you will need to run setup.exe from the root of the CD-ROM drive.)

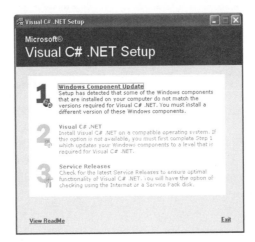

2   Click the Windows Component Update link. You will be prompted to insert the Windows Component Update CD as shown here:

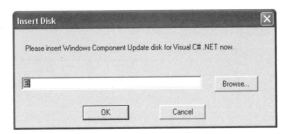

3   Insert the Windows Component Update CD into your CD-ROM drive (changing the drive letter displayed in the dialog box to the letter of your CD-ROM drive if necessary), and click OK. The End User License Agreement (EULA) for the Windows Component Update will appear.

4   Click "I accept the agreement" (you should always read the EULA before agreeing), and click Continue until a list of the components to be installed will appear, similar to what is shown in the following illustration. (Depending on the system you are installing on, more or fewer components might be listed.)

Installing Visual C# .NET

5   Click Install Now! You might be prompted to reboot to complete installation of certain components. The installation will continue after the machine is rebooted. When the installation is complete, the following dialog box will appear:

6   Click Done to complete the installation.

Install Visual C# .NET

1   After you've completed the Windows Component Update installation, the setup dialog box for Visual C# .NET appears.

2 To begin the Visual C# .NET installation, click Visual C# .NET. You will be prompted to insert Disc 1 of Visual C# .NET Standard, as shown here:

3 Insert Disc 1 of Visual C# .NET Standard into your CD-ROM drive (changing the drive letter displayed in the dialog box to the letter of your CD-ROM drive if necessary), and click OK. The setup program will load necessary components and then display the dialog box shown in the following illustration:

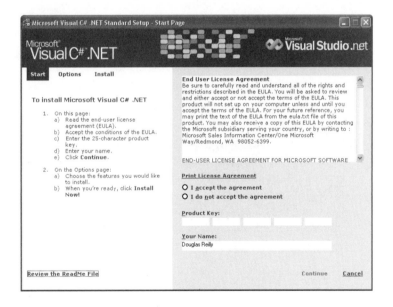

4   Review the EULA, click "I accept the agreement", enter the product key (located on the sleeve of Disc 1) and your name, and click Continue to continue installing. If you are not familiar with installing software such as Visual C# .NET, you should click "Review the ReadMe File" prior to continuing the installation. After clicking Continue, the Options Page will be displayed.

5   Review the available options. You can, for example click the ellipsis button to change the drive on which the software will be installed, or select the Documentation node, and click Run From Source in the Local Path dropdown list to indicate that you want to access the documentation from CD (which saves space on your hard drive). After you're satisfied with the options selected, click Install Now! to continue the installation.

The Install Page dialog box will appear, as shown here:

Ellipsis button

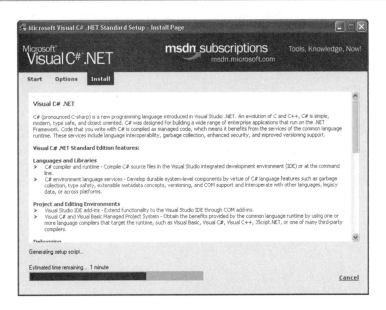

6 When prompted, insert the install disc indicated by the prompt, and click OK.

7 After installation is complete, if there were no problems, the following message will appear. If any errors occurred, you can review the setup log through the link provided to investigate the error.

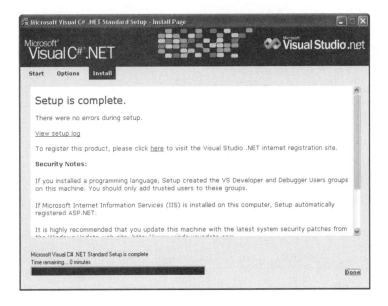

8 Review the installation notes, and then click Done to complete the installation of Visual C# .NET Standard.

Installing Visual C# .NET

C

Install Service Releases

1   After the Visual C# .NET installation is complete, the following dialog box will appear:

2   Visual C# .NET Setup enables you to check for service releases (collections of patches) through the Internet to ensure that your software is up to date. Click the Service Releases link. The Service Releases dialog box will appear, as shown here:

3 If a service release is available, you will be prompted to install it. Otherwise, you will see the dialog box shown here:

4 Click OK to close the Service Releases dialog box.

5 If you want, click the View ReadMe link in the Visual C# .NET Setup dialog box to read about installation and uninstallation, known issues, and other release notes. When you are finished, click the Exit link to exit Visual C# .NET setup.

Install MSDE

A SQL Server-compatible database is required to run the database examples in this book. MSDE, the desktop edition of SQL Server is provided with Visual C# .NET Standard edition, and the setup program for MSDE is copied to the install directory for Visual C# .NET by default. To install MSDE:

1 Locate the setup program (setup.exe) for MSDE. The default location is: C:\Program Files\Microsoft Visual Studio .NET\Setup\MSDE

2 Run setup.exe to install MSDE.

3 To configure MSDE to work with the provided samples, see Chapters 8 and 11 for information about configuring users and database access in MSDE.

Index

Symbols

A

X

About the Authors

Douglas J. Reilly

Ever since he convinced his wife to spend what seemed like far too much money on an Atari 800, Douglas J. Reilly has loved to play with computers. He made a living repairing photocopiers and early personal computers for many years but after a while, the software seemed to be more fun than the hardware.

Doug is the owner of Access Microsystems Inc., a small consulting firm that develops software, using Borland Delphi, Microsoft Visual Studio, Access, SQL Server, and of course the .NET Framework. He has created applications to electronically test job applicants, track retailers' inventory and repair damaged databases. Currently he is working on a variety of health care applications for the St. Barnabas Health Care System as well as applications for a major paint manufacturer, both in New Jersey. In addition to developing software, Doug has written articles published in *Dr. Dobb's Journal* and *Software Development*, wrote a column in the *Pervasive Software Developer's Journal*, and is the author of two Microsoft Press books, *Designing Microsoft ASP.NET Applications* and *Inside Server-Based Applications*.

Doug lives with his wife Jean and their two children, Tim and Erin. When not programming, he enjoys music, reading, and bicycle riding. This summer has been an especially good time for bike riding at the Jersey shore!

Doug can be reached by e-mail at *doug@ProgrammingASP.NET*.

G. Andrew Duthie

G. Andrew Duthie is the founder and Principal of Graymad Enterprises, Inc., providing training and consulting in Microsoft Web development technologies. Andrew has been developing multitier Web applications since the introduction of Active Server Pages. He wrote about developing scalable n-tier applications in *Microsoft Visual InterDev 6.0 Enterprise Developer's Workshop*, also from Microsoft Press.

Andrew is a frequent speaker at events including Software Development, the Dev-Connections family of conferences, Microsoft Developer Days, and VSLive!

In addition to his work for Graymad Enterprises, Andrew enjoys spending time with his wife Jennifer, playing music, and smoking his meerschaum pipe. You can reach Andrew by e-mail at *andrew@graymad.com*.

The manuscript for this book was prepared and galleyed using Microsoft Word 2000. Pages were composed by Online Training Solutions, Inc. (OTSI) using Adobe PageMaker 6.5, with text in Sabon and display type in Syntax. Composed pages were delivered to the printer as electronic prepress files.

Cover Designer

Greg Hickman

Interior Graphic Designer

James D. Kramer

OTSI Team for This Project

R.J. Cadranell

Liz Clark

Joyce Cox

Nancy Depper

Aaron L'Heureux

Joan Preppernau

Lisa Van Every

For more information about OTSI

info@otsi.com

www.otsi.com

Air Gun

The air gun is an essential tool for automotive repair people, woodworkers, contractors, truckers, farmers, or anyone else who needs to clean surfaces quickly. A blast of compressed air from the air gun can quickly blow away dirt, dust, grease, grime, salt, mud, wood chips, or moisture, remove metal shavings from machines, clean moulds on plastic presses, clean gasoline and oil lines, or clean surfaces for painting. Air guns often come with a comfortable pistol grip with easy trigger action and different nozzles for cleaning a variety of surfaces. The power and versatility of a good air gun will just blow you away—just like ASP.NET and Visual C# .NET!

At Microsoft Press, we use tools to illustrate our books for software developers and IT professionals. Tools very simply and powerfully symbolize human inventiveness. They're a metaphor for people extending their capabilities, precision, and reach. From simple calipers and pliers to digital micrometers and lasers, these stylized illustrations give each book a visual identity, and a personality to the series. With tools and knowledge, there's no limit to creativity and innovation. Our tagline says it all: *the tools you need to put technology to work.*

Get the **answers and working code** you need to write
Microsoft Windows–based and .NET-ready applications
with Microsoft Visual C# .NET!

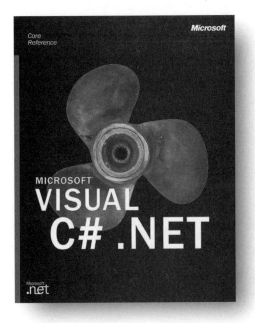

U.S.A. **$59.99**
Canada $86.99
ISBN: 0-7356-1290-0

This core reference delivers essential guidance and comprehensive details for anyone who uses the Microsoft Visual C# .NET development system to produce stand-alone Microsoft Windows®-based and Web-enabled Microsoft .NET applications. The book thoroughly covers the Visual C# .NET language structure, syntax, code wizards, and Microsoft® Visual Studio® development environment for creating both client and server applications. Extensive real-world programming examples and reusable code on a companion CD-ROM enable you to study and implement specific .NET coding solutions.

Microsoft®
microsoft.com/mspress